A Claim For A True Worldview

# A CLAIM FOR A TRUE WORLDVIEW

Spirit of the Natural Law

Victor Leinonen

A Claim For A True Worldview Copyright © by Victor Leinonen. All Rights Reserved.

# Contents

| | | |
|---|---|---:|
| | Introduction | 1 |
| | Dedication | 4 |
| | ACKNOWLEDGMENTS | 8 |
| 1. | THE LAND | 11 |
| 2. | STATE OF NATURE | 18 |
| 3. | IMPERIAL GRAND DUCHIES OF FINLAND | 21 |
| 4. | WORLD WAR I | 25 |
| 5. | SOCIALIST IDEOLOGY | 43 |
| 6. | THE NATURAL RIGHTS | 47 |
| 7. | WHAT IS A WORLDVIEW | 55 |
| 8. | UNIVERSAL DECLARATION OF HUMAN RIGHTS (PART. 1) | 61 |
| 9. | BOLSHEVIK EXPULSION FROM FINLAND 1918 | 64 |
| 10. | REMNANTS OF THE RULE OF LAW | 68 |
| 11. | JOSEPH STALIN WORLD REVOLUTION | 75 |
| 12. | TREATIES TREATY OF BREST-LITOVSK | 83 |
| 13. | NAZI GERMAN-SOVIET PACT OF AGGRESSION | 87 |
| 14. | THE MOSCOW PEACE TREATY MARCH 12th, 1940 | 98 |
| 15. | CONTINUATION WAR 1941 LINE OF DEFENSE | 115 |
| 16. | NUREMBERG PRINCIPLES | 121 |
| 17. | INTERNATIONAL LAW TRIALS | 123 |
| 18. | THE JUST WAR THEORY | 130 |
| 19. | NEW YEARS DAY SPEECH 1940 | 133 |
| 20. | CONSTITUTIONAL LAW | 135 |
| 21. | LAMENTATIONS | 137 |
| 22. | SOVIET CONSPIRACY: WAR AGAINST PEACE | 141 |
| 23. | WAR CRIMES AND GENOCIDE | 145 |
| 24. | WAR RESPONSIBILITY TRIALS IN FINLAND | 159 |
| 25. | NATO ASSURANCE FOR THE RULE OF LAW | 164 |

| 26. | FINLAND ROAD TO EUROPEAN UNION MEMBERSHIP | 168 |
| 27. | WORLDVIEW CONFLICTS IN 2020 | 178 |
| 28. | UNITED STATES LIGHT UPON A HILL | 185 |
| 29. | THE ILLEGITIMATE AUTHORITY | 193 |
| 30. | MOSES DEUTERONOMY CHAPTER 32 (CJB) | 196 |
| 31. | CATEGORICAL MORAL REASONING | 199 |
| 32. | REBELLIOUS ANARCHY | 205 |
| 33. | KARELIAN REFUGEES 1939-1944 | 207 |
| 34. | LEAGUE OF NATIONS | 213 |
| 35. | WHAT DOES THE BIBLE SAY ABOUT THE SATAN? | 227 |
| 36. | HOW DOES THE NEMESIS GET ACCESS TO SOULS? | 229 |
| 37. | ABOUT THE AUTHOR | 234 |
| 38. | GOSPEL ACCORDING TO MATTHEW | 238 |
| 39. | THE ARMOR OF GOD | 239 |
| 40. | TERMINOLOGY | 240 |
| 41. | IMAGE INDEX | 242 |
| 42. | BIBLIOGRAPHY | 243 |
|  | Appendix | 249 |

A CLAIM FOR A TRUE WORLD VIEW

A Claim for A True Worldview book brings forth tools of logic and reason to discern, understand, and define the difference between what is true and what is a false worldview. Truth is knowable; therefore, a True Worldview is knowable also. False worldviews can be examined and revealed by documented world history. Humans inherit or adopt some fundamental basis for their faith and belief, in reality, that automatically creates a Worldview in their mind. It can be a Worldview built upon Truth and reality or corrupted information that is not substantiated with transparent ethics and moral responsibility. This is not making a case for subjective relativism, feeling, or abstract philosophy. It is an axiomatic Truth claim for a 4000-year old biblical and historical Worldview. Having a True Worldview understanding accepts life on earth on the Creator of Life moral terms In the beginning, Elohim Created Time and Space when there was no material Universe of Time and Space. Elohim is a Spirit and has always existed in a higher dimension outside of Time and Space.

A Claim for A True Worldview book explores people's psychological dimension and how rebellious dictators have molded and convinced many generations of people into believing misguided and false Worldviews. False Worldviews planted 100 years ago took root and became established in the minds and hearts of millions of people and was passed on from one generation to the next, without knowing the True Biblical Worldview with the foundational first principles of logic. To think straight, the mind's rational processes need to understand and accept the first principles of logic. Absolutes and precise definitions are vital to a rational thinking human mind. Truth and error distinction, the mind needs to be sharp and reasoning. Another way of thinking it through is to view the necessity of order in meaningful information. The keys of a keyboard are useless if their unique signifying keys are scrambled. Language is a structured system of communication. Language is loaded with detailed information; it can only make sense if the information definitions are accurate and reliable. Arithmetic is only reliable if the definitions of the numbers are reliable.

People have been forced to fight in war's and they died fighting over false worldviews. Their faith was based on a misguided error. They blindly followed their Nationalistic leaders to their grave in vain. Many misguided revolutionists' rebellion, Anarchy, and Nationalism pride are driven by a political agenda with false Worldviews. Even after 100 years, many millions of people have the same mindset and show their allegiance to Nationalism. Even when it was established by despotic dictators foundational belief systems under Socialism's guise, with self-serving agenda for conquest and exploitation of people territory and property. It is unbelievable how many Socialist countries and Socialist people groups in the World will defend and support the Soviet Union's false Worldview. It was false because it contradicts the Jewish Holy Scriptures' core principle instructions of behavior and the exceedingly immoral behavior standards.

The historical records from 1917- 1991 proved that the Soviet Union was established on a seriously erroneous and corrupted false worldview. The Premise of the Bolsheviks rebellion and Anarchy was false. And the actions of the Soviet leaders from 1922- to 1991 further prove that they were morally and spiritually dead wrong. There is a higher authority than rebellious humanity that determines what is morally right and morally wrong. The revelation was given to the people of Israel at Mount Sinai some 3460 years ago. The establishment of the Soviet Union in 1922 and the Soviet Union's track record proves that it was corrupted and erroneous Worldview. You would have to have blind faith or high on Russian Nationalism to believe in something as erroneous as the Soviet Union State atheism, under Soviet leaders.

How is it possible? With the complexity of human psychology, programming is possible. The population of Russia under the communists was programmed, brainwashed, convinced, and coerced into the Soviet Union system. The people's minds were dumped down and altered into making the commitment to sacrifice all to a false worldview. Extreme nationalism, immoral, and idolatrous Worldview; at the core was Soviet Union State Atheism. Soviet Union State Atheism bound up and murdered millions of people with Satan's claws and his diabolical Worldview.

Incorrigible obstinate political Leaders with grandiose illegitimate illusions. Because an error cannot be made to be true, they resorted to mindless means to implement the dictator's false Worldview. They used the Stalin State regime's personality cult to force the Nation people with unethical means such as the collectivization of some 100 million ordinary people's properties and land. Stalin's Communist State Atheism collateral damage between 1932-1933. According to a U.N., a joint statement signed by 25 countries in 2003 declared that 7–10 million perished in the Holodomor famine, a famine created by the Soviet Union regime. The collectivization of the wheat harvest and exporting it to pay for the Soviet Union Socialism's industrialization was a typical demonstration of the hardened criminal nature of the Bolshevik initiative to create a Soviet Union State Atheism at the extreme expense of millions of ordinary people's lives. Soviet Union recurring patterns of people slaughter, 1917-1923. 1936-1938. 1939-1940.

Stalin's political career from early 1900 to 1953 was that of a professional criminal, punctuated by a similar pattern by the slaughter of innocent human beings. Once Stalin had purged the Soviet inner regime and broken their spirit, then he turned to punish the neighbors of Russia. The only way to implement dictators' whims and fantasies was by brutish military power intimidation and threats, whether using divisions of tanks, ships, submarines, bombers, nuclear missiles, hydrogen bombs, or biological warfare. Anyone with a rational mind understands that military power and weapons for extortion, land grabs, occupation, annexation, or invade are motivated by a pathological criminal mind. And their Worldview was abominable. To impose by force a diabolical grandiose delusion, Communism Worldview of leaders onto their imaginary spheres of influence is immoral. The forced evacuation of peoples is always a terrible and unnecessary disruption of people's cultures.

The Good News about a True Worldview is that it offers true justice to all people anywhere in the World. It is the ultimate justice and righteousness Worldview because it is being offered by His Word's Creator of Life to humanity. This book also speaks for the countless innocent people whose lives were cut short and taken away by the capriciousness of the past century dictators. They conjured up theories, philosophies and incubated the seeds for rebellion and Anarchy with a false Worldview. They were ready for the great leap forward, committed to greedy deeds of land grabs and forced evacuations of innocent people. They denied having done anything wrong. They were spiritually blind and oblivious to a human global standard of having human emotions and sensibilities, the heart's strings in tune, and calibrated to moral conscience.

The Western Free World's responsibility and the voting people in Russia with a moral conscience to lift and broadcast the Jewish Holy Scriptures as a foundational moral standard for a correct moral conscience Worldview given by the Creator of Life. In the Books of the Torah, it defines what justice is, what is righteousness and acceptable behavior, and what is abhorrent behavior to the Creator of Life. Human life was assigned intrinsic value. Even one innocent life cut short is too many; how much more dictators in the last century destroyed countless lives, and the dictators are still highly exalted as national heroes in Soviet-Russia and among the Communist sympathizers.

Objective Truth has a significant value. It is the significant value of Truth that needs to be treasured and defended like it was gold. The tabernacle sanctuary at the time of Moses had a holy place and the holiest place. The sanctuary instruments were made of solid gold; also, the walls were lined with gold. Truth and holiness have much in common. They both need to be carefully guarded because they have great value.

# Dedication

In the book Being Logical: A Guide to Good Thinking by McInerny, D.Q. He makes the following point that rings true.

"Truth The whole purpose of reasoning, of logic, is to arrive at the Truth of things. This is often an arduous task, as Truth can sometimes be painfully elusive. But not to pursue Truth would be absurd, since it is the only thing that gives meaning to all our endeavors. It would be equally absurd to suppose that Truth is something forever to be pursued but never to be attained, for that renders our activity purposeless, which is to say, irrational, and turns Truth into a chimera."

How true that is, and there are millions of people in the World today that do not know what objective Truth in logic is, and how it can be used effectively for problem-solving. It is a skill that needs to be acquired and learned by every rational human being.

Here is a paraphrased quote from the McInerny.
"There are three basic components to human knowledge: first, an objective fact (a World); second, the idea of a World; third, the word we apply to the idea, allowing us to communicate it to others (e.g., "Worldview"). It all starts with the World. If there was no real world, there would be no idea about it, and there would be no word for the idea."

McInerny, in his book, Being Logical: A Guide to Good Thinking, stresses the point that ideas (subjective realities) are clear or sound to the extent that they reflect objective realities of the real material world. And that all ideas (human perceptions from the physical environment) have their ultimate source in the objective World. The physical World environment mirrors the 3D space model for the thinking mind to develop a rational 3D conceptualization.

Looking closely at how ideas of the mind relate to the objective World, for that connection is not always straight forward. The most critical question to discover is this: How are bad ideas possible? How is it possible that the people of the World live in the same cause and effect material objective World and often differ so vastly in their interpretation and projection of it? The most apparent immediate answer to the question is found in the human living soul functions, the intellect, consciousness, imagination, will, memory, and emotions. These functions of the human living soul mind from person to person, family to family, culture to culture, nationality to nationality, has potential for millions and billions of variations. One increment + / -, deviation from objective truth, or adding an increment of personal agenda, alters the individual's projection of reality to others. In other words, a person manipulates the objective truth with personal wants, desires, and biases.

The amount of deviation and manipulation away from objective truth is relative to the opportunity and temptation power. If there is no opportunity or power to act, then the level of temptation is weak. When there are opportunity and power, then the temptation to fudge is so much greater. This is true in at least three areas of human life, the lust of the flesh, lust of the eyes, and the pride of life. Without objective moral values and human beings will continue to take the bait that lures them.

Without Moses's first five books (Torah), and the Oracles of God of Abraham, Isaac, and Jacob, the innocent Yeshua from Nazareth, would have been just another Diaspora Jew wandering through life. Yeshua from Nazareth applied his intellect, conscience, imagination, will, memory, and emotions to obey the Torah's written word, that came from the mind and the mouth of Elohim. That is the ultimate objective truth without human agenda and biases. Because the Torah strips away human living soul personal agenda's.

Environmental differences may be one factor, cultural is another, generation gap also influences how people view and share the World. Travel and access to telecommunications devices and videos are factor's that shape's people Worldview. Today people can see with their own eyes how different or similar the World looks like around the globe to their own environment where they live. Other channels also influence the people of the World, it is through education, entertainment, career planning, vocation, and the work environment. Whether the source of information is cultural, tradition and beliefs, history, religious education, voluntary or forced indoctrination, discoveries of science, enlightenment through social psychology, State military coup's, dictators, populist anarchy or rebellion.

The worst suffering and the loss of innocent civilian lives in history, as it is known, the twentieth century was the bloodiest, most destructive century in human history. It came about through illegitimate anarchy and dictators with false Worldviews; they rebelled against the rule of law and legitimate authorities, seized political power with violence, and attempted their great leap forward with a human mind corrupting immoral virus. Dictator Stalin imposed the Bolshevik's rebellious State Atheism Worldview to the Russian people. Force-fed the communist doctrines to all the Soviet Satellite States, even when people wanted no part in it. Stalin also intimidated the independent countries within the realm of the Soviet sphere of Influence with Communist totalitarian doctrines. The Soviet Union used tremendous military power to intimidate the people of countries into surrendering their independence to the State atheism of the Soviet Union. It was a totalitarian political way to take control of other countries through the threat of using military force.

The Soviet Union (USSR) had its roots in the 1917 October Revolution, when the Bolsheviks led by Vladimir Lenin overthrew the Russian Provisional Government. The previous provisional autocratic constitutional monarchy of Tsar Nicholas II was overthrown in the February Bolsheviks agitated Revolution of 1917. The political push to overthrow the Russian autocratic constitutional monarchy of Tsar Nicholas II was a rebellious movement by anarchists. They had worked on it for some 17 years. The spiritual seeds of rebellion were sown by the Bolsheviks agitators and anarchists in Russia from the early 1900. It gained momentum and eventually led to the Russian Civil War that lasted 5 years, 7 months. (November 7, 1917 – June 16, 1923.)

The entire process of transition of power, from the autocratic constitutional monarchy of Tsar Nicholas II, was flawed by a seizure of political power by violence. The removal of Tsar Nicholas from office and the termination of his entire family terminated in a brutal murder. Tsar Nicholas was not a law-breaking criminal deserving of a death penalty at the hands of a murderous mob. The Bolsheviks did not check their emotional impulses through a reasonable and logical Worldview, but instead, they were driven by feverish hate and out of control political leap forward frenzy. They had no cognitive checks and balances in place for determining what is morally right and what is false. They dived deep into lawlessness, rejecting the principles of the rule of law. They refused the lawgiver, who speaks through the Jewish Holy Bible, and through the Spirit, Do not covet, Do not steal, Do not murder, Do not give false testimony.

The affirmative message of the holy scriptures is ageless, instructing humanity about God's character traits and nature. DO acknowledge God and the Holy scriptures, before making any rash decisions. DO not make graven images of personality cults. DO keep the Sabbath and remember to honor your father and mother. It is at the Worldview principles of reason and logic where the aberration and disconnect occurred in the Russian Bolsheviks movement early in 1900. The Soviet Union reaped a spiritually dead and a feral Worldview for themselves that nobody in the Western democratic rule of the law society, with the human rights freedom and a moral conscience thinking mind would touch it with a six-foot stick. That is precisely where the Worldview separation occurred between the East and West.

But the Russian leader's do not get it, they say that the American West is biased, an discriminate against the Soviet-Russian. That is not true. It is only an effect. Why America and the Western World shuns the Soviet-Russian leaders Worldview? Because the Jewish Holy Bible specifically instructs people what is a True Worldview. Soviet-Russian leaders in history are guilty of State Atheism war crimes, guilty of waging aggressive war against peace, they have stolen large areas of territory, perverted the cause of justice, extortion, perjury, and genocide. Russian leaders need to repent for the past century of their godless leaders in Soviet-Russia. To make restitution and return the seized lands and property back to rightful owners, from the Soviet-Russian World War two extortion. Return the territory and wealth to the rightful owners that they have benefited from for the last 81 years. That is precisely what Germany and Japan have done.

The founders of the Soviet State Atheism had no moral conscience, as the universal moral conscience is defined in the Jewish Holy Bible. Not only is it described in the Bible, but it is a commandment from the Creator of Life to humanity. Human beings made in the image of God have the living soul functions of the mind, intellect, consciousness, imagination, will, memory, and emotions. The primary function of human free will is to enable human beings to make moral decisions. By choosing that which is morally right, human beings reflect the mind of their Maker. The flip side is also exact, by deliberate choosing evil and sin deeds, humans transgress more into sin to become more like the enemies of God, on the wrong side of the Holy angels.

Soviet-Russian leaders were thinking in line with their own philosophy, the historical materialism theory. They rejected the primary evidence of the Creator of Life, manifested on earth with Life.
From the early movement of the Bolsheviks to demonstrations to the populist Revolution and blown out the Russian civil war, it says a lot about the nature and the Spirit of the Bolsheviks Worldview. The seeds for change were sown, it became official in divided Russia with the formation of the Soviet Union State Atheism in 1922. In the following 14 years, the seeds produced crops and manifested fruit in 1936-38, the Great Purge by Joseph Stalin. Moscow Trials, and persecution of political prisoners that were not readily conforming to the doctrines of the Soviet utopia and the hidden agenda of the Soviet Union collectivization for the sake of Socialism. The Soviet Union's ideology and communist doctrines were full of contradictions and discrepancies to the expectations of ordinary citizen's idea of a rule of the law society. Because many of the Baltic and the Nordic countries were raised on Christian Bible values. Right to life, right to liberty, and the right to property.

The founding fathers of the Soviet Union were an anomaly, deviant group of renegade men that abolished Godly principles from the Russian civil society. It was a smooth transition for the Bolshevik leader's Worldview, and for the Soviet Union leaders to unite with the Adolf Hitler Nazi Germany proposed Molotov Ribbentrop Pact in 1939, the mutual benefit from the pact was to pillage the small countries of East Europe and the Nordic region. The secret protocol divided East Europe and Nordic countries between the Soviet Union and Nazi Germany material and human labor needs.

This book will bring out many more of the inconsistencies, with the Bolsheviks Soviet Union State Atheism Worldview, and the consistent Soviet-Russian pattern of denial and lying. Their part in the 1939-1945 aggressive war against peace, war crimes, perverting the cause of justice, extortion, perjury, and genocide. Russian leaders refuse to own up to the war crimes of the Soviet Union, which Russia continues to benefit from, even after 81 years. At a time (2020), when the International Criminal Court drags German citizens to courts out of old people's homes because they had some role in Nazi Germany war crimes. It is hypocritical of the Western Allies and the Jewish lawyers to be so partial to their own kindred spirits and turn their back on the Spirit of the Natural law described in the Jewish Holy Bible. Do not show favoritism. Do not covet. Do not steal.

The most shocking fact of the last 100 years is that the modern-day Russian leaders have not been able to progress forward in their Worldview, moral values, in the last 100 years. From the Bolsheviks Worldview to the modern Russian leadership, they still maintain the same pattern of the Bolsheviks and the Soviet Union when it comes to the principles of the rule of law, outside of their own society. They have abstract opportunistic fluid reference points regarding countries outside of their own, and especially the International Law.

They do not acknowledge the principles described in the Jewish Holy Bible, Exodus chapter 20, as having significant desirable merit or usefulness to be considered by the Russian leader's State Geopolitical decisions. What drives the Russian leader's decision is opportunistic convenience at the time. Evidence of that was seen with the annexation of Crimea and East Ukraine in 2014. Similarly, the Russian leader's decision for the intervention in the Syrian civil war since 2015. A civil war that has killed an estimate between 380,000 – 580,000. The number of internally displaced peoples is at 7,600,000. Refugees numbers at 5,116,097 (July 2015/2017).

It is self-evident that the Russian demonstrations of early 1900 led to a spirit of rebellion and anarchy, and to the Russian Civil War that killed some 8 million lives. The formation of the Soviet Union in 1922 by Joseph Stalin as the leader and his followers was a horrible idea. It was a bad idea because the founders were crooks, anarchists, agitators, and hardened professional criminals. That is a fact. From 1922 to 1939, the action of the Soviet Union leaders proves that they indeed were corrupted, immoral professional criminals. Because the principles of the Soviet Union founders were so erroneous and wrong, there was only one way that they could keep the people staying in step with their doctrines. It was through the intimidation tactics of the Secret Police and the Soviet military power. The formation of the Soviet Union was the biggest fiasco of the century. Every step of the way, from 1922, the brutality, imprisonment of innocent civilians, the labor camps, the gulags, the forced conformity of the USSR population by terror, political prisoners, ordinary people with a reasonable peaceful Worldview were seen as a threat to the Soviet State Atheism.

Similarly, the 3360-year Abrahamic religion was seen as a threat to the Soviet State atheism Worldview. Christianity also was seen as a threat to Carl Marx, Vladimir Lenin, and Joseph Stalin's historical materialism philosophy and their State Atheism doctrines.

Citation:
"Humanistic atheists often explain away all moral responsibility of immoral actions. They claim that choices execute without any prior inclinations, prejudice, or disposition. Meaning that there is no significant reason for the choices they make. There is no motivation or motif for a choice. It just happens spontaneously. "Moreover, if that is the way that our choices operate, then we are immediately faced with the absence of the moral problem. How could an action, made by choice, have any moral significance to it at all? The Bible teaching is not only concerned with what we choose but what was our intention. A good deed is not only examined by the outward deed itself, the action but also considers the inner motivation, the intent, behind the deed". – RC Sproul.

The Bible teaches intelligent consciousness and being mindful, self- awareness of one's choosing. History is full of irresponsible leaders of people, fueled by false worldviews and erroneous life philosophies, and they made a grandiose slaughter of humanity during 1900-1953. Globally the attitudes on the intrinsic value of human life are still uncertain and a precarious virtue, an area where the global power geopolitical leaders avoid, deny, suppress, and continuously cheat on.

Quote: Jeremiah 9:23, 24 (CJB)

> ""Here is what Adonai says: The wise man should not boast of his wisdom, the powerful should not boast of his power, the wealthy should not boast of his wealth; instead, let the boaster boast about this: that he understands and knows me — that I am Adonai, practicing grace, justice and righteousness in the land; for in these things I take pleasure," says Adonai.."

# ACKNOWLEDGMENTS

ACKNOWLEDGMENTS

The natural world environment was designed to be an inspiring creative rich soul experience garden for humanity by the Creator of life, Elohim (Genesis 1:1). The universe does not lack space; there is more space than people can imagine or look at. How could 1.5-litre human brain capacity capture the universe in the entirety? Unless humans were designed and created by Intelligent designer according to the image of God, with a mind and capacity for a spirit that can think as God thinks.

Human beings made in the image of God have a natural capacity, with creative skills, talents, attributes, virtues, and powers that are from the Creator of Life. Human's think because God thinks, human's love because God loves, human soul on earth can hate because God can also hate. The difference between the Creator of Life being and the human soul, the Creator of life love, and Creator of Life hate is never in conflict with the infinite character and nature of God. Therefore, the anger of God is according to His Holiness.

The human living soul, with the functions of the mind, the intellect, consciousness, imagination, will, memory and emotions, are vulnerable to pick up lies from the deceiver of humanity. False information and false beliefs deceive the human mind to act according to the false information, causing corruption, lawlessness, and fragmentation of the human mind and the living soul, breaking down the image of God in humanity. Therefore, humans are often at the crossroads of identity, becoming more like the original Creator of life, with the character traits of God, honesty, loyalty, and integrity. Alternatively, humans are digressing with the self-will, rebellion, and stubbornness to willful sin. The human soul is corrupted and changed slowly to the character traits of the devil? Dishonesty, lies, deceit, cover-up and animosity.

Therefore, the right information is vital for a human being to think, act and behave in the right way. The human living soul needs to imitate the Creator of Life. Jesus of Nazareth showed the way back to the Father heart of God. The human thinking mind made in the image of God's mind has a free will with a capacity for self-determination, with intelligent, conscious power for living right according to the quality of information received. Living right according to the right information, with the right worldview, and right life philosophy as designed with intelligent design in mind, by the Creator of Life. The copy of the Creator of Life mind and heart in a template, for the human purpose universally is found in children, it is the only way that humans can become fully human. They have to receive the right information and live and learn as innocent children for at least 12 to 13 years. The spirit of peace respecting the rule of law in a civil society has only been made possible through morally brave people who cared for, encouraged, inspired and defended the spirit of true justice with consciousness to the God-given Spirit of the Natural Law. The Spirit of the Natural Law is impartial for all humanity, the Creator of the universe is not a respecter of persons. He has created laws to govern the universe, life on earth and the human society.

Many people throughout history have given their all-in life to fight the good fight, against ignorance, deception, poverty, depression, sickness, lies, lawlessness, hidden crime, depravity, blatant anarchy, human cruelty, and dictatorial tyranny. Owing moral absolutes, in the fight against every possible form of misleading information, that contains human error and diabolical deceitfulness. Establishing clear communication with meaningful intelligence, establishing the written word that gives hope and reveals God's light for a better-enlightened future, for all those that care about the God-given the spirit of truth with His excellent will plan for humanity. The first victory over deception is achieved in mind and the heart, that is the order of progression, where the deception first began. Followed by the spirit, and the human living soul functions. That is the nature of humanity made in the image of God.

The Harward Law School YouTube channel videos were informative, valuable and helpful during the early stages of the writing this book, especially the David Sandall lecture series on human rights and the natural law connection, to the consent from the state of nature to the rule of human-made law in a society.

Peter Kreeft thought to provoke article on the Karl Marx philosophy, and quoted in this book, titled The Pillars of Unbelief—Karl Marx. Peter Kreeft points out the dangerous deceitfulness of Karl Marx philosophy as a false prophet, with a mind and heart, comparing him parallel to the life of Moses. By clear examples of standard errors in reasoning, which are built upon humanism, with concepts like, Monism, Pantheism, Historicism, Dialectic, Necessitarianism, Statism, Militarism, and Marxism, are topics that reveal the error of the natural human heart and mind reasoning, according to presumptuous human self will. The error of human reason is often in the human unbelief of the prophetic nature of the Spirit of God in the Holy Bible scriptures. Projecting one's unbelief to the people that lived 3400 years ago.

There is the difference between the right information (from God) and the wrong information (from human error). Humans overconfident in the human subjective heart and mind feelings, without understanding the right information from outside time and space, as it is in scriptures inspired by the Spirit of the Creator of Life, which have contained messages from God, since 1500 BC. There is a prophetic element in the Holy Bible that validates the Scriptures as the word of God.

Likewise, the invaluable guidance of the ancient writings of the Bible Books passed on from Moses. The Pentateuch and the Torah, and the recorded historical events that date back to 1500 BC. Moreover, the completion of the promises given in the Bible about salvation for all people that believe and receive the Good News. A promise of Salvation for humanity that was achieved in Yeshua Hamashiach. (Jesus of Nazareth, the Messiah). Truth, love, justice, and faith in Gods covenant promises is the essence that gives integrity to the Holy Scriptures. Which in turn build faith in the believers from active hearing and faith-filled obedience to the written Holy word of God.

[1]

# THE LAND

**THE LAND**

The Nordic people were born into a natural environment, with a cultural connection to the land and the seasonal cycles of life. From the early beginnings, the children raised to learn and interact with the natural environment that stored up lifelong memories of all the seasonal changes. From the hibernating deep snow and ice-covered winters to the awakening sounds of a spring season, with the thousand songs of the migrating birds, singing in the endless sunlight days of the midsummer solstice.

Nordic People instinctively knew the natural environment with its biodiversity, and what the habitats had to offer according to the seasons. Their life depended entirely on natural resources. The people moved and traveled like nomads to optimize the seasonal changes according to local knowledge and the wisdom of the tribe leader's collective experience.

It was a fascinating life environment to be born into, with the unmistakable signs and the unforgiving extreme cold elements of the natural world in charge of the life cycles, commanding respect from people for life in the natural world. Memorable winter night skies that opened high to the star-filled heaven gates, to a mysterious deep dark universe. There were dancing ribbons of light with pastel-like rainbow colors and sounds, creating the atmosphere of awe and wonder in the inquisitive minds as they watched the extravaganza of the aurora borealis lights in the night sky.

The Nordic people did experience the extreme powers of Nature that were so beyond human and animal reach. Stories and myths were inspired and created based on the visible night skies. The same natural phenomenon has presented itself ever since the beginning of the ancient people's collective recorded memory. Over the cycle of seasons, from winter to spring season, the starlit night skies put on an impressive starlight display, which is beyond human capability.

The minds of the observing people wondered as they looked up high into the shifting distant night skies, but they could not unlock the cause of the ribbons of light dancing up and down and all around the panorama above the snow-covered rounded tundra hills. Winter nights were a time for storytelling and sharing the lights with the minds of the younger generation. From there, new ideas formed, and everyday events were placed into future storytelling, which was also developing a bigger worldview in the young people's ever-growing inquisitive imagination. Consciously becoming aware of life and the elements of the natural world.

**SWANS IN FINLAND MYTHOLOGY AND ANTIQUITY**

In the rock art of Karelia, there is a picture outline of swans; the creators of those pictures are sometimes called the "water bird nation" (Fin. Vesilintu kansa). According to the belief of the Karelian people, the white swans not to be harmed; if they were, then the same fate would return to that person as the injured Swan. Because when swans are feeding, their heads are submerging under the surface of the water; therefore it is believed that swans have access to the underworld and hades as well. The White Swans inspire Artists, Musicians, and Poets in Finland.

Jean Sibelius, (8 December 1865 – 20 September 1957) was a composer, violinist of the late Romantic and early-modern periods. Sibelius fame recognized as Finland's most celebrated composer and, through his music, is often credited with having helped Finland to develop a national identity during the early independence years, to the First World War fighting against Russian Bolshevism and Stalinism. (Jean_Sibelius, 2018)

In the Suite, Lemminkäinen is about a vague concept of a mystical swan swimming around Hades, the island of the dead. The mythological figure Lemminkäinen has been tasked with killing the sacred Swan, but on the way, he is shot with a poisoned arrow and dies himself.

Eino Leino (6 July 1878 – 10 January 1926) was a famous poet and journalist. Considered as one of the pivotal pioneers of Finnish poetry. His Swan of the Hades poem, inspirational in the symbolism that first started in picture arts. The poem translated from Finnish brings out thoughts like this:

"Oh! The visiting white birds of the Lapland summer, the great ideological beings, Feel welcomed here! Please stay, make the nest there, and tarry, and do go to the lands of the south! Oh, we do a study and learn from the Swans! They leave in the autumn and return in the spring. There is peace on our shores and safety on the breast of the Tundra." (Leino, 2018)

THE EARLY PIONEERS
The early pioneer's many thousands of years ago traveled northwards, exploring the unknown, uninhabited Nordic north-land. Nomadic peoples were living along the waters of the Arctic Sea, the shores of the Barents and the Norwegian Sea. The indigenous people tribes East and West of Siberia, thousands of years ago, have left cave paintings in Norway, that the modern-day scientific dating methods translate the cave painting to be some 8000 years old. The world of the indigenous peoples is very different from the Imperial States' colonization. A long slow history of humanity lived out before the industrial revolution, which made way to new concepts to enlighten the human conscience, and how people view themselves and the world that they inhabit.

The biblical record of the patriarch Abraham goes back some 4000 years, and the days of Moses and the Exodus of Israel takes us back more than 3460 years. The recorded events and dates of the biblical timeline are a reliable source as a reference because of the context of the five books of Moses are qualified by many generations of spiritual integrity. Two thousand years ago, people were living on the shores of the Gulf of Finland, Bothnia Bay, Lake Ladoga, and the Karelian Isthmus. The region later became known as the Suomi-land and the Suomi people. Translated into English as Finland or Finnish. The word Suomu translates to the English word is scales, as in fish scales.

The alternative autonomy part of a fish is the fin. Therefore, Finland. The original meaning of the word Suomi in Finnish is not precise, but there are several suggestions where the name Suomi originates. The word Suomi is mentioned early in the Treaty of Nöteborg 1323. It was the first settlement between Sweden and the Novgorod Republic regulating their border. A peace treaty of 1323 between Sweden and the Novgorod. (Treaties, 2018)

It was a starting point in the description of the region with a local name, Somewesi or Suomenvesi (Some-wesi, Some-vesi. Translated Fin-land-water). It was describing the area of the Suomi waters in the Bay of Vyborg. The written word Suomi has also appeared at the time of Mikael Agricola (1510 – 9 April 1557), a Lutheran clergyman who worked pioneered the Finnish literary language. Also, a prominent proponent of the Protestant Reformation in Sweden and Finland.

Several words rhyme with the word Suomi, which can be used as a guide for the origin of the word. Here are two suggestions.

- Suo = swamp. Finland has over 100,000 lakes and many more swamps.

- Suomu = scales, as in fish. Clothes made in the Stone Age years from the skin of fish.

The other guide for searching out the meaning of words is anthropology. As in the study of human cultural behavior, in the Finland region nomads, pioneers, language, and societies. The vital clue is found on how and why specific people formed and used their language and named their geographical region, according to the association, according to what their people valued and experienced at the time. Also revealing the specific cultural values from 2000 or more years ago.

In Lapland, there is a town called Kuolajärvi; the word is from the Sami people's language. It means a lake with plenty of fish. Similarly, the Sami people have named the Kuolanmaa. Translated into English as the Kola Peninsula. Meaning; a land with plenty of fish. That is the indigenous people's relationship to the creation, food, and life. Food sources gave freely by the Creator of Life.

Therefore, the Creator of Life instructions for humanity needs to be taken seriously. Otherwise, most likely, people fall onto the wrong side of God's Holy Angels. There is an old cultural connection to the name Suomi land. It refers to the lakes and the fish. From the early hunters and gatherer's perspective, what would be the most paramount concern that they had during the summer season? Naturally, the natural resources for food. There were abundant supplies of food provided by the Creator of Life. Moreover, each person could express their soul in gratitude, according to their soul experience, about the provision that they gathered and hunted.

In the early days, the salmon and pike skins were so plentiful and practical as a waterproof material, once tanned, it is soft and light material to use. The Native Inuits of current Alaska also made Salmon skin clothing. The fish skin leather is waterproof, and waterproofing is vital in the extreme sub-zero temperatures. Wet clothing can be life-threatening in the freezing exposed sub-zero temperatures. If the clothing becomes wet, then it will work like a conductor for body heat to escape; the clothing freezes solid once the physical activity stopped, and the body temperature drops, the clothing freeze solid, and the freezing of skin begins.

The fish skin was processed to be durable leather, especially for the outer waterproof layer. The Alaska region Inuits traditionally used it for boots, mittens, and pants. Waterproof hats are practical. A waterproof fish skin roof for a tent may also be practical because they are very light to carry. Large fish were caught, gutted, skinned; they were scaled and dried. The tanning process cured and manipulated the skin soft. Once the skin was tanned, then it was colored with natural colors. The tanned skins are made into carrying bags, clothes, and other items with various practical uses. The indigenous peoples were creative, living off the land and made use of whatever resources the Creator of life provided them in the natural environment.

Many thousands of years ago, nomadic people's pioneers traveled towards unknown destinations due to seasonal changes that caused people to look for new pastures. Ever growing communities, population, and stock numbers caused nomadic pioneers to explore further West and south from Siberia until they come across the people that were heading northwards, with the same intent in searching for unconsumed natural resources in the wilderness of the natural world. The extreme cold Nordic winters did persuade people to find shelter from the extreme climate to warmer regions. Whether it was 100 km, 500km or more distance, they headed south for winter. Few thousand years ago, there was plenty of room for the nomads to travel the full length of the country from the Kola Peninsula to the shores of the White Sea, all the way to the Gulf of Finland. No Imperial monarchies or ambitious political states were lording it over the early pioneers of the lands. The state of Nature ruled the people, and the people were in tune with the natural environment.

The early pioneers lived amid a natural environment that provided everything that they needed for survival. The spring season bloomed fresh with many millions of migrating water and land birds arriving from the south, as the new living environment was sprouting and welcoming with a vibrant green environment filled with colorful flower-scented meadows. The summer season was the busiest season for building projects, houses, barns for stock feed, boat repairs, and cutting the vital firewood for winter survival. The summer season was the most fun season for children, time for swimming and fishing, and foraging for berries. An old traditional Nordic custom, the entire family would go and forage for wild strawberries, raspberries, bilberries, and mushrooms. The wild berries prepared into conserved jams, concentrated juices, crushed lingonberry barrels, and stored in the underground cellars. The summer season was also crucial for the harvesting of building material timber, gathering up for the winter season firewood stocks, and restoring the old and re-building new projects.

The autumn season was unique for the grains crop harvesting season and foraging of lingonberries, various mushrooms, net fishing, and game hunting for ducks and moose. Planning was the key to survival and healthy living by keeping ahead of the seasonal changes. The stock feed was harvested from the open wild grass meadows, to be cut down and dried. Dry grass then gathered and placed inside the log cabin shelter with water and snow resistant roof. The 6-month long winter consumed much stock feed; it had to be sufficiently dry so that it would not go moldy and rot. With the increase in the human population, there was more demand, and the old forests were thinned out or cleared. Increase of supplies required for all the stock animals for the cold dark winter months. Life for the people of the land was active and busy, even under the most favorable conditions of the natural resources.

The children of families grew to be young adults, the young adults mixed and mingled with other young adults of the communities; there was the natural social life, community life, and commitment for new families. Children were born to young parents; new families created. Children had to be raised and cared for, guided, and instructed, even educated, in the wisdom of the people elders. Life was a fierce struggle in keeping everyone alive. The elements of Nature tested everyone's will, intelligence, and resolved to keep going, regardless of how bitter, cold, how sick, or how miserable, how dark and gloomy the situations turned out to be. There was a strength to be found in the shared values of the community, who respected the Spirit of the Natural Law for the common good. Valued the principles that contributed and ensured survival.

Morality is a resource for inner strength when the circumstances change, and the times are uncertain, even when foreign military powers invade to exploit the local resources. War is often a moment for truth, time for a reality check before the Creator of life, and claim the promises made in the books of the Holy Bible, for the believers. For those that respect the Spirit of the Natural Law in words and deeds and obey the instructions. They do not initiate violence or rely on unscrupulous means for selfish gain.

PIONEER TRAVELLERS
In the early days, small groups of indigenous nomads and pioneers traveled most successfully using boats on the level water highways that reached so far north that the water surfaces froze solid for 3-5 months of the winter. Traveling on the water with equipment, elderly, and the small children during the summer season required less effort than going along the low land lying swamps and tributaries along the shores of the Baltic Sea shores to the Gulf of Finland and the far northern Gulf of Bothnia. The numerous rivers that flow into the Gulf of Bothnia from Finland were an obstacle for the on-land traveler heading north, requiring a swim across the river or a long detour journey eastward to a suitably shallow crossing. The river systems were also water highways to venture far deep into the interior, and even across the entire land. There are four major, far-reaching rivers systems named; Kemi-joki, Kiiminki-joki, Kokemäen- joki, and Oulu-joki (Fin. Joki = river).

RIVER HIGHWAY
Kemi-joki flows westwards through Lapland, from the East Border of Finland and Russia region, through the Lapland city of Rovaniemi westwards to Kemijärvi and from there to the Gulf of Bothnia at the city of Kemi. Kiiminki-joki (Fin. Joki = river) river 170 km length and flows from the Northern vast mid belt of Finland named Ostrobothnia tribunary. Kokemäenjoki 120 km long and joins the Loimijoki River, which is another 114 kilometers in length. Oulujoki drains the Oulu Lake that is 928 square kilometers in size. It is the fifth-largest lake in the country. Saimaa is the largest lake in Finland. Located in southeastern Finland. At approximately 4,400 square kilometers in area (1,700 sq mi), it is the largest lake in Finland and the fourth largest natural freshwater lake in Europe. Believed to have been formed by glacial melting at the end of the Ice Age.

Early pioneers of the Nordic region experienced extreme changes in the seasons when liquid water transformed into a solid mass. Traveling on clear ice is extremely slippery, and with the right kind of contact surface, the traveler could glide on the surface with minimum effort, even with a wind-driven sail. The first types of material used for ice skating were either a block of ice, wood, or bone, strapped to the bottom of an animal leather boot. A sled, or a sleigh, was the apparent transporter to create for convenience sake, used for transporting firewood, household water needs, and for the hunters to carry home their game. Similarly, the concept of skiing becomes evident to the worker from the interaction with the cause and effect material world, with two flat surfaces, pieces of wood under the feet, and two stick poles to push forward. Most likely discovered when attempting to move across the solid snow-covered ground without sinking.

Improvised snowshoes, or for the recreational purpose of gliding downhill. Early hunters would use the skies to their advantage when the snow cover was thick on the ground, and the snow hindered the escaping game animal's progress, the escape of the animal slowed down. Humans fight for survival in the far reaches of the sub-arctic extreme wilderness. The winter snow was entertaining fun for the children to enjoy during the winter season, to master their new-found skill of balance. The workers and the hunters, winter fishers, and travelers that were used to the convenience of traveling on the level surface of the ice. A smooth hard-solid surface can glide over ice due to the layer of ice molecules on the surfaces, are loosely bound as the molecules of the mass of ice beneath. The molecules at the surface area in a semi-liquid state, providing lubrication. Moreover, the stable, smooth surface glides over the surface of the snow, mainly when gravity pushing downhill aids the mass.

Cold winters that freeze the water bodies, including fast-flowing rivers, make the crossing of rivers easy, and the level surfaces for reindeer sleight to travel inland. Skiing on the snow-covered ice was also much less effort in the right conditions for long distances. Even in south Finland, the entire 130 km wide Gulf of Finland would freeze over to about 30-50 cm thick ice. Even more often, the entire Bothnia Bay 100 – 140 km wide between Finland and Sweden would freeze over, and people would cross over from one side to the other during the winter. Either by walking skiing, a reindeer, or a horse-pulled the sleigh.

The lead up to the cold winter months of December to March, the autumn season temperatures could drop down to freezing -15 to -20 Celsius degrees. Freezing the water bodies into clear transparent ice, before there was any snowfall at all, transforming the broad level of flat surfaces to surreal impressions of the transparent yet stable environment. Walking on water was no miracle during the winter months. To an inexperienced traveler to new regions, the autumn and early winter ice could be deceptive, precarious, and dangerous, especially where the river is flowing under the ice cover. The water in the Sea and the lakes are relatively warm during the late summer and autumn season when the cold sub-zero temperatures arrive, the cooling of the water bodies can be slow. The temperatures outside can drop to extreme cold, 20's and 30's, creating a false sense of security regarding the freezing point of water and strength of the ice cover. The deep-water bodies under the ice melt the ice where it is in contact with the water. The experience of the pioneers living through the seasons in the extreme environment would teach them how to navigate and survive in new regions through the various seasons.

The relatively thin ice cover of 5-10 cm on lake water and the heavy snowfalls would work like insulation, preventing the ice from freezing to a safe 20-30 cm thickness. The unsuspecting traveler would make judgments according to the visible weather conditions of the day. Even with clear skies and snap freezing sub-zero temperatures, it can lead to presuming that under the snow cover, the ice is sufficiently stable and safe for travel. The visitor unknowing previous conditions that the snow fell onto the relatively thin ice. Insulated by the snow cover, over relatively warm water, the snow cover is slowing down the freezing of the ice process. Preventing the ice from freezing into a hard solid. Many lives lost while traveling unknowingly on thin ice.

Many thousands of years ago, people explored their environment and noticed the apparent changes in liquid water transformed into solids. Traveling on clear ice is precarious and slippery; with the right kind of contact surface, the traveler could glide on the surface with minimum effort and also conserving energy. The types of material used for children playing on ice could have been anything, such as flat skids made of wood or a flat bone strapped to the bottom of the animal skin. The skin of a hare, fox, wolf, reindeer, moose, or a wolverine made into boots. For the entertainment purposes of children, there is the unlimited creative potential, the golden rule in the winter for children is to stay warm and dry.

Moreover, to have a joyful, creative fun time. Similarly, the idea of skiing would have become evident from the need, with two pieces of wood under the feet and two stick poles to push forward. Whether as entertaining fun for the children to master the environment and the seasons with balance or for the hunter or traveler journeys on ice. In the natural setting of the times, the early pioneers ventured along the clean, fresh waters of Nordic wilderness, surrounded by ancient birch and pine trees of the old forests. The natural rights of a human being are self-evident to a responsible mind; they were born into a state of Nature, with equal natural rights.

To project and to imagine the way that the state of life was in the beginning when people lived in the natural environment entirely dependent on the food provisions that the natural environments provided. The abundant natural resources, along with caring tribal communities, would have created an attitude of gratitude from their good fortune. That in turn, could have pointed the appreciation upwards towards the other, the supernatural Creator of life. The environment biodiversity and provisions, which kept the early pioneer's community alive, active, and healthy. In those days, all of the human five senses were much more engaged and interactive than those of the Western world. People in contact with the continuous sounds of the natural world sounds that could be heard anywhere and everywhere, except during the still quiet winter months. The sound of rustling tree leaves whirling and twirling in the fast-flowing wind currents that sweep through the trees and over the land; the silence of the still night air, echoed by the distant bird calls, in the early hours of the morning. The presence of Nature was everywhere; one could not escape it, even the crackling of firewood was speaking meaning to the observer's senses. At the time of the pioneers of the Nordic region, there was no State government or ruler, dictating human laws onto the people in the state of Nature. There were no other laws besides the Spirit of the Natural Law, interacting with the human intellect, consciousness, imagination, the will, memories, and emotions.

This journey back to many thousands of years in time is exciting; it allows the mind to explore the human Nature and the timeline journey, to ask the question, what are the causes of the human conflict and wars mystery? Where does it originate? What is the energy that drives conflict? Moreover, why is the human history timeline dotted with conflicts and wars, and the same repetition continues to the current day? The answer is in the labyrinth of the human mind and heart. The conscious human mind often ignores the details of human purpose, created in the image of God. It fails to respect the intrinsic value of human life. It is subjectively selective according to individual desires, wants, longings, and soul needs. The human intellect can seek to understand what the difference is between the morally right and the morally wrong. The error is in the repeating of the wrong.

The mind can be taken on a long-compromised ride if it starts to believe in the lies of convenience. The temptation is always bidding on the side of the convenience. It is an easy way, and the broadways of compromise, which draws the mind by diverting attention. Competing elements distracting and drawing for the attention of the intellect, keen focus, and will. The desired outcome of the Nemesis is always fragmentation and confusion, diverting the devotion from a higher moral cause to a human carnal preoccupation.

A parallel to the human conflict can be seen in the animal kingdom; animals fight over partners, food, and territory. They may be the three key areas that relate to the human conflict with Nature as well. There is a difference in the scale; in the animal kingdom, there are no large-scale wars as the human nation wars. The massive battles appear to be a diabolical aberration from even animal behavior, how much more so for the human created in the image of God? To eliminate the existence of a species, is a genocide. Begs the question, why? Is the plan for more partners? Is it for more food? Alternatively, for more territory? The answer of the error can be found in the individual human heart and mind motives.

How much effort and time do people spend in developing their minds? It is, after all, the most highly sophisticated and central organ of all the other human physical ten organs and activities. The mind is not only physical but also spiritual. Many mysteries of the mind are unknown. Is the entire real estate of the mind being used? Alternatively, is it like a storage shed in the backyard, with no real important order, or room to store the latest information items?

THE NATURAL STATE
The Natural State is a neutral state when reflecting upon the early timeline of history. There is no legitimacy to the Imperial power politics and dictators to claim the land on the basis that they have a stronger military force, or

that there are more numerous than the indigenous peoples which they intend to drive out and exploit. The Spirit of the Natural Law justice does not make such provisions for the inequality and exploitation of minorities on the basis that their military force is weaker of people lesser in numbers. The only exception that I have found is in the books of the Bible, the Old Testament Scriptures. God called Moses from the wilderness to deliver the people of Israel out of Egypt. It was God's call to Moses and Israel, followed by 40 years of trials, errors, and failure in the desert; then, the new generation arose and made it to the Promised Land led by Joshua and Caleb. (Moses, Joshua, 2018)

Humanistic atheists may object to the recorded violence in the books of the Old Testament. On the face of it, there is violence. Others make the point that it was God that commanded Moses and Joshua to clear the land of the gross sinful idolatry. How can we know it was God giving the commands? The proof is in the miracles and signs. Only God's will could produce such miracles and signs. That was also the test for the prophets in the Old Testament. If a prophet spoke claiming that the message was from God, and if the message did not come true, then that prophet was to be stoned to death. Deuteronomy 13: (The false prophet). There was zero tolerance in the Old Testament for the deceiver of God's people.

The Holy Scriptures point out that the orders came from God to clear the promised land of the inhabitants because of the gross idolatry of the people of the land. The Promised Land to the people of Israel was a call to a new level of faith and trust in the God of Israel; they had a call to be a Holy Nation that would become a witness to all the people of the world. For better or for the worse, they have a history like no other nation in the world. The future remains bright for the people that remain faithful to the Ten Commandments, the Holy Scriptures, and the life-giving Spirit of God.

> "Now then, if you will indeed obey My voice and keep My covenant, then you shall be My possession among all the peoples, for all the earth is Mine; and you shall be to Me a kingdom of priests and a holy nation.' These are the words that you shall speak to the sons of Israel." Exodus. 19:6. (NAS)

They were destined for a purpose, a call of God for the new generation of believers that were born in the desert during the 40 years exodus. Not necessarily an easy concept to get the mind around to understand. It is good to understand their call, the instructions given in the scriptures, which is impossible for humans to please God without faith.

> "And without faith, it is impossible to please God because anyone who approaches Him must believe that He exists and that He rewards those who earnestly seek Him." Hebrews 11:6. (BSB) (Apollos)

# [2]
# STATE OF NATURE

**STATE OF NATURE**

The state of nature existed for the early inhabitants of the land between the Gulf of Finland and the Bothnian Sea, and along the shore of the Lake Ladoga, freshwater lakes, moss bogs, creeks, and rivers all the way north to the White Sea. Some individual people were in tune with their inner intuitive spiritual being, living among the precious resources of the natural environment and the starlit night skies. We cannot even begin to imagine the interactions that a human spirit—the mind and soul— go through when its life is entirely dependent on the provisions that the natural environment provides. People that lived their lives surrounded by the natural living environment, interacting with the life that was so rich everywhere during the spring, summer, and autumn season that is what shaped their spirits and personalities. God-given life presented with the natural environment; they were the recipients of that life, and they were conscious of it.

June is the beginning of summer in the southern parts of the Nordic countries. It was also hard work at times; shelters were constructed for health reasons and protection. Food had to be gathered, fished, and hunted for provision. Wild berries had to forage for nutritional needs, and water was manually carried for households. Clothing and footwear were repaired, and new items were made. Until the time when the migrating birdlife starts to return south, year after year, return south for the warm summer daylight.

Pioneers most experienced, well prepared, only the brave among them would dare to stay through the Nordic winters, which could be under snow and ice for six months (some regional variations), November to May. During the cold dark winters, wild game animals are tracked and hunted, moose and deer. Fire is essential to stay healthy and alive in the Nordic cold winters. During the Nordic winter, the environment is often dead still and quiet, not a sound heard. A winter environment covered with snow insulating and trapping any sounds from the pine trees. Blue haze appears around mid-morning with no sunrise during the day, and the darkness returns at mid-afternoon. Six hours of grey blue haze daylight is a sign of the Nordic midwinter solstice.

The season changes, and the daylight hours go closer to midnight, the winter snow and ice soon melt away as the migrating birds arrive from their South Europe and African winter escape. The green vegetation starts to thrive, and soon the wild berries start to flower, giving birth to wild strawberries, bilberries, lingonberries, thorn-buck berries, and cloudberries. The environment is full of the sounds of singing bird calls and songs. Game animals such as reindeer, whitetail deer, brown bear, and the moose, they mate and give birth to their young; food is abundant during the three short months of the Nordic summer season.

The life of the natural environment speaks with narrative to a rational, intelligent human mind. It is the Creation, the works of God. Who could have measured the depth, the length, and the width of human understanding some 4500 years ago? From season to season, the people of the far north walked, boated, climbed, skied, journeyed, foraged, trapped, fished, and hunted. There was an abundant food supply of water and firewood. During the summer nights, they listened to the echo of the calls made by the water birds at a distance, endless daylight lasting all through the nighttime hours.

Through belief, faith, myth, and imagination, the nomad people's minds began to join dots and to draw charcoal sketches of the fuller expansive imaginary world beyond their experience. A world where all the clouds of the sky glide from, and a world where all the rivers and lakes flow. An imaginary world filled with a countless number of lakes filled with the vigorous life, a world where all the migrating birds fly to and fly from, feeding and nesting amongst the reeds, green swamps, meadows filled with wildflowers, and rolling hills with virgin forests, with the dark soil trails of the majestic moose.

THE PEOPLE OF SUOMI

The story of the Ingria people, groups, and Cultures. "The recent studies have rejected the old theories that the Baltic Finns had come to the shores of the region in waves of migrations in the early part of the first century, from East to the south-east. The results of the research had revealed that the North-European people were of Finn stock (Kanta Suomalainen). Not to be confused with the Finn-Ukraine stock (kantasuomlais-Ugrilaista), as they also moved to the north as the Indo-European people groups began to settle there. They also have a relatively recent history, integrated with the Indo-European Nations. Similarly, the Baltic Finn tribes and their Nationality are a representation of the local indigenous people of the Baltic Sea, in the same way as the Sami people represent the Indigenous people who found their habitation environment in the south and the far north. The Baltic Sea Finns, the Ingria land people (Inkeriläiset), also have roots that go far back in history. (Saressalo, 2000) Lassi Saressalo:

IMPERIAL GRAND DUCHIES OF FINLAND 1581

An extended Southwest Finland was made a titular grand duchy in 1581, when King John III of Sweden, who as a prince had been the Duke of Finland (1556–1561/63), extended the list of subsidiary titles of the Kings of Sweden considerably. The new title Grand Duke of Finland did not result in any Finnish autonomy, as Finland was an integrated part of the Kingdom of Sweden with full parliamentary representation for its counties. (Sweden, Grand Duchy of Finland, 2018)

FINNISH WAR 1808

The Finnish War fought between the Kingdom of Sweden and the Russian Empire from February 1808 to September 1809. As a result of the war, the eastern third of Sweden established as the autonomous Grand Duchy of Finland within the Russian Empire. (Sweden, Finnish War, 2018)

EMPEROR NICHOLAS II

Nicholas II (1868 – 17 July 1918) was the last Emperor of Russia, ruling from 1 November 1894 until his forced abdication on 15 March 1917. The people of the Russian revolution rejected their Monarchy system. (Russia, Nicholas II of Russia, 2018)

THE PEOPLE FINLAND IN THE IMPERIAL POWER VICE

The people of Finland grew up on land, located between a rock and a hard place. The two Imperial Superpowers were Sweden on the West side of the Bothnia Sea, and Russia on the East side of Lake Ladoga and the Neva River. Both Imperial superpowers have influenced, intimidated, invaded, educated, and betrayed a trust with the people and the government of Finland over the last 500 years. These two-imperial superpowers were not equal; they have a very different history, cultural values, and people's national identity and destiny.

Nordic countries have been spiritually inspired and influenced by the evangelical Christian values, not a dead religion. The two Imperial superpowers also had different ambitions, inclinations, prejudices, dispositions, and motives in invading the people of the Nordic countries. It is refreshing to think about how Sweden has managed to stay within its national skin. The Soviet Union was not able to stay within their Russian national skin, almost like a giant snake eating up others outside their borders, and always restless, and never satisfied or settled.

The ability to stay within one's skin takes self-control. There must be the ability to see some good in what they have. They have acquired vast natural resources, mostly from indigenous people's lands. What is Moscow? If all the indigenous people like the Sami people of the Kola Peninsula and the Sami people of Siberia and further East were given their original ancestral lands back? It is reasonable to say that those that have much should be the most hospitable and generous. The USSR was never generous, was never hospitable to their neighbors. They caused unimaginable suffering and heartache for millions of people that lost their neighbors, parents, husbands, wives, and children to labor camps and the persecution of political prisoners.

The Imperial powers did not always just come randomly or impulsively to the territory of the Suomi people. They came after calculated strategic war planning was complete. The Imperial Russian leaders had planned far in advance for their territorial, material, or political ends. At other times the Superpower leaders were driven by personal ambition, impulsions, and fantasies as dictators do. The superpowers have always included the use of military force; once the military force is sufficiently built up and intimidating, then right to human nature, they exploit that intimidation and make outrageous demands for territory or other material wealth. If the Imperial demands were not met, then they keep going on rolling destruction, which flattens whatever that is sticking up in their way to be flattened. It is sinister and ruthless exploitation, history of full of such exploits committed by imperial superpowers and hungry dictators.

THE GOOD NEWS
It was through Sweden that the Good News Gospel came to Finland after the first millennium. The First Swedish Crusade is said to have taken place with a military expedition, around the year 1150 AD. It was the first attempt by Sweden to convert Finnish pagan culture to Christianity. According to the legend, it was by King Eric IX of Sweden with an English bishop by the name of Henry of Uppsala, who also remained in Finland, but was killed by a pagan Finn. (Bishop of Finland)

The Second crusades from Sweden, according to Eric's Chronicle from 1320-1340, the crusade took place between Birger Jarl getting elevated to the position of jarl in 1248 and the death of King Eric XI of Sweden in 1250.

The Third Crusade was far-reaching in the East Finland region Karelia. The Viborg Castle was established in the Gulf of Finland Bay Viborg Karelia, and western Karelia remained under Swedish rule for over 400 years. It was an expedition focused on the pagan Karelians in 1293.

It is fair to say that the Swedish influence on the early Finnish culture has been positive, and one of nation-building. The Swedish Royalty certainly did lord it over their subjects and kept their subjects in their little place. Until 1800 when the Russian got the better of the Swedes militarily, the nation of Sweden never again glorified its nation with military supremacy and conquering exploits. Sweden today is more pre-occupied with their export home brands, making the world news with product brand like HUSGAVARNA, SAAB, VOLVO, SCANIA, IKEA, Electrolux, Ericsson, H & H, and Skype. Consistent quality control, production, and global distribution are respected worldwide. Sweden is still today one of the two official languages in Finland.

## [3]

# IMPERIAL GRAND DUCHIES OF FINLAND

IMPERIAL GRAND DUCHIES OF FINLAND

An extended Southwest Finland was made a titular grand duchy in 1581, when King John III of Sweden, who as a prince had been the Duke of Finland (1556–1561/63), extended the list of subsidiary titles of the Kings of Sweden considerably. The new title Grand Duke of Finland did not result in any Finnish autonomy, as Finland was an integrated part of the Kingdom of Sweden with full parliamentary representation for its counties.

FINNISH WAR 1808

The Finnish War fought between the Kingdom of Sweden and the Russian Empire from February 1808 to September 1809. As a result of the war, (as the current Finland territory), regarded as the eastern third of Sweden in 1809, established as the autonomous Grand Duchy of Finland within the Russian Empire. The Russian military conquest took the land off Sweden's control and claimed to have the right to control and dominate the land and the people of Finland. (Sweden, Finnish War, 2018)

EMPEROR NICHOLAS II

Nicholas II (1868 – 17 Jul 1918) was the last Emperor of Russia, ruling from 1 Nov 1894 until his forced abdication on 15 Mar 1917. The people of the Russian revolution rejected their Monarchy system.

MUTINY AFTER THE 1917 REVOLUTION

After the Russian revolution, the monarchist was hounded, including the organized military, Royal Russian navy ships were in the port of Finland for the winter, Russian sailors mutinied over 100 Russian Navy officers stationed in Helsinki 1917. The Russian revolution fever spiked with the spirit of anarchy. The revolution that started in Russia raged out of control with drunken violence. The spirit of anarchy was contagious, and the fever caught people everywhere, where ever the Royal Russian military was present. It ruthlessly split and polarized the two sides by the lawlessness and bloody violence. There was a protest as early as 1914 as Russian was starting to engage in World War 1. Russia declared war on Turkey on 2 Nov 1914.

In Finland, by 1917, there was severe poverty, hunger, also the Bolsheviks rebellion, anarchy, and mutiny. There were about 100,000 Russian military troops in Finland for World War One strategic reasons. Russian leaders feared the Germans, believing that the Germans would go north and land in Finland, and push back the Russian to where they had come from, East side of Lake Ladoga, and East of Neva River.

TSAR RUSSIA TERRORISM

Alexander II Born 29 Apr 1818 – 13 Mar 1881) was the Emperor of Russia from 2 Mar 1855 until his assassination on 13 Mar 1881. Alexander's most significant reform as Emperor was the emancipation of Russia's serfs in 1861, for which he is known as Alexander the Liberator. In foreign policy, Alexander sold Alaska to the United States in 1867, fearing the remote colony would fall into British hands if there were another war.

ASSASSINATION ATTEMPTS ON ALEXANDER II

"During the 1867 World Fair, Polish immigrant, Antoni Berezowski attacked the carriage with Alexander, his two sons, and Napoleon III. His self-modified, double-barreled pistol misfired, and a bullet struck only a horse of an escorting cavalryman. On the morning of 20 Apr 1879, Alexander was briskly walking towards the Square of the Guards Staff and faced Alexander Soloviev, a 33-year-old former student. Having seen a menacing revolver in his hands, the Emperor fled in a zigzag pattern. Soloviev fired five times but missed. Was sentenced to death by hanging, on 28 May."

"On the evening of 5 Feb 1880, Stephan Khalturin, also from Narodnaya Volya, set off a timed charge under the dining room of the Winter Palace, right in the resting room of the guards one story below, killing 11 people and wounding 30 others." "Fortunately for Alexander, dinner was delayed by the late arrival of the tsar's nephew, the Prince of Bulgaria, so the tsar and his family were not in the dining room at the time of the explosion and were unharmed." "After the last assassination attempt in February 1880, Count Loris-Melikov was appointed the head of the Supreme Executive Commission and given extraordinary powers to fight the revolutionaries..."

"On 13 Mar 1 March. 1881, Alexander II fell victim to an assassination plot in Saint Petersburg"....

"As he was known to do every Sunday for many years, the Emperor went to the Mikhailovsky Manège for the military roll call. He traveled both to and from the Manège in a closed carriage accompanied by five Cossacks and Frank (Franciszek) Joseph Jackowski, a Polish noble, with a sixth Cossack sitting on the coachman's left. The Emperor's carriage followed by two sleighs carrying, among others, the chief of police and the chief of the Emperor's guard.."........

"The explosion, while killing one of the Cossacks and seriously wounding the driver and people on the sidewalk, had only damaged the bulletproof carriage, a gift from Napoleon III of France... The Emperor emerged shaken but unhurt". "Nevertheless, a second young member of the Narodnaya Volya, Ignacy Hryniewiecki, standing by the canal fence, raised both arms and threw something at the emperor's feet"....

"His Majesty was half-lying, half-sitting, leaning on his right arm. Thinking he was merely wounded slightly, they tried to lift him, but the Czar's legs shattered, and the blood poured out of them. Twenty people, with wounds of varying degrees, lay on the sidewalk and the street. Some managed to stand, others to crawl. Still, others tried to get out from beneath bodies that had fallen on them. Through the snow, debris, and blood, the fragments of clothing, epaulets, sabers, and bloody chunks of human flesh were visible".

"Alexander was taken by a sleigh to the Winter Palace to his study where almost the same day twenty years earlier, he had signed the Emancipation Edict freeing the serfs. Alexander was bleeding to death, with his legs torn away, his stomach ripped open, and his face mutilated. Members of the Romanov family came rushing to the scene. Alexander It's death caused a significant setback for the reform movement. The assassination triggered significant suppression of civil liberties in Russia, and police brutality burst back in full force after experiencing some restraint under the reign of Alexander II, whose death was witnessed first-hand by his son, Alexander III, and his grandson, Nicholas II".

ALEXANDER III
*Alexander III 10 1845 – 1 Nov 1894) was the Emperor of Russia, King of Poland, and Grand Duke of Finland from 13 Mar 1881 until his death on 1 Nov 1894. During Alexander's reign, Russia fought no major wars, for which he was styled "The Peacemaker." In 1894 Alexander III became ill with terminal kidney disease (nephritis).*

*Soon after, his health began to deteriorate more rapidly. He eventually died in the arms of his wife, in the presence of his physician, Ernst Viktor von Leyden. At Maly Palace in Livadia on the afternoon of 1 Nov [O.S. 20 Oct] 1894 at the age of forty-nine, and was succeeded by his eldest son Tsesarevich Nicholas, who took the throne as Nicholas II.* (Russia, Alexander III of Russia, 2018)

NICHOLAS II
When Nicholas II was but thirteen years of age, his grandfather, Czar Alexander II, was assassinated by an insurgent group intent on overthrowing the czarist rule of Russia.

"On 1 Mar 1881, Czar Alexander II traveled to military roll call, as he did, predictably, every Sunday. Members of the *terrorist group known as Narodnaya Volya, meaning "People's Freedom," was waiting for the Czar's carriage at the point the route narrowed and crossed the Pevchesky Bridge. The first explosive thrown damaged the Czar's carriage, killed one of his guards, and injured bystanders. It also had the effect of inducing the Czar to leave the smoke-filled protection of the bulletproof carriage. In the confusion of noise, debris, and panic, a second assassin threw another bomb, which exploded in the group of guards and police surrounding the Czar. When the smoke cleared, Czar Alexander II lay in the street, hideously mutilated, covered in blood, with both legs torn away in the explosion."....*

*"Ironically, the assassination of Czar Alexander II ended his plan to enact sweeping social reforms that might have satisfied the goals of groups agitating for the rights of the people. On the previous day, before being killed, the Czar had drafted a plan for creating an elected legislative body to represent the citizens of Russia. He had intended to release these plans the following day. His son, Alexander III, destroyed these plans when he became a Czar."*

*"The new ruler Alexander III considered his father's murder justification for the more brutal suppression of civil liberties instead of increased liberty. He vowed, "I shall never, under any circumstances, agree to a representative form of government because I consider it harmful to the people whom God has entrusted to my care."*

*"An attempt was made to assassinate Nicholas II while the group was traveling in Japan, causing the trip to be cut short. Nicholas's father, Czar Alexander III, refused to appoint Nicholas to a position in government, feeling his son was too young to take on the burden of such responsibility." "In 1894, the Czar was diagnosed with terminal kidney disease. Though he received the best treatments available and spent time recuperating in the warmer clime of the summer palace in Livadia, nothing seemed to ease his condition. The Czar was forty-nine years old when he passed away from his illness. Nicholas was just twenty-six, and he was the first to admit he was not prepared to take over as ruler of Russia."*

*"Less than a week after the passing of Czar Alexander III and his ascension to the title of Czar Nicholas II, Nicholas was married. The bride was to his long-time love, Alexandra, a princess of Hesse and the Rhine, whom he had met at his cousin's wedding in London. Czar Alexander II had opposed the match before his illness but relented when it was clear that his health was failing. Alexandra herself had also had reservations about the marriage. She was reluctant to give up on her Protestant faith to convert to Russian Orthodoxy, as it would be required. After the encouragement of her parents, the princess marriage went ahead; the couple appeared to be devoted to each other."*

*"Czar Nicholas II ruled Russia much as his father Alexander II had. He strongly believed in the absolute autocracy of the crown. In hindsight, but also in reviewing political trends in Europe and the populist violence his own family had suffered."*
Source: – Russian Revolution: A Concise History From Beginning to End. (History H., 2016)

ABDICATION (1917)
At the end of the "February Revolution" of 1917 (February in the Old Russian Calendar), on 2 Mar (O.S.) / 15 Mar (N.S.) 1917, Nicholas II chose to abdicate.

IMPRISONMENT
*"The Governor's Mansion in Tobolsk, where the Romanov family held in captivity between August 1917 and April 1918. "Nicholas desperately wanted to go into exile in the United Kingdom following his abdication. The British government reluctantly offered the family asylum in the UK on 19 Mar 1917; the suggestion was that it would be better for the Romanovs to go to a neutral country. News of the offer provoked uproar from the Labour Party and many Liberals, and the British ambassador Sir George Buchanan advised the government that the extreme left would use the ex-Tsar's presence "as an excuse for rousing public opinion against us."...*

On 1 Mar 1918, the family was placed on soldier's rations, which meant parting with ten devoted servants and giving up butter and coffee as luxuries. Nicholas and Alexandra were appalled by news of the Treaty of Brest-Litovsk, whereby Russia agreed to give up Poland, Finland, the Baltic States, Ukraine, the Crimea, and most of the Caucasus. What kept the family's spirits up was the belief that help was at hand. The Romanovs believed that various plots were underway to break them out of captivity and smuggle them to safety.

THE WEST TO THE ROMANOV RESCUE?

The Western Allies lost interest in the fate of the Romanovs after Russia left the war. The German government wanted the monarchy restored in Russia to crush the Bolsheviks and maintain good relations with the Central Powers. "On the 30 Apr 1918, the Romanovs were transferred to their final destination: the town of Yekaterinburg, where the prisoners were in the two-story Ipatiev House, the home of the military engineer Nikolay Nikolayevich Ipatiev, which ominously became referred to as the "house of special purpose." (Russia, Nicholas II of Russia, 2018)

### EXECUTION

*"According to the account of Yurovsky (the chief executioner), in the early hours of 17 Jul 1918, the royal family was awakened around 2:00 am, got dressed, and were led down into a half-basement room at the back of the Ipatiev house. The pretext for this move was the family's safety, i.e., that anti-Bolshevik forces were approaching Yekaterinburg, and the house might come under fire. Nicholas was carrying his son; when the family arrived in the basement, the former empress complained that there were no chairs for them to sit on. Yurovsky ordered two chairs brought in, and when the empress and the heir were seated, the executioners filed into the room. Yurovsky announced to them that they had been condemned to death by the Ural Soviet of Workers' Deputies. A stunned Nicholas asked, What? And turned toward his family. Yurovsky quickly repeated the order and shot the former Emperor outright. The executioners drew handguns, and the shooting began. Nicholas was the first to die; Yurovsky shot him several times in the chest. In 1981, Nicholas and his immediate family were recognized as martyred saints by the Russian Orthodox Church Outside Russia."* (Russia, Nicholas II of Russia, 2018)

Robert K. Massie provides a more sympathetic view of the Tsar: ... *"there still are those who are for political or other reasons continue to insist that Nicholas was "Bloody Nicholas." Most commonly, being described as shallow, weak, stupid—a one-dimensional figure presiding feebly over the last days of a corrupt and crumbling system. Descriptive of the prevailing public image of the last Tsar. Historians admit that Nicholas was a "good man"—the historical evidence of personal charm, gentleness, love of family, deep religious faith and strong Russian patriotism is too overwhelming to be denied—but they argue that personal factors are irrelevant; what matters is that Nicholas was a lousy tsar ... Mainly, the tragedy of Nicholas II was that he appeared in the wrong place in history"*. (Russia, Nicholas II of Russia, 2018)

# [4]
# WORLD WAR I

*"The European colonial period was the era from the 15th century to 1914 when Spain, Portugal, Britain, Russia, France, the Netherlands, Germany, Italy, and Belgium established colonies outside Europe."* (History, 2018)

Historically it is the Imperialists that are the primary source of global conflict. They had risen with rebellion and lawlessness and violated the Spirit of the Natural Law. Certain fundamental individual human rights are so important that no government, even a representative government, even democratically elected government can override them. They are inalienable human rights. A natural right to life, liberty, and property. The right to property is not the creation of government or law; the right to property is a natural right, in the sense that it is pre-political. It is a right that attaches to individuals, as human beings, even before any government comes on the scene, even before parliaments and legislature enact laws, define rights, and to enforce them, according to John Locke.

*"For me, being all the workmanship of one omnipotent, and infinitely wise maker, they are his property, whose workmanship they are, made to last during his, not one another's pleasure."* (John Locke, 2018)

The books of the Old Testament taught the people of Israel to choose life, by their conscious mind and the active free will to make the right choice according to the Torah of Moses every time. The will needs to be exercised, just like the pinkie finger it is weak without exercise. Not so for musicians, whether a keyboard player, a stringed instrument, or a brass instrument musician, the pinkie has an equal role in playing notes according to the demand of the score. It takes training to master.

THE BIG FIVE
The five biggest culprits in the last 500-year history of Europe that caused the large-scale destructive wars have been Britain, France, Russia, Germany, and Sweden. Those nations were extraordinarily ambitious and hungry to win the race in colonizing the world and beat other efforts. Small state countries and the indigenous people usually keep to themselves and get going with the toil of life and would instead prefer to be left alone than to be manipulated and invaded by the Imperialists. However, that is often far from reality; the large imperial nations manipulate the small ones to join the Allied forces to outdo the other imperialists, they get sucked into the Imperialists wars. Instead, (the Imperialists) they should have more genuine faith in the Creator of Life. Moreover, obey the Creator of life, Adonai Elohim given Torah instructions.

What is the driver of the Imperialistic ambitions to gain more power than they need? It is the exploitation of ordinary people of the land. Compared to the life and teaching of Yeshua Hamashiach, the Imperialists are too power-hungry and avaricious. Therefore, the small nations of the world should join forces and boycott the five large imperialists states and hold them accountable for their manipulative history that ratchets up tensions, conflicts, and wars. The small countries became collateral damage in the imperial conflicts.

The core problem of the Imperialists is that they do not respect the natural human rights to life, liberty, and property. The Imperialists always have agendas that preceded the natural human rights. That is the cause of wars. State of nature is a state of liberty; human beings are free and equal beings; no human-made hierarchy can take away life, liberty, or property. Even when individuals agree to come out of the state of nature and enter into society through consent and contract, the natural human rights do not get revoked. The only way to have the natural rights revoked is through lawlessness.

Similarly, in the state of nature, the natural lawbreaker would lose his or her natural rights to life, liberty, and property. Similarly, to the tooth for tooth, an eye for an eye, and life for a life principle. That does not reinforce a stable and secure society. It puts everyone on edge, defending their life in case of aggression because there were no police forces or army to control unexpected external aggression and violence. Everyone looked after themselves, similar to the animals in the natural environment.

Human beings were created in the image of the Creator of LIfe; they have Intellect, consciousness, imagination, will, memory, and emotions. Therefore, their existence is supposed to be on a higher moral plane than mere predator animals. Believe it or not, they have a God-given capacity for it. How many animals or humans do we know? That eat their offspring? There is a conscious sense, a pre-designed intellect with genuine respect and balance for life, given from outside of self-determination and will.

How often do we hear early in the morning the birds complaining about their lot in life? They sing a new song each morning as an expression of their living soul life experience from within, and they fill the environment with musical sounds, communicating melodically with other creatures of creation. Human character traits are different from animals at many levels.

One example of that was the occupation and the Russification of the Baltic States, 1940-1991. Horrible manipulation of independent states and people with natural human rights that wanted no part of the Russian Imperial expansionism. The Baltic states and the Nordic countries had their history and heritage, with their own people's shared values, beliefs, traditions, culture, human rights, and life priorities. What is even worse when the imperialists manipulate the cause of the wars and later blame others by taking the small states to their kangaroo courts of law and judge them to be guilty. The table should turn around and the small states to take the Imperialists to court and judge them on the unresolved World War 2 war crimes. 1939-1940.

The educated and learned people of the Modern world seek privilege. The causes of World War I remain controversial and debated questions. Scholars looking at the long-term seek to explain why two rival sets of powers – Germany and Austria-Hungary on the one hand, and Russia, France, and Great Britain on the other – had come into conflict by 1914. Scholars doing short-term analysis focused on summer 1914 ask if the conflict was possible to stop or whether it was out of control. Consensus on the origins of the war remains elusive since historians disagree on critical factors and place differing emphasis on a variety of factors. That point is compounded by changing historical arguments over time, particularly the delayed availability of classified historical archives. There was extreme chaos, disorder, and violent lawlessness happening all over Europe? The core reason for conflict and wars is the general disrespect for the sanctity of human life. Human consciousness can be diverted and distracted to value material things more than the central miracle of life, made in the image of God.

Here are some of the causes and effects of Europe that affected Finland directly: World War 1.

- Russian Revolutions, 1905 and 1917.
- Tsar of Russian permits the creation of the Duma in 1905 and abdicates in 1917.
- Russian sailors dissent, rebel, and mutiny in Russia and Helsinki, Finland.
- Socialist street guard controls the street as a militia. Ordering shops to close during Worker strikes. Manipulating people to join in the Russian revolution marches.
- Government Police Officers all over Finland sacked out of office. Replaced by Bolshevik Socialists.
- Poverty, hunger, and high unemployment in Finland in 1917. Workers are getting increasingly frustrated.

- Socialists use the Russian military presence in Finland to bolster their political causes.
- Parliament in Turku is held against their will in their work offices for 37 hours. Socialist leaders demand more Socialists to have seats in the parliament. If they do not accept the demands, Socialists will get the Russian military to make a coup. There were some 100,000 Russian military troops stationed in Finland in 1917.
- The Queen of England blessings, to give support to the Russian revolution Red Bolsheviks. By forming two troops in the Archangel White Sea region. They warred and killed dozens of Finnish white soldiers.
- The Brits went to the same side with the Russian revolution Bolsheviks, which murdered the entire Romanov family. As a preventative action to block the Germans from making their way towards the White Sea city of Archangel region.
- Russian civil war 1918 -1922.
- Brits in bed with the Romanov family murderers. It was an immoral compromise on the lawless side of the angels.
- Murmansk legionnaires in 1918 (Russian Reds)
- Murmansk Legion, also known as the Finnish Legion, was a British Royal Navy organized military unit during the 1918– 1919 Allied North Russia Intervention. It was composed of Finnish Red Guards who had fled after the Finland Bolsheviks expulsion from White-dominated Northern Finland to Soviet Russia and of some Finns working on the Murmansk Railroad. The Legion fought the 1918 Viena expedition of Finnish White Guards and defended the Murmansk Railroad along with British troops. Again the Brits supporting the lawlessness of the Bolsheviks.
- Karelian regiment recruitment.
- The Karelian regiment was another communist recruiting by British troops, which consisted of red socialists who had fled to the Soviet Union during the Bolsheviks ousting from Finland. It fought in Viena Karelia, alongside Bolshevism, a group of Finnish red tribal warlords led by Toivo Kuisma, against the Kuisma expedition, which was returned. The slogan of the Karelian regiment was "for the freedom of Karelia."
- In August 1918, the hope of Kuisma, the 250-man tribal troop leader, moved to Vienna and held Uhtula. The 300-400-member Karelian regiment of the Karelian Republic, which was equipped and trained by the English brits, commenced military action against tribal soldiers by killing the intelligence and security forces.
- 

## DISRESPECT FOR THE SPIRIT OF THE NATURAL LAW

There was no respect for the rule of law, no respect for natural rights. No one was declaring true Justice and declaring the same law to all. The out of control spirit of anarchy raged against the Spirit of the Natural Law and propagated violence. With rage, they hated those that believed in human rights, the civilized rule of law. The Bolsheviks extreme anarchy demanded the highest seat of authority for themselves.

Imperial England generally presumed that they had the moral high ground worldwide, based on their privileged reputation and royalty status.

Moreover, the arrogance of it, when any nation offended them militarily, then they would condemn that country, and not only the country that directly offended them militarily, but also any other country that had an alliance and mutually respectful relationship with the country, in their economic interest. The pride of the imperials leads them to serve serving arrogance.

## INWARD-LOOKING IMPERIALISTS

The Allied forces, especially England, were very narrow-minded, inward-looking, prejudiced, insular, utterly blind to the facts of reality and experience that Finland and the Baltic States had regarding Russia from the previous 500 years. How could the British leaders be so pride-filled smug and delusional that the independent

States would put aside their country's interest? Moreover, neglect their own militarily self-defense for the sake of England's prestige and foreign policies? The level of selfishness and indifference was absurd.

The Nordic countries and the Baltic people had to survive from early 1307 to 1917. For 500 years, the Nordic countries in a harmonious working relationship and has remained so to this day. The most predominant military aggressor during those 500 years was the Russian expansionism and Stalinism. There were many conflicts between Russia and Sweden. Russia has persistently pushed the boundaries westwards since 1807.

Europe has been like a material cash magnet for Moscow. Russian has often been desperate to compete with Western materialistic economic successes and compromised the integrity of its national soul in the process. The enemy of Finland people's Independence for the last 200 years has been Russia, not Germany. Historically there was much common ground between Finland and Germany. In the industries and tourism interest generally and the State Lutheran Church teachings. The relationship between the two countries developed early years through the Christian teaching and interpretations of the biblical doctrine of Martin Luther. Both countries rejected the Catholic heresies of the middle ages.

*"Martin Luther, (10 November 1483 – 18 February 1546) was a German professor of theology, composer, priest, monk, and a seminal figure in the Protestant Reformation. Luther came to reject several teachings and practices of the Roman Catholic Church. He strongly disputed the Catholic view on indulgences. They escorted Luther to the security of the Wartburg Castle at Eisenach. During his stay at Wartburg, which he referred to as "my Patmos," Luther translated the New Testament from Greek into German and poured out doctrinal and polemical writings. The Wartburg is a castle built initially in the Middle Ages. the place where Martin Luther translated the New Testament of the Bible into German."* (Luther, 2018)

*"A written agreement between the Evangelical Lutheran Church of Finland and The German Evangelical Church. The year 1500. The theological foundation. Conscious of its common roots in the history of the Western Church and the reformation of the 16th century. The Evangelical Lutheran Church of Finland and Germany evangelical church by the Lutheran member churches and the Evangelical Lutheran Church in Finland have a religious connection with the Lutheran World Federation as members, reinforce the existing and practically implemented connection."*

PIETISM
*"Pietism, from the word piety, was an influential movement in Lutheranism that combined its emphasis on Biblical doctrine with the Reformed emphasis on individual piety and living a vigorous Christian life. Pietism originated in modern Germany in the late 17th century with the work of Philipp Spener, a Lutheran theologian whose emphasis on personal transformation through spiritual rebirth and renewal, personal devotion, and piety laid the foundations for the movement. Pietism spread from Germany to Switzerland and the rest of German-speaking Europe. Scandinavia and the Baltics (where it was heavily influential, leaving a permanent mark on the region's dominant Lutheranism, with figures like Hans Nielsen Hauge in Norway. Peter Spaak, and Carl Olof Rosenius in Sweden, Katarina Asplund in Finland, and Barbara von Krüdener in the Baltics), and the rest of Europe. It was further taken to North America, primarily by German and Scandinavian immigrants. There, it influenced Protestants of other ethnic backgrounds, taking part in the 18th-century foundation of Evangelicalism, a vibrant movement within Protestantism that today has some 300 million followers."* Pietism. (encyclopedia, 2018)

Early 1900, the Finland government sought help from Germany for the expulsion of the Bolsheviks from Finland, at a time when the Bolsheviks attempted to influence and take charge of Finland society, just as they did later in Russia 1917. To understand the dilemma of being occupied for 100 years, from 1807 to 1917, Finland was not permitted to have an independent defense force.

The Russian Grand Duchy governors were determined to subjugate small countries; the russification process developed early in the interest of Russian expansionism. The Soviet Union continued to use russification as a Morphosis process in Finland and the Baltic States territory. So that the ordinary people of the land and the independent constitutions would morph from the original people's cultural identity, values, and the government constitution into a different political species and become loyal to a foreign constitution.

Why would they plan such a sinister corkscrew conspiracy? They were not on a leisure holiday; they were on an assignment. They were hungry to exploit other national resources, government offices, people, land, and territory. In other words, coveting everything from the high offices and the transport to the silk stockings and the kitchen sink. So, doing subjugating the peoples to become an extension of the broader Russia, with the same purpose and objectives as the communist worldview and life philosophy 1922 -1991.

The Western world, by large, does not understand the nature of the East European spiritual battle or the diabolical source that powers it into lawlessness. It has a spiritual source, which people yield to and empower it. The power of Satan that has been raging for the last 500 years. The dots are everywhere from the early 1900 to 1991. It starts with the core lawlessness, rebellion, and anarchy. To steal away authority from legitimate jurisprudence spiritual authority. As a cause, who has been stealing? Killing?

Moreover, destroying? How difficult is it to join those dots to the past 100-year history? The cause was from 1900-1922. Moreover, from 1939-1945. The wild conspiracy between Germany and Soviet Russian leaders to pillage East Europe. It was the spirit of Satan with temptations that got into the heads of Joseph Stalin, with totalitarian state atheism, under the guise of pseudo-socialism, and Adolf Hitler with the totalitarian Nazi regime.

In so doing, Satan was able to cause extreme destruction to people, animals, land environment, and human civil society. All in the spirit of animosity, against the Creator of life, Elohim. Spiritual forces are continually influencing and tempting a leader's mind egos to take sides with the lawlessness of the Nemesis. Testing the borders and the will of the people seeking out broken walls. The nature of the spiritual battles on the borders of countries, and humanity made in the image of God, clearly described in the Bible.

> "For our struggle is not against flesh and blood, but against the rulers, against the authorities, against the powers of this dark world and the spiritual forces of evil in the heavenly realms." Ephesians 6:12. (Apostle Paul)

What is he talking about? Who is the ruler? Satan. Who is the authority? Demonic spiritual forces. Powers of the dark underworld.

It is the Nemesis, Satan, and his demon host. That can only destroy the earth through tempting people to do evil, people that are given to the demon spirit influence. There is a mark of the Nemesis in those minds that partake in the spirit of the lawless one, those that are guided by the spirit of Satan, to do his bidding. In so doing, making war against the kingdom of the Creator of Life.

By reason alone, immoral actions can be forensically inspected and identified as being irrational because it is a severe error of moral judgment. How is it possible? Why would ambitious politicians, government leaders, servants of people's society make such severe errors in moral judgment? Violating the principles found in the Bill of Rights? The spirit of the Natural Law. In conflict with the principles of International Law. Moreover, and to deny any wrongdoing?

How is it possible? The dark side of the coin causes it. The Deception of the Nemesis, the demon spirits that get into the hearts and minds of leaders and uses them for evil on earth. That is also the blind corner, the failure to see and understand the spiritual reality of moral values. Causing spiritual vacuum in the mind and heart, with the absence of the absolute moral code.

No animal of the wilderness would divert from natural to such extreme behavior, from their natural habitat. Humans are commanded by God in the Bible to behave more like humans and less like animals. Dictators have surpassed the behavior of wild animals by far, considering the many millions of innocent lives that their actions have destroyed. What is behind it all? It is the influence of the Nemesis, the devil, and the spirit of Satan that empowers the dictator's lust after political and military power, as if it was their highest throne and destiny in life, at the feet of Satan.

One explanation is that the dictator's minds were blinded by the deceitful temptations of the Nemesis. They became filled by his spirit and therefore deceived into believing lies. They trusted their mind and gave no respect to the Creator of Life. They certainly did not believe or respect the natural human rights or respect the sanctity of human life. The covetousness of Imperial Russia and the USSR expansionism was viewed by the people as the Russian bear eating up the smaller neighbors on the fringes. Who would find any evidence? Alternatively, have a voice to call for Justice? In a lawless world, where rebellion and anarchy are often voices heard the loudest, with the most authority, by servants of the devil.

Welcome to the dark dungeons of the Nemesis. Fighting for the cause of the prince of darkness called Satan. That diabolically manipulates people's minds, denying them of life, liberty, and destiny. In 1914-17 the Brits had an enemy, but because they were so preoccupied with their royalty status and pride, they could not see the larger picture, how the Nemesis had been active in the life of the East European States over the 200 years since 1807. What are the priorities between nations when dealing with others Internationally? It is most commonly commerce and trade. Should the priority always be economics? Chasing after the Trade and Goods markets? Not really! They are a secondary priority in life. The most greedy people will fight and start wars over territory.

LAMENT OVER BABYLON

> Revelation 18: 11-14. (NIV) "The merchants of the earth will weep and mourn over her because no one buys their cargoes anymore— cargoes of gold, silver, precious stones and pearls; fine linen, purple, silk and scarlet cloth; every sort of citron wood, and articles of every kind made of ivory, costly wood, bronze, iron and marble; cargoes of cinnamon and spice, of incense, myrrh and frankincense, of wine and olive oil, of fine flour and wheat; cattle and sheep; horses and carriages; and human beings sold as slaves."

The priority should be balance with integrity, be faithful to the Spirit of the Natural Law, and represent true Justice. According to the interpretation of the Natural Law, John Locke wrote.

*"Every man has a property in his person. This nobody has any right to but himself. The labor of his body, and the work of his hands, we may say, are the property of his".*

*"We own ourselves, and we have property in ourselves, to the idea that we own our labor."*

*"whatever then he removes out of the state that nature has provided, and left it in, he has mixed his labor with, and joined to it something that is his own, and thereby makes it his own"*

How and why?

*"For this labor being the unquestionable property of the laborer, no man but he can have a right to what that is once joined to."* (Locke, John Locke, 2018)

UNREST

There was unrest, rebellion, lawlessness brewing, that flared up with the spirit of anarchy in early 1900-1922. The Imperial Superpowers had no conscience or political will to put out any civil anarchy firestorms such as the Russian Revolution and the Russian civil war. It was ballistic violence on the Spirit of the Natural Law. They just stood back and watched it as a price fight, or a street brawl, and let it burn out by itself. Indifferent to which side won and came on top. They were going to reward the winner regardless, who, what, when was violated.

As it turned out, lawlessness won big time. It was a victory on many fronts for Satan for 50 years, from early 1903 – 1953. To understand it, one just needs to join the dots that sink below the rule of law, according to the Spirit of the Natural Law, of the last 100-year history of East Europe. Generally, in the West, any rebellion, lawlessness, or dictator's anarchy are not seen, mentioned, or understood to have any spiritual connection to the dark side, or the force influencing the human agents to be lawless. The bottom line in Western thinking is their motivation and drive, convenient interpretation of economics, and progress. Law and Justice are seen according to their own short-sighted self-satisfied objective goals.

The characteristic of the Nemesis at work in history are not always observed because human minds are full of economics and are deceived into believing two-dimensional reality. The oversimplified 2-dimensional reality that has been skewed by the Nemesis to hide Satan in the human blind corners, of three and four dimensions, where he can hide and nobody notices anything. He has become nonexistent to the preoccupied human conscience.

Germany was a Godsend to Finland in the early 1900, providing means of support in the fight against the violence of the Russian Bolsheviks, which was ever-growing chaos to 1922. Suppressing and fighting against the spirit of anarchy that would spill out over the borders of Russia. Pride filled Imperialists saw them themselves as all-knowing God on earth; they did not see the big picture according to the Spirit of the Natural Law. Finland was discreetly requesting and petitioning behind the Russian Governor-General for weapons from Germany for self-defense purposes. Germany was discreetly selling weapons for self-defense purposes and secretly providing military training for the young university students of Finland. They were getting training to become organized military officers in the fight against the Bolsheviks spirit of lawlessness. The rising tide of anarchy, which became the future hardcore stronghold of State Atheism by Stalin, in the Satan ruled USSR. Similarly, 20 years later, Germany providing vital military equipment in the fight against Stalin's totalitarian regime war against peace in 1940.

Moreover, much more hardware support from 1941 to 1944. Finland purchasing German military hardware, equipment; with the strong spirited will to remain independent, Finland was able to defend against USSR aggressive invasion attempts in 1939 and 1944. It was the appropriate solution to Stalin's methods.

Russian leaders calloused hearted culture to the Spirit of the Natural Law. in the minds and the hearts of the Russian leaders for the last 500 years. The same land bridge, where the Karelian and the Ingrians lived, was not left alone and allowed the people of the land to live in peace.

The Russian leaders did not have the ears to hear or the eyes to see what was the will of the Creator of life for humanity. Peace on earth. The same self-driven bellicose spirit was repeating violence and crime against humanity over and over. Stalin's rule characterized aggressive politics, violence, and the military force when his foreign politics failed to deliver on-demand. The manipulative demands by Moscow politics were far-reaching, into the Baltic States and Finland. The constraints came from several levels.

They were denied self-determination and denied Independence and constrained from developing robust self-defense. The constraints came from several directions. Unlike the Baltic States, occupied for 50 years. That was a dismal scenario for the Baltic States, to be occupied by the Soviets for 50 years, by the Allied forces partners in crime from 1941 to 1945. A severe error of judgment, and a blind corner beyond the allied forces conscience. 1939-1953.

The Russian revolution fever finally peaked into total anarchy over the Monarchy rule. The Royal Romanov family execution preplanned, manipulated and approved by the Bolsheviks leaders. The Royal family portrayed by the Bolsheviks as being the ultimate enemies of the people of Russia. That was an apparent nefarious link to the heart of the Nemesis, to steal, kill and destroy. To twist and remove the spirit of truth, to make the morally right into the wrong (reject truth), and to make the morally wrong (accept lies) into the accepted standard in the society.

To make the core influencing spirit of the Nemesis, as some legitimate kindred ruling spirit of values in society. The Deception of the destructive forces, in the spirit of rebellion, lawlessness, and anarchy. Is that not a familiar pattern? Created by all dictators who perpetuate lawlessness? There is a familiar pattern to the influence and the dark deeds of the Nemesis, another mark of the Nemesis, planned and approved by the Bolsheviks leaders, portraying the Royal family as the ultimate enemies of the people of Russia.

How many political executions of Kings and Tsars does it take to believe that there are rebellion, lawlessness, and the spirit of anarchy raging, being whipped up by the spirit of Satan and his demon hosts? There were many political executions before the Romanov family executed in 1918. Therefore, that Bolsheviks propaganda about Nicholas II being the enemy of the peoples was no news; the revolutionists had been singing the same anarchist tune for 50 years.

God and the Holy Bible make clear that rebellion, lawlessness, and the spirit of anarchy is from the pit of hell. So, why should people give it more power? When is it condemned by the infinite mind wisdom of the Creator God? Aggression and violence do not deserve the respect of intelligent people. Furthermore, it is in the domain of the evil one. The loser of a life. The Russian people could not read the future and do not realize that what was going to come from the Bolsheviks perpetuated revolution and the totalitarian State Atheism leader Joseph Stalin, that would require the people of Russian many more millions of lives between 1917 to 1967. The destruction of humanity was far worse during the USSR than the Nicholas II Tsar of the Russian Monarchy.

The Bolsheviks rejected the God-given principles of the Spirit of the Natural Law and sided with the enemy of God, the Nemesis. They were doing deliberate violence to the Creator of Life on earth. The fundamental individual rights that are intrinsic values of human life, so important that no government, even a representative government, the even democratically elected government can override them. They are the natural right to life, liberty, and property. So, what if the Russian Tsar did not respect the rights to life, liberty, and property? What could people do? They could protest peacefully and make their complaints heard. Such was the result of the 1905 demonstrations. The Russian Duma formed as the result of those requesting, petitioning through the communication of the demonstration.

LAWS CONCERNING ISRAEL'S KINGS
A king has a responsibility to hear the complaints of the people. They were not to put a foreigner over them, who was not their brother. There was the clear guidance of the responsibilities and principles given to a King in Israel; he was accountable for his office as a king. These instructions and laws were given in 1400 BC. There is no excuse for any ruler to be irresponsible, only self-appointed dictators and despots position themselves above the Spirit of the Natural Law, such as Joseph Stalin and Adolf Hitler.

> "The king, moreover, must not acquire great numbers of horses for himself or make the people return to Egypt to get more of them, for the Lord has told you, "You are not to go back that way again." He must not take many wives, or his heart will be led astray. He must not accumulate large amounts of silver and gold. When he takes the throne of his kingdom, he is to write for himself on a scroll a copy of this law, taken from that of the Levitical priests. It is to be with him, and he is to read it all the days of his life so that he may learn to revere the Lord his God and follow carefully all the words of this law and these decrees and not consider himself better than his fellow Israelites and turn from the law to the right or to the left. Then he and his descendants will reign a long time over his kingdom in Israel." Israel." Deuteronomy 17:18-20

The same principles of responsibility apply for human reason, to engage in, and to take it as a priority value in life.
Quote: John Locke. *"The state of nature has a law of nature to govern it which obliges every one: and reason, which is that law, teaches all mankind, who will but consult it, that being all equal and independent, no one ought to harm another in his life, health, liberty or possessions. The reason is that law, of nature. And the human capacity to reason together."* (Locke, 2018)

The disconnect between the Russian monarchy rule of law and the spirit of anarchy in the Russian revolution became an infectious fever that was caught on by people who were given to the Bolsheviks inciting and rousing revolution and violence with the Russian Seamen. Then came dissent, defiance, rebellion, and mutiny. The Russian Seamen in the port of Finland mutinied their officers on the ships and the shore.

The Russian engagement in World War 1 took its toll on the people. The intolerance and unrest grew by the military failures and setbacks during the three and a half years of World War 1. Russia was engaged in World War One for 3 1/2 years. After the Russian setbacks, came to the realization that it was an enormous loss, a wasted effort, and the unbearable misery for the wounded and for the families of the lives lost. A waste of valuable national resources to continue the mindless slaughter at the front lines of World War 1.

## RUSSIAN REVOLUTION

Looking back at the events, the 1917 Russian revolution can be compared to 26 April, 1986, the Chernobyl disaster, which was a catastrophic nuclear accident. Those people that romanticize the Russian revolution are irresponsible and out of touch with the intelligent human purpose design. They are mostly lefties, like those in the Australian Broadcasting Corporation.

What is there romantic about the Chernobyl disaster, that was a catastrophic nuclear accident? People that romanticize the Chernobyl nuclear accident do not think laterally of the people who live in Nordic countries and East Europe when the radioactive contamination from the Chernobyl accident was scattered. There were Russian, Ukraine and the international spread of radioactive substances, much of it deposited in mountainous regions such as the Alps, the Welsh mountains and the Scottish Highlands, where adiabatic cooling caused radioactive rainfall.

*"Approximately 100,000 km² of land was significantly contaminated with fallout, with the worst hit regions being in Belarus, Ukraine, and Russia. Slighter levels of contamination detected over all of Europe except for the Iberian Peninsula".* (Wikipedia E., Chernobyl disaster, 1986)

The Nordic pine forests along East Finland, Estonia, and Russia are used during the summer months for foraging wild berries, and for mushroom during the autumn season. Every wild berry and mushroom foraging Finn along the East Finland and Russian border, has had his quiet moments in the summer season, listening to the song of birds, singing in the natural forest. The connection with the natural environment with wild berries and mushroom to the Chernobyl nuclear disaster was never seen as being romantic. No health respecting person is so delusional or vain.

How destructive was the Russian revolution and the Civil war to the Russian society spiritually? It was morally, spiritually and socially a catastrophic disaster event, from 1917 to 1922? It effected not only the regions of Russia, but also other regions outside of Russian were significantly contaminated with fallout. The spirit of lawlessness fallout was horrific in 1917-1922. It was there the USSR State atheism was given birth. Then the grim reapers began their harvest of human souls between 1922 to 1944; it was unlike anything before or since. How many people lost their lives? Far too many.

## SOCIALIST PUSH FOR INDEPENDENT FINLAND IN JULY 1917

The forced abdication of the Russian Tsar Nicholas II was seen as a window of opportunity for the Bolsheviks and Socialists. When the Russian temporary government was set up in Petrograd, the Socialists attempted to drive a wedge between Russia and Finland governance, and there by the Bolsheviks getting the control of Finland political power. There appeared an opening, a window of opportunity during the unrest caused by the Russian revolution, for a political party to take advantage of. Would future Finland have the Bolshevik socialist agitators as the majority in Finland parliament? As it was already pushing for before the Russian Revolution of 1917?

The Bolsheviks had been working at it and agitating for change in the political environment for 17 years. The conservative bourgeois society harrowed against it. The conflict between the two opposing worldviews flared up with a crescendo in 1917; the lawless anarchists were using unscrupulous means to seize government authority and power. Their worldview was atheism, no respect for the Spirit of the Natural Law, no respect for the rule of law, and no respect for the Biblical worldview. There was a fundamental contrasting difference in their life philosophy difference. The Bolsheviks were ready to steal. Kill and destroy to satisfy the will and desires of the Nemesis heart and mind.

## SUMMER OF 1917 FINLAND

The society of Finland was affected by the political turbulence going on in Europe and Russia, in the summer of 1917. There was the 100-year unpleasant air of foreign Imperial Russia, hanging over the people of Finland. It was not by choice of Finland people that Russian rule had landed on Finland society. On the contrary, it was Imperialist power politics, and the influence of the Nemesis, coveting and greed, to grow Russia bear bigger and bigger by eating up the indigenous people's territories. Russian rule over the affairs of Finland was an uninvited encroachment of the early 1800 conflict.

In 1917 there was high unemployment; there were poverty and hunger, people and communities were caught up in the flux of the uncertainty, the ebb, and flow of open rebellion, the rule of law and anarchy. Here are some of the prevailing circumstance of the times.

- Socialist Party had a majority in the "autonomous" Finland parliament in 1917.
- More than 50% of all the party representatives supported SDP.
- Tsar Nicholas II abdicated. Russia was being led by the temporary government.
- Russia was still engaged in the World War One from 1914 to 1917.
- There was over 100,000 Russian military personnel in Finland in 1917. Finland did not have Independence, and not allowed to have any organized military armed forces.
- There was much unsettling uncertainty caused by the World War 1 in Europe.
- Unemployment was very high in Finland in 1917; there were much poverty, shortage of food, and hunger inside the society.
- 

There was a strange spirit of confusion, caused by the revolution fever. That affected the people's living soul constitution. There was the one-sided coin illusion, the letter of the law, formalities, hysterical peoples, obsessive minds, no peace, no contentment, and no spiritual reality. There was no knowledge of the Spirit of the Natural Law. No understanding or respect for the Creator of Life design. Only agitated people are demanding their own will, their way for the future. The Bolsheviks got it their way from 1917 to 1922.

The socialist was demanding change to the law that determined the length of work hours per day. Demand was to reduce the work hours down to 8 hours per day. The standard work week at the time was officially six days. The Socialist worker's organization representative struck and formed radical guards to dominate the public streets. The Senate Square in Helsinki was often filled with Socialist and work for striking crowds. Socialist organization guards evolved to be the radical Red guards.

The supreme authority in Finland government during the Russian Tsardom was the Russian Governor General and Tsar himself. When Nicholas II was removed from power, then the political fight began for power between the temporary government in Petrograd. And Bolsheviks, which were driven by the socialist ideology inspired to take all authority and power off the Russian government altogether and began to be self-governed as an independent nation run by the Bolsheviks. Behind the scenes, a spiritual driving force, the dark side of the coin. The same dark, a diabolical source that feeds rebellion, lawlessness, and does violence to the Spirit of the Natural Law, of the Creator of Life. The nature of the Creator of Life does not change. His laws do not change; they are consistent forever. Socialist pushed for changes in the authority law and planning to declare themselves as the highest authority in Finland. It would remove authority from the Russian temporary government. Excluding the Russian foreign policy and the military matters.

Oskari Tokoinen of the Social Democrats Party, Spring 20 April, 1917. In his speech, he encouraged his party and spoke of the opportunity for Finland to declare Independence. Mr. Tokoinen believed the Russian Revolution was a legitimate demonstration of the people. Moreover, Finland should do likewise to declare Independence.

The Bolsheviks leader's viewpoint was that the Bolsheviks was the only political party in Russia that showed empathy to the idea that Finland should become independent of the established Russian Monarchy. They believed that the Finland declaration of Independence was foreseeable shortly. However, the Russian temporary government in Petrograd was sharply opposed to the idea of Finland independence from Russia.

Again, the same one-sided coin illusion. On the surface presenting ideas and concepts, that are false principles. They hide the dark side of the coin; they hide their diabolical hidden agenda, they hide the global socialist ideology, the socialist revolution, where the leaders gravitate and become great in the eyes of the socialist world history.

At the time Lenin had returned to Petrograd from his Russian exile in Europe and Finland, and he was voicing his radical ideas openly in his letters and speeches, that the small oppressed countries should have their self-determination granted to separate from Russian monarchy.

"but not for the reason that we fantasize about the ideals of small countries becoming independent, rather the contrary, we want large governments, but on a democratic foundation." – Vladimir Lenin.

The Vladimir Lenin political campaign speeches that mentioned the Baltic States self-determination to be separate from Russian monarchy did not necessarily mean becoming an independent country, or separate from the more "fabulous Russian future." They were purely political speeches, with hidden agendas, without the spiritual reality of liberty. What the people of Finland and the Baltic States wanted, was for the Bolsheviks, the socialist, and the Russian communist agitators to go home, and leave the Independent aspiring people alone in their own country. Both Vladimir Lenin and Joseph Stalin were highly motivated politically; they were false spirit BS artists, they were speaking as false prophets, speaking for the cause of the Nemesis, the will of Satan on earth. They did not have the spirit of truth.

> "The thief comes only to steal and kill and destroy. I have come that they may have life, and have it in all its fullness." John 10:10.

Peace loving people should be left alone in their natural state and allow them to live their lives under the spirit of God's rule. Away from the ambitious politician's misguided false spirits, that only cause confusion, loss, and destruction. A sample of the false spirits misleading is the pseudo-socialism and communist ideology. From the 1917 campaign speeches, Finland and the Baltic States were in for a rude shock, in 1939-1941. The aggression of the totalitarianism, Stalinism, and the hardcore State Atheism, with the violent military invasion and occupation, followed.

RURAL WORKERS STRIKES, CONFLICT
People in the cities were queuing in bread lines, expecting handouts to keep families with young children in health with little food and nutrition supply. There was an underlying card ration system allocating food. People went without bread for several days at a time; rye bread was a standard food stable. The agricultural workers strike at the same time as the shortage of food supplies caused much anger in the rural communities. The environment of uncertainty in 1917 caused people to congregate and form groups and networks for united effort. This is understandable from the people of Finland perspective, the population of Finland in 1917 was just over 3.1 million.

At the same time, the population of Russia was 125,000,000. The ratio alone over 40 to 1 can cause an enormous amount of defenselessness, especially in those people that are on the edge of vulnerability, poverty and unemployment people of the society. A minority people group being pushed around by the lawless anarchists.

For some people, it may have been the decider that decided to swing over to a fantasy of being under the wing of a foreign superpower such as Russia. Destitute, unemployed people were expecting relief to their misery from the visibly grand Russian monarchy affluence to be the savior of the poor. In reality, it was a misguided illusion that only got worse from 1922-1950, when the Lenin and Stalin Marxist ideology masqueraded as pseudo-socialism and was implemented as a hardcore State atheism.

## THE HAKANIEMEN RIOT 1906

The Hakaniemen riot is considered to be the first of the clashes between the white Finns guardianship and the Red Guards. The involvement of Finnish Reds in support of the revolt of the Viapora revolt led to a more profound interplay between the Finnish workers' movement and the Russian revolutionaries and the more explicit confrontation with the bourgeoisie.

On 2 August, 1906, the Hakaniemen riot was an armed incident in Hakaniemi, Helsinki. The parties involved in the interrogation of the Viapora rebellion were the white guardianship of the students opposed to the Red Guards and the rebels of the Russian Seamen. The incident began when the Red Army tried to stop the tram in Hakaniemi. The conflict required nine deaths, seven of which belonged to the white guard's arena and two red guards. Dozens of people were injured in the riot. (Encyclopedia, Red Guards, 2018)

## HUITTINEN DAIRY INDICENT 1917

Huittinen (Swedish: Vittis) is a town and municipality of Finland. It is located in the Satakunta region. 61°10.5′N 022° 42′E. The Huittinen's skirmish between the Russian revolution supporters and the white Finn guards at the Dairy Co-Op in July 1917. The strike efforts by the reds were similar to the all-out strikes during 1905 Russian demonstrations. The skirmish was between the dairy owners and the dairy workers that were of the same mind as the Russian revolutionists. On 12 July, 1917, an 8-hour strike was called by the workers. The following day a 400-500 mob came with clubs, rocks to support the strikers. At the dairy was a rural police officer with 50 armed guards. Several guards were injured, including the police officer. The striking mob wanted Huittinen dairy to stop production. The owners refused to stop the dairy production. It was the first violent political confrontation in Finland since the riot of Hakaniemi in 1906. Seven strikers were shot and wounded by the dairy guards as the strike supporting mob encroached on the farm and started throwing rocks and clubs, and bashing the guards at the dairy farm, several guards were seriously injured. (Encyclopedia, Huittisten meijerikahakka, 1917)

## THE WHITE GUARDS VERSUS THE BOLSHEVIKS RED GUARDS

Russian revolution patronizing socialists, on one side, and the right winged bourgeois on the other side. Supported by the Workers Union, the strikers demand police off the street in Helsinki, with the help of the Russian revolutionist military and Russian Seamen. Socialist strikers formed organized street militia guards, to make sure the shop owners were closing shop during the socialist workers strikes. The socialist militia guards controlled the street of Turku. The militia street guards were a precursor of the armed conflict that flared up against the right-wing Finns.

There was conflict amongst the university students, the socialists arresting the right wing supporting students, and often attempting to change the right wings political views over to the left-wing socialists. There was animosity on the street of Turku during the early spring of 1917, deep-seated hatred that went two ways. On one side the arrogance of the Russian Socialist militia guards, which encroached on Finland society and imposed Russian rule in 1808, were some Finnish Russians sympathizers, they were a minority. The opposite side was the home grown Finnish people of the land. People of the land that the Russians had encroached upon. They were the Right-winged liberal Finns.

Russian government rule over the people of Finland for 100 years had marinated the Finnish society culture. Previously the society was under the Swedish Grand Duchy government influence for 400 years. The 1917 strikers at Turku leader Tuomas Myrsky suggested that the Turku parliamentarians should be taken as prisoners. There were thousands of strikers surrounding the parliament house in Turku and would not allow the parliamentarians to come out of the building. Parliamentarians were held on lockdown. Until the strikers, demands were implemented. The socialist strikers surrounded the city of Turku representative council member's offices. Moreover, held captive for 37 hours inside the government building office space. The socialist demanded their party representatives be given more seats in the parliament, even though during the elections they had not won enough support. The strikers threatened the parliament, saying that the socialist representation had to receive more seats in the parliament. Otherwise, the Russian military will take control of the government, in others words they were threatening a military coup by the Bolsheviks and the Russian military. The sitting Parliament in Turku resisted the threats of the strikers and stayed firm on the principles of the rule of law, and the democratic voting process.

### SOCIALIST LEADER OSKARI
"The SDP (Socialist Democratic Party) was founded as the Finnish Labour Party (Finnish: Suomen Työväenpuolue) in 1899. The name was changed to the present form in 1903. SDP was closely affiliated with 1907 established Finnish Trade Union Federation (SAJ), as all of its members were also members of the party."

The spirit of the Bolsheviks rebellion and lawlessness from Russia paved the way for the pseudo-socialism and pseudo-social democratic party. From the beginning, it was a revolutionist movement, rebellion, lawlessness, and anarchy. A counterfeit created by the Nemesis his demon host. They did not recognize or respect the authentic spirit of the Creator God. The SDP did not perceive or understand the Spirit of the Natural Law. They resorted to brute force, self-will, and the spirit of the Nemesis. "The party lost its majority in the 1917 election, and in 1918, started a rebellion that escalated into the Finland Liberation war. SDP members declared Finland the Socialist Republic but were defeated by the forces of the Finnish Senate. The war resulted in most of the party leaders being killed, imprisoned or left to seek refuge in Soviet Russia."

*"In addition, the process leading to the Civil War and the war itself had stripped the party of its political legitimacy and respectability in the eyes of the conservative majority. However, the political support for the party remained strong, and in the election of 1919, the party, reorganized by Väinö Tanner, received 80 of the 200 seats of the parliament. Former exiled SDP members founded the Communist Party of Finland in Moscow in 1918."*

*"Although the Communist Party was banned in Finland until 1944, it was represented by front organizations, leading to the support of the Finnish working class being divided between the communist party and the SDP."* (Encyclopedia, Social Democratic Party, 2018)

Government organization authorities were being challenged by the Bolsheviks brutish tactics on the street of Finland early in 1917. Workers street militia ruled the streets. With the help of the Russian military rebels and Seamen. 1917 was a time for unsettling uncertainty; workers street militia let everyone know who was in charge of the streets in the city of Turku. Socialist Workers organized militia which evolved into the Communist Red militia. The community worldviews became more and more polarized. Russia was in turmoil, and the Russian Governor General in Finland was losing authority fast. As it happened, the Finns sprang out from underneath the death grip, of the dead carcass of the Russian bear. For a time, Finland was free from the Governor-general authority.

### THE SUPREME AUTHORITY LAW
Previously the supreme law was under the Tsar of Russia. After the Russian revolution, the power authority elapsed. Who would take the reins of power in Finland?

The most coveted burning question during the transfer of power. Should the power over Finland go to the temporary government in Russia? Alternatively, to the Finland parliament?

The parliament in Finland prepared to declare the parliament to be the highest authority in Finland affairs. It was the first step towards Independence from Russian rule. The Russian temporary government would only have foreign affairs and the military matters to be concerned. Socialist minister Oskari Tokoinen had openly talked about Finland becoming independent.

### RUSSIAN REVOLUTION
Much earlier on in 1905, the Russian Revolution was causing mass political and social unrest that spread through vast areas of the Russian Empire. The rebellion included worker strikes, peasants and also military mutinies. It led to Constitutional Reform in Russia including the establishment of the State Duma, a multi-party system, and the Russian Constitution of 1906.

In 1917 the Russian military eventually refused to follow Russian Nicholas II orders to put down the rebellion, at times had even used their weapons against the protestors. There was a tectonic shift of loyalties, in the military ranks, the force of the moving loyalties was cracking and splitting by the forces of lawlessness and anarchy.

Fiction.
*From 1917 to 1922, on the other side of the coin, the demonic cauldron was being filled and fired up for five years with countless tormented human souls. The spirit of betrayal, bitterness, and treason flowed, and hissed like the melted lava of an erupting volcano, releasing the escaping pressure under the earth mantle, and shooting up hot lava through the red heart of a black volcano.*
End of fiction.

It was John Stuart Mill that made a clean break with bright intelligence, between the potential spiritual mind, and the carnal mind of the flesh. He said,

*"It is better to be a human being dissatisfied than a pig satisfied. Better to be Socrates dissatisfied than a fool satisfied. And if the fool or the pig is of a different opinion, it is because they only know their side of the question."* – John S Mill (Mill, 1863)

A clear contrast between spiritual free will, and a succumbing to the carnal desires of the flesh. To be spiritually and morally strong with the power of a rational mind. The freedom of choice by the free will is possible when it is consciously exercised. Children learn to use their mind and the capacity of the free will to make choices as they are instructed and guided by their parents, teachers, and spiritual leaders.

Wise parents instruct and guide their children to spiritual values and moral ethics, explaining why it is important to listen? The point of listening is to learn how to do it the right way. And to learn how to live a life in the right way. Too many people have lived their lives the wrong way, not according to the Spirit of God. They did not listen to His voice of wisdom. The importance of having an ability to think rationally and morally is vitally important for successful life skills. Personal, spiritual and social health. The thinking mind and heart need to be in the right order. It starts with listening to spiritual leaders that explain what the right order of life is. In the beginning God, Elohim.

The wrong order starts with self-will. It creates frustration, setbacks, suffering, depression, and can possibly lead to a life of crime. The wrong sequence order is rammed through even when it does not fit. Understanding the Biblical worldview, with Biblical life philosophy, and to live in the will of the Creator of life, as Adonai and Elohim.

The most unfortunate children are those that get no education, no instruction or training on how to think about the world that they live in. Does it make a difference in how people think? The nature of the human living soul is very easily programmed to deceive self; there are six functions of the mind, the Intellect, will, imagination, consciousness, memory, and emotions.

In the Hebrew custom, children become responsible at 12 to 13 years old.
*"According to Jewish law, when Jewish boys become 13 years old, they become accountable for their actions and become a bar mitzvah. A girl becomes a bat mitzvah at the age of 12 according to Orthodox and Conservative Jews, and at the age of 13 according to Reform Jews."*

*"Passages in the books of Exodus and Numbers note the age of majority for army service as twenty. The term "bar mitzvah" appears first in the Talmud. The codification of the Jewish oral Torah compiled in the early first millennium of the common era. To connote "an [agent] who is subject to the law," and the age of thirteen is also mentioned in the Mishnah as the time one is obligated to observe the Torah's instructions (commandments):*

*"At five years old, a person should study the Scriptures, at ten years for the Mishnah, at 13 for the commandments".*

*"The Talmud gives 13 as the age at which a boy's vows are legally binding and states that this is a result of his being a "man," as required in Numbers 6:2. The term "bar mitzvah," in a sense is now used, cannot be clearly traced earlier than*

*the 14th century, the older rabbinical term being "gadol" (adult) or "bar 'onshin" (legally responsible for own misdoings)."* (Encyclopedia, Bar Mitzvah, 2018)

REVOLUTION BOLSHEVIKS IMPOSE CONFORMITY

The rebellious activists, the professional Bolshevik revolutionists, worked at it from early 1900 to 1917, and finally overthrow the Russian Royal authority by the spirit of rebellion and anarchy. Once they had overcome the ruling authorities and got into the position of power, they imposed their political views on everyone that were of different political, or worldview. Hard-line politics, back flips, extortion, and brute force cruelty, everything sliding away from ethics, morality and the rule of law in the Russian society 1917 to 1922. Everyone locally had to conform and join in the Socialist political movement for the local political leaders will. The importance of understanding the difference between authentic spiritual life values and a purely materialistic life philosophy. One is a biblical spiritual life philosophy, and the other is purely materialistic worldview and at the core with a dialectic materialism agenda.

The fundamental problem for the last 100 years at the core is Deception. Human minds blind to the spiritual reality of life. Life is not like a one-sided coin. How could they miss it, when there is an entire material world of God's works as evidence? They missed it because they did not listen, they were full of unbelief, not listening to the voice of wisdom. Their minds were under the power of Deception, of the carnal mind, and the deceitful influence of the Nemesis.

DECEPTION

*"Deception is the act of propagating a belief that is not true or is not the whole truth (as in half-truths or omission). Deception can involve dissimulation, propaganda, and sleight of hand, as well as distraction, camouflage, or concealment. There is also self-deception, as in bad faith. It can also be called, with different subjective implications, beguilement, deceit, bluff, mystification, ruse, or subterfuge."* (Encyclopedia, Deception , 2018)

In 1922 the collective brain-child of Karl Marx Dialectic Materialistic philosophy, V. Lenin political theory for the Socialist global domination, and Stalin's political ambitions for conquest was the formation of the State Atheism, Union of Soviet Socialist Republics (USSR). It was a diabolical rebellious deception, contrived by the influence of the prince of darkness. For maximum destruction and the suffering of creation, the USSR state atheism was defiant and making war on everything that the Holy Bible represented. A purely materialistic worldview, by people without faith, or goodwill, towards the Creator of Life. The Natural rights of people were removed and demolished; people had no right to life, liberty, or property.

The spirit of anarchy in the Bolsheviks got its way and took over the political authority and the military power in Russia and used it capriciously in the Russian civil war from 1918 to 1922. There were no civil authority obstacles, no more moral constraints or boundaries for their materialistic worldview or their atheistic philosophies to be denied faith and implementation.

The Russian Monarchy had faith in the principles of the rule of law but had lost the faith of the people. The Spirit of the Natural Law, and the Natural rights, and the civil rule of law has been passed down to humanity from the transcendent Creator God of the Universe. Law is not a material entity; it has a transcendent source, principles according to the mind and the Spirit of God. Laws do get enforced materially, restrictions, constraints, denial of entry and law enforcement. The origin of the Spirit of Law is transcendent. So is the intelligent design of the human mind. Made in the image of God. If the human mind was not designed by the Creator God, we would not be able to understand the created things and the nature of God. Intellect, consciousness, imagination, will, memory and the emotions, are the functions of the living soul mind. Both in humans and mammals. Once Bolshevik leaders got into governmental power, they immediately began to represent the beginnings of totalitarian state values, traits that appeared in 1922 as The Soviet Union (USSR).

What happened to the people that were loyal to the Russian Royalty, or for other reasons they did not want to rebel with the spirit of anarchy or a bloody revolution? They become the diametrical enemies of the Bolshevik

Socialist movement. Therefore, many the loyal Russian authority representative officers were executed, and military offices mutinied by their subjects, the Russian seamen.

## LAST GOVERNOR-GENERAL OF FINLAND 1917

*Nikolai Vissarionovich Nekrasov 1871, Saint Petersburg – 7 May, 1940, Moscow) was a Russian liberal politician and the last Governor-General of Finland. (Wikipedia E. , Franz Albert Seyn, 2018) Before he became a Governor-General, Seyn had been a staff officer in the military district of Finland, as an aide to the previous Governor General. Seyn contributed in the Russification of Finland as he followed in the footsteps of his assassinated (1904) predecessor, Governor General Nikolai Ivanovich Bobrikov. Finnish autonomy was further limited and in laws passed in 1908 and 1910 the Duma, instead of the Finnish Diet, was given rights to make laws concerning the Grand Duchy of Finland. (Encyclopedia, Nikolay Bobrikov, 2018)*

*After the February Revolution, the Russian Provisional Government arrested Seyn on 16 March, 1917, and brought him to Saint Petersburg where he was apparently killed the next year. Nikolai Vissarionovich Nekrasov 1871, Saint Petersburg – 7 May, 1940, Moscow) was a Russian liberal politician and the last Governor-General of Finland.*

*On 17 September Nekrasov was appointed Governor-General of Finland after Mihail Aleksandrovich Stahovich quit from his post. Nekrasov's job was to negotiate between the Finnish Senate and the Russian Provisional Government. The Senate wanted to secure the Finnish autonomy with a treaty. Kerensky approved it in September, but in October the Senate came with a new proposal which would further increase Finnish Independence.*

*On the morning of 7 November Nekrasov, on his way to Saint Petersburg to hand over the proposal to Kerensky, found out that the Bolsheviks had overthrown Provisional Government during the October Revolution. He informed the Senate that he would not return to Finland. March 1917. Approximately 100 Russian Navy officers were executed in Helsinki by the Bolsheviks inspired Russian mutineers.*

## THE BALTIC SEA FLEET GENERAL PA PENNE

Early in the Russian revolution, the General of the Russian Baltic Fleet Navy had turned sides to the Bolsheviks revolutionary side. After switching sides, he received orders from the Bolsheviks leaders in Petrograd to arrest the Governor General Grand Duchy of Finland, arrest the Governor-general Sienna, and he was arrested. However, the Russian Baltic Fleet General changing sides and proving it with action did not appease the Bolsheviks for long. Only one day after he had arrested the Governor General Seynne, he was executed by the seamen. (Encyclopedia, Baltic Fleet, 2018)

## LOYALTY TO THE RED ARMBANDS

Red arm bands and red ribbon on the chest were used publicly as an open symbol of loyalty to the Russian revolution in Finland. Red armband and a red ribbon on the chest. Protestors wore red armbands and ribbons as a sign of their support for the revolution.

## SELF-JUSTIFICATION AFTER ENGAGING IN CRIME

It is believed that the Russian workers grabbed the power of the Tsar by force, and it has been said that it was the poor people fighting against the rich people, as in social class struggle. It is also used as a justification for lawlessness and immorality. No law breaker or wrongdoer wants to admit that they have engaged in crime or done something immoral. Stalin denied it with his unbelief, willful self-justification, from as early as the Tbilisi Spiritual Seminary 1894, all the way to his death in 1953. 59 years of denial in spiritual reality. If their heart and mind reject the Spirit of the Natural Law. That also is just another form of subjective relativism deception, deceiving people into thinking that they are justified by doing lawless deeds. After all the Spirit of the Natural Law does not change, whether it is the poor people or the rich people, the Spirit of the Natural Law remains the same always. Those that break the spirit of the Natural law become guilty of lawlessness. This is clearly spelled out in the first five books of Moses. God is not a respecter of persons. There can be no self-justification for doing evil to others, the only confession before God can bring forgiveness. The redemption of sin has been made possible in the New Testament through the redemptive work of Jesus Christ. (Romans 3:23, Romans 5:8, 1 John 5:.11-12).

> "You shall not show partiality in judgment; you shall hear the small and the great alike. You shall not fear man, for the judgment, is God's. The case that is too hard for you, you shall bring to me, and I will hear it." Deuteronomy 1:17.

> "For the LORD your God is the God of gods and the Lord of lords, the great, the mighty, and the awesome God who does not show partiality nor take a bribe." Deuteronomy 10:17.

> "Now then let the fear of the LORD be upon you; be very careful what you do, for the LORD our God will have no part in unrighteousness or partiality or the taking of a bribe." 2 Chronicles 19:7.

> "Then Peter opened his mouth, and said, Of a truth, I perceive that God is no respecter of persons". ACTS 10:34.

This same truth and principle are made clear in the Book of Deuteronomy. Moses declared the blessings, and the curses, blessings from moral obedience, and curses from moral disobedience, and the same applies to the Jews and Gentiles alike, inside the covenant, or outside the covenant. It is at the core of moral, spiritual law. Deuteronomy chapter 27 and 28.

The disobedience of the people of Israel did not save them from the destruction of the first temple, second temple and the genocide in Europe during 1939-1945. The only guarantee of protection to people claiming God's promises is obedience to the Holy Spirit and the Torah Law (instructions) of God. It is a deflective umbrella of protection for the believers. The destruction of the Jerusalem temples were extremely severe judgments by God. Those two events in history alone make the strong point that obedience alone assures protection from being deceived. Even when people have fallen under the spirit of Deception and unable to see the truth, even that is one form of judgment, received and filled with the spirit of idolatry. People are caught up in their own folly; they will sow the seeds of their mind and heart, by their free will volition, and reap the spiritual consequences in time.

RUSSIAN SEAMEN

October Revolution and Russian Civil War 1917–22). Main article: Baltic Fleet during the October Revolution and Russian Civil War. "During the October Revolution, the sailors of the Baltic Fleet (renamed "Naval Forces of the Baltic Sea" in March 1918) were among the most ardent supporters of Bolsheviks and formed an elite among Red military forces. The fleet was forced to evacuate several of its bases after Russia's withdrawal from the First World War, under the terms of the Treaty of Brest-Litovsk. The "Ice Cruise" of the Baltic Fleet (1918), led by Alexey Schastny, saw the evacuation of most of the fleet's ships to Kronstadt and Petrograd." Some ships of the fleet took part in the Russian Civil War, notably by clashing with the British navy operating in the Baltic as part of intervention forces. Over the years, however, the relations of the Baltic Fleet sailors with the Bolshevik regime soured, and they eventually rebelled against the Soviet government in the Kronstadt rebellion in 1921 but were defeated, and the Fleet de facto ceased to exist as an active military unit. (Encyclopedia, Baltic Fleet, 2018)

## ALFRED KORDELIN

Finnish industrialist Kordelin became entangled with the spirit of the Russian revolution that was whipped up by the Bolshevik agitators and the Russian Seamen in Finland. During the final stages of the First World War when the peasants began to strike, and the political workers started moving among the farmers. Kordelin understood the demands of the people who had no land to farm, but the yields of the mansions were also significant for him. During the Russian revolution troubled times, he was demonized and made a symbol of the money power. (Wikipedia, Alfred Kordelin, 2018)

During the German and the Russian Empire, the Seamen were used politically to implement actions. Due to its technical nature, the fleet required a moderate level of general education from its crew. On the other hand, the navy in the Baltic Sea was quiet, and both the German and the Russian fleets lay for long periods at the pier, when the crew was at port often bored. In the Soviet historiography, the Seamen were used at the front line of the revolution. Already in 1905, the Russians seamen rebelled against Taurian Prince Potjomk's armor ship.

Industrialist Kordelin died in the so-called Mummila Manor skirmish. Russian Seamen had been commanded to send 3,000 men to St. Petersburg to support the Revolutionists. The Seamen invasion of the Mummilla Manor and kidnapping the Finnish industrialist Alfred Kordelin has been defended by the Russian Seamen, saying that they had been given misguided information about the presence of the city of Lahti region's white guards.

If that story were true, then surely after arriving at the Manor they would have seen that the Mummila Manor was not a stronghold of the white guards, after all, they did go inside the Manor during the Kordelin birthday party and interrupted it. If the objective was the white guard stronghold suspicion, then the suspicion proved wrong at the point when they had inspected the Manor.

True to the human nature the Manor status and the industrial Kordelin Birthday party was most likely the temptation pull that attracted the Russian Seamen to go out of their way to visit the Manor. There surely would have been food and alcohol at the Manor, at the home of the wealthiest entrepreneurs in Finland at the time. The Seamen had been ordered to go to Petersburg, to support the Russian revolution, they were going into a potential warfare situation with 3000 men. Maybe some convincing comfort and consolation to their mission journey were needed, to make the step lighter to the 350 km journey East to Petersburg.

The same principle of the Natural law was in force, which side was the Russian Seamen on? On the side of the spirit of the Natural law, or on the side of the spirit of anarchy, the answer is obvious. The Russian Seamen were anarchists taking the law into their own hands; they were under the guidance and the spiritual power of the Nemesis. By their own volition at some point in time, they gave their souls to lawlessness and the spiritual power of Satan.

It was said at the time, that the Seamen thought that the whites civil guard had established the Mummila Manor as a military camp base and were about to break the railway line between Helsinki and St. Petersburg. So the Seamen went to invade the Mummila Manor to look for weapons and on 7 November 1917 and arrested Kordelin and some of the guests who had been in the mansion to celebrate Kordelin's birthday. The seamen kidnapped Alfred Kordelin and took others as prisoners and went to transport their prisoners to Otto train station, but they got into a firefight with the white guardians. In the chaos situation on, one of the Russian Seamen fired at Kordelin and killed him.

What was the purpose of the Seamen to take the Industrialist Kordelin to the railway station? Take him to Petersburg? As a trophy? Who knows? The intent of kidnapping the riches entrepreneur in Finland at the time was a severe crime. *"Alfred Kordelin (6 November 1868, Rauma – 7 November 1917, Kordelin had little formal education. He was the son of a poor seaman from Rauma. Kordelin invested wisely in the fields of weaving, shipbuilding, and metalworking, becoming one of Finland's wealthiest men. Risto Ryti, who later became President of Finland, was Alfred Kordelin's legal advisor and close friend. Kordelin owned the Mummila and Jokioinen manor houses and a steam mill in Reposaari."* (Wikipedia, Alfred Kordelin, 2018)

## [5]
# SOCIALIST IDEOLOGY

SOCIALIST IDEOLOGY
During the Finnish Civil War (27 January – 15 May 1918) concerned the transition of leadership and the control of Finland during the transition from a Grand Duchy of the Russian Empire to an independent state of Finland.

UNION OF SOVIET SOCIALIST REPUBLICS SOCIALISM
In theory, the core ideology of socialism is when a population collectively owns and controls the means of production and distributes the result proportionally. The control delegated to the State. While the distribution usually comes in the form of underlying social welfare to satisfy everyone's basic needs, like housing, education, and healthcare. The ideals end goal and purpose of socialism were to guarantee a level playing field for members of society, thereby removing class distinctions based on ownership. In reality, it was like a one-sided coin. An ideology that was rooted in unbelief, lawlessness, and atheism. The founders resorted to rebellion, violence, and anarchy. Committing murder, for their godless political ends. USSR was a vile manifestation of the erroneous human carnal nature, heart, and mind corruption. The only objective for the fruits of the sinful man and the Nemesis of humanity to manifest on earth.

THE RUSSIAN REVOLUTION TO COMMUNIST
Their ideology was delusional, and it was a purely materialistic worldview; it became defined as a Dialectic Materialism philosophy, not people-centered with spiritual values, but instead purely 100% materialistic worldview.

THE SOURCE OF KARL MARX CREED?
Karl Marx had a Jewish heritage, but he deliberately turned 180 degrees around from the (1) supernaturalism and (2) distinctiveness of his Jewish heritage to embrace (1) atheism and (2) communist ideology. Marxism retains all the major structural and emotional factors of biblical religion in a secularized form. He is a false prophet in every sense of the word. (Encyclopedia, Karl Marx, 2018)

> MOSES. "So remember that the Lord is the only true Elohim, whether in the sky above or on the earth below." Deuteronomy 4:39. (1446 BC)

KARL MARX DOCTRINE
"Marx, like Moses, is the prophet who leads the new Chosen People, the proletariat, out of the slavery of capitalism into the Promised Land of communism across the Red Sea of bloody worldwide revolution and through the wilderness of temporary, dedicated suffering for the party, the new priesthood."

*"The revolution is the new "Day of Yahweh," the Day of Judgment; The party spokesmen are the new prophets, and political purges within the party to maintain ideological purity are the new divine judgments on the waywardness of the Chosen and their leaders. The messianic tone of communism makes it structurally and emotionally more like a religion than any other political system except fascism".*

*"Just as Marx took over the forms and the spirit of his religious heritage, but not the content, he did the same with his Hegelian philosophical heritage, transforming Hegel's philosophy of "dialectical idealism" into "dialectical materialism!" "Marx stood Hegel on his head," the saying goes. Marx inherited seven radical ideas from Hegel:*

**Monism**: the idea that everything is one and that common sense's distinction between matter and spirit is illusory. For Hegel, the matter was only a form of spirit; for Marx, the spirit was only a form of matter.

**Pantheism**: the notion that the distinction between Creator and creature, the distinctively Jewish idea, is false. For Hegel, the world is made into an aspect of God (Hegel was a pantheist); for Marx, God reduced to the world (Marx was an atheist).

**Historicism**: the idea that everything changes, even truth; that there is nothing above history to judge it; and that therefore what is right in one era becomes false in another, or vice versa. In other words, Time is God.

**Dialectic**: the idea that history moves only by conflicts between opposing forces, a "thesis" vs. an "antithesis" evolving a "higher synthesis." This applies to classes, nations, institutions, and ideas. The dialectic waltz plays on in history's ballroom until the kingdom of God finally comes-which Hegel virtually identified with the Prussian State. Marx internationalized it to the worldwide communist State.

**Necessitarianism**, or fatalism: the idea that the dialectic and its outcome are inevitable and necessary, not free. Marxism is a sort of Calvinistic predestination without a divine Predestinator.

**Statism**: the idea that since there is no eternal, trans-historical truth or law, the State is supreme and uncriticizable. Marx again internationalized Hegel's nationalism here.

**Militarism**: the idea that since there is no universal natural or eternal law above states to judge and resolve differences between them, war is inevitable and necessary as long as there are states." (Kreeft, 2018) www.peterkreeft.com/pillars_marx.

SOVIET UNION BEGINNINGS 1900-1917

The Soviet Union had its ideological and nationalistic roots in the Russian unrest years that started bubbling in the Russian human souls during the demonstrations of 1905. The failure of the Russian leadership to deliver anything significant to the nationalistic fever, that they had when they went into the world war 1. They experienced setbacks at the front lines, with the enormous losses to the military soldiers and the society at large. The Russian souls came back to their senses and reacted with violence and lawless, against their nation monarchy and leaders. Those circumstances were ideal for the Nemesis to get a grip on the people and lead them further into rebellion, lawlessness, and anarchy.

That enabled more of the revolution fever momentum led by Vladimir Lenin, to overthrow the Russian Tsar and the Provisional Government in Petersburg. They were determined with the spirit of the revolution fever to overthrow the established authorities. It was blatant anarchy, which violated the principles of the rule of law. The primary spiritual driver of the USSR ideology was the Nemesis, the lawless one called Satan.

"He seized the dragon, that ancient serpent, who is the devil, or Satan, and bound him for a thousand years. He threw him

> into the Abyss, and locked and sealed it over him, to keep him from deceiving the nations anymore until the thousand years were ended." Revelation 20: 2, 3.

> "For rebellion is as the sin of divination, and the presumption is as iniquity and idolatry. Because you have rejected the word of the Lord, he has also rejected you from being king." 1 Samuel 15:23. (ESV)

> "An evil man seeks only rebellion, and a cruel messenger will be sent against him." Proverbs 17:11. (ESV)

## REBELLION

The Bolsheviks were determined to overthrow the Russian Monarchy; they worked at it for some 17 years. The provisional Government eventually replaced Tsar Nicholas II towards the end of World War I. It was the beginning of 1900, with the unrest in Russian society, manifesting with demonstrations of soldiers and civilians. That led to a rebellious and lawless revolution spirit that the Bolsheviks fed and perpetuated to their advantage. The Bolsheviks minded agitators worked to get the political support of the people with momentum for a better future; their victories would blossom for a brief moment, and then would finally implode into the full-blown anarchy of the Russian Civil War, lasting four years, and 2 million people dead.

It was later refined and proudly declared as State Atheism with collective communism. The totalitarian regime disconnected itself from the Spirit of the Natural Law. The State Atheism remained so until Adolf Hitler's military forces started knocking at the gates of Moscow. It soon changed Stalin's attitude towards religion, and the churches, the believers that they had been mocking, suppressing, murdered and imprisoned the pastors. Desecrating and destroying the church buildings. The Russian people were once again after 1941, allowed to go and pray to God openly for a brighter Russian future.

Stalin's willful atheism gave way to the reality of God's sovereignty over the affairs of men. It is almost ironic that the arrogance of Stalin during 1939-41 soon boomeranged back; he received that which he had willfully committed himself. Deliberately ordered the executions of innocent victims in Poland, and orchestrated a war against peace in Poland, Finland, Estonia, Latvia, and Lithuania.

Just like the Pharaoh of Egypt, when his arrogance and hard-hearted attitude rebound, after 1945, when the allied forces supported Stalin to fight back the Nazi Germany military invasion. There is a direct correlation between the 1939 Nazi German-Soviet Pact of Aggression with Stalin's violent actions against the innocent victims in the war against peace, against Poland and Finland. They were war crimes against the Baltic States and genocide against Polish nationals in 1940. There can be seen a direct judgment of God visible for all to see. In the crime does not pay principle.

Both Hitler and Stalin planned war crimes and genocide from 1939 to 1940. From the partnership in the conspiracy, 1939 Molotov & Ribbentrop Nazi German-Soviet Pact of Aggression, that did turn against Stalin in 1941. Stalin was punished for his 40 years of lawlessness, anarchy, arrogance, cruelty, and violence. Hitler likewise was punished and eventually destroyed in 1945. Stalin's arrogance, idolatry, and war crimes live on in the inner circles of the Russian leadership. That is the spirit that enables lawlessness at the government lever, Ukraine territory annexation in East Ukraine, Ukraine Crimea Peninsula occupation, and the Russian activities in Syria, are only possible when the leaders are motivated by the spirit of rebellion, lawlessness, and anarchy. The same spirit as the Bolsheviks Revolution, and the USSR State Atheism.

Nazi Germany and Adolf Hitler's war crimes and sin's do not live on, they died in Nuremberg 1945, in the court of law, with the conviction of the war criminals, the guilt of crime is therefore removed by the admission, and confession of the crime in the court of law. The penalty, restitution, or the sentence is an acknowledgment of the guilty agent having broken the Spirit of the Natural Law. The same cannot be said for Soviet Russian war crimes. Russia is still profiteering from the Soviet Stalin's 1939-45 war crimes in 2018. The current Russian leadership and the Russian spirit of nationalism are proud of Stalin. Stalin's Soviet Union is looked up and esteemed as being a great model for the Russian future. Carnal hearts and minds can only appreciate it, when it is disconnected from the Spirit of the Natural Law.

The carnal nature of human mind and heart often glorifies the deceitful gain, just like Stalin did in 1939, 1941. Soviet and Russian leaders have not acknowledged their 1939 – 1945 war crimes. Therefore, they are still outstanding war crimes. Why would they not be? Only people living in denial of the spiritual reality would suppress or repress facts. It is an old spiritual truth from the book of Proverbs chapter 16, verse 4. "The LORD has made everything for its own purpose, Even the wicked for the day of evil." Adolf Hitler was used by God to achieve his goals, according to his Holiness. Matthew Henry's Commentary on Proverbs 16:4.

*"God makes use of the wicked to execute righteous vengeance on each other, and he will be glorified by their destruction at last."*
*"Though sinners strengthen themselves and one another, they shall not escape God's judgments.*
*"By the mercy and truth of God in Christ Jesus, the sins of believers are taken away, and the power of sin is broken.*
*"He that has all hearts in his hand can make a man's enemies be at peace with him."*
*"A small estate, honestly come by, will turn to better account than a great estate ill-gotten." "If men make God's glory their end, and his will their rule, he will direct their steps by his Spirit and grace." "Let kings and judges of the earth be just, and rule in fear of God." "To observe justice in dealings between man and man is God's appointment."*

Political theory has little meaning and value for people if human lives become worthless. The theory of Karl Marx, Lenin, and Stalin are unthinkable as a rational theory for the people of a nation. They declared State atheism from the beginning, idolatrous core philosophy. Without any respect for God's Creation, made in the image of God. The intrinsic value of human life with God-given rights. In their ideology, there was no acknowledgment of human beings created in the image of God, and therefore having no God-given respect and human worth. That was a severe error of judgment, and it only appealed to those that wanted quick results, without work, and were rebellious and given to lawlessness. It was a sure sign of the influence of the Nemesis.

NEMESIS IDENTIFIED

What are the ancient old patterns of human history? That causes the living human souls to break down? Furthermore, the human soul in a broken state, in turn, inflicts suffering on other human beings? It is seen in the fragmentation of the living soul mind functions, the intellect, consciousness, imagination, will, memory, and emotions.

# [6]
# THE NATURAL RIGHTS

THE NATURAL RIGHTS

What are natural rights? *"Natural rights are those that are not dependent on the laws or customs of any particular culture or government, and therefore universal and inalienable."* What are the legal rights? *"Legal rights are those bestowed onto a person by a given legal system (i.e., rights that can be modified, repealed, and restrained by human laws)."* (Wikipedia, Natural Rights, 2020)

NATURAL LAW

The Spirit of the Natural Law exists first; the natural human rights derive from the Spirit of the Natural Law. In the beginning God, Elohim (Genesis 1:1).

*The Natural Law first appeared in ancient Greek philosophy and was referred to by the Roman philosopher Cicero. The concept and the Spirit of the Natural Law can be seen in the events of the Bible; it is there as surely as a canvas in a classical oil painting. It is seen in the actions, behavior, manner and the living soul of Abraham, interacting with the Spirit of the Natural Law. Similarly, Moses sensitivity to true justice, compassion, and mercy for the innocent. Moses teaching in the first five books of the Bible (the Pentateuch) reveals the Spirit of the Natural Law is active. It exists with the presence and the nature of Elohim instructions to humanity. The Spirit of the Natural Law is like a buffer, an interface that provides knowledge and grace to the human living soul mind. The Spirit of the Natural Law appeals to the human soul mind. It is good to have understanding, to weight up the options. To listen to the voice of reason and wisdom, or to act out on an impulse of the emotions. The human mind and heart can be a receiver, meditating on the Spirit of the Natural Law. God that instructs and guides humanity, according to the wisdom in His word, Elohim. The Natural Law concepts.* "It was developed in the Middle Ages by Catholic philosophers such as Albert the Great and his pupil Thomas Aquinas." (Encyclopedia, Natural Law, 2018)

STATE OF NATURE – JOHN LOCKE

*John Locke reasons that in the beginning humans lived in the State of Nature. State of nature where there were no overlord State or government to impose the Law of men onto their subjects.* "The lawbreaker was dealt with one on one, about who broke the Law and how. If confronted by a lawbreaker, or catching a lawbreaker doing violence to an individual, then the lawbreaker was punished directly without a third party". (Wikipedia, State of Nature, 2020)

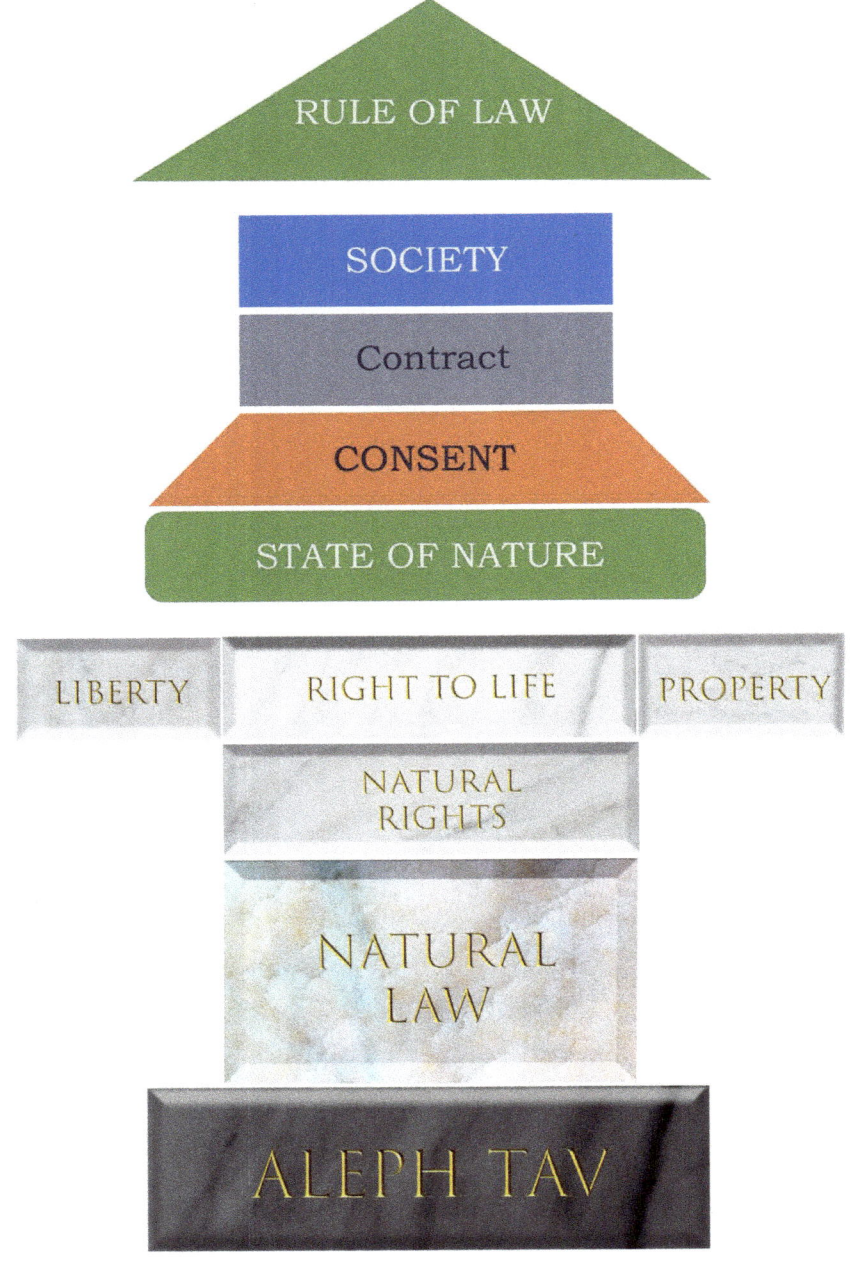

Graphic. All Rights Reserved. Victor Leinonen. 2020.

The same law principles are written in the book of the Exodus, some 1460 AD.
LAWS CONCERNING PERSONAL INJURY AND HOMICIDE

> "Whoever strikes a man so that he dies certainly to be put to death." "If he did not lie in wait, but God let him fall within his reach, then I will appoint for you a place to which he may flee. "If a man acts deliberately against his neighbor, to kill him by treachery, you are to take him to die even if he is at my altar." Exodus 21: 12-14.

The State of Nature has a Spirit of the Natural Law to govern it, and that Law is the reason. Locke believes that reason teaches that "no one ought to harm another in his life, liberty, and or property." The way out of the state of nature is through consent, to join a society is through consent. The consent takes on to the social contract, and to the Law of the society/State. According to the John Locke philosophy of law human's inherent natural rights when they are born. Due to the intrinsic value of human life. Rights can be forfeited, through willful sin. To deliberately flaunt sin, is to disrespect the Creator of life. God is Holy.

## THE NATURAL STATE

The building blocks of a stable society are illustrated here in the graphic below. The rule of Law derived from the Spirit of the Natural Law.

Also, Natural rights in civil society are derived from the Spirit of Natural Law principles. The right to life, liberty, and property. The Spirit of the Natural Law protects the people in the Natural State before the population explosion on earth. Since then, people have joined the society through consent and through the social contract. Responsibly submitting to the laws of that particular society. It is the rational, logical, linear order of native people entering from the natural state, into civil society with the law-abiding society of people submitted to the Rule of Law.

The rule of Law is only valid when it depends on the Spirit of the Natural Law; It provides the Natural rights to people in the society. The right to life, right to liberty, right to property. The natural Law protects the people in the natural state, before the population explosion on earth. Since then people have joined the society through consent, through the social contract. Responsibly, submitting to the rule of Law in a society.

## RULE OF LAW

The term Rule of Law is often used all over the world in various countries and states. It may be legitimate Law, or it may not be a legitimate law. Just like the currency of money is produced, some are legitimate, and others are counterfeit. The same Spirit of corruption and lawlessness is active with the counterfeit currency and the counterfeit Law. It leads to the same source, the underworld of the Nemesis and the demon host.

Law can also be a false counterfeit. It depends on the power enforcing it. Moreover, whether it respects the Spirit of the Natural Law. How can one tell the difference between State laws? At the most basic level, to check whether people have Natural rights:

- Right to life
- Right to liberty
- Right to property

Most nations have laws; some are arbitrary; the worst-case scenario in the last 100-year European history was the leader's that introduced State Atheism, with the lawless totalitarian military regime, which denied people their right to life, liberty, and property. Such was the revolution created by the Bolsheviks pseudo socialism in Russia from 1922 to 1991.

The Bolsheviks and the USSR roots were a mixed bag from Karl Marx's philosophy, Lenin's philosophical theories, and Stalin's ego ambitions for political and military power conquest as the man of steel. Stalin was not in it for humanity or welfare. Stalin was in it for the sake of power, materialism, and national glory. Stalinism followers were doomed to fail, for the same reason Lucifer failed. There is a parallel between the Spirit of Lucifer that led to the fall and the Spirit that tempted Stalin to become what he became, utterly given to violating the Spirit of the Natural Law.

> "How you have fallen from heaven, morning star, son of the dawn! You have been cast down to the earth, you who once laid low the nations! You said in your heart, "I will ascend to the heavens; I will raise my throne above the stars of God; I will sit enthroned on the mount of assembly, on the utmost heights of Mount Zaphon. I will ascend above the tops of the clouds; I will make myself like the Most High." Isaiah 14:12-14 (NIV).

It was the Spirit of Lucifer that worked the hearts and minds of Karl Marx, Vladimir Lenin, and Joseph Stalin, to the same end as Lucifer and his demon host. In violent conflict with the Creator of Life. They were all deceived to the wrong side of the angels.

It was an aberration of the true Spirit of the Natural Law. A counterfeit created for the Nemesis, a pseudo-law that twisted and deceived people's minds away from the spiritual truth. It also denied many generations of people the opportunity to have the impartial rule of Law, in a respectful, law-abiding, peaceful society. The pseudo-law did not respect the natural rights, the Natural Law, or the Creator of Life. They had ambitiously rejected the Biblical worldview and commenced creating a hardcore State Atheism, supported by narrow-minded subjective relativism. At the very core center where the Law is manufactured for society, the Spirit of the Natural Law should be respected, establishing a moral duty of the government, as being a central core value serving the people. There was violence done to the Spirit of the Natural Law; the Spirit was evicted out of the national governance by the leaders of State atheism. It was built purely on materialistic life philosophy. Human life had little significance compared to the ambitious goals of the dictators.

There the watershed in the worldview and life philosophy can be seen clearly between the East and the West. It was played out and proclaimed openly by the Satan's State Atheism representatives. Their diabolical lawless deeds were recorded in the historical records, some of them released, others suppressed. How can it be that people generally do not see the evidence of Satan's representatives all over the world history? The reason is that they do not even understand the parables spoken by Jesus from Nazareth. How could they then understand anything outside of their hand reach?

> "Then Jesus said to them, "Don't you understand this parable? How then will you understand any parable?" Gospel According to Mark 4: 1-41.

The dots of history are everywhere, waiting to be joined with understanding. However, there is an obstacle to understanding the truth and facts of life; that obstacle is the deception of the heart and mind. The deceiver works in a way that it appears to be in control and ahead of human consciousness time, orchestrating events ahead of manifestation. It is only a matter of perspective, observing viewpoint.

Time is a constant flow; it waits for no man or woman. Humanity cannot do anything to change the flow of time, of the planet earth, the other planets, or the galaxy. The one thing that individual people can change or alter, for better or for worse, is their living soul consciousness. The exercise of the Intellect, imagination, will, and memory. To train their mind, and to exercise the free will selectively. Away from the idiot box, the passive trance meditation on the television, without thinking, is all negative as far as the Intellect and the free will is concerned. The internet is selective, enabling creative use of the mind intellect, imagination, consciousness, will, and memory. Suppose people manage to control the many temptations. People are not equal; nothing is equal in a material world.

Individual people with a free will cut their own fingernails and brush their own teeth. Generally, no one else will do that, which a person can do for themselves. Therefore, the minds of people are not equal. People will need to exercise and train their minds because no one else will do that for them. People are not even equal physically; some are physically stronger than others. Similarly, in the animal world, they are not equal; a wombat is not equal to a rhinoceros, salmon is not equal to a marlin. Every artist trains their imagination by the power of their will.

Musicians exercise their hearing to distinguish notes, set of notes, groups of notes, scales, modes, and their relationship to a given key. To consciously intelligently distinguish notes, major, minor, diminished, augmented, or suspended notes in a chord of notes, is achieved through intelligent consciousness. Consciousness, similarly to intelligence, is malleable within the personality. Use it, or lose it, applies for everyone. There are no exceptions to the Law of exercise; it can reach anywhere and everywhere.

That was already discovered some 3400 years ago; they learned to write and share their life experiences with the following generations. That fact is supported by the need for young people to be educated by teachers and educators. Classical musicians and composers would inevitably develop their hearing sense and the consciousness of listening to music. That, in turn, shapes and develops the functions of their mind and the living soul to enjoy and to master their craft in music. To fine-tune consciousness, and to sharpen the mind? Or to blunt it into oblivion? Fine-tuning of consciousness with logic and reason enables responsibility. Responsibility cannot exist without having a keen sense of consciousness and the knowledge of exercising free will with logic and reasoning. The Nemesis has the advantage of having an army of volunteers for his cause, millions, hundreds of millions of willing volunteers, going blindly with the flow to the more significant (illusion) cause of the Nemesis, just by volunteering to do lawlessness. That is all it takes; voluntary actions can become habits that can lead to sin. Sin and lawlessness are the only reward that is offered for those that offer their will to serve Satan's will on earth.

There is a rational and logical explanation of the conflict, the very core reason for the conflict, it is visible, from history for everyone to see. It has manifested again and again, also been recorded for thousands of years. Only those people that deny the Spiritual reality and their minds are under the deceitful power of Satan, deception by convoluted explanations and philosophies, which defend immoral actions and lawless deeds. They fail to see and understand the profound spiritual nature of the Spirit of the Natural Law. It requires a personal relationship attitude to the Creator of Life.

Technology is God's mercy and grace to humanity. Satan would not have allowed technologies to advance from the dark ages. No text printing of the Good News Bible. No global transport for distribution. No medical breakthrough would serve the purposes of Satan. No communication devices serve the purposes of Satan, the dark ages with heresies, sickness and disease, black plague, and other horrendous diseases that are some of the Nemesis ointments to put on God's creation and humanity.

What are the benefits of digital technologies for dictators? If there were no global communications? No public reporting of atrocities. No Spiritual light from the lantern to the dark corners of spiritual darkness. The evidence of this reasoning can be seen in the Iron Curtain and the Bamboo Curtain. The internet does not serve the purposes of Satan on earth primarily; there are counterfeits for everything that is good and useful for people to grow and become educated for a better world, with less suffering.

SALT AND LIGHT

> "Neither do people light a lamp and put it under a basket. Instead, they set it on a lampstand, and it gives light to everyone in the house." "In the same way, let your light shine before men, that they may see your good deeds and glorify your Father in heaven." -Yeshua. Matthew 5:15,16.

The most important question to ask is how to use modern technology wisely because it is a window of opportunity. To use it for education, teaching, and training in righteousness, directly with a search keyword? Serving and communicating with people who are seeking God's Kingdom and sharing the Good News of the Gospel? Immanuel Kant puts the pressure on the carnal mind and proving an excellent state of mind, which is the rational mind. He makes the point that there is no alternative to the basic command given by God to be rational moral thinking of human beings.

We must believe in the rational moral model of the human mind. To obey means to think more spiritually, and the actions become less carnal. Carnality succumbs to the influencing power of the Nemesis; it blocks the minds of people from thinking spiritually, the carnal mind becomes a slave to Satan, leading to lawless deeds of ignorance. To be given to a carnal mind means that the meditations of the mind are carnal. To be spiritual, minded means for the meditations of the mind to be of the Spirit. The Natural rights, derived from the Spirit of the Natural Law, do have a Spiritual source.

*"Immanuel Kant characterized the Categorical Imperative as an objective, rationally necessary, and unconditional principle that we must always follow despite any natural desires or inclinations we may have to the contrary. All specific moral requirements, according to Kant, are justified by this principle, which means that all immoral actions are irrational because they violate the CI. Other philosophers, such as Hobbes, Locke, and Aquinas, had also argued that moral requirements based on standards of rationality."* (Immanuel Kant. Encyclopedia, 2020)

JOHN LOCKE

Fundamental individual human rights. No government, not even a democratically elected government, has the right to override natural rights. However, they can be revoked by the person's own willful lawlessness. In rebellion, violating the Spirit of the Natural Law.

No government can override:

- The fundamental rights
- The natural right to life
- Right to liberty
- Right to property.

"The Natural inherent rights are not just for the sake of creating a government and a set of human laws for a civil society. Already activated in the Natural State". – John Locke.

*"The case for fundamental individual rights. No government, not even a democratically elected government, has the right to override them. John Locke argues that the right to property is not just for the sake of creating a government and political mandate. The right to property is a natural right in the sense that it is pre-political."*

*"It is a right that attaches to individuals, as human beings, even before the government comes on the scene, even before parliaments and legislatures enact laws to define rights, and to enforce them. John Locke says to think about what it means to have a natural right; we have to imagine the ways things are before the government, before the Law. That is what Locke means by the state of nature".*

*"John Locke says that the state of nature is a state of liberty, human beings are free and equal beings, there is no natural*

hierarchy, it is not the case that some people are born to be kings and others were born to be serfs we are free and equal in the state of nature." David Sandell. Harward University. (School of Law).

Consistent with the intrinsic value of human life.
*"Nor am I free to take my own life, liberty, or property. Even though I am free, I am not free to violate the Law of nature. I am not free to take my own life, or to sell myself into slavery, or to give someone else arbitrary absolute power over me.?"*. – David Sandell. Harvard Law School.

Where does the constraint come? By design in the design of the human mind, by the Creator of life.
*"For men, being all the workmanship of one omnipotent, and infinitely wise maker, they are his property, whose workmanship they are, made to last during his, not one another's pleasure."* – John Locke.

Why can't we give up our rights to life, liberty, and property? Why? Because they are not individual rights to use on self. Because we as humans are the creature of God, in the beginning, God created a human in His image.

## THE NATURAL LAW. EMMANUEL KANT

"Immanuel Kant (1724–1804) argued that the supreme principle of morality exists as a standard of rationality that he dubbed the "Categorical Imperative" (CI)."

*"However, these standards were either instrumental principles of rationality for satisfying one's desires, as in Hobbes or external rational principles that are discoverable by reason, as in Locke and Aquinas. Kant agreed with many of his predecessors that an analysis of practical reason reveals the requirement that rational agents must conform to instrumental principles. He also argued that conformity to the CI (a non-instrumental principle), and hence to moral requirements themselves, can nevertheless be shown to be essential to the intelligent agency".*

*"This argument is based on his striking doctrine that a conscious will must be regarded as autonomous, or free, in the sense of being the author of the Law that binds it. The fundamental principle of morality, the CI — is none other than the Law of an autonomous will. Thus, at the heart of Kant's moral philosophy is a conception of reason whose reach in practical affairs goes well beyond that of a Human 'slave' to the passions. Moreover, it is the presence of this self-governing reason in each person that Kant thought offered decisive grounds for viewing each as possessed of equal worth and deserving of equal respect".* (Stanford, 2020)

*"Kant's analysis of common sense ideas begins with the thought that the only thing good without qualification is a "goodwill." While the phrases "he is good-hearted," "she is good-natured," and "she means well" are common, "the goodwill" as Kant thinks of it is not the same as any of these ordinary notions. The idea of goodwill is closer to the idea of a "good person," or, more archaically, a "person of goodwill."* (Stanford, 2020)

*"The Basic function that drives human to become the basic idea, as Kant describes it in the Groundwork, is that what makes a good person good is his possession of a will that is in a certain way "determined" by, or makes its decisions by, the moral Law. The idea of goodwill is supposed to be the idea of one who is committed only to make decisions that she holds to be morally worthy and who takes moral considerations in themselves to be specific reasons for guiding her behavior. This sort of disposition or character is something we all highly value, Kant thought".*

*"First, unlike anything else, there is no conceivable circumstance in which we regard our moral goodness as worth forfeiting merely to obtain some desirable object."*
"Second, possessing and maintaining a steadfast commitment to moral principles is the very condition under which anything else is worth having or pursuing."(Stanford, 2020)
*"In Kant's terms, an ethical will is a will whose decisions are wholly determined by moral demands or, as he often refers to this, by the Moral Law. Human beings inevitably feel this Law as a constraint on their natural desires, which is why such Laws, as applied to human beings, are imperatives and duties".*

*"To act out of respect for the moral Law, in Kant's view. It is to be moved to act by a recognition that the moral Law is a*

*supremely authoritative standard that binds us and to experience a kind of feeling, which is akin to awe and fear when we acknowledge the moral Law as the source of moral requirements." (Stanford, 2020)*

*"According to Kant, what is singular about motivation by duty is that it consists of bare respect for the moral Law. What naturally comes to mind is this: Duties are rules or laws of some sort combined with some felt constraint or incentive on our choices, whether from external coercion by others or our powers of reason".....*

*"Kant's account of the content of moral requirements and the nature of moral reasoning, based on his analysis of the unique force moral considerations have as reasons to act. The force of moral requirements as reasons is that we cannot ignore them no matter how circumstances might conspire against any other consideration".*

*"Necessary moral requirements retain their reason-giving force under any circumstance; they have universal validity. So, whatever else may be said, of necessary moral requirements, their content is universal."*

*"Only a universal law could be the content of a requirement that has the reason-giving force of morality."*

*"This brings Kant to a preliminary formulation of the CI: "I ought never to act except in such a way that I could also that my will maxim should become a universal law" (G 4:402). This is the principle which motivates a goodwill, and which Kant holds to be the fundamental principle of all of the morality". (Stanford, 2020)*

## [7]

# WHAT IS A WORLDVIEW

WHAT IS A WORLD VIEW?

Worldview is a concept, demarcation, rendition of our conscious perception. With a reasonable interpretation of the overall world experience that we live in. It has to be proven by experiential knowledge. And not only philosophized with theoretical knowledge. Life itself is impacting, interacting, and engaging in all levels of the conscious experience of life. To repress one aspect of material world objective truth from the mind, conscience acknowledgment is possible. To suppress inconvenient truth is most often favored.

To understand the value of accurate rendering of conscience selection, the intellect needs to be guided, instructed, and trained. According to the ultimate truth and reality by the First Cause of Life. The instructions have been spelled out over 3460 years ago. The journey starts with conscious integrity. God of the Bible demands uncompromising integrity from humanity. In effect, YHWH is saying, clean the chalk board of your conscience, and keep it clean, so that I can write my Torah instruction on your conscious mind. To make it easier, there is a fast track to having the sinful human conscience mind cleared. By the redeemer, the lamb of God. Yeshua Hamashiach. Jesus from Nazareth walked with YHWH and showed the way to a meaningful relationship with the God of Abraham, Isaac, and Jacob. He did not endorse impersonal "dead religious rituals." He said there was much more to life, living a meaningful life spiritually, according to the Spirit of YHWH.

The human living functions of the mind, intellect, consciousness, imagination, will, memory, and emotions, with the inalienable human rights. Right to Life, right to liberty, and property right give people the false confidence every human subjective perception is a correct worldview. The living human mind functions are highly subject to misleading imaginations and erroneous worldviews. Partly because people think with their passions, ambitions, hormones, feelings, and emotions. They make a common mistake, thinking that they can imagine and conjure up their own Worldview. And nobody has any right to correct anybody else's subjective mind errors for an artist sketching, painting, and making sculptures that may be true. It may not violates anybody else's rights.

When a populist leader rises within a nation, the problems arise in the national arena, it may arrive by political, nationalistic, or military means. The rise of a leader may be a reaction, just like the rise of the Bolsheviks and Joseph Stalin was a reaction to the Russian monarchy rule of law. Similarly, the rise of Adolf Hitler was a reaction by the German people to how they, as the German people, were dealt harshly with after World War One. The armistice on 11 November 1918 until the signing of the peace treaty with Germany on 28 June 1919.

The Imperialist spirit of pride-filled nations of Europe, such as England, France, Germany, and Russia, are the culprits for causing wars by their imperial spirit of pride and arrogance. They have always dragged others into their Imperial wars. That alone is a great evil and a disgrace for the spectator side of humanity. Not one of the above Imperials will admit that they were misled by a false spirit. There was a better way, but they missed it. They missed it because of their spirit of pride and arrogance.

The people of England have an English Worldview. The people of France have a French worldview. The people of Germany have their own subjective Worldview. Soviet-Russia's people also a Worldview that is imparted to them by the Soviet Russian leaders over the last 100 years. People are homegrown into a nationalistic worldview. That four Imperial powers with people can be categorized as having subjective worldviews. That is problematic if they cannot find any common ground outside of their subjective emotional minds. It is irrational behavior by people with a rational mind capacity. Still, it refuses to focus their rational thinking mind on a common denominator, described as the First cause of Life.

The First cause of Life has an overview of humanity like none other. He also has rational logic and wisdom like none other. He has proven His superior wisdom over the last 3460 + years. The ten instructions were given at Mount Sinai over 3460 years ago, and they are still upheld by people who respect Life and the life-giver. If the people of nations made it a priority to acknowledge the God of Abraham, Isaac, and Jacob. To take Him at His word, they would discover the First principles of logic and discover that humanity's problems are rooted in human self-will and erroneous worldviews.

no surprise that the nations do not fight and quarrel over arithmetic?

They all agree rationally that number values, identities, and operations of numbers are consistent with understanding reasonable Universal laws. The operation of numbers with addition, subtraction, division, and multiplication. They agree that there are constant laws that enable a level play-field for all. Since the early chapters of this book, I have recalled events and moments in Finland's 500-year history. Again and again, the same pattern arises with the Soviet-Russian leader's Worldview. They have violated the basic moral laws of humanity. Denied and refused to be accountable as lawbreaking criminals. They have sided with corruption and committed criminal deeds, and deny having done anything wrong. The same pattern of criminal mind surfaces again and again over the last 100 years. The violation of the leaders of Soviet-Russia are shocking, and the repression of truth is brazen.

Evidence of the Soviet-Russian criminal mind behavior is in their characteristic traits; some have been presented in this book. It has to be realized that the Soviet-Russian leader's behavior has a pattern of pathological liars and professional criminals. Their glory is their shame. That does not mean that the people of Russia are the same as their political leaders. The Soviet Union was controlled with an iron fist. It was the only means to keep the people submitted to such an evil totalitarian regime.

The Soviet-Union leaders knew they were criminals, and they willfully repressed it to the end. The following generation also knows that the Soviet-Union leaders were criminals, but they continue to suppress it. Similarly, people who do evil deeds know that there is a Creator of Life. As visibly seen the primary evidence of God, found in the living things. Still, they use their free will to suppress the spirit of truth. They have sided with their wilfulness to do evil deeds. And to keep God's spirit away from them at a distance. They are committed to doing evil on the planet earth. And do not welcome the Kingdom of God on to earth.

An Objective Worldview according to the Spirit of the Natural Law

A reality-based worldview defended here is logical and rational:

- Reality. Truth based, factual knowledge about human nature and life on earth.
- Beliefs. What is True? Objective truth, with the First Principles of Logic.
- Values. What is Right? Morally right, including the intrinsic value of human life.
- Behavior and habits. What is the right behavior? Morally right behavior. According to a Holy Creator of Life, Elohim.

Why is the right choice an intelligent choice? Because it is giving space to the priori wisdom of the Creator of life, and it is giving priority to the right outcome. The right outcome is objectively verifiable. The right outcome is always competed for by many distractions, temptations, and compromise. The need to have absolutes for intelligent decision outcomes for problem-solving. Artificial intelligence also requires absolute values and absolute definitions. Also, for mathematics and geometry. 2+2 = 4. A square is a square, and a circle is a circle; they are not equal in shape or in meaning.

Nobody complains that there are absolutes in arithmetic or absolutes in scientific engineering; it makes much sense. Absolute values are also rewarding when purchasing a thing or a machine or flying overseas at 10,000 meters altitude in a crowded passenger jet. Who cares about the absolutes of engineering? The controlled flight is maintained by the precision engineering of aviation technology, science, and human knowledge.

The most common controversial area where people complain about absolutes is moral ones. They protest the idea that there are absolute values in human conduct and morality. Why is that? Because their self-determination is heading south? Moreover, the God-given moral law, in the situation, is pointing north? That creates a conflict of interest, a dilemma.

> "Do not store up for yourselves wealth here on earth, where moths and rust destroy, and burglars break in and steal. Instead, store up for yourselves wealth in heaven, where neither moth nor rust destroys, and burglars do not break in or steal. For where your wealth is, there your heart will be also." Matthew 6:21. (CJB)

The intelligence at the individuals living soul core, the intellect, the will, and the heart. Are there absolute master plan Laws given by the Creator of Life for humanity to follow? Yes, there are. What is the origin of such laws? The origin is from outside space and time, from the Intelligent mind of the Creator God. Humanity, in the beginning, was made in the image of God. With an Intellect, consciousness, imagination, will, memory, and emotions.

This is how John Locke describes them.
*"The law of nature constrains what we can do, even when we are free in the state of nature."*
We are not free to do whatever we feel or desire to do. There have to be constraints in a multi-people society.

What are the constraints?
*"The only constraint in the state of nature is that the rights that we have, we cannot give them up, nor can we take them from someone body else. Under the law of nature, I am not free to take them from someone else". (Locke, THIS LAND IS MY LAND, 2009)*

Life, liberty, or property. Nor am I free to take my own Life, liberty, or property. Where does the law of nature constraints come from? John Locke gives two answers.
"For we, being all the workmanship of one omnipotent, and infinitely wise maker, they are his property, whose workmanship they are, made to last during his, not one another's pleasure." (John Locke)
*"For we, being all the workmanship of one omnipotent, and infinitely wise maker, they are his property, whose workmanship they are, made to last during his, not one another's pleasure."(John Locke)*

### LOCKE AND NATURAL RIGHTS
*"Locke says to think about what it means to have a natural right, we have to imagine the way things are before the government, before the law, and that is what Locke means by the state of nature."*
*"He says the state of nature is a state of liberty. Human beings are free and equal beings. There is no natural hierarchy. It is not the case that some people are born to be kings, and others are born to be serfs. We are free and equal in the state of nature, and yet, he makes the point that there is a difference between a state of liberty and a state of license".*
*"And the reason is that even in the state of nature, there is a kind of law. It is not the kind of law that legislatures enact. It is a law of nature. Moreover, this law of nature constrains what we can do even though we are free, even though we are in the state of nature." (Sandel, 2009)*

It means that just because we have a consciousness, imaginations, and a free will that enables us to be physically mobile and free, with the ability to determine where and when we move from point A to point B. That does not give license to do whatever, to self or others.

Free will is not self-sufficient, it is only as useful with the consciousness, and the intellect is working together. The will of the mind is a blind mechanism that needs the other functions of the mind: Intellect, consciousness, imagination, and memory, to bring content, value, and meaning to evaluate the decision, that it intends to execute according to consciousness instructions. Human and mammal animal intelligence is extraordinary, highly tuned to evaluate the object of decision making. How does a pilot of an Airbus 380 land it on tarmac safely? It requires high intelligence to evaluate the situation and conditions. Moreover, a free will to optimize circumstances to the desired objectives, under the Creator God laws on the planet earth.

The realization of the intrinsic human life value is vitally essential for the development of human self-identity and the mind's development. It provides self-worth and self-respect. To agree with the Jewish Holy Scriptures of the Bible. That a human being is made in the image of God, then I will make decisions in my Life according to God-given instructions. That is a rational and logical response to information that I have accepted to be logical, rational, and correct.

Exercising faith and obedience. Reading instructive books, studying scripture and learning with other believers, and being a dedicated representative of the Heavenly Father that Yeshua represented almost 2000 years ago. A follower of the teaching of Yeshua from Nazareth. Learning to become more like him in life values, priorities, goals, and attitudes with the help of His Spirit of grace.

> "Come to me, all of you who are struggling and burdened, and I will give you rest. Take my yoke upon you and learn from me, because I am gentle and humble in heart, and you will find rest for your souls. For my yoke is easy, and my burden is light."
> Matthew 11:28-30.

The knowledge of the Creator of Life brings up an association, a relationship idea, between the Creator of the material world and the living things that we observe in nature. In the beginning, Elohim created the universe, life, and human beings here on the planet earth.

There are also benefits for all in the visible created world for all to inspect, the world of the living things, plants, trees, animals, insects, birds, fish, and more. It is the primary evidence of the existence of God. also known as the works of God. Observation of the living plants, to see how they grow from seeds. Season to season, they are very persistent living things. The designs of plants and flowers are highly artistic, colorful, refined in detail, and practically functional. In the Jewish Holy Scriptures, we can read.

> "Birds build their nests nearby and sing in the trees. From your home above you send rain on the hills and water the earth. You let the earth produce grass for cattle, plants for our food, wine to cheer us up, olive oil for our skin, and grain for our health".
> Psalm 104: 12-15.

### WHY DO PEOPLE OBJECT TO MORALITY?
Why did the Bolsheviks resort to rebellion, anarchy, and murder? It was a gradual process; the Bolsheviks worked at it for 17 years; they were determined to cause a revolution and overthrow the Russian Monarchy. Many

bystanders were caught up in the revolution fever, believing that they were justified in taking part in lawlessness. They were wrong and seriously deceived. The failure to adhere to absolute moral values makes them feel guilty. They have strong desires for various pleasures, but they compromise many other values for the sake of their own chosen pleasure. The human mind requires a conscious effort to plan for the future. To think about the future requires accurate sound projection and planning ability; they are a cognitive function of the mind.

Not all people are equal. Therefore, the level of the person's Worldview varies from person to person. Similarly, conscious logical thinking varies from person to person. Some people are so busy with Life or always working that they have no time to be thinking much else than the list of things they must get done in the day's cause. Others may have more time to read, study, talk to friends, and enjoy meaningful company. Age and education also impact the amount of thinking that individual people do and whether they can explain and share their Worldview in a meaningful way.

### UNDERSTANDING A WORLDVIEW
*"A worldview is a framework from which we view reality and make sense of life and the world." [It is] any ideology, philosophy, theology, movement or religion that provides an overarching approach to understanding The Creator, the world and man's relations to God and the world"* (Noebel)Understanding the Times.

### IN DEFENSE OF THE NATURAL LAW
This book, A Claim for A True Worldview, is written in defense of the Natural Law's Spirit. In this book's argument, I am standing in the position of defending the Spirit of the Natural Law. The Spirit of the Natural Law provides Natural rights, which are also included in the International Declaration of Human Rights.

### WHY DO PEOPLE OBJECT TO MORALITY?
Why did the Bolsheviks resort to rebellion, anarchy, and murder? It was a gradual process; the Bolsheviks worked at it for 17 years; they were determined to cause a revolution and overthrow the Russian Monarchy. Many bystanders were caught up in the revolution fever, believing that they were justified in taking part in lawlessness. They were wrong and seriously deceived. Because of the failure to adhere to absolute moral values makes them feel guilty. They have strong desires for various pleasures, but they compromise many other values for the sake of their own chosen pleasure. The human mind requires a conscious effort to plan towards the future. To think regarding the future, it requires accurate sound projection, planning ability; they are a cognitive function of the mind.

Not all people are equal. Therefore, the level of the person's worldview varies from person to person. Similarly, conscious logical thinking varies from person to person; some people are so busy with life, or always working that they have no time to be thinking much else than the list of things that they must get done in the cause of the day. Others may have more time to read, study, talk to friends, and enjoy a meaningful company. Age and education also impact the amount of thinking that individual people do and whether they can explain and share their worldview in a meaningful way.

### UNDERSTANDING A WORLDVIEW
*"A worldview is a framework from which we view reality and make sense of life and the world." [It is] any ideology, philosophy, theology, movement or religion that provides an overarching approach to understanding The Creator, the world and man's relations to God and the world,"* (Noebel) Understanding the Times.

### IN DEFENSE OF THE NATURAL LAW
This book, A Claim for A True Worldview, is written in defense of the Spirit of the Natural Law. In this book's argument, I am standing in the position of defending the Spirit of the Natural Law. The Spirit of the Natural Law provides Natural rights, which are also included in the International Declaration of Human Rights.

> 2 Chronicles 20:5,6. "Lord, the God of our ancestors, are you not the God who is in heaven? You rule over all the kingdoms of the nations. Power and might are in your hand, and no one can withstand you". (Jehoshaphat, 1450 BC)

The facts are known; we have the information and knowledge to share what is right, what is fair, and what is true justice. In 1948 the Declaration of Human Rights was prepared.

Why, then, is there so much ignorance of moral rights? Many blatant violations of fundamental law, conflicts, and wars in the world? The answer is found in the unconstrained human will. The incorrigible obstinate human will violates God's laws naturally. Unless the mind is enlightened to serve God with joy, with a free will, it is like a mule with a bridle.

The mystery of wars and conflict is convoluted in the human life soul experience. The subjective mind is going backward. In reality, it is direct and straightforward; individuals and national leaders do not give due respect to human Life. The economy rules the roost. International trade compromised look the other way when the cargo ships come into offload and to load. Which industry has the most significant slice of the human labor pie? Certainly not humanities.

## THE MYSTERY OF WARS AND CONFLICT?

It is so apparent and straightforward, nothing mysterious about it at one level. There is the Spirit of the Natural Law, in the beginning, God, Elohim. Followed by people with self-will. The self-will can be so loud and dominant in people that it overrides the Creator of Life and the Spirit of the Natural Law. So? Who is at fault? Who is the cause of violence and conflict? What value do they place on humanity? What is the intrinsic value of human Life? Created by the Creator of Life.

The minds of children do not plan wars. They do not march off in the children's army to fight until death. So, who does plan wars? Who are they that march off to fight wars until death? They are ambitious adult politicians. They have always been ambitious politicians that planned and caused wars in the last 100 years.

Adult politicians are good at making excuses. It is always the other at fault. The most greedy one. The one that came to steal, kill, and destroy is at fault. The cause of conflict and wars is direct and straightforward. Individuals and national leaders do not give sufficient respect to human Life. The economy and materialism rule the global roost. International trade compromised look the other way when the cargo ships come into offload and to load. Which industry has the most significant slice of the human labor pie? Certainly not humanities. People expect more convenience for life, at what cost? "It is the economy, stupid."

[8]

# UNIVERSAL DECLARATION OF HUMAN RIGHTS (PART. 1)

Adopted by General Assembly resolution 217 A (III) of 10 December 1948
(UN, 2018)
"The Declaration consists of a preamble and 30 articles, setting forth the human rights and fundamental freedoms to which all men and women, everywhere in the world, are entitled, without any discrimination.

**Article 1**, which lays down the philosophy on which the Declaration is based, reads:
All human beings are born free and equal in dignity and rights. They are endowed with reason and conscience and should act towards one another in a spirit of brotherhood.

The article thus defines the underlying assumptions of the Declaration: that the right to liberty and equality is man's birthright and cannot be alienated: and that, because man is a rational and moral being. He is different from other creatures on earth and therefore entitled to individual rights and freedoms which other creatures do not enjoy.

**Article 2**, which sets out the fundamental principle of equality and nondiscrimination as regards the enjoyment of human rights and fundamental freedoms, forbids "distinction of any kind, such as race, colour, sex, language, religion, political or other opinion, national or social origin, property, birth or other status".

**Article 3**, the first cornerstone of the Declaration, proclaims the right to life, liberty, and security of person -a right essential to the enjoyment of all other rights.

This article introduces articles 4 to 21, in which other civil and political rights are set out, including freedom from slavery and servitude; freedom from torture and cruel, inhuman or degrading treatment or punishment; the right to recognition everywhere as a person before the law; the right to an adequate judicial remedy; freedom from arbitrary arrest, detention or exile; the right to a fair trial and public hearing by an independent and impartial tribunal; the right to be presumed innocent until proved guilty; freedom from arbitrary interference with privacy, family, home or correspondence; freedom of movement and residence; the right of asylum; the right to a nationality; the right to marry and to found a family; the right to own property; freedom of thought, conscience and religion; freedom of opinion and expression; the right to peaceful assembly and association; and the right to take part in the government of one's country and to equal access to public service in one's country."
(UN, 2018)

USSR INTERNATIONAL HUMAN RIGHTS
That is the core reason for the mystery of conflict and wars. It is willful lawlessness and disrespect for the sanctity of life.

Joseph Stalin's life would have been much more meaningful and rewarding to him eternally as a human being made in the image of God if he had stayed at the seminary, where he started his theological studies. Potential to know what the will of God for him and humanity in general. He could have also found personal salvation and become righteous before God, living in submissive obedience to the Creator of life, through the redemption of Yeshua Hamashiach.

### LENIN A JEW?

"The declassification of documents since the collapse of the Soviet Communist tyranny in 1991 has brought irrefutable proof that Lenin's maternal great-grandfather was a shtetl Jew named Moshko Blank. Whether or not Lenin himself was aware of this piece of information is uncertain, but by the time of his death in 1924, his sister had possession of the facts—and, by order of the Central Committee of the Communist Party, was forced to keep them secret. The order held firm until the dissolution of the Soviet Union in the early 1990's". (Wisse, 2018) My Jewish learning.com

### KARL MARX

"Marx was ethnically Jewish. His maternal grandfather was a Dutch rabbi, while his paternal line had supplied Trier's rabbis since 1723, a role taken by his grandfather Meier Halevi Marx".(Encyclopedia, Karl Marx, 2018)

Karl Marx, with Jewish ancestry, would have served people much better by believing in the teaching of the Torah, instead of being a false prophet of humanism, teaching the people of the world atheism. The Bolsheviks failed their calling in life, by their obstinate self-will, willfully trusting their understanding, more than the written word of God. That is the difference.

> "Trust in the Lord with all your heart and lean not on your understanding; in all your ways submit to him, and he will make your paths straight." Proverbs 3:5-6. (NIV)

### SURE FOUNDATIONS

The Spirit of the Natural Law is a sure foundation for the rule of law and eternal law principles respecting societies. Without accepting the Spirit of the Natural Law principles, it is impossible to have legal principles for the International Law. It is only the Spirit of the Natural Law that provides true justice impartial to all people worldwide.

People that deny the Spirit of the Natural Law do so because their will and their spirits are not willing to submit to the impartial Spirit of the God-given Natural Law principles. The truth, similarly, a convicted lawbreaker will often repress or deny having broken any laws. Many simply will not accept the Spirit of the law that commands the human will to submit to the Spirit of the Natural Law's transcendent origin, Creator of Life. The same point made earlier; the law is not a material entity; it is immaterial. Transcendental Spirit of the Natural Law. In the beginning, Elohim, the Creator of life. Created the material world according to the Spiritual reality Law outside time and space.

Meaning to use the intellect and the will to make the right choice, consciously to do the right thing. It is a matter of realization and awareness to make an intelligent, higher conscious choice in a finite material world. Mostly, it is not a tug-a-war between the human will and human law, but rather a battle between human intellect, will, and the human carnal nature, pulling each way, and not giving the due respect to the Spirit of the Natural Law.

The intellect should be informed and enlightened to accept the knowledge of the more significant, the prior, Spirit of the Natural Law. The old analogy of the cart, the driver, or the horse? Which entity acts as the engine? Which has a more significant role in the steering? The metaphysical Spirit of the Law, or the subjective human will? What is its logic? Which has priority? Which is secondary?

Moreover, what purpose does it serve? Do spiritual laws serve random human behavior? Alternatively, does the random human behavior learn to submit to the metaphysical Spirit of the Natural Law? Moreover, learn the right priority and submit the human will to God's will to the higher priority order. It is like a small Copernican Revolution of the discovery of the other. The other being greater. The other being the will and the Spirit of Elohim.

It is a question of information, knowledge, understanding, and cognitive intelligence. A knowledge problem, with the intellect, that drives the individual self-determination. Almost 2000 years ago, 12 disciples made a free choice; after they were asked to follow Yeshua from Nazarene, they were invited to follow Jesus. The 12 to be disciples intuitively sensed that it was an invitation of a lifetime, worth taking. So, they committed themselves to follow the teaching Rabbi called Yeshua. It changed their lives forever.

The global community has always been a violent place, ruled by violent individuals. It is no different in the last 100 years. They do not accept the Spirit of the Natural Law as a reliable guide for civil government. Many dictator leaders have attempted to shut down the Spirit of the Natural Law and re-write the meta-narrative of the rules for human existence, according to the dictator's political ambitions, self-seeking glory, egomaniac fantasies, military power trips, and other imaginary extremities, like global domination.

### CLEAR LOGICAL THINKING EXPLAINED
Quote: *"The whole purpose of reasoning, of logic, is to arrive at the truth of things."*
*"This is often an arduous task, as truth can sometimes be painfully elusive. But not to pursue truth would be absurd, since it is the only thing that gives meaning to all our endeavors." "It would be equally absurd to suppose that truth is something forever to be pursued but never to be attained, for that renders our activity purposeless, which is to say, irrational, and turns truth into a chimera."* (McInerny, 2004) Being Logical: A Guide to Good Thinking.

### WHY DO HUMAN BEINGS DECEIVE ANIMALS?
Human deceptive methods are used for trapping animals and fish. The fish are caught by deceptive means to make the fish believe that bait is harmless when there is a hidden hook to snare the fish. During the stone age, wild animals were hunted, trapped for the food and the furry skins. It was beneficial for the survival of humanity, especially in the Northern Arctic regions of the globe. People that lived on the Pacific Islands would not need to hunt animals for their furry skins. There was no need for such extravagance; palm tree leaves skirt would suffice in the tropics. The fruits of the trees, and the root vegetables of the land, along with the fish and seafood of the ocean was nutritious and plentiful for people to survive on. It is revealing how humans treat animals with respect or disrespect. The quality that humans treat animals is learned and can also become part of human traits. Animals have character traits such as the adaptable, shy and timid, the laid back, happy, independent, and confident. Animals deserved to be respected. It is also commanded so in the Holy Scriptures.

> "For six days, you are to work. But on the seventh day, you are to rest, so that your ox and donkey can rest, and your slave-girl's son and the foreigner be renewed." Exodus 23:12. (CJB).

### OBJECTIVE FACTS
*"There are two basic types of objective facts, things, and events. A "thing" is an actually existing entity, animal, vegetable, or mineral.*

*A subjective fact, to the subject experiencing it, self-evident under normal circumstances. However, through such mechanisms as self-delusion or rationalization, a person could fail to get straight a fact even about himself.*

*We all tend to favor our ideas, which is natural enough. They are, after all, in a sense our very own babies, the conceptions of our minds.*

*However, conception is possible in the thinking subject only because of the subject's encounter with the world. Our ideas owe their existence, ultimately to things outside and independent of the mind, to which they refer: objective facts."*

*"Our ideas are clear, and our understanding of them is clear, only to the extent that we keep constant tabs on the things to which they refer. The focus must always be on the originating sources of our ideas in the objective world. We do not really understand our own ideas if we suppose them to be self-generating, that is, not owing their existence to extramental realities."*
(McInerny, 2004) Being Logical: A Guide to Good Thinking.

# [9]
# BOLSHEVIK EXPULSION FROM FINLAND 1918

BOLSHEVIK EXPULSION FROM FINLAND 1918

Finland's 1918 internal conflict has been described in many ways by the people of Finland and Russia for the last 100 years. It tells that the Bolsheviks Reds see the conflict from a different 180-degree angle than what the Blue Finns do. For the Bolsheviks, the event in Finland was a rude awakening to the Respect Rule of Law that they had become accustomed. The forces behind the Bolsheviks lawlessness people movement and the anti-monarchy ideology planned, conjured up, and orchestrated the Russian Revolution as early as 1900, by the full-time agitators and activist. Stalin was working as a revolutionist as early as 1902. The Bolsheviks lawless arrogance did not expect any opposition to their brazen murder of the Russian Monarchy.

- Liberation war
- Internal war
- A war between the Reds (Bolshies) and Blues (Finns)
- Extraction of the Bolsheviks spirit of lawlessness from Finland 1918
- Civil war does not sit regarding the Bolsheviks 18 years agitation in Russia (1900 -1918)

All of the above descriptions have some truth in them. However, the conflict's primary cause was the Bolsheviks exporting the Russian revolution fever and the Spirit of anarchy into Finland. Deliberate foreign lawlessness was not welcome in Finland.

The conflict between the Bolsheviks and the Blue Finns flared into ballistic warfare with military weapons on the January 27 and lasted until the Bolsheviks, and the Reds expulsed and driven out of Finland back to Russian on May 15, 1918. The war fought between the two opposing sides. The Russian Revolution's effects caused polarization in Finland's society; the Russian society collapses into rebellion and the anarchy of a Russian Civil War 1918 after the Bolshevik leaders murdered the Russian Tsar Romanov family, the royal couple, and their five children, including their servants.

It was a pre-planned 17 old rebellion in the making. The Spirit of anarchy was rebuffed and stopped in Finland. The Spirit of the law-abiding people of Finland had zero tolerance for the Bolsheviks lawless worldview and their State atheism philosophy. It was morally responsible for the people of Finland and the future government to defend self-preservation and stop the Spirit of anarchy spreading and gaining control in Finland. After hearing the reports of the Romanov family murders. Who would welcome the Bolsheviks into their country? Not likely. The general Spirit of the Nordic country's society, respect for law and order, would not accept such immoral and lawless behavior.

The Spirit of the Natural Law points out who the criminals were, and who was encouraging lawlessness. Since early 1900 there were individuals, like Josef Stalin, that was a habitual anarchist. A revolutionist that was doing everything in his power to undermine the authority of the Russian monarchy. The Spirit of the rule of law must be respected. It is a command in the Holy Scriptures. It is the Spirit that enables a society to have a universal respect for peace and order. That does not mean that a monarchist can self-indulge in privilege. No human is outside of the law, regardless of the status in society. Be it a leader, a king, or a prime mate, a husband or a wife, a manager or a business owner, every individual need to respect the Spirit of the law and abide in the rule of law, as long as the rule of law is morally responsible and respectful.

Even if the law becomes arbitrary and is immoral, that does not give license to murder the human-made lawmaker. It does mean that people are not obliged to obey immoral laws. That is another reason why it is essential to understand and know the Spirit of Natural Law. Understanding enables us to make the right decisions consciously. The people of Finland in 1918 declared explicitly that the Bolshevik gangsters had no authority over the peace respecting the people of Finland. Therefore, they were driven out of Finland, back to the Bolsheviks ruled Russia. That was the rational Worldview of peace-loving and law respecting the people of Finland. There was no question that the Bolsheviks were off the moral rails.

## 1918 BOLSHEVIKS EXPULSION FROM FINLAND

The conflict was directly from the Russian Revolution fever in 1917, which perpetuated the Spirit of anarchy to spread out into surrounding countries where the Russian military occupied in 1917. People had lost sight of what was normal moral behavior. Violent aggression is not a healthy state for the human mind and heart. Aggressive minority individuals do not have the authority to claim that their state is average. It only reveals their abnormal state. The normal human state can be studied in the 66 books of the Holy Bible. Let the word of God judge people as being deceived liars, and only God can ultimately judge rightly. The influence of the nemesis confused people with losing track of spiritual reality and cognitive facts. The most confused people are those that were tempted by influence and gave into the Spirit of rebellion and anarchy. They participated in the rebellion and overthrew the legitimate rule of law that was in Russia at the time.

Fueled by the Russian revolution fever events, it caused a domino effect, which was about to unravel the giant coil spring under tension and ready to release the trapped energy at the trigger. That would release a vast amount of stored spiritual dark energy and express itself with the mindless Nemesis rage's violence. There were ambitious political leaders, the criminal revolutionists, and the soldiers' tormented souls returning from the madness of the World War One Russian front lines ready and ripe to unravel.

## WHAT CAUSED THE RUSSIAN REVOLUTION?

On October 7, 1917, the Revolution of October moved the power according to the words of the Bolsheviks to the workers and gave birth to the dictatorship of the proletariat in Russia. The primary revolution goal was to create the first communist state country system in the world. The Bolshevik praetors were on the road to progress; those who stood in the way and prevented socialism's historical fate were not welcomed in the construction; it was a zero-tolerance closed group.

Bolsheviks emerged from power to abolish opposition parties and eliminate the enemies of the Revolution. The long-under-surface society tension developments triggered armed clashes around Russia since 1917. The war for the Revolution and against raged for a long time on numerous fronts between 1917 and 1921, which drove Russia to the brink of collapse. The seeming red powers in the core areas of Russia were even weaker in the periphery of the Russian land, which was warring against mixed counter-revolutionary armies.

War operations spread across a wide area of Soviet Russia, which consisted of the culmination point of the Civil War in the summer of 1919. Only in the area of the Grand Duchy of the Old Moscow, but even then, the Bolshevik leaders could not ignore, leave, or forget the Russian side of the socialist construction viewpoint. Bolshevik's earlier promise of people to the right of self-determination contained an affectionately underlined obligation to establish a new one instead of the bourgeois administration, based on the new, modern "working councils."

A regime that would operate either in the context of Soviet Russia or in its counterpart under the tutelage of the promised self-determination was just the right of working classes. If so, bourgeois forces seek to "prevent" the realization of this right; the Bolsheviks sent them ever-growing Red Army to "protect" the proletariat of the various regions in their own class struggle. The Civil War in Russia was not just a war, but by the war, the Bolsheviks were trying to dominate the system by any means. According to Bolshevik's ideas, the warfare described as "class struggle" came to extol the everlasting peace and security.

### WHO WERE THE BOLSHEVIKS?

One of the leaders of the Bolsheviks was Josef Stalin; he becomes a personality cult in Soviet Union-Russia. It is revealing to study the early years of his political career to get an insight into his life values, Worldview, and his character. What was the integrity of his character? And why on earth was he as a leader being worshipped as a personality cult idol? Was it because he represented the Dialectic Materialism worldview to the people? The political profile of Josef Stalin is far from Western standards in the 20 century. Stalin had a serious criminal record, including the armed robbery of a bank and a mail carriage; he was an ordinary streetwise gangster between 1900-1917. His name at birth was Ioseb Jughashvili. His father's name was Besarion Ivanes dze Jughashvili. Who was a successful shoemaker by trade, but later in life he slid into alcoholism and became a vagrant? His wife and Stalin's mother was Ekaterine Geladze.

*"The Jughashvili family were ethnically Georgian, and Stalin grew up speaking the Georgian language. Gori was then part of the Russian Empire and was home to a population of 20,000, the majority of whom were Georgian but with Armenian, Russian, and Jewish minorities. Stalin was baptized on December 17. He earned the childhood nickname of "Soso," a diminutive of Iosif (Joseph)."* – Wikipedia.

Joseph Stalin was sixteen in 1895; he received a scholarship at the Georgian Tbilisi Spiritual Seminary. Which was a religious training institution that operated from 1817 to 1919 in the Georgian Exarchate of the Russian Orthodox church? Stalin joined the 600 trainee priests who boarded at the seminary; Joseph is said to have been academically successful and gained high grades there.

### STALIN'S CHANGE OF HEART AT THE SPIRITUAL SEMINARY

As Stalin grew older, at the seminary, he lost interest in the subject of his studies; his grades dropped, and he was repeatedly confined to a cell for his rebellious behavior. Teachers complained that he declared himself an atheist, chatted in class and refused to doff his hat to monks.

*"Stalin joined a forbidden book club active at the school; he was particularly influenced by Nikolay Chernyshevsky's 1863 pro-revolutionary novel, What Is To Be Done? Another influential text was Alexander Kazbegi's The Patricide, with Stalin adopting the nickname "Koba" from that of the book's bandit protagonist. He also read Capital, the 1867 book by German sociological theorist Karl Marx. Stalin devoted himself to Marx's socio-political theory, Marxism, which was then on the rise in Georgia, one of the various forms of socialism opposed to the empire's governing Tsarist authorities."* (Encyclopedia, Joseph Stalin,)

### THE OPEN REBELLION OF AN OUTLAW

*Stalin co-organized a secret mass meeting of workers for May Day 1900, at which he successfully encouraged many of the men to take strike action.*

*The empire's secret police—the Okhrana—were aware of Stalin's activities within Tiflis' revolutionary milieu. They attempted to arrest him in March 1901, but he escaped and went into hiding.*

*Remaining underground, he helped to plan a demonstration for May Day 1901, in which 3,000 marchers clashed with the authorities.*

*In November 1901, he was elected to the Tiflis Committee of the Russian Social Democratic Labour Party (RSDLP), a Marxist party founded in 1898.*

*After several strikes, leaders were arrested, he co-organized a mass public demonstration that led to the storming of the prison; troops fired upon the demonstrators, 13 of whom were killed.*

*Stalin organized a second mass demonstration on the day of their funeral, before being arrested in April 1902.*

*He was initially held at Batumi Prison and later moved to the more secure Kutaisi Prison. In mid-1903, Stalin was sentenced to three years of exile in eastern Siberia.*

*Stalin left Batumi in October, arriving at the small Siberian town of Novaya Uda in late November. He lived in a two-room peasant's house, sleeping in the building's larder. Stalin made several escape attempts; on the first, he made it to Balagansk before returning due to frostbite.*

*His second attempt was successful, and he made it to Tiflis.*

*Stalin married Kato Svanidze in a church ceremony at Senaki in July 1906.*

*By the year 1907—according to the historian Robert Service— Stalin had established himself as "Georgia's leading Bolshevik."*

*After returning to Tiflis 1907, Stalin organized the robbing of a large money delivery to the Imperial Bank in June 1907. His gang ambushed the armed convoy in Yerevan Square with gunfire and home-made bombs. Around 40 people were killed, but all of his gang escaped alive.*

*After the heist, Stalin settled in Baku with his wife and son. There, Mensheviks confronted Stalin about the robbery and voted to expel him from the RSDLP, but he took no notice of them.*

*In Baku, he had reassembled his gang, the Outfit, which continued to attack Black Hundreds and raised finances by running protection rackets, counterfeiting currency, and carrying out robberies.*

*They also kidnapped the children of several wealthy figures to extract ransom money.*

*In March 1908, Stalin was arrested and interred in Bailov Prison, where he led the imprisoned Bolsheviks, organized discussion groups, and ordered the killing of suspected informants.*

*He was eventually sentenced to two years in exile in Solvychegodsk, Vologda Province, arriving there in February 1909. In June, he escaped the village and made it to Kotlas disguised as a woman and from there to Saint Petersburg.*

*In March 1910, arrested again and sent back to Solvychegodsk. There he had affairs with at least two women; his landlady, Maria Kuzakova, later gave birth to his second son, Konstantin.*

*He proceeded to Saint Petersburg, where he was arrested in September 1911, and sentenced to a further three-year exile in Vologda.*

*In February 1912, Stalin escaped to Saint Petersburg, tasked with converting the Bolshevik weekly newspaper, Zvezda ("Star") into a daily, Pravda ("Truth"). The new newspaper was launched in April 1912, although Stalin's role as editor was kept secret.*

*In May 1912, arrested again and imprisoned in the Shpalerhy Prison before being sentenced to three years exile in Siberia.*

*In July, he arrived at the Siberian village of Narym where he shared a room with fellow Bolshevik Yakov Sverdlov. After two months, Stalin and Sverdlov escaped back to Saint Petersburg.*

*During a brief period back in Tiflis, Stalin and the Outfit planned the ambush of a mail coach, during which most of the group— although not Stalin—were apprehended by the authorities.*

*In February 1913, Stalin was arrested while back in Saint Petersburg.*

*He was sentenced to four years exile in Turukhansk, a remote part of Siberia from which escape was particularly tricky.*

*In March 1914, concerned over a potential escape attempt, the authorities moved Stalin to the hamlet of Kureika on the edge of the Arctic Circle.*

*In the hamlet, Stalin had an affair with Lidia Pereprygia, who was thirteen at the time and thus a year under the legal age of consent in Tsarist Russia.*

*Circa December 1914, Pereprygia gave birth to Stalin's child, although the infant died soon after*

*While Stalin was in exile, Russia entered the First World War, and in October 1916 Stalin and other exiled Bolsheviks were conscripted into the Russian Army, leaving for Monastyrskoe.*

*They arrived in Krasnoyarsk in February 1917, where a medical examiner ruled Stalin unfit for military service due to his crippled left arm. Aged 12, he was seriously injured after being hit by a phaeton, resulting in a lifelong disability to his left arm.*

*Stalin was required to serve four more months on his exile, and he successfully requested that he serve it in nearby Achinsk. Stalin was in the city when the February Revolution took place; uprisings broke out in Petrograd—as Saint Petersburg had been renamed—and Tsar Nicholas II abdicated to be replaced by a Provisional Government.* (Wikipedia, The early life of Joseph Stalin, 2018)

[10]

# REMNANTS OF THE RULE OF LAW

In 1920 the Treaty of Tartu was signed in Tartu (Estonia) at the Estonian Students' Society building. The ratifications of the treaty were exchanged in Moscow on December 31, 1920. The Tartu treaty confirmed that the Finnish-Soviet border would remain and follow the old border which was established between the autonomous Grand Duchy of Finland and Imperial Russia. (Wikipedia, Treaty of Tartu (Russian–Finnish), 1920)

## A WAR BETWEEN THE TWO COUNTRIES 1918

The diplomatic relations between the repatriated Finland and Soviet Russia broke down following the Finland Liberation War outbreak. The Council of Russian People's Commissars recognized that the Revolutionary People's Delegation would be the future Finnish Government. The 42nd Army of Russia in Finland had also started military operations against White troops, and some of the Russian militaries became Reds military. There were no significant battles between Finland and Soviet Russia during the Finland Liberation War because the Reds of Finland played a significant role in the battles. Under the Brest-Litovsk Peace Treaty signed in March 1918 between Russia and the German Empire, Russian troops were withdrawn entirely from Finland except for a few volunteers. (Encyclopedia, Treaty of Brest-Litovsk, 1918)

The Finnish Senate, as the Government, for the first time declared that Finland was at war against Russia, at the beginning of April 1918, justifying the imprisonment of the Levis Kamenev of Bolsheviks in Åland. Relations between the two countries could not be restored after the Bolsheviks expulsion from the Finland war. In April 1918, Soviet Russia appointed colonel Konstantin Kovankon as a diplomatic representative to Helsinki, but the Finnish authorities imprisoned him at the end of May and did not allow his successors to enter the country.

After the Finland Liberation War, Finland asked for assistance from Germany to solve the conflict issues of Eastern Karelia and Municipality in the Barents Sea port of Petsamo. After several requests, Germany agreed to host the peace talks between Finland and Russia, which took place in Berlin in August 1918 for three weeks. Negotiations ended unsuccessfully due to the uncoordinated regional requirements of both countries. Also, Soviet Russia did not accept the Finnish interpretation of the state of war between the two countries, as all Russian state property left in Finland would have been transferred and interpreted as Finland's property.

Over the next two years, the leadership of Soviet Russia declared that it wished to maintain peaceful neighborly relations with Finland for the time being. Usually, diplomatic relations were not possible even though the occasional informal exchange of notes between the country's foreign ministries. The Finns considered the state of war to continue and held informal contacts with the Russian White Leaders.

## PEACE NEGOTIATIONS 1920

Peace negotiations over a Peace Treaty began in Estonia, Tartu, on June 12, 1920. The negotiations were held at the University of Tartu Student Organization Eesti Üliõpilaste Seltsi. J. K. Paasikivi led the Finnish Delegation. The Delegation consisted of the same people as the Committee that had previously prepared the Finnish peace rules. The presidency was initially offered to Carl Enckell, but he refused because he opposed the Bolsheviks' peace agreement. When the members' views on the need to link East Karelia to Finland varied, the Paasikivi Committee, as a compromise, intended to require the Eastern Karelians to decide by referendum to either side with Finland or with Russia. Meanwhile, foreign Finland minister Holsti gave the Finnish Delegation the goal of pulling the eastern border to the line of Laatokan- Syvärin-Ääninen- the White Sea and linking Petsamo Municipality and the entire Kola peninsula to Finland.

Only the requirements of Kirjasalo or Ingria have left aside because their pursuit was not considered realistic due to the continued Russian expansion location of St. Petersburg. The city had outgrown and expulsed the local population. It was decided to recommend the use of cultural autonomy to the Ingrians. Before starting the negotiations, Soviet Russia occupied the area between Murmansk Railway and Finland. It announced the establishment of a Karelian Workers' Commune, led by Socialist Edvard Gylling, who had fled from Finland. According to Bolshevik, this was a demonstration that the people of East Karelia had solved the content of their sovereignty, and no referendum would be needed.

Finland delegation 1920

### THE COURSE OF THE NEGOTIATIONS

In the beginning, the negotiations stalled in place on regional issues. The Russians insisted on maintaining the borders of 1914, except for the municipality of Repola and the municipality of Porajärvi, which could have been negotiated, as well as obtaining part of the Gulf of Finland Islands and the Karelian Canal.

The Finns did not want to retreat from their demands for eastern Karelia because they suspected that Soviet Russia wanted peace as soon as possible with the war in Poland and the rest of its neighbors and would agree to concessions. The negotiations stalled for several months before the parties were ready to overthrow their demands when the Red Army in Poland's anti-war invasion near the Warsaw neighborhood in late summer, negotiations with Finland were suspended in mid-July from both sides' wish for two weeks. During the break, President K. J. Ståhlberg lowered demands.

Finland still wanted the municipality of Petsamo while the population of Repola and Porajärvi had to decide on their own fate, but the sovereignty of East Karelia could be resilient. After the negotiations resumed, the Finnish

Delegation was deliberately delayed, as expected, to clarify the global situation. Finally, on August 9, Foreign Minister Rudolf Holsti allowed Finland's delegates to start negotiations with realism, as Poland had already begun negotiations with the Council of Russia.

The truce was concluded between Finland and Soviet Russia in August in Poland; the Red Army was able to hit back at the Polish border, so Tartu's negotiating arrangements began to compromise. Soviet Russia was ready to hand over Petsamo to Finland. However, it was still waiting for Finland to return the municipality of Repola and Porajärvi, closer to the Muurman railway track, the northernmost, year-round railroad to the north of Russia.

Soviet Delegation 1920.

For Finland, however, two broad areas of the eastern bloc municipality were not as crucial as the year-round ice-free port of Petsamo. From Finland, possession of Repola and Porajärvi was also a way to improve the likelihood of being taken over by Petsamo. This consensus was contributed by confidential Vaino Tanner, a representative of the Social Democrats of the Finnish Delegation, with Plato Keržentsev, a member of the Russian Delegation. Along with Tanner, only Paasikivi knew about these conversations. Tanner suggested to Kerzenville that the acquisition of Petsamo was a priority for the Finns concerning the preservation of Repola and Porajärvi. On Tanner's suggestion, the Russian Delegation presented its last bid to replace these areas, to which the Finns agreed on September 7, 1920. Foreign Minister Holsti, who was pressurized by public opinion, still insisted on keeping Repola and Porajärvi in a hurry. However, the Finnish Delegation did not want to tear apart the reconciliation that had taken place after months of work. The latest disagreements concerned the borderline in the Fisham fishing island of Petsamo and the fate of the Gulf of Finland's outer islands required by Russia. On October 2, Vladimir Lenin, the Bolshevik Party's politburo, ordered his representative to conclude peace with Poland and Finland as soon as possible.

## TREATY OF TARTU 1920

The Treaty of Tartu was between Finland and Soviet Russia. It was finally signed on October 14. 1920. After the negotiations that lasted four months. The treaty confirmed the border between Finland and Soviet Russia, after the 1918 Bolsheviks expulsion from the Finland war and the Finnish volunteer expeditions in Russian East Karelia. The treaty was signed in Tartu (Estonia) at the Estonian Students' Society building. Ratifications of the treaty were exchanged in Moscow on December 31, 1920. The treaty registered in the League of Nations Treaty Series on March 5, 1921. The treaty confirmed that the Finnish-Soviet border would follow the old border between the autonomous Grand Duchy of Finland and Imperial Russia. Finland additionally received Petsamo, with its ice-free harbor on the Arctic Ocean.

As far back as 1864, Tsar Alexander II had promised to join Petsamo to Finland in exchange for a piece of the Karelian Isthmus. Finland also agreed to leave the joined and the occupied areas of Repola (joined to Finland during the Viena expedition) and Porajärvi (joined during the Aunus expedition) in Russian East Karelia. The treaty also had some articles besides area and border issues, including a Soviet guarantee of free navigation of merchant ships from the Finnish ports in Lake Ladoga (Laatokka in Finnish) to the Gulf of Finland River Neva. Finland guaranteed land transit from the Soviet Union to Norway via the Petsamo area. Also, Finland agreed to disarm the coastal fortress in Ino, opposite the Soviet city Kronstadt located on the island of Kotlin. The Finnish outer islands in the Gulf of Finland were demilitarized. (Wikipedia, Treaty of Tartu (Russian–Finnish), 1920)

EAST KARELIAN AGAINST BOLSHEVIKS

The Karelian region. After Finland declared independence from Russia, some Finnish nationalists supported the idea of a Finland expansion Eastwards. It was an attempt to block the Russian encroachment on the Karelian region. The Karelians were much closer culturally to Finland than Russia. More Karelians spoke Finnish than the Russian language. The Finnish culture, the Karelians, the Ingrians, and the Swedish Kingdom had seen and experienced Moscow's push since the 17 Century. In the early days of the calendar years, people lived along the Gulf of Finland, along with the Karelian Isthmus, Lake Ladoga, North Karelia, and the Kola Peninsula. People lived in these areas and spoke their language for thousands of years before Moscow or Russia existed. Both Russia and Moscow are latecomers, peoples from the Slav regions migrating East. They have no rightful claims to the Nordic indigenous people's regions, only military conquest. State atheism claims regions that do not belong to them, so they resort to extortion and ruthless totalitarianism and genocide. Every evil deed committed by evil dictators against the Spirit of the Natural Law is felt, seen, noticed, and recorded by the Creator of Life. Justice will come one day to the millions of innocent lives lost between 1900 to 1991. This planet's soil never forgets the murders, and the innocent lives blood, committed by godless atheists.

The Karelian regions have a long cultural history parallel with the Finnish peoples; they are regarded as Finnish tribes. The USSR made a significant effort to forcefully remove the people of Karelia and replace the peoples with Socialist Russians during the 1930–1950s. The systematic ethnic cleansing with communism obsession and political tactics for expanding the socialist ideals into Europe. They were ruthless with the Ingrian people in the Karelian Isthmus. Eradicating the Ingrian population and culture from their home region, all because of a war between Sweden and Russia. Peter the Great started building his new city on a swamp named Petersburg. It was the first established location by Sweden and the Finns, a fortress named Nyenschantz, at the Gulf of Finland shore, at Neva's river mouth.

NYENSCHANTZ FORTRESS 1611

*"Nyenschantz fortress was built in 1611 to establish Swedish rule in the Ingria land, which was initially pioneered and populated by peoples, later to be conquered by the Novgorod or Moscow expansionism towards West. It was taken away from the Russians by Sweden during the Time of Troubles. The town of Nyen, which formed around Nyenschantz, became a wealthy trading center and capital of Swedish Ingria during the 17th century. In 1702, Nyenschantz and Nyen were conquered by Russia during the Great Northern War, and the new Russian capital of Saint Petersburg was established by Peter the Great in their place the following year".* (Nyenschantz, 1611)

The Finnish people effort in the 1920s to push back the Russians from the Karelian region was an effort to push back the forces that had slowly crept up and pressing on the eastern borders of Finland since the 16th century.;

It is a strange, bizarre concept indeed; why would such a giant Imperial Empire that reaches from East Europe to the Sea of Japan want to torment indigenous peoples and small independent nations such as Finland, Estonia, Latvia, and Poland? It is the immoral, insane madness of the Russian leader's foreign policy spirit to consider the countries' areas in comparison.

- Russia. 17,075,200. Expanded to 17 Million square kilometers.
- Finland. 338,424. Square kilometers (2018).
- 372,266. Square kilometers during 1939.
- Estonia. 45,227. Square kilometers.
- Latvia. 64,589. Square kilometers.
- Poland. 312,679. Square kilometers.
- 

The activist Finns tried to free the Karelia of Russian domination. It was seen as an effort to form a unified country for Finnic tribes, who were regarded as kindred by these activists. The resulting two incursions by Finnish volunteers into Russia called the Viena and Aunus expeditions, are not considered wars against Russia in Finnish historiography. In Russia, this conflict, as well as the Finnish expeditions into East Karelia and the Petsamo in 1918–1920, is considered a military intervention and called the First Soviet–Finnish War. This period of disagreement and uncertainty about borders was ended with the Treaty of Tartu, where Finland and the Baltic states first recognized the Russian Soviet Federative Socialist Republic as a sovereign state and established the border between Finland and RSFSR.

The motivation for the uprising was East Karelians' year-long experience of the Bolshevik regime – not respecting promises of autonomy, food shortages, the will of nationalistic kindred activists to amend the results of the "shameful peace" of Tartu, and the wish of exiled East Karelians. Finnish kindred activists, notably Jalmari Takkinen, the deputy of Bobi Sivén, the bailiff of Repola, had been conducting a campaign in the summer of 1921 to rouse the East Karelians to fight against the Bolshevik belligerents of the ongoing Russian Civil War. East Karelian paramilitary units called themselves Karjalan metsäsissit (English: Forest Guerrillas), and by autumn of 1921, a notable part of of White Karelia was under their control.

### BEFORE THE TREATY OF TARTU
The parishes of Repola and Porajärvi of the Olonets Governorate had voted in favor of secession from Bolshevist Russia, and had been occupied by Finland later that year. In late 1919, the Russian White Army retreated towards the Finnish border to the Repola-Porajärvi area. The Finnish government led by Juho Vennola decided in February 1920 that Finland should intervene to help the dissidents by diplomatic means.

Foreign minister Rudolf Holsti sent a message to his counterpart Georgy Chicherin stating that Finland would disarm the retreating Russian White troops if the Red Army does not occupy the parishes. The agreement was honored by both parties, although there were minor skirmishes between Finnish troops and the Red Army. This fights led to armistice negotiations in Rajajoki, which ended unsuccessfully after two weeks.

There had been uprisings in White Karelia as early in 1920. After British forces left Karelia, Karelian ethnic nationalists arranged a meeting in Ukhta (now Kalevala, Russia) in March–April 1920 where they elected 117 representatives. In the meeting, they decided that White Karelia should become an independent nation. Some parishes of Olonets Karelia joined in, and the Väliaikainen toimikunta (Temporary Commission) renamed itself to Karjalan väliaikainen hallitus (Temporary Government of Karelia). However, the Red Army suppressed this uprising, and in summer 1920 the Temporary Government fled to Finland. In its place, the Karelian Worker's Commune was formed, a autonomous oblast of the RSFSR.

During the treaty negotiations, Finland proposed a referendum in East Karelia, through which its residents could choose whether they wanted to join Finland or Soviet Russia. Due to opposition from Russia, Finland had to withdraw the initiative. In return for ceding Repola and Porajärvi back to Russia, Finland acquired Petsamo and a promise of cultural autonomy for East Karelia. However, this cultural autonomy was poorly carried out.

### PREPARATIONS
Following the signing of the treaty, irredentists of the Repola county devised a contingency plan with the silent approval of the Finnish ministry of foreign affairs, titled Karhunpesäsuunnitelma (Project Bear's Den). They acquired a shipment of 500 Japanese rifles and 100 000 cartridges from Elmo Kaila, one of the Jäger Movement leaders. They

also had two Maxim machine guns and four Lewis Guns. Weapons shipments for Project Bear's Den was an open secret and overlooked by Finnish customs officials.

On January 6, 1921, an aide of the Finnish minister of foreign affairs Rudolf Holsti demanded an official account for the weapons. Eventually, the leader of the Repola irredentists, Bobi Sivén, received a letter from the Finnish foreign ministry stating: "Due to extraordinary circumstances you must do your utmost to prevent the people of Repola and Porajärvi from arming themselves." On January 12, Sivén committed suicide with his service pistol. In several suicide letters he left behind, he expressed his resentment at Finland "betraying" the East Karelians, and his wish to rather die for East Karelians than return to Finland. He had answered earlier requests from Finnish government to return to Finland by stating he resigns from his bailiff office, and prefers to live as a civilian in Repola. Due to succeeding events Sivén was elevated to a status of a minor Finnic national hero and martyr akin to Eugen Schauman, whose method of suicide he also imitated either on purpose or coincidentally, shooting himself in the heart instead of head in addition to the similar nationalistic pathos letters. Gradually these early uprisings and Finnish government's interest in supporting them dwindled.

## THE UPRISING

The pivotal moment in the uprising was the council meeting of Karelian Forest Guerrillas in mid-October 1921. It voted in favor of secession from Soviet Russia. The key leadership was formed by military leaders Jalmari Takkinen, Finnish-born, aka. Ilmarinen, and Ossippa Borissainen. Particularly Vaseli Levonen aka. Ukki Väinämöinen, who had prominent Karelian features and general resemblance to the Finnish mythical character, was deemed suitable for the role as an ideological leader. Some 550 Finnish volunteers joined the uprising, acting mostly as officers and squad leaders. Most famous of them was Paavo Talvela and Erik Heinrichs of the Jäger Movement who later served as a high ranking staff officer in the Winter War and Continuation War.

The uprising is a peculiarity among heimosodat (tribal wars) at this time the initiative was, not taken by Finnish insurgents, but by East Karelian separatists, and Finnish government remaining officially passive. After the treaty of Tartu and Finnish government retreating from covert separatist support, the uprising was started by East Karelians, with Finnish volunteers joining afterward. The uprising began with the immediate summary execution of anyone who was or was suspected to be a Bolshevik. The uprising escalated into a military engagement in October–November 1921. The 2 500 Forest Guerrillas were initially reasonably successful, despite their lack of proper equipment.

The East Karelian rebels got some publicity in international media, but they had expected Finland to intervene with its defense forces. However, the Finnish government denied requests for arranging official enlistment, but it did not prevent private Finnish volunteer activists from crossing the border. Finland did agree to send humanitarian aid to the East Karelian rebels, taking the risk of provoking a war with the RSFSR. Soviet historians, however, stipulated that the Finnish government did militarily support the uprising, and was intervening in an internal conflict. In Northern White Karelia the smaller Vienan Rykmentti (Viena Regiment) was formed. Combined, the East Karelian rebels numbered 2500.

On November 6, 1921, the Finnish and Karelian forces began an incursion into East Karelia. According to Finnish historians, on that day Karelian guerrillas and Finnish volunteer forces attacked in Rukajärvi. Russian historian Alexander Shirokorad claims this force was 5 000– 6 000 strong, which is twice the total strength of East Karelians and Finnish volunteers combined according to to Finnish records.

The first Finnish volunteers reached Repola at the end of November 1921. The volunteers acted as private citizens, and were not considered a government intervention by Finland, but the Russian view differed. This controversy caused considerable friction in diplomatic relations between Finland and RSFSR. Most of the volunteers joined the Repolan Pataljoona (Repola Battalion). Command of the Battalion in Olonets Karelia was first taken by Gustaf Svinhufvud and after that by Talvela, at the middle of December 1921.

By, the end of December 1921, the Finnish volunteers and Karelian Forest Guerrillas, had advanced to the Kiestinki Suomussalmi – Rukajärvi Paatene, Porajärvi lines. Meanwhile, the ca. 20 000 troops of the Red Army led by Alexander Sedyakin have reached Karelia and mounted a counterattack. The Red Army also had Red Finns within its ranks. These Finns had emigrated to Soviet Russia after their defeat in the Finland Liberation War. One such unit was a ski battalion of 200 Red military school cadets under the command of Toivo Antikainen.

DEFEAT OF THE UPRISING

Finnish support of the uprising with volunteers and humanitarian aid caused a notable regression on Finnish-Russian diplomatic relations. Leon Trotsky, the commander of the Red Army, announced that he was ready to march towards Helsinki and Soviet Russian troops would strike the East Karelian rebels with a 20 000 strong army via the Murmansk railway. At the onset of winter, the resistance of Forest Guerrillas collapsed under superior numbers of the Red Army, famine, and cold. The rebels panicked, and their troops started to retreat towards the Finnish border.

According to Shirokorad, the troops of the Red Army had crushed the main group of the Finnish and Karelian troops by the beginning of January 1922 and had retaken Porosozero and Reboly. On January 25, the northern group of the Soviet troops had occupied Kestenga and Kokkosalmi, and by the beginning of February occupied the settlement Ukhta.

During the final stages of the uprising, the Red "Pork mutiny" occurred in Finland, sparking a hope among the rebels and Finnish volunteers that this would cause the Finnish government to intervene and provide military aid to the insurgents. This did not happen; on the contrary, the minister of interior, Heikki Ritavuori, tightened border control, closed the border preventing food and munitions shipments, and prohibited volunteers to cross over to join the uprising. The assassination of Ritavuori on February 12, 1922, by a Finnish nationalist activist, did not change the situation. The last unit of the uprising, remnants of of Viena Regiment, fled Tiirovaaraon February 16, 1922, at 10:45 am and reached the border at one pm.

AFTERMATH

On June 1, 1922, in Helsinki, Finland and Soviet Russia signed an Agreement between RSFSR and Finland about the measures providing the inviolability of the Soviet–Finnish border. Both parties agreed to reduce the number of border guards and to keep those who do not reside permanently in the border zone from freely crossing the border from either side to the other. Towards the end of the uprising, some 30 000 East Karelian refugees evacuated to Finland.

*"The Karelian Worker's Commune was renamed into the Karelian Autonomous Soviet Socialist Republic in 1923, and its autonomy further expanded. However, the cultural autonomy practically ended in 1933 – 1935 when the émigré Finnish leaders Edvard Gylling and Kustaa Rovio were purged, and teaching of Finnish language was prohibited."*

*"Gylling had promoted Finnish's adoption rather than Karelian within the KASSR as he and the other émigré Finns who dominated the leadership of Karelia before 1935 did not consider Karelian to be anything more than a rustic dialect of Finnish. It may also be argued they held the same view of the essential unity of the Karelians and Finns as one Finnic people as their nationalist counterparts, and also wished that they are unified (albeit in somewhat different political circumstances)."* East Karelian Soviet–Finnish conflict of 1921–22. (Karelia, 1921)

[11]

# JOSEPH STALIN WORLD REVOLUTION

*"Socialism in One Country was a theory put forth by Joseph Stalin and Nikolai Bukharin in 1924 and after. The Soviet Union eventually adopted it as state policy. The theory held that given the defeat of all the communist revolutions in Europe in 1917–1923 except Russia's, the Soviet Union should begin to strengthen itself internally. That turn toward national communism was a shift from the previously held position by Classical Marxism that socialism must be established globally (world communism). However, the proponents of the theory contend that it contradicts neither world revolution nor world communism. The theory was in opposition to Leon Trotsky's theory of permanent Revolution."*

*"The defeat of several proletarian revolutions in countries like Germany and Hungary ended Bolsheviks' hopes for an imminent world revolution and began promotion of "Socialism in One Country" by Stalin. In the first edition of the book Osnovy Leninizma (Foundations of Leninism, 1924), Stalin was still a follower of Vladimir Lenin's idea that Revolution in one Country is insufficient. Lenin died in January 1924. By the end of that year, in the second edition of the book, Stalin's position started to turn around: the "proletariat can and must build the socialist society in one country." In April 1925 Nikolai Bukharin elaborated the issue in his brochure Can We Build Socialism in One Country in the Absence of the Victory of the West-European Proletariat? The Soviet Union adopted "Socialism in One Country" as state policy after Stalin's January 1926 article On the Issues of Leninism."* wikipedia.org/wiki/Socialism_in_One_Country

*In his 1915 article "On the Slogan for the United States of Europe," Lenin had written: "Uneven economic and political development is an absolute law of capitalism. Hence, the victory of socialism is possible first in several or even in one capitalist Country alone. After expropriating the capitalists and organizing their socialist production, the victorious proletariat of that Country will arise against the rest of the world...."*

Again, in 1918, Lenin wrote:

*"I know that there are, of course, sages who think they are very clever and even call themselves Socialists, who assert that power should not have been seized until the Revolution had broken out in all countries. They do not suspect that by speaking in this way, they are deserting the Revolution and going over to the side of the bourgeoisie. To wait until the toiling classes bring about a revolution on an international scale means that everybody should stand stock-still in expectation. That is nonsense."* (Speech delivered at a joint meeting of the All-Russian Central Executive Committee and the Moscow Soviet, May 14 1918, Collected Works, Vol. 23, page. 9.)

After Lenin's death, Stalin used these quotes and others to argue that Lenin shared his view of Socialism in One Country.

Grigory Zinoviev and Leon Trotsky vigorously criticized the theory of Socialism in One Country. In particular, Trotskyists often claimed, and still claim, that Socialism in One Country opposes both the basic tenets of Marxism and Lenin's specific beliefs that the final success of socialism in one Country depends upon the Revolution's degree of success in proletarian revolutions in the more advanced countries of Western Europe. At the Seventh Congress in March 1918 Lenin explained that:

*"Regarded from the world-historical point of view, there would doubtlessly be no hope of the ultimate victory of our Revolution, if it were to remain alone if there were no revolutionary movements in other countries ... I repeat, our salvation*

*from all these difficulties is an all Europe revolution ... At all events, under all conceivable circumstances, if the German Revolution does not come, we are doomed."*

However, in the Political Report of the Central Committee to the Extraordinary Seventh Congress of the R.C.P.(B.) Lenin wrote that:

*"Yes, we shall see the international world revolution, but for the time being it is a very good fairy-tale, a very beautiful fairy-tale—I quite understand children liking beautiful fairy-tales. However, is it proper for a serious revolutionary to believe in fairy-tales?"*

*"There is an element of reality in every fairy-tale. If you told children fairy-tales in which the cock and the cat did not converse in a human language they would not be interested. In the same way, 'if you tell the people that civil war will break out in Germany and also guarantee that instead of a clash with imperialism we shall have a field revolution on a worldwide scale, the people will say you are deceiving them."*

*"In doing this, you will be overcoming the difficulties with which history has confronted us only in your minds, by your wishes. It will be a good thing if the German proletariat can take action. However, have you measured it, have you discovered an instrument that will show that the German Revolution will break out on such-and-such a day? No, you do not know that, and neither do we. You are staking everything on this card. If the Revolution breaks out, everything is saved."*

*"Of course! However, if it does not turn out as we desire, if it does not achieve victory tomorrow—what then? Then the masses will say to you; you acted like gamblers—you staked everything on a fortunate turn of events that did not take place, you proved to be unequal to the situation that arose instead of the world revolution, which will inevitably come, but which has not yet reached maturity."*

Also, in a Letter to American Workers, 1918 he wrote:

*"We are banking on the inevitability of the world revolution, but this does not mean that we are such fools as to bank on the revolution inevitably coming on a definite and early date..."*(Vladimir-Lenin, 1918)

### JOSEPH STALIN PROFILE
1918 – From March, the Bolsheviks refer to themselves as Communists. Their party is the Communist Party.

1919 – Stalin is elected as a member of the Politburo, the inner circle of the Central Committee and principal policy-making body in the Soviet Union.

1922 – Stalin is given the newly created post of general secretary of the Central Committee. The position places him in control of party appointments and allows him to develop his power base. He consolidates his influence further by spying on his colleagues, a tactic that becomes a hallmark of his dictatorship.

When Lenin suffers a stroke in May, a troika (triumvirate) composed of Stalin, Lev B. Kamenev, and Grigorii V. Zinoviev assume leadership.

Lenin recovers after three months and reasserts control. In letters written at the end of 1922 and the beginning of 1923, Lenin singles Stalin out for criticism.

"Comrade Stalin, having become general secretary, has unlimited authority concentrated in his hands, and I am not sure whether he will always be capable of using that authority with sufficient caution," Lenin writes.

*"Stalin is too rude and this defect, although quite tolerable in our midst and in dealing with us Communists, becomes intolerable in a general secretary. That is why I suggest the comrades think about a way of removing Stalin from that post and appointing another man in his stead, who in all other respects differs from Comrade Stalin, in having only one advantage, namely, that of being more tolerant, more loyal, more polite, and more considerate to the comrades, less capricious, etc.."*

*"This circumstance may appear to be a negligible detail. But I think ... it is not a detail, or it is a detail which can assume decisive importance. Lenin also criticizes Stalin for using coercion to force non-Russian republics to join the Soviet Union, saying he has behaved like a "vulgar Great-Russian bully."*

"I think that Stalin's haste and his infatuation with the pure administration, together with his spite against the notorious 'nationalist-socialism,' played a fatal role here," Lenin writes. "In politics spite generally plays the basest of roles."

However, the party takes no action. Stalin remained as general secretary when Lenin died on January 21, 1924

1925 – Following Lenin's death, the Kamenev-Zinoviev-Stalin troika again comes to prominence. Stalin consolidates his power base until he can break with Kamenev and Zinoviev. He has the city of Tsaritsin renamed Stalingrad (now Volgograd) and allows the development of a Stalin personality cult and propaganda campaign. From 1926 to 1930, he progressively ousts his opponents on the left and right of the party, silencing debate about options for the development of communism and the USSR. By the end of the decade, Stalin has emerged as the supreme leader of the Soviet Union.

Cultists hail him as a "shining sun," "the staff of life," a "great teacher and friend," the 'hope of the future for the workers and peasants of the world" and the "genius of mankind, the greatest genius of all times and people." 1928 – Stalin introduces the first five-year plan, the "revolution from above," to develop the USSR. "We are 50 to 100 years behind the advanced countries," he said in 1931. "We must cover this distance in 10 years. Either we do this, or they will crush us."

The state takes control of the economy, introducing a program of rapid industrialization and agrarian consolidation and setting unrealistic goals for development. Industry and commerce are nationalized. All social, political and regulatory power is centered on the state. Twenty-five million peasant farmers are forced to collectivize their property and then work on the new state-controlled farms. Wealthy peasants (kulaks) and the uncooperative are arrested and either executed or deported to work camps in Siberia. The collectivized farms are required to meet ever-increasing production quotas, even if this results in starvation on the farm.

In the Ukrainian Republic, up to five million peasants starve to death in the famine of 1932 to 1933, when the state refuses to divert food supplies allocated to industrial and military needs. About one million starve to death in the North Caucasus.

By 1937, the social upheaval caused by the "revolution from above" has resulted in the deaths of up to 14.5 million Soviet peasants.

1929 – The Politburo begins to discuss the expansion of the work camp system set up by Lenin following the Bolshevik Revolution. The system comes to be known as the Gulag Archipelago or Gulag. (Gulag is an acronym of Glavnoe Upravlenie Lagerei – Russian for Main Camp Administration.)

1932 – Although the industry has failed to meet its production targets, and agricultural output has dropped in comparison with 1928 yields, Stalin announces that the first five-year plan has successfully met its goals in only four years. The second five-year plan was introduced in 1933 and the third in 1938.

On November 8, Stalin's second wife, Nadezhda Alliluyeva, commits suicide following Stalin's argument during a party at the Kremlin.

Her suicide also reportedly comes after a group of students she is teaching are arrested for sedition after attempting to inform Stalin of the plight of the peasants.
Nadezhda Alliluyeva's suicide and the scathing personal note she leaves him are believed to have had a shattering effect on Stalin.

1934 – Stalin's purges of party members suspected of disloyalty begin in December after Leningrad party chief Sergei Kirov is assassinated. Thousands from the Leningrad party office are deported to work camps in Siberia. Not many returned alive.
At show trials held in Moscow between 1936 and 1938 dozens of former party leaders are forced to confess to crimes against the Soviet state. They are then executed. Among those put to death are Kamenev and Zinoviev,

the former members of the troika that included Stalin. By the end of 1938, almost every leading member of the original Bolsheviks has been killed.

The campaign of terror, flamed by the secret police (the NKVD, or People's Commissariat of Internal Affairs – the forerunner of the KGB, or Komitet Gosudarstvenoi Bezopasnosti), extends throughout the party and into the general community, including the military high command. Also targeted are scientists, artists, priests, and intellectuals.

All told, about one million are executed in what comes to be known as The Great Terror, The Great Purge, or the Yezhovshina (after the head of the NKVD, Nikolai Yezhov). At least 9.5 million more are deported, exiled or imprisoned in work camps, with many of the estimated five million sent to the Gulag never returning alive. Other estimates place the number of deported at 28 million, including 18 million sent to the Gulag. Stalin personally orders the trials of about 44,000 and signs thousands of death warrants. He also ends early release from work camps for good behavior.

1936 – The Spanish Civil War began on July 18 when Spanish Nationalists led by Francisco Franco staged a coup against the Country's left-leaning Republican Government. Stalin provides support to the Republicans but is wary about antagonizing Germany's Nazi dictator, Adolf Hitler, who is backing the Nationalists.

1937 – On July 30, the NKVD issues Order No. 00447, setting out the "means of punishment of those to be repressed, and the number of those subject to repression." The operation is to begin on August 5 and be completed in four months. "All kulaks, criminals, and other anti-Soviet elements to be repressed are to be divided into two categories," the order stats.

"a) The first category is the most hostile of the enumerated elements. They are subject to immediate arrest, and after their cases have been considered by a three-person tribunal (troika), they are TO BE SHOT.

"b) In the second category is the other less active though also hostile elements. They are subject to arrest and imprisonment in a camp for 8 to 10 years, and the evilest and socially dangerous of these, to incarceration for the same period in prison, as determined by the three-person tribunal."

The order then lists the numbers of individuals from regions around the Soviet Union to be "subject to repression." 75,950 are to be executed and 203,000 exiled. At the same time, the purge of the Red Army begins. The purge results in the execution, imprisonment or dismissal of 36,671 officers, including about half of the 706 officers with the rank of brigade commander or higher. Three of the Army's five marshals and 15 of its 16 top commanders are executed.

On November 7, during a toast to mark the anniversary of the October Revolution, Stalin states that every enemy of the state will be destroyed. "Even if he were an old Bolshevik, we would destroy all his kin, his family," he says. "We will mercilessly destroy anyone who, by his deeds or his thoughts, yes, his thoughts, – threatens the unity of the socialist state. To the complete destruction of all enemies, themselves and their kin!"

1938 – On September 29, Britain, France, Germany, and Italy sign the Munich Agreement. The agreement, which cedes the German-speaking area in the north of Czechoslovakia to Germany, is an ill-fated attempt to avoid the Second World War. Stalin interprets the agreement as a sign that he will not be able to count on either Britain or France if Germany becomes hostile.

1939 – On August 23 the Soviet Union and Germany sign a nonaggression pact carving up Eastern Europe into German and Soviet spheres of influence, with the USSR claiming Estonia, Latvia, Lithuania, Finland, part of the Balkans and half of Poland. German troops invade Poland on September 1. Britain and France declare war on Germany two days later. The Second World War has begun.

Stalin acts to secure the USSR's western frontier without antagonizing Hitler. Soviet forces seize eastern Poland in September and enter Estonia, Latvia, and Lithuania in October. Stalin's war against starts on November 30, without a declaration of war. The declaration of war on Finland comes later after the fact in December 1939.

In Poland, soldiers and others who might resist the Soviet annexation are arrested en masse. By 1941 about two million have been imprisoned or deported to the Gulag. More than 20,000 Polish officers, soldiers, border guards, police, and other officials are executed on Stalin's orders. The largest massacre takes place at the Katyn Forest near the Russian city of Smolensk. About 4,500 military personnel are executed and buried in mass graves in the forest.

Meanwhile, Stalin helps supply the German war effort, providing the Nazi regime with oil, wood, copper, manganese ore, rubber, grain, and other resources under a trade agreement between the two nations. Stalin views the war against Germany as a conflict "between two groups of capitalist countries," saying there is "nothing wrong with their having a good fight and weakening each other."

Stalin is named 'Time' magazine's person of the year for 1939 for switching the balance of power in Europe by signing the nonaggression pact with Hitler, a decision that is described as "world-shattering." "Without the Russian pact," the magazine says, "German generals would certainly have been loath to go into military action. With it, World War II began."

In December 1939, to celebrate his 60th birthday, he is awarded the Order of Lenin and given the title Hero of Socialist Labour. 1940 – The war with Finland ends on March 8. Finland loses 10% of the countries territory but retains its independence. In the south, the Soviets occupied part of Romania in June."
Source: Harris, Bruce. Sydney, Australia. (Harris, 2018) www.moreorless.net.au/killers/stalin.html. Last modified: February 12 2017.

SOVIET PROPAGANDA. FINLAND RUSSIFICATION

The process of Russification of the people of Finland. Nikolay Ivanovich Bobrikov (Governor General).
In 1898, Tsar Nicholas II appointed Bobrikov as the Governor-General of Finland. Bobrikov quickly became very unpopular and hated in Finland as he was an adamant supporter of the curtailing of the grand principality's extensive autonomy, which had in the late 1800s come into conflict with Russian ambitions of a unified and indivisible Russian state.
In 1898, Tsar Nicholas II appointed Bobrikov as the Governor-General of Finland. Bobrikov quickly became very unpopular and hated in Finland as he was an adamant supporter of the curtailing of the grand principality's extensive autonomy, which had in the late 1800s come into conflict with Russian ambitions of a unified and indivisible Russian state. In 1899, Nicholas II signed the "February Manifesto" which marks the beginning of the first "Years of Oppression" from the traditional Finnish cultural perspective. (Wikipedia, Russification, 2018)
In 1900, Bobrikov issued orders that all correspondence between government offices was to be conducted in Russian and that education in the Russian language was to be increased in schools. The Grand Duchy of Finland army was abolished in 1901, and Finnish conscripts could now be enforced to serve with Russian troops anywhere in the Russian empire. To the first call-up in 1902, only 42% of the conscripts showed up.

In 1905, conscription in Finland was abolished, since the Finns were seen as unreliable for the Russian cause. Who was involved? First World War was said to be the War to End All Wars; it was a global war originating in Europe that lasted from July 28, 1914, to November 11, 1918. The war drew in all the world's major economic powers. Two opposing sides and two opposing alliances:
The Allies (based on the Triple Entente of the Russian Empire, the French Third Republic, and the United Kingdom of Great Britain and Ireland).
Versus the Central Powers of Germany and Austria-Hungary. Although entered the war: Italy, Japan, and the United States joined the Allies, while the Ottoman Empire and Bulgaria joined the Central Powers. More than 70 million military personnel. Over nine million combatants died. Seven million civilians died as the result.

The Victims of genocide.

There was civil dissent, authority defiance, community lawlessness, left politics driven anarchy and military mutiny. Those manifestations at the human spiritual level were not only isolated to Russian disorder and chaos, but they flowed right through across regions and cultural borders into the Russian occupied society of Finland. How could the rebellious Spirit of anarchy that erupted in Russian contained spreading and affecting the minds of rational peace-loving people? It was the moral duty of the rule of law respecting people to stop the revolution fever of anarchy from spreading.

Strong-willed people drove the mindless, bloodthirsty mob revolution with emotions of anger and bitterness for revenge. The emotional paybacks, with danger and risk adrenalin, ultimately fragment and disconnect the souls of a stable society. They lacked the Spirit of respect for a peaceful solution, that comes with respect for the rule of law, from the Spirit of the Natural Law. They chose the path of the Russian civil war from 1917 to 1922. The man-made law letter does not bring peace when it is used arbitrarily as a human thumb screw.

Fiction section.
*World War One had started in 1914; by 1917, the cauldron of violence was heating uprising and bubbling, and about to boil over. The mindless violence and random innocent human suffering damaged the human spirits, minds, bodies, and souls everywhere in the conflict zones. At the dragon's hive of demons, a filthy cauldron of sin, rebellion, anarchy, and violence was full of ghastly diabolical brew, and it was affecting all the worshiper conscious beings with frenzied drunkenness, for everyone who drank the vile demon filth of lawlessness. The diabolical climax event of a century, the fallen angels, proclaimed the highly anticipated feast on the stench of human flesh. Satan's throne at the far end of the tunnel of thick darkness. The most significant mass exodus of human souls, from the planet earth in 50 years, to be released over to death, and the howling and screaming feeding frenzy of demons, like the screaming howl of hundreds of Stalin's Katyusha rockets, launched for the destruction of humanity.*
End of fiction.

It was the Bolsheviks brainchild's anticipated fruit, after many years of agitation and labor, just as Stalin proclaimed on November 7, 1937, during a toast to mark the anniversary of the October Revolution. *"Stalin stated that every enemy of the state would be destroyed."*
*"Even if he were an old Bolshevik, we would destroy all his kin, his family," he said."*
*"We will mercilessly destroy anyone who, by his deeds or his thoughts, yes, his thoughts – threatens the unity of the socialist state. To the complete destruction of all enemies, themselves, and their kin!"*

Stalin had sold his heart, mind, and soul to the demons of darkness. Without realizing it, he had stepped over the line of no return and was well favored by his demon host. He gave his all for the cause of Satan on the planet earth. The primary mission being, the destruction of that which is good, whether the creation works of God in the living things of nature, or the human beings made in the image of God. Stalin was obsessively in love with the kingdom of darkness. Europe would be embroiled in the hot seat of total war, piece by piece the rebellion and anarchy were orchestrated from as early as 1900, 1905, 1917, 1918-1922, 1936-38, 1939-1945, 1945-1955. The dots of progression during those years are pointing towards mindless destruction. And there are two main culprits being played by Satan; they are Adolf Hitler and Joseph Stalin. How mindlessly stupid can people be to miss the obvious?

Why Military Conflict on such a Large Scale? Why the two rival sets of powers: Germany and Austria-Hungary on the one side. Russia, France, and Great Britain on the other side. Conflict of 1914.
Who was at fault? Satan cannot do anything without willing volunteers.
Satan requires people to insult the Creator of Life, the Elohim. He cannot do it himself directly. He can only do it indirectly, deceiving, and tempting human beings to indulge in lawlessness and sin. In so doing, to lose their mind, becoming slaves to all kinds of sinful lust, and becoming willing volunteers to play out the evil plan on earth. That is the hidden mystery of evil on earth. The minds of people are being deceived, perverting that which is made in the image of God. To lead them away from the purpose of the first creation, which was right on the planet earth.

> "The one who practices sin is of the devil because the devil has been sinning from the very start. This is why the Son of God was revealed, to destroy the works of the devil". 1 John 3:8.

People created in the image of God must have sufficient faith to walk as innocent children of God. And therefore, avoiding the trappings of temptations and sin. Like all human endeavors and the apes of the jungle, on the planet earth, there is the alpha male, filled with human pride, and the ego of the military leader, that are often precarious as leader of a nation. They are trained to be cocky and arrogant; military might, military pride, that can lead to extreme nationalism. Nationalism is not the end all, of human life values. Nationalism should not be on the highest level of personal moral values. A person cannot get to heaven through nationalism. The military is vital for defense, the world is a wild place with lawlessness, and ambitious dictators waiting for an opportunity to strike at any weakness.

## TERRITORIAL DISPUTE

*"A territorial dispute is a disagreement over the possession/control of land between two or more regional entities or the possession or control of the property, usually in a new state and the occupying power. Territorial disputes are often related to the possession of natural resources such as rivers, fertile farmland, mineral or oil resources although culture, religion and ethnic nationalism can also drive the disputes. Territorial disputes often result from vague and unclear language in a treaty that set up the original boundary. Territorial disputes are a primary cause of wars and terrorism as states often try to assert their sovereignty over a territory through invasion, and non-state entities try to influence the actions of politicians through terrorism. International law does not support the use of force by one state to annex the territory of another state".* (Encyclopedia, Territorial Dispute, 2018)

## WORLD WAR CAUSES?

People that study the cause of world wars, they look at such factors as political, territorial and economic conflicts, militarism, a complex web of alliances and alignments, imperialism, the growth of nationalism, and the power vacuum created by the decline of the Ottoman Empire.

## CORRUPT AND THE IMBALANCE OF MILITARY POWER

Finland's 100 Year Fight for Independence is direct evidence of the Imperial leader's predatory behavior and moral corruption, that will take advantage of any weaknesses that become apparent to their advantage. It happened in real life in the Baltic states between 1940 to 1991. Fifty years of occupation by the Soviet Union military. Loss of independence and loss of hundreds of thousands of people's lives between 1939 to 1991. And none of the members of the allied forces are willing to compensate for the losses caused by one member of the Allied forces. Soviet Union from 1941 to 1945. The allied forces were punishing the Axis powers in the Spirit of Stalin, even when they were innocent of any war crimes. Where are truth and justice? When the Imperialists dictate the law?

*"At times of political uncertainty and civil chaos, apparent political uncertainty, military indecision, spiritual vacuums are filled and exploited for the utilitarian "greater good."* (Wikipedia, Utilitarianism, 2018)

The balance of power theory in international relations suggests that national security is enhanced when a military capability is evenly distributed so that no one state is strong enough to dominate all others. Sweden and Russian Imperial domination caused issues for the land working peasants; the Nordic people of the land life, 2000 years ago, they had no concept of Imperial dominance? The Imperial dominance had gone on for many centuries before 1917, which had left tensions high. The Finnish Culture worldview can be traced to changes in the balance of power in Europe, Sweden, and Russia since the beginning of the 11-century record.

## THE CAUSE AND EFFECTS KARELIAN REGIMENT

There was much unrest in Europe and Finland; the uncertainty with human misery contributed further to the Spirit of rebellion and anarchy. Here are some of the events listed.

WW1. Russian Revolution. The Tsar of Russian dethroned by the anarchist rebellion. Russian sailor's dissent, rebellion, and mutiny in the Ports.

Socialist street guard controls the street as a militia. Ordering shops to close during Worker strikes.

Police Officers all over Finland kicked out of office. Replaced by Socialists militia. Poverty, hunger, and high unemployment in Finland in 1917. Workers are getting increasingly frustrated. Socialists use the Russian military presence in Finland to bolster their political objectives.

Parliament in Turku is held against their will in their work offices for 37 hours. Socialist leaders demand more Socialist to be given seats in the parliament. If they do not accept the demands, Socialists will get the Russian military to make a coup. There were some 100,000 Russian military troops stationed in Finland in 1917.

The Queen of England gives her blessing to give support to the Russian Revolution Red Bolsheviks. By forming two troops in the Archangel White Sea region. They warred and killed dozens of Finnish white soldiers.

The Brits went to the same side with the Bloody Revolution Bolsheviks that murdered the entire Romanov family. To block the Germans from making their way towards the Archangel region. Murmansk legionnaires in 1918 (Russian Reds)

Murmansk Legion, also known as the Finnish Legion, was a British Royal Navy organized military unit during the 1918– 1919 Allied North Russia Intervention. It was composed of Finnish Red Guards who had fled after the Finnish Civil War from White-dominated Northern Finland to Soviet Russia and some Finns working on the Murmansk Railroad. The Legion fought the 1918 Viena expedition of Finnish White Guards and defended the Murmansk Railroad and British troops.

KARELIAN REGIMENT

*"The Karelian regiment was another communist recruiting by British troops, which consisted of red socialists who had fled to the Soviet Union during the Civil War. It fought in Viena Karelia, alongside Bolshevism, a group of Finnish red tribal warlords led by Toivo Kuisma, against the Kuisma expedition, which it was called back. The slogan of the Karelian regiment was "for the freedom of Karelia."*

*In August 1918, the hope of Kuisma, the 250-man tribal troop leader, moved to Vienna and held Uhtula. The 300-400-member Karelian regiment of the Karelian Republic, which was equipped and trained by the Brits, commenced military action against tribal soldiers by killing the intelligence and security forces.* (Encyclopedia, Viena Expedition 1918, 2018)

There was no justice with authority. The Russian revolution fever with anarchy raged against law and order. They demanded the highest authority of the land for themselves. The Russian revolution fever peaked, and the Romanov family executed as the Bolshevik socialist mob's enemies. The Bolsheviks perpetuated the Russian revolution fever, and it was caught by many everywhere where there was a Russian military presence. Then came dissent, defiance, rebellion, and mutiny. Russian Navy sailors in the port of Finland mutinied their officers on the ships and the shore. Russia was engaged in World War 1 for 3 1/2 years. Then came the realization of the insane waste of human life to continue the mindless slaughter. The fighting over land and territory of East Europe has been ongoing for the last 1000 years; at the same time, there have been sensible people appealing for the rule of law, with a conscious awareness of the Natural Law's Spirit.

No consciously healthy thinking man, woman, or child on the planet earth, would willingly accept the encroaching foreigners, the military forces that arbitrarily come to invade peaceful people of the land homes and livelihood. Self-respecting people do have a sense of justice, family, community, civil law, and society, they object to lawlessness. People's appeal for justice, there is the Spirit of the Natural Law, which provides the Natural rights to exist. A rational, logical sense of justice for those that respect the legitimate rule of law derived from the Spirit of the Natural Law. At the same time, they detest the counterfeit dictators that are imposters of spiritual authority for a community civil law. Understanding a legitimate spiritual authority, there needs to be respect for the First Cause Spirit of the Natural Law. From the ultimate lawgiver, In the beginning, Elohim.

[12]

# TREATIES TREATY OF BREST-LITOVSK

The outcome of World War I was disastrous for both the German Reich and the Russian Soviet Federative Socialist Republic. During the war, the Bolsheviks struggled for survival, and Vladimir Lenin gave provision for some independence of Finland, Estonia, Latvia, Lithuania, and Poland, to get a broader support base. He did not encourage small independent States. Moreover, facing a German military advance, Lenin and Trotsky were forced to enter into the Treaty of Brest-Litovsk, which ceded vast western Russian territories to the German Empire. After Germany's collapse, a multinational Allied-led army intervened in the Russian Civil War (1917–22).

The Treaty of Brest-Litovsk was a peace treaty signed on 3 March 1918 between the new Bolshevik government of Soviet Russia and the Central Powers (Germany, Austria-Hungary, Bulgaria, and the Ottoman Empire), which ended Russia's participation in World War I. In the treaty, Bolshevik Russia ceded the Baltic States to Germany; they were meant to become German vassal states under German princelings. Russia also ceded its province of Kars Oblast in the South Caucasus to the Ottoman Empire and recognized the independence of Ukraine. (Encyclopedia, Treaty of Brest-Litovsk, 1918)

THE TREATY OF RAPALLO
The Treaty of Rapallo was an agreement signed on 16 April 1922 between Germany and the Russian Soviet Federative Socialist Republic (RSFSR) under which each renounced all territorial and financial claims against the other following the Treaty of Brest-Litovsk and World War I. (Wikipedia, Treaty of Rapallo, 1922)

TREATY OF BERLIN 1926
Treaty of Berlin (German-Soviet Neutrality and Nonaggression Pact) is a treaty of 24 April 1926 under which Germany and the Soviet Union pledged neutrality in the event of an attack on the other by a third party for the next five years. The treaty reaffirmed the German-Soviet Treaty of Rapallo signed in 1922. (Encyclopedia, Treaty of Berlin, 1926)

THE GERMAN-SOVIET FRONTIER
The German-Soviet Frontier Treaty was a second supplementary protocol, of the 1939 Hitler-Stalin Pact (known as the German-Soviet Treaty of Nonaggression, or by its original name of the German-Soviet Treaty of Friendship, Cooperation, and Demarcation). It was a secret clause as amended on September 28, 1939, by Nazi Germany and the Soviet Union after their joint invasion and occupation of sovereign Poland. (Encyclopedia, German-Soviet Frontier Treaty, 1939)

THE ALLIED INTERVENTION 1918
The Allied intervention was a multi-national military expedition launched during the Russian Civil War in 1918. The stated goals were to help the Czechoslovak Legion, to secure supplies of munitions and armaments in Russian ports, and to re-establish the Eastern Front. After the Bolshevik government withdrew from World War I, the Allies militarily backed the Bolsheviks forces in Russia. (Wikipedia, Allied intervention in the Russian Civil War, 1918-25)

## LEGAL TREATY OF TARTU 1920

The Treaty of Tartu between Finland and Soviet Russia was signed on 14 October 1920 after negotiations that lasted four months. The treaty confirmed the border between Finland and Soviet Russia after the Finnish civil war and Finnish volunteer expeditions in Russian East Karelia. The treaty signed in Tartu (Estonia) at the Estonian Students' Society building. Ratifications of the treaty were exchanged in Moscow on 31 December 1920. The treaty registered in the League of Nations Treaty Series on 5 March 1921.

The treaty confirmed that the Finnish-Soviet border would follow the old border between the autonomous Grand Duchy of Finland and Imperial Russia. Finland additionally received Petsamo, with its ice-free harbor on the Arctic Ocean. As far back as 1864, Tsar Alexander II had promised to join Petsamo to Finland in exchange for a piece of the Karelian Isthmus. Finland also agreed to leave the joined and then occupied areas of Repola (joined to Finland during the Viena expedition) and Porajärvi (joined during the Aunus expedition) in Russian East Karelia. (Wikipedia, Treaty of Tartu (Russian–Finnish), 1920)

## THE SOVIET–FINNISH NON-AGGRESSION PACT 1932

The Soviet–Finnish Non-Aggression Pact was a non-aggression treaty signed in 1932 by representatives of Finland and the Soviet Union. The pact was unilaterally renounced by the Soviet Union in 1939 after it had committed the deception operation Shelling of a town called Mainila, shelling its own troops inside a village and claimed Finland to be responsible. It was a false flag operation.

The Soviet Union had started non-aggression pact negotiations with its neighboring countries in Europe during the Invasion of Manchuria, due to which the Soviet Union wanted to secure its borders. Although Finland was the last to sign the pact on January 21, 1932, after Estonia, Latvia, and Poland, it was the first to ratify it in July 1932. Both parties guaranteed to respect the borders between the countries and agreed to stay neutral. Disputes were promised to be solved peacefully and neutrally. The pact was extended to December 31, 1945, in Moscow on April 7, 1934.

It was signed by the Finnish foreign minister Aarno Yrjö-Koskinen and the Soviet foreign minister Maxim Litvinov. The pact was renounced by the Soviet Union on 28 November 1939, two days before its invasion of Finland, claiming Finland had shelled a Soviet village. According to the Article Five,[2] parties should have called for a joint commission to examine the incident, which Finland tried to call but the Soviet Union refused. (Encyclopedia, Soviet–Finnish Non-Aggression Pact, 1932)

## FALSE FLAG OPERATION 1939

On 26 November 1939, an incident was reported near the Soviet village of Mainila close to the border with Finland: A Soviet border guard post had been shelled by an unknown party resulting, according to Soviet reports, in the deaths of four and injuries of nine border guards. Research conducted by several Finnish and Russian historians later concluded that the shelling was a false flag operation carried out from the Soviet side of the border by an NKVD unit, with the purpose of providing the Soviet Union with a casus belli and a pretext to withdraw from the non-aggression pact of 1932. Trail of the Nemesis. The contemporary term, false flag, describes covert operations that are designed to deceive in such a way that activities appear as though they are being carried out by individual entities, groups, or nations other than those who planned and executed them. (Encyclopedia, Shelling of Mainila, 1939)

## CASUS BELLI

Casus belli is a Latin expression meaning "an act or event that provokes or is used to justify war" (literally, "a case of war"). A casus belli involves direct offenses or threats against the nation declaring the war, whereas a casus foederis involves offenses or threats against its ally, usually one bound by a mutual defense pact. Either may be considered an act of war. (Wikipedia, Casus belli, 2018)

## THE MOLOTOV–RIBBENTROP PACT 1939

The Molotov–Ribbentrop Pact, also known as the Nazi German-Soviet Pact of Aggression. On the official formality paperwork, it was written as: Treaty of Non-aggression between Germany and the Union of Soviet

Socialist Republics). On the favorable light, it was a neutrality pact between Nazi Germany and the Soviet Union, signed in Moscow on 23 August 1939 by foreign ministers Joachim von Ribbentrop and Vyacheslav Molotov. It had a commercial dimension to it also. Followed by the German-Soviet Commercial Agreement in February 1940.

## A COIN WITH TWO SIDES

A physical coin has two sides, so did the Molotov and Ribbentrop Pact. On the face of it on paper, it was presented as the means of securing peace in Europe between Stalin's military power and Hitler's Nazi Germany military might. That was the face side of the coin. The Time magazine in New York in 1939 also presented the M & R Pact with the face of Stalin on the front cover of the Time magazine. But, in their thinking mind, they over simplified reality and were ignorant of the Stalin track record, between 1905 and 1939, and misjudged the criminal nature of Stalin. Stalin's nature was that of a hardened criminal. The criminal nature can be seen as early as 1905, and his violent actions reinforce that all the way to 1939. The people at the Time magazine saw the event in a narrow two-dimensional way as if reality was only being played out in two-dimensional space, on the paperwork. The Time magazine used the commercial opportunity to deceive the American public and others globally for their commercial interest, to sell their magazines with the misguided reality of Europe in 1939.

The two-dimensional reality is used by criminals to deceive people's minds, into believing a lie. And when the time is convenient, the criminal mind comes up with an alibi, then rip's up to the paper contract and throws the paper contract into a bin. Saying to the audience, the other party of the contract has neglected their obligation to the contract, therefore making it invalid. That is the nature of corruption; it uses unscrupulous methods for self-gain. How many million times has that been played out in the last 100 years? Criminals are proud of their ability to deceive people into believing lies, and they maximize all opportunities to mislead people's thinking to their own advantage. The back of the coin was the dark side of the coin; it had the Nemesis all over it. It was the underworld, the lawlessness, spiritually corrupted, criminal intent to exploit the innocent people of the land.

It was not the idea or intention of peace in Europe that brought the forces of Stalin and Hitler together in August 1939. On the contrary, it was exploitation and further territorial gains for both parties, that lured their spirits with irresistible temptation, that they could multiply their gains with the help of the Nemesis lawlessness synergy. The Pact between Stalin and Hitler was a criminal conspiracy to do crime against the innocent peoples of the Baltic States and Finland. That was the core idea that brought them to the negotiating table.

The Soviet leaders went along with it because it gave them a license to lawlessness, to demand whatever they wanted from the Baltic countries and Finland. There was no State, Nation or institution that would stop the Russians from achieving their objective goals. Previously it was the German military power that had intervened against the Bolsheviks lawlessness in Finland 1918. They provided moral balance to the imbalance 3.4M : 185M ratio, between Finland and the Soviet Union. The Soviets wanted Germany to stay out of Finland defense. Germany was often seen as a big brother that went to help Finland when there was a military conflict with the Russian in the Nordic countries. That is precisely how it played out in 1939 and 1940.

The West (France, England, United States), did nothing to stop the Soviet Union from exploiting the Baltics and Finland. The Imperial West approved the Bolsheviks lawlessness from 1917 to 1922. Including the Russian civil war that slaughtered 2 million lives. In the West, it was most likely seen as a process that would weaken Russia as a threat to the West. The reasoning was based on two-dimensional reasoning, without considering the effect of the violations against the Spirit of the Natural Law, that would remove the legal rule of law from Russia. By removing the legitimate spirit of the rule of law, that opened the gates to further lawlessness, rebellion, and anarchy. Russia would become a haven for the Nemesis lawlessness, and their leaders declare themselves to the rule of State Atheism and dialectic materialism.

The violence against Poland and Finland commenced in 1939. Violent aggression with shameless lawlessness. At the core of their beings, the same spirit was active as the Bolsheviks spirit of anarchy, shamelessly murdering the Russian Tsar family. What followed was the bloody Russian civil war from 1917 to 1922. That destroyed 2 million lives, in the name of "socialism." The only way to understand what was honestly going on in 1939 to 1941. Is to review the life, and the political career of Stalin, it needs to be scrutinized and studied in the context of social psychological truth, and not the Soviet propaganda lies. To understand the spiritual war between light and darkness. How deep Stalin was given to the dark powers of the Satan. Most people will be shocked to discover the exact contents of the diabolical mind, heart, and spirit that he had given himself over to be possessed. His long list of decisions and actions were only possible with a mind, heart, and soul that was given to the devil's cause on earth. Clearly, he chose to be on the wrong side of the righteous angels. Therefore, his life was an open conduit, for the worship of demons.

The problem with 3-dimensional spiritual reality is this, people are ignorant of the human true spiritual life, in their living soul. Therefore, they escape into their oversimplified two-dimensional mind space. They meditate on the 1939 cover page of Stalin, in the Time magazine. Glorifying it, and rendering all kinds of subjective and soulish make-believe, Stalin as the father sun, that gives light to the Russian peoples.

Communist ideology worldview, socialist utopia, that the Soviet propaganda has propagated to a person that was glorified with a personality cult. The actual timeline from 1905 to 1953 is entirely different, what most Russian's are led to believe. Stalin was undesirable human being, a diabolical atheistic to the core, a human monster, given to a dialectic materialism philosophy. After 17 years as a Bolshevik, led to his upgrade as Soviet leader in 1922, only deepened his core values, as seen in the Stalin purges 1936-38. Only a few years later in 1939 he comfortably slotted into the same groove as Adolf Hitler and the Nazi regime, to exploit Europe. They were full of the same spirit and the values of the dark side of the coin

The M & R Pact treaty included a secret protocol that divided territories of Poland, Lithuania, Latvia, Estonia, Finland, and Romania into German and Soviet "spheres of influence," anticipating "territorial and political rearrangements" of these countries. After that, Germany invaded Poland on 1 September 1939. Soviet Union leader Joseph Stalin ordered the Soviet invasion of Poland on 17 September, one day after a Soviet-Japanese ceasefire at the Khalkhin Gol came into effect. In March 1940, parts of the Karelia and Salla regions in Finland were annexed by the Soviet Union after the 1939 Winter War. This was followed by Soviet annexations of Estonia, Latvia, Lithuania, and parts of Romania (Bessarabia, Northern Bukovina, and the Hertza region)." (Wikipedia, Nazi German-Soviet Pact of Aggression, 1939)

[13]

# NAZI GERMAN-SOVIET PACT OF AGGRESSION

The Pact between Adolf Hitler Nazi Germany and Joseph Stalin USSR was an evil conspiracy, with an aggressive war against peace. Starting with Poland and Finland in 1939. Poland suffered extreme losses after being attacked from the West by Germany and the East by the Soviet Union. War prisoners of war were executed from 1939 to 1940 by the tens of thousands.

The Molotov & Ribbentrop Pact was a conspiracy hatched between Joseph Stalin and Adolf Hitler regimes. The effect of the M & R Pact caused enormous human loss and casualties. Also, large-scale material loss and damages. The Fact caused severe war crimes and Genocide by the Soviet leaders against the Polish nationals and their government. They did not want to be a target or to have anything to do with the two dictator's political ambitions and power politics in East Europe. When Stalin led the Soviet Union, he was steeped in the conspiracy with Hitler, fully aware of their share in the spoils of war. Both parties of the Pact had expectations by expanding their influence over East Europe territory, occupying the land, pillaging, and taking control of the Baltic States and Finland.

THE BENEFITS FOR NAZI GERMANY AND SOVIET RUSSIA

- Territory conquest and eliminate resistance.
- Politically demolish the Independence of the Baltic's
- Dialectic Materialism. Roll out communism.
- 

Soviet Union Stalin leadership were equal partners with Nazi Germany in the Molotov Ribbentrop Pact. The effects of the implementation and the maneuvering of the M & R Pact 1939 to 1941 caused tremendous damage to the Baltic States, Finland, and East Europe. Joseph Stalin and the Soviet Union leaders who participated in the Molotov & Ribbentrop Pact on the Soviet side walked away in 1945 without guilt in their role in the war crimes. Stalin simply shrugged it off as not real; he completely denied any existence of a secret protocol.

At a two-dimensional reality, the Allied partners took it at face value and did nothing more about it. They distanced themselves from the Spirit of the Natural Law. The war against Finland was started by the Soviet Stalin and his military Generals on November 30, 1939, without any war declaration. Winter had already started with a thick snow cover on the ground. The Soviet Union had a well thought out plan for the military takeover of Finland. Their plan included the entire 1100 km border between the Soviet Union and Finland.

# Nazi Germany and Soviet Union Pact of Aggression 1939.

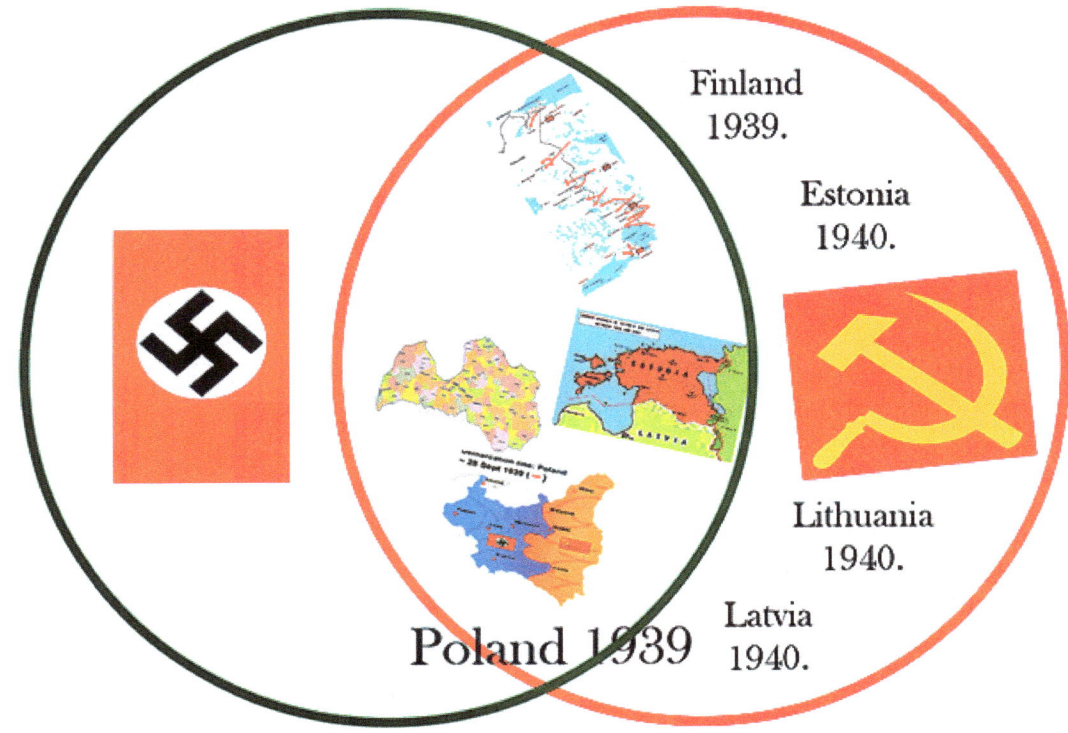

Soviet Invasion Attempt November 30, 1939-March 1940.

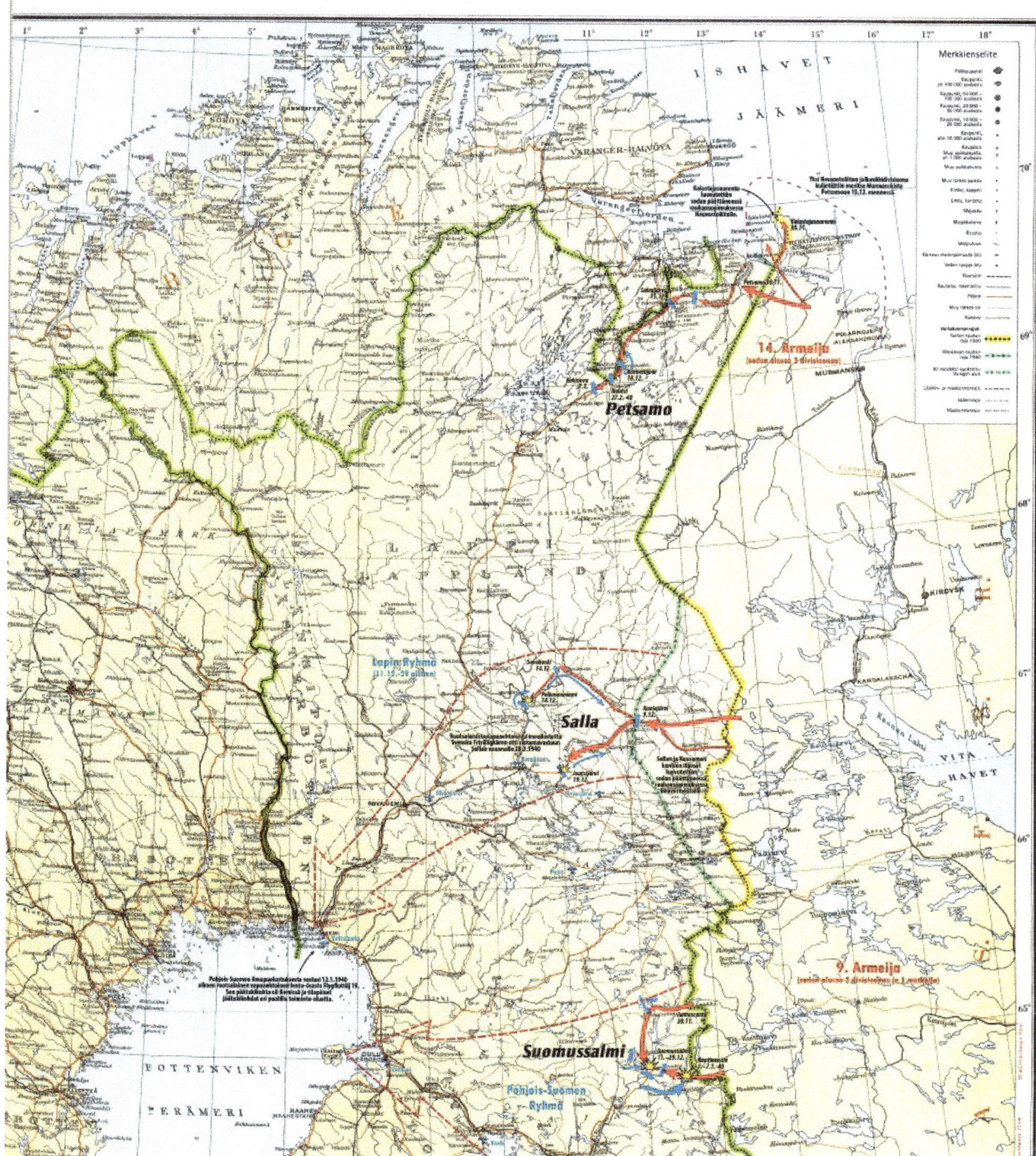

## SOVIET FORCES PLANNED TO MOVE IN AND TAKE OVER

The Soviet military forces organized as follows:

**The 7th Army**, comprising nine divisions, a tank corps, and three tank brigades, was located on the Karelian Isthmus. Its objective was the city of Vyborg. The force was later divided into the 7th and 13th Armies.

**The 8th Army**, comprising six divisions and a tank brigade, was located north of Lake Ladoga. Its mission was to execute a flanking maneuver around Lake Ladoga's northern shore to strike at the rear of the Mannerheim Line.

**The 9th Army** was positioned to strike into Central Finland through the Kainuu region. Composed of three divisions with one more on its way. Its mission was to thrust westward to cut Finland in half.

**The 14th Army**, comprising three divisions, was based in Arctic Port of Murmansk. Its objective was to capture the Arctic port of Petsamo and the Nickel mine and then advance south to Rovaniemi's town.

On November 30, 1939, Soviet forces crossed over the Finland border with 21 divisions, a total of 450,000 troops. That takes a lot of logistics to maintain for a fortnight. It was a deliberate military takeover attempt of Finland.

SOVIET TAKE OVER PLAN IN 1939

The takeover of Finland plan was not only at the military level; there was preparation done at political, cultural, and psychological levels. Satan used many levers to manipulate the human living soul to his advantage, intellect, consciousness, imagination, will, memory, and emotions. Psychologically and politically the Soviets had prepared Soviet puppet State representatives for the Finland government after the occupation. The de-facto Kuusinen's government was a Soviet puppet set up as future Finland's people's government. They called it the Finnish National People's Government. It was signed on December 1, 1939.

Soviet Foreign Affairs Commissar Vyacheslav Molotov officially signed the agreement. Approved by the spirit of the Nemesis. The Soviets mustered up vast resources for their push westwards towards Europe. Bolsheviks lawless energy, Socialist ideology, and the Communist State Atheism megalomania for global domination. The goals of the war against peace became blatantly clear as soon as the invasion had begun in 1939. The goal was an occupation takeover, followed by a russification process. Subjugating people to Soviet Russian pseudo-socialism. Spiritually it was the corrupting influence of the Nemesis, using temptations, exploiting others, and using political means and military power to move obstacles away from the communist leadership goals. The Nemesis tempted both Hitler and Stalin into an agreement to exploit the territory and property of the East European States. (Molotov-Ribbentrop-Pact, 1939)

The Soviets set up a fake government for Finland's future, led by Otto Ville Kuusinen, to his predecessor Terijo. The Soviets armies also brought along their army brass bands. To play at ceremonies. Mr. Ville Kuusinen's history goes back to 1918 to the time of the Expulsion of the Bolsheviks from Finland. They did not accept the Independence of Finland as a reality. They were obstinate to make Finland a communist country, with Russia in charge of Finland's governance. The de-facto Kuusinen's Government was signed by the Soviet foreign minister and Joseph Stalin. And Foreign Minister, Kuusinen, moved from Finland to Soviet Russia and created a political career as the Soviet Union in 1922 in the communist party of a changed state. Mr. Ville Kuusinen had signed an agreement with the Soviet Union leaders to replace the democratically elected government in Finland, that was elected into parliament in 1939.

The earlier years of Joseph Stalin strengthened his resolve from 1894. He had no excuse for ignorance. He studied at a religious seminary environment, where there were 600 trainee priests and spiritual monks. By his own rebellious will, he had the thought, the idea, what he wanted to become, and he chose to love lawlessness. He continued to make the same choices and left the seminary. He could have chosen to humble himself to obey the spirit of the scriptures that they were taught at the seminary. To humble himself is a choice; similarly to rebelling is a choice also.

SOVIET AGGRESSION 1939

The beginning of the Trail of destruction. Early on the morning of August 24, 1939, the Soviet Union and Germany signed a ten-year non- aggression pact, called the Molotov–Ribbentrop Pact. The Pact contained a secret protocol by which the states of Northern and Eastern Europe divided into German and Soviet "spheres of influence...."

*"In the north, Finland, Estonia, and Latvia assigned to the Soviet sphere. Poland partitioned in the event of its "political rearrangement"—the areas east of the Narev, Vistula and San Rivers going to the Soviet Union while Germany would occupy the west."*

*"Lithuania, adjacent to East Prussia, would be in the German sphere of influence, although a second secret protocol agreed in September 1939 assigned the majority of Lithuanian territory to the Soviet Union. According to this secret protocol, Lithuania*

*would regain its historical capital Vilnius, previously subjugated during the inter-war period by Poland."* (Wikipedia, Nazi German-Soviet Pact of Aggression, 1939)

Following the end of the Soviet invasion of Poland on October 6, the Soviets pressured Finland and the Baltic states to conclude mutual assistance treaties.

The Soviets were rolling westward empowered by their nationalism and lawlessness; they were searching out cracks in the Baltic states, a way to get in and start their Russification process under the pretense of pseudo "Socialism." The spiritual power push of the Nemesis always gives alibis of deception, to lead people into thinking something else, then the actual intent, perceived by the human mind. In so doing, they obscure the actual activity of Satan, which is to steal, kill, and destroy. Any excuse to doubt the neutrality of Estonia; they found one in the escape of an interned Polish submarine on September 18, 1939. It is the most obvious thing if anyone signs up for the Nazi German-Soviet Pact of Aggression that the neighbors will run and scream wolf! So, therefore Soviets did not need to wait long after August 23, 1939, before they were spotted one.

### ESTONIA
*"A week later on September 24, the Estonian foreign minister was given an ultimatum in Moscow. The Soviets demanded the conclusion of a treaty of mutual assistance to establish military bases in Estonia. The Estonians had no choice but to accept naval, air, and Army bases on two Estonian islands and at the port of Paldiski. A similar agreement was signed on September 28, 1939".* (Invasion, Occupation of the Baltic states, 1940)

### LATVIA
*"Latvia followed on October 5, 1939, and Lithuania shortly after that, on October 10, 1939. The agreements permitted the Soviet Union to establish military bases on the Baltic states' territory for the duration of the European war and to station 25,000 Soviet soldiers in Estonia, 30,000 in Latvia and 20,000 in Lithuania from October 1939."*....(Invasion, Occupation of the Baltic states, 1940)

### PACTS
*"In September and October 1939, the Soviet government compelled the Baltic states to conclude mutual assistance pacts which gave it the right to establish Soviet military bases. In May 1940, the Soviets turned to the idea of direct military intervention but still intended to rule through puppet regimes. Their model was the "Finnish Democratic Republic,"*....(Invasion, Occupation of the Baltic states, 1940)

### LITHUANIAN
*"On June 15, 1940, the Lithuanian government had no choice but to agree to the Soviet ultimatum and permit the entry of an unspecified number of Soviet troops. President Antanas Smetona proposed armed resistance to the Soviets, but the government refused, proposing their candidate to lead the regime. However, the Soviets refused this offer and sent Vladimir Dekanozov to take charge of affairs while the Red Army occupied the state."*....(Occupation of the Baltic states, 1940)

*"On June 16, 1940, Latvia and Estonia also received ultimata. The Red Army occupied the two remaining Baltic states shortly after that. The Soviets dispatched Andrey Vyshinsky to oversee the takeover of Latvia and Andrei Zhdanov to oversee the takeover of Estonia. On 18 and 21 June 1940, new "popular front" governments were formed in each Baltic country, made up of Communists and fellow travelers.[57] Under Soviet surveillance, the new governments arranged rigged elections for new "people's assemblies." Voters presented with a single list, and no opposition movements were allowed to file, and to get the required turnout to 99.6% votes were forged."* (Invasion, Occupation of the Baltic states, 1940)

### SOVIET PUPPET ATTEMPT ON FINLAND
Teri-River (Teri-joki) pseudo Government was a Soviet set up intended to lead future Soviet Finland. Obtrusive and brutish, push and a shove to remove the rule of law from a democratic republic of Finland. A diabolical blunting and disregard for any genuine spiritual quality or effort for the human moral consciousness, for the democratic process. When Joseph Stalin and Adolf Hitler had agreed to the Nazi German-Soviet Pact of Aggression, of the Baltic States, and Finland, on the diabolical Satan scale, 1-10, it is already peaking from the 1939 Poland invasion at around 8 points. It peaks further for the Soviet leadership in 1940 with the Genocide of the

22,000 Polish nationals. And for the Soviet troops heading to Germany, it spikes to a climax 10 with the citizens of Berlin 1945. (Rape in Berlin, 1945)

The Government of Terijoki, also called the Kuusinen Government, was "officially" called by the Soviet leadership of the Finnish People's Government. The government was intended to become the new government of the Finnish Soviet Union republic. It was also a carryover from the 1918 Bolsheviks failed revolution of Finland along with the Russian revolution. The Bolsheviks failed to score in Finland 1918. The expulsion of the Bolsheviks from Finland in 1918, the Red Russian Socialist Finns, never got over. They had some spiritual bonds with the communist minded Russians.

> "Woe unto them that call evil good, and good evil; that put darkness for light, and light for darkness; that put bitter for sweet, and sweet for bitter!" Isaiah 5:20. (700 BC)

## OTTO VILLE KUUSINEN
"*Otto Wilhelm (Wille) Kuusinen Otto Vilgelmovich Kuusinen) (October 4, 1881 – May 17, 1964) was a Finnish and, later, Soviet politician, literary historian, and poet who, after the defeat of the Reds in the Finnish Civil War, fled to the Soviet Union, where he worked until his death.*" (Kuusinen, Otto Wille Kuusinen, 1939)

*The Kuusinen government was announced on the date of the Winter War on November 30, 1939. At that time, the Moscow Radio announced that an "unknown radio station somewhere in Finland" had announced that SKP had set up a "Democratic Government." The following day it was announced that "diplomatic relations between this government and the Soviet government were established in the" city of Terijoki.*" (Kuusinen, Terijoki Hallitus, 1939)

The aggressive war against peace in the Winter War of 1939, was a brutish move to take over the entire country under further russification process converting subjects to the communist ideology. Soviet Russia was on the same Lenin & Stalin global communist doctrine for 70 years. It was seriously erroneous false leading ideology, from a one-sided coin delusion presented by Marx, Lenin, and Stalin, that accumulated to the status of Stalin being glorified as a personality cult. Only to be torn down and demolished by angry mobs with heavy trucks, winch cables, wielding heavy sled hammers in 1991. They put away the blatantly pagan idolatry of the Stalin personality cult in the ex-Soviet States.

## HOW CAN WE SEE SATAN TRACKS IN HISTORY?
There is always a disguised lie, a cover-up, a smokescreen, an alibi, a counterfeit, casus belli, or a false flag operation. That tries to manipulate an honest person's mind. It is all about relative positioning; from a corrupted lawless environment, there is no respect for human dignity. Everything is disgusting, filthy lies and corruption. To move out of that to a normal law-abiding society where people have integrity in their living soul. A corrupted person can only communicate and interact with an honest person through deceit. To pretend to be honest. Fake it, as a law-abiding respectful person. For a time, until some goodness has been extracted, consumed, or violated from the person of integrity.

Two realities on the planet earth. One distributes, the other consumes and corrupts the moral good that is vital for humans to be qualified as human beings. There is an effort and a cost to be an honest human being. Taking advantage of the trusting, the presumption of innocence standard society. Fraudulent operators disguise themselves as honest, innocent, law-abiding, ordinary moral citizens. Fraudulent operators are faking it; by their choosing, they belong to the underworld of corruption. It is the realm of demons and Satan. How do the two worlds coexist at the same time? While their spirituality and moral values are a world apart. The underworld would consume itself and be depleted if the honest, hard-working daylight world people of the world did not provide and feed the underworld.

The progression is always downwards, from higher intelligence, innocent moral values starting point, as in the honest, transparent innocent children's minds, to corrupting influences and corroding down to where there are no intelligent absolutes left. And everything has corroded down to pagan, idolatrous, and carnal level, without any intelligent meaning. The Nemesis, or Satan, works through corrupting spiritual influence. That way, Satan deceives the mind of the person into believing that a lie is a better option than the truth option. The path of the deception influences the human carnal nature; the mind is deceived when it is given to carnality. Seeing the carnal human reality as being the one and only dimension to life. To elevate the human carnal reality as the primary and ultimate world of pleasure, defended by subjective relativism, and throw the absolute moral truths out of the window. Then the corrosion continues to work in the human living soul, of the intellect, consciousness, imagination, will, memory and emotions.

Insatiable greed, coveting for the neighbor's territory, natural resources, is a human carnal reaction to the material world. Joseph Stalin and the Soviet Union leadership were given to the carnal material world. They were willing to steal, kill, and destroy in order to get more of it. However, they never say that upfront. They fabricate a lie. They don't declare themselves to be organized criminals, even when every honest person knows the difference between an honest person and a criminal. It is feasible to think that the idea behind why the Bolsheviks chose their brand name to be "Socialism" is a strategic agenda-driven lie from the pit of hell, to maximize the power of deception. Unthinking naïve people will fall for it, believing that they have something useful to offer to society. Not so during the Soviet Stalinism years. 1922 to 1991.

The difference is in the human living soul; intellect, consciousness, imagination, will, memory, and emotions. Any honest person can ask themselves, what state occupies their living soul? Is it more like an honest person? Or is it more like a dishonest criminal? It is the choice of the will, of the free will, what one chooses to become? God's grace with responsibility is like a dissolvent that can release a human soul from the power of sin.

By the Nuremberg Principles, the indicted Nazi war criminals were declared guilty. Many of them were given a death sentence and hanged. By the International law, and the Nuremberg Principles, and the International Bill of Rights, the Soviet Russian World War 2 war criminals are to be indicted. There is no alternative because it is only the Soviet Russians leaders that the Allied forces patronized from 1941 to 1945, which gave them amnesty over their war crimes, by welcoming the Soviet Stalin to their club, with all the privileges, including the 120 Billion USA (in today's value) aid to the Soviets over 4 years.

The Allied forces, England, France, the United States, played God. They did not have the right to say to the Soviet Stalin, regarding their war crimes and Genocide, she'll be right mate, it was no big deal, just keep going, as usual, the Allied forces club has forgiven you. The Allied forces patronized because they were morally corrupted and showed favoritism to the members of their own "club." That is the core reason why Russian leaders have become more brazen in East Europe in the twenty-first century. Soviet Russian war criminals have not learned the fundamental lesson regarding crime and lawlessness. They boast and gloat with the spirit of Stalin arrogance, with the spoils of war that they took from 1939 to 1945. They have no spirit of respect to share with their neighbors, such as Ukraine. So, they help themselves to other's territory as if they were a roaming bear feeding on natural resources. They are a law onto themselves. Redefining laws mindlessly suits their own leader's ego desires, power politics, and military power conquest and domination.

They continue to deny the Spirit of Natural law. Because it has not registered in their mind intellect and consciousness, they were given free reins after serious war crimes and Genocide from 1939 to 1940. The Allied forces rewarded Joseph Stalin for the Pact that was made with Adolf Hitler in 1939. They rewarded Stalin for the Moscow extortion that he committed in 1940, and they rewarded Stalin's Genocide of the 22,000 Polish nationals in 1940. The Allied forces gave Stalin a license to do it and to get away with such atrocities.

There is no government or political power on Earth that has the authority to nullify the absolutes that are written words in the Holy Bible and the Spirit of God's authority. And it has flowed down from Soviet Russian to North Korea and Iran. The same moral compromise political favoritism infused with lawlessness is expected today in the communist-inspired countries, as it was granted to Soviet Stalin in 1945.

> "Why do you contend with me? You have rebelled against me," declares the LORD." Jeremiah 2:29.

Nothing profound has changed in their core communist ideology worldview. They are confronted by the western community leaders over the same lawlessness actions as 75 years ago. Why is that? It is because they were never held accountable for their war crimes and Genocide. They were told indirectly by the Allied leaders with inaction that "you can get away with it." If the lawless spirit can get away with crime, they will try it repeatedly until they learn that crime does not pay.

Does the rain from clouds fly upwards or fall downwards towards the Earth? Likewise the luring temptation of ill-gotten gain, to irresponsible, immoral minds, are like sharks going into a feeding frenzy. They live for it. By their actions and deeds, the Bolsheviks and the Soviet leaders are to be indicted and declared war criminals. There is no shadow of a doubt, them having committed war crimes and Genocide between 1939 to 1945. The facts are documented. Also available online.

An alternative view, they the Russian leaders have been deceived, and consciously they don't know it because they don't have any other reality reference than Joseph Stalin and the USSR nationalism. The world of corruption has overcome them like a tsunami, washed them up into a confused Soviet Russian lagoon. Regardless, it is the responsibility of the Russian Christians and the people of the free world that have minds that are not deceived by Satan to let their nation leaders deceived minds know; what is it? Where is it? What does it mean to have a mind duped by Satan lies? In a nutshell, it is a sin of idolatry. To give heart, mind, and soul to loving complete lawlessness is the sin of idolatry.

Stalin's mind, heart, and soul were grotesque because he loved the demon host that occupied him. He loved the lusts of the carnal nature, greed, cruelty, lawlessness, control, stealing, violence, and hate. They get away with it for a time because of the spiritual power of the Nemesis. Satan gives the power of temptation to people to deceive more minds, to win over more people to the carnal kingdom of Satan. The Russian leadership has accepted and received the spiritual baton of power from the Bolsheviks Soviet Stalin, with the curse of the Nemesis. The same power as the Soviet Union authority Joseph Stalin possessed. Spiritually it is a direct transfer of the dark spiritual power of Satan.

And the Kremlin is proud of the dark power manifested by the Soviet's "father sun," Joseph Stalin, from 1917 to 1953. It can be proven very quickly by the manifested principles that their nationalism adheres to and what they covet and boast about. The Russian leadership has made many hard decisions since the year 2000. Many of them are the exact same copy of the Soviet Stalin spirit of the Nemesis. The activity of the Nemesis can be traced from the last century of history. The year 1917 to 2017. It is ghastly, frightening, and blinding contrast for anyone with interest to know how the Nemesis influences people's thinking, minds, hearts, and activities. How to unravel the devil's work? By using the available resources for understanding; intellect, consciousness, imagination, will, memory, and emotions. To use the functions of the human soul, to learn the Torah, the instructions of God to believers. That is how Yeshua Hamashiach stayed on track with his calling. The Torah led the way to his first love. Obedience to the Word of God.

## THE 10 INSTRUCTIONS ARE A HUMAN BACKBONE FOR MORAL VALUES

There is always a definite pattern to be discovered that is being projected onto the wall of the evil one. The Nemesis influence is pushing national leaders to action, actions that are lawless, cruel, violent, inhuman, discriminating, and blatantly sinful. The above list does not sanctify humanism when humanism violates the written instructions of the Torah. Humanism has value, but the humanist's worldview and life philosophies are often naturalist, postmodernism, subjective relativism, and off the wall, when they are in line with the unbelieving atheists and give no credit to the Holy Bible.

Another clue is how they cover, protect, and hide the influence of the devil with corruption. Therefore, in reality, the devil hides his own tracks and influence and uses street sweepers to hide all evidence. Soviet Russian leaders have a habit of coveting and lusting after more territory in the Baltic States, East Europe, Finland, Karelian Isthmus, Salla municipality, Petsamo municipality, Gulf of Finland Islands, Kuril Islands of Japan, Crimea Peninsula of Ukraine, and East Ukraine region. These regions are clear signs of the corrupted Soviet Russian leaders and the temptation power of Nemesis, to persuade the corrupted leaders to wage war, with their coveting lusts and belief in their demonic delusions.

During the Soviet Union, their landmass was 22 million square kilometers (22,402,200 km2). Yet they were invading, annexing, or occupying relatively small neighboring countries during 1939-1945. Poland, Finland, Estonia, Latvia, Czechoslovakia. Today in 2020, Russia claims to have occupied 17 million square kilometers of God's Earth's surface. They have taken it by force from others and claimed it as their own (17,098,246 km2). There is a problem with the Russian claim because they conflict with the Creator of life and the Universe. The Creator of the Universe says in His word that he will not take the hand of the wrongdoer because God, in his nature, has moral absolutes in his Holiness.

> "Behold, God will not reject a blameless man, nor take the hand of evildoers." Job 8:20. (ESV)

> "There are six things the Lord hates, seven that are detestable to him: haughty eyes, a lying tongue, hands that shed innocent blood, a heart that devises wicked schemes, feet that are quick to rush into evil, a false witness who pours out lies and a person who stirs up conflict in the community." Proverbs 6:16-19. (NIV)

How does the soul decisions of Joseph Stalin rate against the instructive words of the Proverbs 6:16-19.

There is a severe problem with truth and integrity with the Bolsheviks leadership track record and the Soviet Russia roots, from the year 1900 to 2018. Every action, deed, and philosophy they established was anti-biblical and anti-God. They proclaimed the Soviet Union to be hard-core State Atheism and a pseudo-socialist utopia at the same time. Right there, the Soviet leaders rejected the wisdom and the love of God. Cruelty, lawlessness, suppression of truth, and corruption thrived. The Holy Bible was forbidden, Christian ministers locked up in jails, tortured, and doing time for long sentences. Churches burnt down and blown up. Christian believers persecuted and murdered because of their faithfulness and the testimony of Jesus Christ. If that is not recognized as a sign of an evil empire, then the observes minds are seriously deceived by the spirit of the world and the influence of the devil.

Many people, including Christians in the West and Russia, have very little knowledge of world history. They have not bothered to train their minds to think rationally and logically. Not taking the time to learn the instructions of the Holy Bible. Therefore, they are ineffective and silent, not able to impact the leaders of their nation. Then the Nemesis with the demon host, and the devil's volunteers, take charge, take over the society, and there is no one to call out his bluff, and his true colors, as being an enmity to truth and justice, an enemy of God.

> "All Scripture is God-breathed and is useful for instruction, for conviction, for correction, and for training in righteousness," 2 Timothy 3:16.

Yet the current Russian leaders with the military have invaded Ukraine territory. The Crimea Peninsula of Ukraine and annexed sections of East Ukraine in 2014. They helped themselves to a large piece of the Ukraine territory as if it was a Russian made pie. History reveals that they are always creating conflict with their neighbors over territory. Russian leader's paranoia of other human beings invading and stealing the "Russian" land. People do not live on a Russian planet called Earth; people live on the Creators planet called Earth. While the Russians have been coveting and stealing land from the indigenous peoples between the Gulf of Finland, Arctic Sea, Black Sea, China, and the Pacific Ocean, it has been ongoing for the last 500 years. How are they influencing the world? What was their contribution? Between 1900 to 2000? The current Russian leaders don't even respect or understand the most fundamental or basic principles of integrity and transparent honesty as leaders.

In relation to their neighbors in the International community, the Russian leaders react to real-time, more like street kids without guiding parents, and they hate the policemen with a personal vengeance that defends the rule of civil law. The connection between truth, integrity, and justice is beyond their intellect and moral responsibility consciousness level. The least they owe to themselves, and to the intelligent people of the global community, to accept the God-given pure spirit of truth taught in the books of the Bible. And to stop spreading the Stalin pseudo-socialist lies on God's planet earth.

The Soviet pseudo-socialist philosophy had no absolute moral values, no beginning for the planet earth, no beginning to the universe, and no end. Their philosophy had no Creator of Life, no Creator of the human being, and no social-psychological definitions with meaning for the human being and mind identity that could give meaning and hope for the future generations. They had a plethora of hidden agendas and temptations of the Nemesis, as they presented the one-sided coin to Russian society.

Everything in the Stalinist worldview and life philosophy thinking was dialectic materialism. The human mind can project onto others that it sees in his or her own mirror of the conscience. A dirty mirror is a dirty mirror that reflects a blurred picture. The conscience is like a closed loop, like a board game; every smartboard game has rules, same rules for each player. Only the irrational and the insane would play a board game with no rules. Where do the world dictators sit alone with the demons of the Nemesis? What board games do they play? Does it not have rules? Go figure.

The Soviet Russian leaders have been extraordinarily totalitarian and nationalistic since 1917, and not good at giving glory to God for the gift of life or creative in using the God-given materials for making friends. Instead, they covet, hoard, steal, and destroy other people's lives. Taking by a force other people's territory, homes, properties, stocks, and other natural resources. Why? Because of their false worldview, state atheism, and erroneous life philosophy of their national leaders. They are under the curse of Stalin's godless Revolutionism, Bolshevism, Stalinism, and State Atheism, 1917 to 2018.

# [14]

# THE MOSCOW PEACE TREATY MARCH 12th, 1940

The Moscow Peace Treaty March 12th, 1940
The Treaty of Peace between The Republic of Finland and The Union of Soviet Socialist Republics.
This MPT article list is not complete; only 4 Articles are shown here.

### Article 1
Hostilities between Finland and the U.S.S.R. shall cease immediately in accordance with the procedure laid down in the protocol appended to this treaty.

### Article 2
The national frontier between the Republic of Finland and the U.S.S.R. shall run along a new line in such fashion that there shall be included in the territory of the U.S.S.R. the entire Karelian Isthmus with the city of Viipuri and Viipuri Bay with its islands, the western and northern shores of Lake Ladoga with the cities of Kexholm and Sortavala and the town of Suojärvi, a number of islands in the Gulf of Finland, the area East of Märkäjärvi with the town of Kuolajärvi, and part of the Rybachi and Sredni peninsulas, all in accordance with the map appended to this treaty.

A more detailed determination and the establishment of the frontier line shall be carried out by a mixed commission made up of representatives of the contracting powers, which commission shall be named within ten days from the date of the signing of this treaty.

### Article 4
The Republic of Finland agrees to lease to the Soviet Union for thirty years, against an annual rental of eight million Finnish marks to be paid by the Soviet Union, Hanko Cape and the waters surrounding it in a radius of five miles to the south and East and three miles to the north and west, and also the several islands falling within that area, in accordance with the map appended to this treaty, for the establishment of a naval base capable of defending the mouth of the Gulf of Finland against attack; in addition to which, for the purpose of protecting the naval base, the Soviet Union is granted the right of maintaining there at its own expense the necessary number of armed land and air forces.

Within the days from the date this treaty enters into effect, the government of Finland shall withdraw all its military forces from Hanko Cape, which together with its adjacent islands shall be transferred to the jurisdiction of the U.S.S.R. in accordance with this article of the treaty.

### Article 7
The government of Finland grants to the Soviet Union the right of transit for goods between the Soviet Union and Sweden, and, with a view to developing this traffic along the shortest railway route, the Soviet Union and Finland consider it necessary to build, each upon its own territory and insofar as possible in the year 1940, a railway which shall connect Kantalahti (Kandalaksha) with Kemijärvi. (Treaty, 1940) These articles reveal the severity of Stalin's extortion demands.

**Article 2. Territory demands. Entire cities and towns.**

- The entire Karelian Isthmus, the city of Viipuri and the Viipuri Bay with its islands.
- Western and northern shores of Lake Ladoga, the cities of Kexholm, Sortavala and the town of Suojärvi.
- Many major islands in the Gulf of Finland
- Area east of Märkäjärvi with the town of Kuolajärvi, and part of the Rybachi and Sredni peninsulas

**Article 7.** This one set the alarm bells ringing louder in people's minds.

- The government of Finland grants to the Soviet Union the right of transit for goods between the Soviet Union and Sweden with a view to developing this traffic along the shortest railway route, the Soviet Union and Finland consider it necessary to build,
- each upon its own territory and insofar as possible in the year 1940, a railway which shall connect Kantalahti-Soviet (Kandalaksha) with Kemijärvi-Finland.
- Soviet Moscow Demanded Finland to Build the Railway from Kemijärvi to Salla.

The new railway construction demand on Finland in 1940 was another extortion demand by Moscow. There was an entire hidden world of agendas in the Soviet leader's as their demands unfolded. The new railway demand was located at a strategic location, useful for the fast mobilization of troops. It was located far north Finland, half of it inside the Arctic region. Useful for:

- Transportation of Soviet troops to the Sweden border. Transportation of Soviet tanks into Finland interior. Transportation of supplies and munitions to Soviet troops in Finland.

The new Railway on the Finland side was to be built 86.8 kilometers long, heading East from the city of Kemijärvi to the Soviet border. That would have allowed the Soviets to get access to the Finland interior railway grid and cut through Finland from East to West, at the narrowest section of Finland, between Russia and Sweden.

Article 7 of the 1940 Moscow peace treaty made people in Lapland nervous. They instantly knew that the Russian bear was up to no good; they could smell it. With the new 86.8-kilometer-long Railway, connecting the old town of Salla to Kemijärvi. There was already a railway line from Kemijärvi to Rovaniemi, and from there towards West to Sweden. The Soviet had already started building a railway from Kantalahti to the Finnish border in 1939, before the M & R Pact.

The responsibility of construction on the Soviet part of the Railway was the Main Board of the GULAG under the NKVD of the Soviet Interior Commissar. They built the Soviet Railway using prisoners.
In the Soviet railway construction, there were GULAG prisoners used:

- May 1940 – 58,198 prisoners in the building project
- August – 31,808,
- November – 26,469
- January 1941 – 31,618.
- The construction project was terminated on January 30, 1941.

At the same time, the Soviet Union built a track from Rutsy to the Muurmann line through Alakurtti to the national border. The Soviet Union began construction of its 171 km long section on January 19, 1940, and completed on February 25, 1941, while Finland's share was completed and merged into Alakurtti on May 15, 1941.

Finland commenced building the Railway as the Moscow extortion demanded; the work commenced in June

1940. At one time, the most workers on the Finland side of the new railway project were 3200 workers at various locations of the Railway. The Soviet diplomats kept on the pressure to speed up the new railway building progress and to have it completed in 1940. There were many scenarios being considered behind government doors. The intelligence was seeking out information behind the Soviet lines to find out what was Stalin up to next?

The previous November 1939, the Soviet failed invasion attempt was a shocker for all the ordinary peace-loving people of the Nordic countries. Everybody was on edge; once again, he or she had lost trust in the Soviet leadership. The Soviet leadership proved themselves one more time that they were professional criminals. Agents of lawlessness, going about with no respect for the rules. Planning violence to the innocent law respecting people of the land.

RAILWAY PROJECT FROM THE CITY OF KEMIJARVI TO SALLA TOWN 1940

SA Picture. War Archives. War Museum of Finland.

### INSULT TO INJURY

There is a strikingly familiar pattern of the Bolshevik's violent lawlessness in mind, heart, and Spirit, that emerges out of Soviet Union leaders during 1940. Their hard-line nefarious criminal minds, demanding shamelessly outrageous appeasements from Finland nation, that was nothing short of treacherous extortion. It is unbelievable how the allied forces leaders would be so blind to the spiritual reality of the Bolsheviks USSR leaders, that they would provide support to the Soviet leaders after the events of 1939 to 1940. The state of the Soviet Stalin USSR degenerate depravity was so shocking that it must be projected back to the Imperials spirits of England, France, and the USA. What is there to stop them from being just as aloof as they were in 1940?

It is indeed not their intelligence. Or their respect for the Spirit of the Natural Law. Their respect for politics was like their respect for the golden calf; they did not recognize the war crimes and genocide of the Soviets when it happened to others. They only recognized it when they were at the receiving end. Therefore, it was not the Spirit of the Natural Law that they were defending, their military actions were only defending themselves economically and politically. The end of 1939 to 1940 was a horrendous year for Poland and Finland. The actions of the Soviets in 1939, is followed up by adding insult to injury. Here is a list that the Soviets demanded in 1940. It reveals the nature of the beast, behind the Soviets. Shamelessly violating everything that is moral and virtues.

### STALIN EXTORTION 1940

Moscow demands were an insult to injury. It is clear where it was all going in 1940. The same Spirit of the Bolsheviks lawlessness from 1917 to 1922. When they murdered the Romanov family, in the name of "Soviet Socialism."

- 10% of Finland land area to be ceded to Soviet Russia
- All of the Karelian Isthmus to be ceded to Soviets, all 24,700 square kilometers
- There were 37 municipality divisions in the ceded area
- The city of Vyburg to be ceded, with some 80,000 inhabitants that evacuated
- The city of Sortavala to be ceded to Soviets
- The city on Kakisalmi. In 1939, Käkisalmi had a population of 5083.
- Gulf of Finland Islands to be ceded
- The Island of Petsamo to be ceded to the Soviets
- Port of Hanko to be leased to the Soviets for 30 years.
- Enso Pulp mill factory was clearly inside Finland 1940 agreed border. But through extortion ceded to the Soviets.
- All machines that were removed from the Karelian Isthmus to be returned and surrendered
- Financial compensation for missing machines from Karelian Isthmus to the Soviets
- 75 train locomotives had to be handed over to the Soviets
- 2000 rail cars had to be surrendered to the Soviets
- Finland Port of Petsamo nickel mine production was a Canadian British production company. Soviet leadership demanded the nickel production right to be transferred to Soviet Russia.
- Finland was demanded to build a new 87 km railway between kemijärvi and the Salla town.
- The Soviet Union placed sanctions of Finnish grain imports from Russia. Caused by the nickel mine.

The Soviets did not want peace. They shot down Finnish transport plane Aero Oy Jungers Kaleva, over Gulf of Finland 14 June 1940. The flight from Tallinn, Estonia to Helsinki was shot down by two attacking Soviet fighter planes. The plane crashed in the sea, and all nine people perished. The remains of the plane were picked up by Estonian fishing boats, but a Soviet submarine appeared at the crash site and confiscated all the crashed plane materials from the Estonian fishermen. On the same day, 14 June. 1940. Latvia and Estonia were given an Ultimatum by Moscow for the Soviet military occupation of their countries.
Karelia Ladoga Isthmus 1917-1939 border.
Next Page maps. Ladoga Isthmus and Karelia Isthmus. Copyright © KARTTAKESKUS.fi

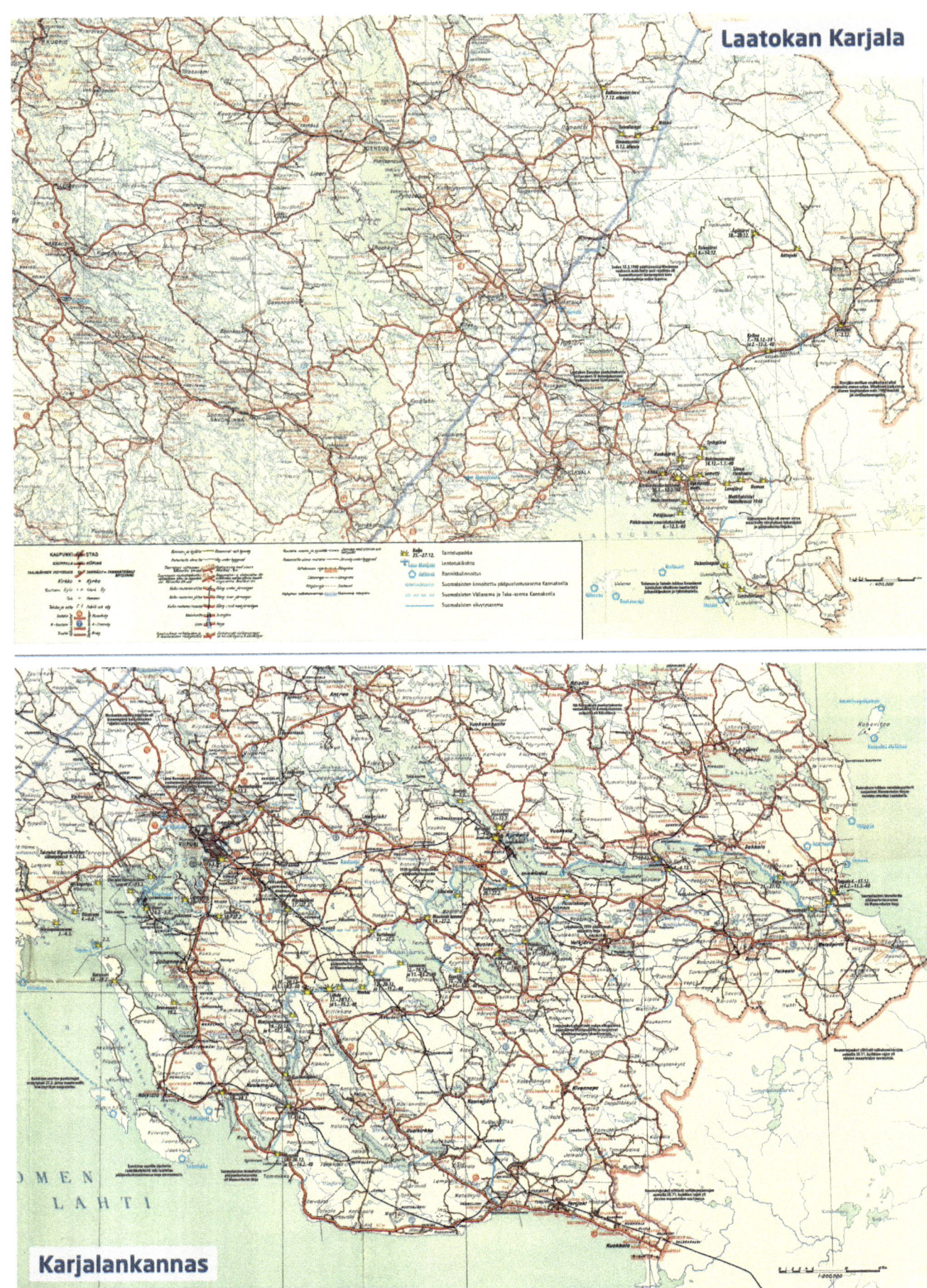

## Karelian Isthmus

In May 1940 established the Soviet Union and Finland friendship club started working against the government of the Finland rule of law. At the Hakaniemi market square in Helsinki, August 6, the demonstrating Socialist revelers lit up the massive firewood storage area. They became known as the socialist wood storage arsonists. The Socialist underground movement moles, at Helsinki, were supported by the Soviet Russian sources. The demonstrating agitators were made up of partly lefties, socialists, communist and drunken revelers. Soviet pressured and manipulated Finland's internal affairs. Accusing Social Democrat Party MP Vaino Tanner of being anti-Soviet. Demanding that Mr. Tanner be removed from the Parliament. Finland obeyed and removed Mr. Tanner from his MP office on August 15.1940.

Finland was not self-sufficient in 1940. Needed grain, fertilizers, and petroleum products. They were not available due to the conflict in Europe. Export from Finland was reduced by some 70%, compared to the previous year before the winter war in 1939. Rebellion, lawlessness, and the Spirit of anarchy in the form of despotic dictators were once again rearing up its ugly head. 1922 to 1940. There were only three options for imports at the time. Sweden, the Soviet Union, and Germany. Sweden was also in difficulty, therefore not much joy for Finland. Soviet was putting sanctions on Finland grain import. In June 1940, Finland managed to secure a trade agreement with Germany. Denmark and Norway were out of the action due to German aggression. Finland was in the grip of sanctions. The only source for the domestic needs was Germany.

## THE LAST FRONTIER

The last frontier for humanity is in human minds and hearts. Humanity to submit to the Spirit of the Creator of Life and to the Natural Law. Thereby forsaking rebellion and lawlessness against the will of the Creator. In the beginning, God, Elohim as it is written in the Torah and the books of the Bible. The process has been ongoing for about 3400 years. The blueprint has made its way to all continents and to most countries. The blueprint of the Bible has also been translated into 640 different languages. The New Testament alone translated into 1521 languages. There are some 8000 people groups on earth in different languages.

What does the Spirit of the Natural Law have to do with the Bible? The fact is that the Spirit of the Natural Law was present each day during the past 3400 years, as the Bible text was written and the scrolls unfolded. It has been present in the historical events, from the days of the Bible to the current day. The problem is with the human living soul; the intellect, consciousness, imagination, will, memory, and emotions. Each individual human spirit needs to receive the original meaning of the message in the Bible. The wisdom in the text can speak to the intellect and convince the mind to amend behavior, to behave in line with God's will on earth.

## FINLAND IN THE CONTINUATION WAR 1941- 1945

There were many moral and ethical reasons why Finland defended their country from 1939 to 1940. Many moral reasons why Finland took the opportunity for a pre-emptive strike at the Soviet Union leader's despotic lawlessness in 1941. Finland's leaders were unwilling to stand by as the Western allies, England, France, and the USA were indifferent to the Soviet war crimes and genocide from 1939 to 1940. Only self-defense would stop the Soviet lawlessness, a madman. And not Western superpowers leaders patronizing. They were not willing to let an immoral, lawless madman get away with the extortion of the entire Karelian Isthmus region and parts of Lapland, that caused the evacuation of 430,000 civilian people of the land. Stalin invaded with the purpose to steal, kill, and destroy.

Finland's leadership was responsible for fighting against such lawless Bolshevik as Joseph Stalin. All his planning and actions from 1905 to 1922, and from 1922 to 1940, caused massive destruction and suffering of innocent peoples of the land. Stalin had it all wrong from his political career beginning; by his own choosing, as an anarchist, he had nothing going for him as a moral human being. He went off the right track and became a renegade campaigner as a totalitarian communist. A hard-core State atheism model. Stalin was spiritually immoral, unethical, and had an erroneous worldview, and his life philosophy was off the rails with the dialectic materialism. He was given to extreme nationalistic idolatry that gave no thought or glory to the Creator of Life.

There was no difference between Finland as a target for the Molotov & Ribbentrop Pact from Poland, Estonia, Latvia, or Lithuania? They were all in Pact's "Soviet Sphere of influence." The genocide of 20,000 Polish nationals reveals the evil Spirit of the Soviet leadership; they had the same violent animosity as the Bolsheviks during the Russian Revolution and the Russian Civil war from 1917 to 1922. At no point in time has that lawlessness been stopped since 1900. It is glorified in the extreme Soviet Russian nationalism.

Independent Finland leadership was no different from any other country leadership; they needed to defend their national territory from being attacked indiscriminately by the Soviet Stalin totalitarian military machine or Adolf Hitler's Nazi regime. Why would anybody think any differently about Joseph Stalin and Adolf Hitler? There is no difference between the two dictators. They were both given to immoral lawlessness. The victims will be biased, according to the aggressor. The subjective biases do not set the rules for discerning true justice. The Spirit of the Natural Law can separate between the right of law and the lawlessness of wrong.

Can anyone show from the books of the Holy Bible, where are the scriptures that differentiate between the two dictators, Joseph Stalin and Adolf Hitler? It does not exist. Both of their minds and hearts were deceived into the siding, ultimately with sin and deeds of lawlessness. Both trusted their own understanding more than the instructions given in the Holy Bible. Neither of them feared God sufficiently to stop their volition ambitions and actions from advancing the course of destruction.

There has been a lot of biased nationalistic propaganda that portrays the two dictators very differently. Western propaganda demonizes Hitler and glorifies Stalin. The Western Hollywood style propaganda is not according to the Spirit of the whole truth; it is only a one-sided coin. It is also subjective and soulish; it was playing the same tune as the Allied forces in 1945. Joseph Stalin is the model and hero of extreme Russian nationalism, that the current Russian leadership glorify their support for extreme Russian nationalism. The attitude was already set in the Imperial Western leader's minds in 1917 when the Western leaders sided with the Bolsheviks Russian revolution and the Reds in the Russian civil war. There is a more profound truth of division to be found between the morally right and the morally wrong. It is found with the Spirit of the Natural Law. There was an ongoing war between the supporters of the rule of law and the supporters of rebellion and lawlessness. The supporters of lawlessness won the Russian civil war of 1917 to 1922. But they lost out in Finland in 1918. The same Spirit of lawlessness continued from 1917 to 1940. The same Spirit of the Bolsheviks in Stalin tried to invade Finland in 1939. The Spirit of the Bolsheviks militarism was expulsed from the Finland society in 1918.

What does the Bible say about initiating violence? Against the innocent people of the land? It says, don't even think about it. It forbids arbitrary violence against innocent people. The ten commandments are a backbone of justice and understanding the importance of moral integrity. People that respect and understand the Spirit of the Natural should not make judgments on morally right and morally wrong based on their own nationalistic biases. Or debate over preferred personality types as with Hitler or Stalin. Unfortunately, people are too often blinded by the emotional power of nationalism. It is like an emotional marinade or drunkenness from red wine. It bends truth and reality. Truth and justice go a lot deeper than nationalism and personalities. It looks at the intent, actions, deeds, and the effects caused by the initiator of violence.

Why is it important? It is essential because of the identity of their crimes. They crossed the same line, to the side of lawlessness. They went to the wrong side, the forbidden side of the law. Their actions are equally immoral and lawless. The Creator of the Universe does not show favoritism. He is not a respecter of persons. He can see through the heart and minds of people as spiritual vessels. Are they filled with clean oil? Or are they filled with willful sin and idolatry? The core point of condemning individual dictators is not their personality, talents, giftings, or lack of. No. It is because of the intensity of their immoral, violent actions. Their deliberate actions to harm others caused unimaginable destruction and human suffering. Without any gain towards a more peaceful civilized existence for humanity.

## IN RELATION TO THE SPIRIT OF THE NATURAL LAW
Dictators are blatantly violating the Spirit of the Natural Law. There is an imprint of connections wired in their minds. They are willingly using political power for the wrong reasons. They are also using military power capriciously to do violence against innocent people. The lawless dictator's mind wires have everything back to front. Volitiously they have wired their minds to an error by the actions of their evil imaginations. That is why Isaiah wrote.

> "Woe to those who call evil good and good evil, who turn darkness to light and light to darkness, who replace bitter with sweet and sweet with bitter." Isaiah 5:20.

The point being, people who respect and know the truth, they are open to the Spirit of truth. The people that are given to lies and falsehood, they end up with a false spirit within. It goes deep into the human mind and Spirit. The intellect, consciousness, imagination, will, memory, and emotions. To know the truth requires sacrifice, time, and effort. Values have a price tag. The truth is not cheap. Lies and falsehood are cheap. They pervert real-life values into disposable commodities. Any favoritism between Hitler and Stalin, as in the case of the Allied forces showing favoritism to Joseph Stalin from 1941 to 1945. It is because they viewed the World Wars through their own nationalistic interests and political lenses. Finland leaders were merely taking back the territory for more than 407,000 Karelian civilians that were robbed of their homes, land, and heritage in 1939-40. Too many westerners know very little about East Europe and even less about the Nordic countries 500-year history. The same old encroachments and invasion of Nordic people's territory by Russia.

Finland took their own border's interest in the military strike back as a co-belligerent along with the German military as a pre-emptive strike against the Spirit of Bolsheviks madness in Joseph Stalin in 1941. It was simple as arresting a criminal, taking him to court, and recovering that which the thief had stolen, according to the legitimate rule of law. Established by the Spirit of the Natural Law. The moral reasons cannot be fully understood without understanding the true evil intentions that Joseph Stalin and Adolf Hitler had when they signed up for the benefits of the Nazi German-Soviet Pact of Aggression. They both had the same level of lawlessness. Both were morally corrupted. Both were spiritually dead. They had no life to give to humanity, only death and destruction. That is the reason why Finland fought against the evil that Stalin represented.

His intent for others was only evil. ; The conflict in eastern Europe between Moscow and East Europe has been ongoing for 500 years. The cause at the root level is a primitive one. It can be traced back in time to the early primal forces working out from the human primitive Stone Age mind, with internal and external conflicts, that the Nemesis can exploit. At the root, it is the fallen human carnal nature, with willfulness, that leads to lawlessness, rebellion, and anarchy. There is disrespect for the Spirit of the Natural Law. The problem is also inside the Russian society. In part caused by a false worldview, the dialectic materialism as a worldview is false. It is an atheistic worldview. The Biblical worldview has a Creator of life. In the beginning, Elohim. Russian history timeline and their leader's record reveals that they find it very difficult to stay inside their own skin. They spill their problems over the borders, even to their next-door neighbors, like Ukraine. Poland, Estonia, Latvia, and Finland. Why is that? It is the nature of the beast.

## THE POWER OF THE NEMESIS TO INFLUENCE LAWLESSNESS
The last hundred-year history clearly points out where the lawlessness manifested. Who were the lawless leaders of people? The culprits that were perpetuating rebellion and anarchy. The murders of the Romanov family clearly portray the nature of the beast. The substance of the Spirit that was inside the Bolsheviks spirits. It was developed and taken to a new level of destruction with Joseph Stalin State Atheism, 1922 to 1953. Horrendous diabolical destruction of humanity and society. Some people romanticize the Communist State Atheism model by saying they were searching for the real utopia.

The real utopia is found in the Creator of Life. It was already discovered 3500 years ago. Moses found it in the desert in the form of a burning bush, and also on Mount Sinai. The Torah, given by Elohim. There is no reason to rewrite the Creator of Life. We just need to accept the true spiritual nature of reality. There is a God, the Creator of life. He knows best what is right for humanity. The ten commandments are a reliable guide to knowing the backbone of God's will. Instead of going back 3400 years to square one, to discover God in the desert, there is an easier way to discover who God is. Although God is a Spirit, time is no obstacle for Him. The short route to the discovery of the nature of God in the past history is found less than 2000 years ago. To the days of Yeshua from Nazareth. It is much easier to discover God from someone who really knows God personally. It was the mission of Yeshua on earth to introduce people to God. He is like a road map to the Creator of Life.

> "Now this is eternal life: that they know you, the only true God, and Jesus Christ, whom you have sent." John 17: 3. (NIV)

## CO-BELLIGERENT

*"Co-belligerence is the waging of war in cooperation against a common enemy without a formal treaty of military alliance. Co-belligerence is a broader and less precise status of wartime partnership than a formal military alliance."*

*"Co-belligerents may support each other materially, exchange intelligence, and have limited operational coordination. The aims of war in which co-belligerents participate may differ considerably".*

*"The term co-belligerence indicates remoteness between the co-belligerent parties, cultural, religious, ideological or otherwise, whereas alliance indicates a corresponding closeness."* Wikipedia.

## THE CONTINUATION WAR

The Continuation War began 15 months after the end of the Soviet Russian aggression against Finland in 1939 Winter War. It was fought for the sole reason of taking back the territory that Soviet Stalin had used with violence against Finland. There were extreme demands from Moscow, material and territory extortion in exchange for peace in 1940. First of all, Stalin demanded that the entire land bridge of the Karelian Isthmus, including the entire historical Finnish and Swedish city of Viipuri (Vyborg).

The Viborg Castle was built during the so-called "Third Swedish Crusade" in 1293 on an older Karelian fort, which burned down. The castle was fought over for decades between Sweden and the Novgorod Republic. By the Treaty of Nöteborg in 1323, Vyborg belonged to Sweden from 1323 to 1819, and to Finland from 1917. The city was demanded by Stalin with the threat of the Continuation of the war in 1940.

The Finns and the Swedes built Vyborg's city; it was a central cultural hub for commerce. Stalin's threats were not empty; at the same March 1940, the USSR NKVD chief Lavrentiy Beria's proposal to execute all the Polish officer corps' captive members, dated 5 March 1940. The proposal was approved by the Politburo of the Communist Party of the Soviet Union, including its leader, Joseph Stalin. The number of victims executed between May and April 1940 is estimated to be 22,000. Only 2 to 4 years earlier, Stalin had undertaken the Stalin purge and the Moscow trials in the Soviet Union. The proposal was approved by the Politburo of the Communist Party of the Soviet Union, including its leader, Joseph Stalin. The number of victims executed between May and April 1940 is estimated to be 22,000. Only 2 to 4 years earlier, Stalin had undertaken the Stalin purge and the Moscow trials in the Soviet Union. Not only was there the great loss of life (25,227 Finnish soldiers killed) but over 22,000 square miles of Finnish land was turned over to the USSR. The Finns lost the entire Karelian Isthmus which included Finland's second largest city Viipuri. The militarily important section of Hanko lost, as were many of the areas that had previously been fortified against possible Soviet aggression.

Industries related to timber, chemicals, textiles, and various refining plants were all greatly affected by the loss of Finnish territory. The loss of important port areas would also have lasting effects on the Finnish way of life. Over 407,000 Karelian Finns were displaced from their homes. There were also extraordinary Soviet demands for war reparations in 1944 which the Finns would be stretched to meet. In the succeeding months, Soviet meddling in Finnish internal politics and other overbearing actions indicated the continuing Soviet objective was to subjugate Finland. Among other actions, the Soviets demanded the demilitarization of the Aland Islands (not called for by the Peace of Moscow), control of the Petsamo nickel mines, and the expulsion of Vainö Tanner from the Finnish government. More ominously, the Soviets demanded to send an unlimited number of troop trains through Finnish territory to the Soviet base at Hanko.

Occurring at about the same time that the Soviets annexed the Baltic states in June and July 1940, the Finns began to fear that they would be next. When Soviet foreign minister Viacheslav Molotov visited Berlin later that year, he admitted privately to his German hosts that the Soviets intended to take Finland. The Finnish-Soviet Peace and Friendship Society (Suomen-Neuvostoliiton rauhan ja ystavyyden seura–SNS), a communist-front organization that quickly gained 35,000 Finnish members, conducted subversive activities in open defiance of the Finnish government. The SNS was banned in August, thus preserving public order, but on other matters of concern to the Soviets, the Finnish government was forced to make concessions. Unknown to the Soviets. However, the Finns had agreed with Germany in August 1940 that had stiffened their resolve.

Hitler soon saw the value of Finland as a broader Russian front line for his forthcoming invasion of the Soviet Union. The informal German- Finnish agreement was formalized of August 1940 in September, and it allowed Germany the right to send its troops by railroad through Finland, ostensibly to facilitate Germany's reinforcement of its forces in northern Norway. A further GermanFinnish agreement in December 1940 led to the stationing of German troops in Finland, and in the coming months, they arrived in increasing numbers. Although the Finnish people knew only the barest details of the agreements with Germany, they generally approved of the pro-German policy, and they were virtually unanimous in wanting to recover the ceded territories.

By the spring of 1941, the Finnish military had joined the German military as a co-belligerent in the German plan for the invasion of USSR- Russia. In mid-June, the Finnish armed forces were mobilized. It was not politically expedient for the Finnish government to appear as the aggressor. However, so Finland at first took no part in the Nazi invasion of the Soviet Union on June 22. Three days later, Soviet aerial attacks against Finland gave the Finnish government the pretext needed to open hostilities, and war was declared on June 26. Finland thus appeared to be defending itself against an act of Soviet aggression, a posture that helped unite the Finnish people for the war effort.

The Finns called this conflict the Continuation War because it was seen as a continuation of events that began with the Winter War. What began as a defensive strategy, designed to push back Soviet aggression with the German counterweight to Soviet pressure, was seen by the Soviet propaganda machine as an offensive strategy, aimed at invading the Soviet Union Truth to be known, the Soviet Union was the aggressor 1939- 1940, making war against peace. The Finnish leadership by the conscious decision took a preemptive strike at regaining the lost territories and ridding themselves of of any further Soviet threat. In July 1941, the Finnish army began a major offensive on the Karelian Isthmus and north of Lake Ladoga and by the end of August 1941, Finnish troops had reached the prewar boundaries. By December 1941, the Finnish advance had reached the outskirts of Leningrad and the Svir River (which connects the southern ends of Lake Ladoga and Lake Onega).

By the end of 1941, the front became stabilized, and the Finns did not conduct major offensive operations for the following two and one-half years. Finland's participation in the war brought significant benefits to both Finland and Germany. First, the Soviet fleet was blockaded in the Gulf of Finland, so that the Baltic was freed for training German submarine crews as well as for German shipping activities, especially the shipping of vital iron ore from northern Sweden and nickel from the Petsamo area. Second, the sixteen Finnish divisions tied down Soviet troops, put pressure on Leningrad, and cut one branch of the Murmansk Railroad. Third, Sweden was further isolated and was forced to comply with German wishes. Finland went along with Germany as co-belligerent to make a preemptive strike against the Bolshevik spirited Soviet madman. Stalin 1939 to 1940 war crimes and genocide were nothing short of a mad man actions against the innocent people of the land

- 430,000 war evacuees relocated to live elsewhere
- Lost homes, properties, and heritage

- 25,904 defenders of Finland dead or missing
- 43,557 wounded
- 800–1,100 captured
- 24,700 square kilometer extortion
- 75 locomotives
- 2000 train cars

BRITAIN DECLARED WAR AGAINST FINLAND

As a result of 1941, Britain declared war against Finland. Providing supplies to the USSR. Between June 1941 and May 1945, Britain delivered to the USSR:

- 3,000+ Hurricanes
- 4,000+ other aircraft
- 27 naval vessels
- 5,218 tanks (including 1,380 Valentines from Canada)
- 5,000+ anti-tank guns
- 4,020 ambulances and trucks
- 323 machinery trucks
- 1,212 Universal Carriers and Loyd Carriers (with another 1,348 from Canada)
- 1,721 motorcycles
- £1.15bn worth of aircraft engines
- 1,474 radar sets
- 4,338 radio sets
- 600 naval radar and sonar sets
- Hundreds of naval guns
- 15 million pairs of boots

In total, 4 million tons of war material, including food and medical supplies delivered to Joseph Stalin. Wikipedia.

UNITED STATES MATERIAL SUPPORT FOR THE USSR 1941-1945

The United States did not declare war on Finland; they did not need to. United States provides for the Joseph Stalin USSR war efforts was humongous.

- More than 14,000 U.S. airplanes 8,000 came from Alaska
- 44,000 American jeeps
- 375,883 cargo trucks
- 8,071 tractors
- 12,700 tanks
- Additionally, 1,541,590 blankets
- 331,066 liters of alcohol
- 15,417,000 pairs of army boots
- 106,893 tons of cotton
- 2,670,000 tons of petroleum products
- 4,478,000 tons of food supplies made their way into the Soviet Union.

Lend-Lease Program

In the United States, the people of Finland were regarded as hard-working, honest people of the land. Finland also earned respect in the West for its refusal to allow the extension of Nazi anti-Semitic practices in Finland. Jews were not only tolerated in Finland, but some Jewish refugees also were allowed asylum there. In a strange paradox, Finnish Jews fought in the Finnish army on the side of Hitler. Finland began to seek a way out of the war after the disastrous German defeat at Stalingrad in January-February 1943. Negotiations were conducted intermittently between Finland on the one side and the Western Allies and the Soviet Union on the other, from 1943 to 1944, but no agreement was reached.

As a result, in June 1944 the Soviets opened a powerful offensive against Finnish positions on the Karelian Isthmus and in the Lake Ladoga area. On the second day of the offensive, the Soviet forces broke through Finnish lines, and in the succeeding days, they made advances that appeared to threaten the survival of Finland. The Finns were equal to the crisis, however, and with some German assistance, halted the Russians in early July, after a retreat of about one hundred kilometers that brought them to approximately the 1940 boundary at the city of Vyborg. Finland had been a sideshow for the Soviets, however, and they then turned their attention to Poland and the Balkans. Although the Finnish front was once again stabilized, the Finns were exhausted, and they needed desperately to get out of the war. Finland's military leader and national hero, Gustaf Mannerheim, became president, and he accepted responsibility for ending the war.

In September 1944, a preliminary peace agreement was signed in Moscow between the Soviet Union and Finland. Its major terms severely limited Finish sovereignty. The borders of 1940 were reestablished, except for the Petsamo area, which was ceded to the Soviet Union. Finland was forced to expel all German troops from its territory. The Porkkala Peninsula (southwest of Helsinki) leased to the Soviets for fifty years, and the Soviets were given transit rights to it. Various rightist organizations were abolished, including the Civil Guard, Lotta Svard, the Patriotic People's Movement, and the Academic Karelia Society. The Communist Party of Finland (Suomen Kommunistinen Puolue– SKP) was allowed legal status. The size of the Finnish armed forces was restricted. Finland agreed to pay reparations to the Soviet Union.

Finland agreed to hold war crimes trials. Finally, an Allied Control Commission, which was dominated by the Soviets, was established to check Finland's adherence to the terms of the preliminary peace. This preliminary peace treaty remained in effect until 1947, when the final Soviet-Finnish peace treaty was signed. Although Finland had been defeated for a second time, it had managed to avoid military occupation by the Soviets. The reason the War is known as the Continuation War in Finland is that most Finns viewed these actions as the second part of the Winter War. While there were some in Finland that wanted to take land "in mass" from the Soviets, most Finns viewed this as the chance to take back just the land that was lost in the Winter War. The Finnish and German militaries also acted on their behalf. In most cases, there were not many Finn-German joint actions.

The main Finnish hoped the outcome was one of the following:
Germany defeats the USSR, and Finland regains the lands lost in the Winter War. Finland might also acquire more territory, but overall these gains would be rather small and were not on the minds of of most Finns since the main goal was to regain what was lost.
Germany and the USSR become involved in a bloodbath with neither side able to win. A stalemate would work for Finland as well since Finnish troops would have already taken the land lost in the Winter War. This would force a Soviet attack to displace the Finns. If there were a stalemate, this would be hard for the Soviets to do and if a treaty ended the war, Finland felt it would be able to keep what it had regained. Germany inflicts massive damage on the Soviet Union and a quick peace is made. This also would allow Finland to keep the regained land.
The world has gone crazy; Nothing compares to the scale of lawlessness when the Super Powers start warmongering. They have the power to do the worst damage globally, even in the days of the handguns, bullets, and gunpowder. The world seriously needs true justice with the Spirit of Natural Law. Only by being submissive to the Spirit of the Natural Law can the lawbreakers be identified.

WORLD NEEDS TRUTH AND JUSTICE
Moreover, the Allied forces protected Joseph Stalin from admitting his role in the conspiracy, almost as if given amnesty. The violation of the natural law did boomerang back to the Western Alliance, especially the Americans.

They did pay with time and money after the Soviets Joseph Stalin withdrew behind the iron curtain, the Nemesis was back on the throne of Russia. It was the beginning of the cold war of denial; the Soviets repressed the spiritual Natural Law and suppressed people's voices from speaking out for the truth. The new phase began with the suffering of hundreds of thousands of political prisoners denied their freedom to believe as the Creator of life intended.

### WESTERN IMMORAL BACKFLIP

What happened to the Western Alliance triumphalism in 1945? At the defeat of Nazi Germany leadership? Was all the evil eliminated and removed from the world? Hardly, it was alive and well hiding in the corrupted underworld of carnal human nature, sowing seeds of corruption and reaping deeds of organized crime and sin. On a large national scale, the Nemesis went into hiding behind the Iron Curtain. There was the existing partnership in crime, between Joseph Stalin and the Nemesis, the small beginnings partnership that may have developed much earlier than 1894 when he joined the Spiritual Seminary in Tiflis. At his teachers' recommendation, Stalin proceeded to the Spiritual Seminary in Tiflis. At the age of 16, he joined the 600 trainee priests who boarded at the seminary. Stalin is said to have lost interest in his studies, and his grades in the studies dropped; he was repeatedly confined to a room for his rebellious behavior. Teachers complained that he declared himself an atheist, chatted in class, and refused to doff his hat to monks. Stalin' studies took a turn to the other side, to the opposition. He reportedly joined a forbidden book club members that were active at the seminary. (Joseph-Stalin, 1894)

The Allied Forces drank their cup of victory and partial justice until it was empty in 1945. They drank from the same cup as victors with the 1939-45 Soviet war criminal Stalin. That had denied millions of people their right to life, liberty, and property, since 1922-1941. The Nemesis that had walked in the shoes of Hitler was not defeated. The same old Nemesis continued to walk in the shoes of Joseph Stalin for another ten years, until 1953. And from there walked in the shoes of the Soviet Union until 1991. The Spirit of the Nemesis is protected there where willing human souls give in to corruption, sin, and organized crime. He works through his Spirit in people that entertain such spirits as dishonesty, deceitfulness, cruelty, fraud, false witness, and many other undesirable traits that corrupt the minds of people even further to the wrong side. Satan deceived people's minds into hiding evil deeds, bad behavior and to glorify bad behavior. To be a sinner and proud of it is a short-sighted prideful condition. The Spirit of the world encourages people to glorify their freedom and to focus that freedom on indulging in carnal human pleasures. It is not new that human carnal nature is prone to sin. But there needs to be balanced in the living soul with the intellect, consciousness, imagination, will, memory, and emotions.

All humans have a carnal nature, so they need a redeemer and power to overcome sin. Yeshua came to save the world, not to condemn the world. However, there is no excuse for people to hide sin or to glorify sin, or to be a slave to sin. People have to deal with it personally and to have a new spiritual birth, where they know they have given their heart to follow and obey Yeshua Hamashiach as the Lord of their life.

> "For God so loved the world that He gave His one and only Son, that everyone who believes in Him shall not perish but have eternal life. God did not send His Son into the world to condemn the world but to save the world through Him." (Good-News)

True spirituality, as Yeshua Hamashiach taught it, and the Spirit of the Natural Law, they are in harmony. It is easy to see when the Spirit of Natural law is being violated. The Soviet Union Joseph Stalin war crimes of 1939-1945 have not been resolved, openly confessed as war crimes. No restitution was made.

The Russian leadership continues to profit from Joseph Stalin's war crimes, the annexation of land in Finland Karelia, Estonia, and the Japanese Kuril Islands today in 2018. Russia invaded the Kuril Island after 2 days of the atom bombs being dropped on Hiroshima in 1945. (Kuril, 1945) (Sakhalin, 1945)

### THE IMPERIAL SUPERPOWERS LAWLESSNESS

Imperial superpowers form alliances and fabricate their own rules and regulations that advance their own interests. They use military power as a license to commit immoral deeds against innocent people's lives. The

Soviets were guilty of war crimes, and the Western Alliance protected war criminal Joseph Stalin. The Soviet prosecutors committed perjury in the court of law at Nuremberg. Falsely accusing the innocent regarding the 1940 Katyn Forest massacre. While they, the Soviet leadership, by approving and documenting the genocide and the war crimes against the 22,000 Polish nationals in April-May 1940. That was perjury, committed by the Soviet Judges, in the house of the court of law, at Nuremberg 1945.

## THE EARTH IS THE LORD'S

> A Psalm of David. "The earth is the LORD'S, and all it contains The world, and those who dwell in it."

How is the Nemesis active in that? Temptation, to materialism, to covet, to steal, to kill and destroy other people's lives, land, and property.

When the servants of the Nemesis give their heart, soul, and mind entirely to blatant lawlessness. They glorify Satan's evil. They love the lust of being united with Satan. Therefore, they are the sons of the devil. Their deeds are evil, and their ways are corrupted through the spiritual influence of Satan. (John-3:20, AD) Democratic society gives people the freedom to exercise their free will. The exercise of free will should be morally responsible. Also, theologically responsible, reading, and knowing what is the written word and will of God for humankind. Acknowledging the Creator of life and giving God the respect that He deserved for the life that He has given to proportionally to humans, mammals, animals, fish, birds, and all living plants and things.

## SIGNS OF THE NEMESIS

There are parallel similarities in the following events.

- Russian demonstrations 1905
- Russian Revolution 1917
- Russian Civil War 1918-1822
- State Atheism USSR 1922-1953
- Stalin Show Trials 1936-38
- Nazi German-Soviet Pact of Aggression 1939
- Poland Invasion 1939
- War against Peace 1939 Finland
- Genocide of Polish Nationals 1940
- Soviet Invasion of the Baltics.1940-41. 1944 – 1991.
- Czechoslovakia (1968–1989)
- The Invasion of Chechnya 1994. 1999.
- The Georgia Invasion of 2008.
- Invasion of Crimea 2014
- Invasion of East Ukraine 2014
- Military Support for Syrian government 2011-1018 (Invasions, 2018)

Each of the above events, whether it is an invasion, atrocity, lawless acts, rebellion, or anarchy, the perpetrator always blames the deeds on the innocent or the defensive side. That means the Nemesis always pushes servants of Satan to act out violence. Whether it is a demonstration, revolution, by the people, or an invasion by a military dictator, they commonly fabricate a smokescreen, a pretense, to cover up what they love to do. They love to steal, kill, and destroy. That is precisely what Joseph Stalin during the Soviet Union days did. Most often had a pretense, an excuse, alibi, planned out before they did the dirty deed. It is also entrenched deep in twisted organized crime. The Bolsheviks were organized criminals. There is a connection to the underworld, lawlessness, crime, rebellion, anarchy, and servants of Satan. They love to do evil, and often they are compelled to do evil because of their spiritual connection to the father of all evil.

> "Ye are of your father, the devil, and the lusts of your father ye will do. He was a murderer from the beginning, and abode not in the truth, because there is no truth in him. When he speaketh a lie, he speaketh of his own: for he is a liar and the father of it." John 8:44. (Bible Gateway.com, 2018)

The characteristic that is typical of the Nemesis is compelled to do evil; it is the only thing that satisfies his being. He is restless without the evil destruction, suffering, and death occurring on the planet earth. So he puts pressure on people to do evil. People do have free will unless they have give away their free will to some extreme physical addictions or idolatry. Therefore, the only way for Satan to access to humans is through temptation.

HOW DID THE TEMPTATION WORK IN HISTORY?
What was the carrot? Territory. Wealth. Power? Unlimited material resources?
Temptation can be like a carrot, on the outside, appealing to the inside. Or temptation can be internal temptation seeking to satisfy it on the outside. Or it can be a compromising diversion of the will to do the right thing. Either way, temptation needs to be controlled by the power of the cognitive mind and self-control. Reading, meditating, praying on the word of truth with understanding, with the relevant topic of the Holy Bible.

> "Finally, brothers and sisters, whatever is true, whatever is noble, whatever is right, whatever is pure, whatever is lovely, whatever is admirable—if anything is excellent or praiseworthy—think about such things." Philippians 4:8. (NIV)

CREATOR OF LIFE
A world that has a beginning, by an intelligent Creator of life. We do not need to redefine life; it has already been defined by the Creator of life, as it is written. And been given as a free gift to enjoy. Therefore we need to respect the gift giver of life.

LITHUANIAN
*"On 15 June 1940, the Lithuanian government had no choice but to agree to the Soviet ultimatum and permit the entry of an unspecified number of Soviet troops. President Antanas Smetona proposed armed resistance to the Soviets, but the government refused, proposing their candidate to lead the regime. However, the Soviets refused this offer and sent Vladimir Dekanozov to take charge of affairs while the Red Army occupied the state."*...(Occupation of the Baltic states, 1940)

*"On 16 June 1940, Latvia and Estonia also received an ultimatum. The Red Army occupied the two remaining Baltic states shortly after that. The Soviets dispatched Andrey Vyshinsky to oversee the takeover of Latvia and Andrei Zhdanov to oversee the takeover of Estonia. On 18 and 21 June 1940, new "popular front" governments were formed in each Baltic country, made up of Communists and fellow travelers. Under Soviet surveillance, the new governments arranged rigged elections for new "people's assemblies." Voters presented with a single list, and no opposition movements were allowed to file, and to get the required turnout to 99.6% votes were forged."* (Invasion, Occupation of the Baltic states, 1940)

STALIN'S CHANGE OF HEART AT THE SPIRITUAL SEMINARY
As he grew older, Stalin lost interest in his environment of studies; his grades dropped. He was repeatedly

confined to a cell for his rebellious behavior. Teachers complained that he declared himself an atheist, chatted in class, and refused to doff his hat to monks.

*"Stalin joined a forbidden book club active at the school; he was particularly influenced by Nikolay Chernyshevsky's 1863 pro-revolutionary novel What Is To Be Done?. Another influential text was Alexander Kazbegi's The Patricide, with Stalin adopting the nickname "Koba" from that of the book's bandit protagonist. He also read Capital, the 1867 book by German sociological theorist Karl Marx. Stalin devoted himself to Marx's socio-political theory, Marxism, which was then on the rise in Georgia, one of the various forms of socialism opposed to the empire's governing Tsarist authorities."* (Joseph-Stalin, 1894)

The life of Stalin developed his character from the early 1900. He had no excuse for ignorance. He studied at a religious seminary, where there were hundreds of spiritual monks. By his own rebellious nature, he had the thought, and the idea, to become lawlessness.

He continued to make the same choices and left the seminary. He could have chosen to humble himself, to obey the Spirit of the scriptures that they were taught at the seminary. To humble himself is a choice, similarly to rebelling is a choice also.

THE OPEN REBELLION OF AN OUTLAW

He co-organized a secret mass meeting of workers for May Day 1900, at which he successfully encouraged many of the men to take strike action.

The empire's secret police—the Okhrana—were aware of Stalin's activities within Tiflis' revolutionary milieu. They attempted to arrest him in March 1901, but he escaped and went into hiding.

Remaining underground, he helped to plan a demonstration for May Day 1901, in which 3,000 marchers clashed with the authorities.

In November 1901, he was elected to the Tiflis Committee of the Russian Social Democratic Labor Party (RSDLP), a Marxist party founded in 1898.

After several strike leaders were arrested, he co-organized a mass public demonstration that led to the storming of the prison; troops fired upon the demonstrators, 13 of whom were killed.

Stalin organized a second mass demonstration on the day of their funeral before being arrested in April 1902.

He was initially held at Batumi Prison and later moved to the more secure Kutaisi Prison. In mid-1903, Stalin was sentenced to three years of exile in eastern Siberia.

Stalin left Batumi in October, arriving at the small Siberian town of Novaya Uda in late November. He lived in a two-room peasant's house, sleeping in the building's larder. Stalin made several escape attempts; on the first, he made it to Balagansk before returning due to frostbite.

His second attempt was successful, and he made it to Tiflis.

Stalin married Kato Svanidze in a church ceremony at Senaki in July 1906.

By the year 1907—according to the historian Robert Service— Stalin had established himself as "Georgia's leading Bolshevik."

After returning to Tiflis 1907, Stalin organized the robbing of a large delivery of money to the Imperial Bank in June 1907. His gang ambushed the armed convoy in Yerevan Square with gunfire and home-made bombs. Around 40 people were killed, but all of his gang escaped alive.

After the heist, Stalin settled in Baku with his wife and son. There, Mensheviks confronted Stalin about the robbery and voted to expel him from the RSDLP, but he took no notice of them.

In Baku, he had reassembled his gang, the Outfit, which continued to attack Black Hundreds and raised finances by running protection rackets, counterfeiting currency, and carrying out robberies.

They also kidnapped the children of several wealthy figures to extract ransom money

In March 1908, Stalin was arrested and interred in Bailov Prison, where he led the imprisoned Bolsheviks, organized discussion groups, and ordered the killing of suspected informants.

He was eventually sentenced to two years in exile in the village of Solvychegodsk, Vologda Province, arriving there in February 1909. In June, he escaped the village and made it to Kotlas disguised as a woman and from there to Saint Petersburg.

In March 1910, arrested again, and sent back to Solvychegodsk. There he had affairs with at least two women; his landlady, Maria Kuzakova, later gave birth to his second son, Konstantin.

He proceeded to Saint Petersburg, where he was arrested in September 1911, and sentenced to a further three-year exile in Vologda.

In February 1912, Stalin escaped to Saint Petersburg, tasked with converting the Bolshevik weekly newspaper,

Zvezda ("Star") into a daily, Pravda ("Truth"). The new newspaper was launched in April 1912, although Stalin's role as editor was kept secret.

In May 1912, arrested again and imprisoned in the Shpalerhy Prison before being sentenced to three years of exile in Siberia.

In July, he arrived at the Siberian village of Naryn; there, he shared a room with fellow Bolshevik Yakov Sverdlov. After two months, Stalin and Sverdlov escaped back to Saint Petersburg.

During a brief period back in Tiflis, Stalin and the Outfit planned the ambush of a mail coach, during which most of the group— although not Stalin—were apprehended by the authorities.

In February 1913, Stalin was arrested while back in Saint Petersburg.

Stalin was sentenced to four years exile in Turukhansk, a remote part of Siberia from which escape was particularly tricky.

In March 1914, concerned over a potential escape attempt, the authorities moved Stalin to the hamlet of Kureika on the edge of the Arctic Circle.

In the hamlet, Stalin had an affair with Lidia Pereprygia, who was thirteen at the time and thus a year under the legal age of consent in Tsarist Russia. Circa December 1914, Pereprygia gave birth to Stalin's child, although the infant died soon after.

While Stalin was in exile, Russia entered the First World War. In October 1916, Stalin and other exiled Bolsheviks were conscripted into the Russian Army, leaving for Monastyrskoe.

They arrived in Krasnoyarsk in February 1917, where a medical examiner ruled Stalin unfit for military service due to his crippled left arm. Aged 12, he was seriously injured after being hit by a phaeton, resulting in a lifelong disability to his left arm. (Encyclopedia, Joseph Stalin, 2018)

Stalin was required to serve four more months in his exile, and he successfully requested that he serve it in nearby Achinsk. Stalin was in the city when the February Revolution took place; uprisings broke out in Petrograd—as Saint Petersburg had been renamed—and Tsar Nicholas II abdicated, to be replaced by a Provisional Government.

# [15]

# CONTINUATION WAR 1941 LINE OF DEFENSE

CONTINUATION WAR 1941 LINE OF DEFENSE

The Finnish military defense frontlines in 1939 to 1940 were held in many areas; they kept the territory for three months. The cessation of territory came through extortion at the negotiations; Stalin threatened to continue the aggression of war if his territorial demands were not agreed to. In the event of the new border demands, the military troops and some civilians were evacuated to inside the new border. A total of 422,000 Karelian civilians, 12% of Finland's population, lost their homes. After only six weeks from the above 1940 Moscow treaty, Joseph Stalin, and Molotov (Foreign minister), and other Soviet leaders approved the genocide of 22,000 Polish Nationals that took place in April /May 1940. The consequence of the massacre was from the Soviet Union invasion of Poland in 1939 (M&R Pact). The Soviets then had 30,000 Polish nationals as prisoners of war. They executed 22 000 of them. A series of mass executions of Polish nationals carried out by the Soviet Union secret police (NKVD, 1940)

Generally, people in the Western world do not understand the reality and the severe consequences of the 1939 Molotov & Ribbentrop Pact. Because of the Western Alliance short-nearsightedness and often naïvetivity with the USSR. It had obscured the spiritual reality of the deceitful nature of the Nemesis. The truth has not been told in the West because it was not their loss. Therefore, they have looked the other way and been indifferent to the Polish Nationals genocide.

SOVIET UNION AND THE NAZI GERMANY LEADERSHIP CORRUPTION RUSSIAN GOLD

The only difference between the Soviet Union Russian leadership, and the Nazi Germany leadership, regarding the severe war crimes from 1939 to 1945, is that the Nazi Germany leaders were arrested and taken to court.

RUSSIAN GOLD

Simultaneously, the Allied forces supported the Soviet Union during the World War 2 effort by supplying munitions, transport, planes, ships, clothing, and food supplies to the Soviet military forces that committed war crimes only a few years earlier. In total, the U.S. deliveries through Lend-Lease amounted to $11 billion in materials:

- Jeeps and trucks over 400,000
- 12,000 armored vehicles (including 7,000 tanks, about 1,386 of which were M3 Lees and 4,102 M4 Shermans);
- 11,400 aircraft (4,719 of which were Bell P-39 Airacobras)
- 1.75 million tons of food.

US DELIVERIES TO THE SOVIET UNION
Allied shipments to the Soviet Union
Year    Amount         (tons) %

- 1941 360,778 t 2.1
- 1942 2,453,097 t 14
- 1943 4,794,545 t 27.4
- 1944 6,217,622 t 35.5
- 1945 3,673,819 t 21
- Total 17,499,861 t 100

American deliveries to the Soviet Union can be divided into the following phases:

**"Pre Lend-lease"** June 22, 1941, to September 30, 1941 (paid for in gold and other minerals)

**First Protocol period** from October 1, 1941, to June 30, 1942 (signed October 7, 1941), these supplies were to be manufactured and delivered by the UK with US credit financing.

**Second Protocol period** from July 1, 1942, to June 30, 1943 (signed October 6, 1942)

**Third Protocol** period from July 1, 1943, to June 30, 1944 (signed October 19, 1943)

**The Fourth Protocol** period from July 1, 1944 (signed April 17, 1945), formally ended May 12, 1945. Still, deliveries continued for the duration of the war with Japan (which the Soviet Union entered on August 8, 1945) under the "Milepost" agreement until September 2, 1945, when Japan capitulated. On September 20, 1945, all Lend-Lease to the Soviet Union was terminated. (Lease, 1941)

## UNCLE SAM NEEDS RUSSIAN RUBLES

The United States delivered to the Soviet Union from October 1, 1941, to May 31, 1945, the following:

- 427,284 trucks,
- 13,303 combat vehicles,
- 35,170 motorcycles,
- 2,328 ordnance service vehicles,
- 2,670,371 tons of petroleum products (gasoline and oil) or
- 57.8 percent of the High-octane aviation fuel,[24]
- 4,478,116 tons of foodstuffs (canned meats, sugar, flour, salt, etc.),
- 1,911 steam locomotives, 66 Diesel locomotives,
- 9,920 flat cars, 1,000 dump cars,
- 120 tank cars, and 35 heavy machinery cars.

Provided ordnance goods (ammunition, artillery shells, mines, assorted explosives) amounted to 53 percent of total domestic production. One item typical of many was a tire plant that was lifted bodily from the Ford Company's River Rouge Plant and transferred to the USSR. The 1947 money value of the supplies and services amounted to about eleven billion dollars.

## 11 BILLION US DOLLARS IN 1943. TODAY EQUIVALENT TO 160 US BILLION DOLLARS
## AMERICA MADE BIG MONEY DURING THE SECOND WORLD WAR

What were the Americans thinking? Why did they support the Bolshevik's lawlessness from 1905 to 1945? When the day would come that they turn against them. It is the spiritual battle essence; both sides have opposing forces that demand allegiance. Spirit of the Natural Law on one side, and lawless anarchy on the other. It was only five short years later that the Soviets supplied China with T34 tanks and other military hardware, weapons and jet pilots, officer training in the North Korean war from 1950 to 1953. The Korean War between North Korea, with the support of China and the Soviet Union, and South Korea with the support of the United States.

The American reputation would do much better, and they would advance the course of justice if they themselves stayed on the right side of the Spirit of the Natural Law. And stopped supporting lawlessness. Stopped giving aid to lawlessness as they did with Bolsheviks. How did they justify it? Maybe it was all humanistic reaction, without any knowledge of the Holy Bible instructions. Alternatively, it may have been a numbers game. Opportunity to make money selling American goods. One does not need to be a rocket scientist to read the Holy Bible and consider where the Spirit of the Natural Law is speaking true justice. Soviet Union leader Joseph Stalin was part of the same 1939 to 1941 conspiracy with Adolf Hitler that started World War 2 with Nazi Germany. The Allied forces protected Joseph Stalin's 1939-1945 war crimes and genocide. The Allied forced did nothing to bring the Russian war criminals to the court of law and real justice to the innocent victims.

The Allied forces inaction provided the environment to incubate the seeds of further corruption that continue to bloom into the 21 century. The annexation of Crimea and East Ukraine is one more example of what has followed from the Soviet Union leadership passing on the spiritual baton of Joseph Stalin USSR to the Kremlin, and from there to the current Russian leadership. The Syrian crisis is another example of a coin with two sides. Nemesis influence, with the same USSR Russian leadership values, deceit with the production and supply of chemical weapons to Syria. Also, possibly a fear of the Syrian Government collapse, with information leaking to the West from the USSR Syrian connections. In any case, they are protecting the dictator Assad interests in the Syrian Government militarily. There is apparent moral corruption in the leadership in relation to the intrinsic value of human life. Dictators protect other dictators; they have many life values in common. Complete disregard for the humanitarian crises in Syria. The Russian economic interests are a priority in supporting the Syrian Assad regime with the Russian military equipment, radar, and missile systems. Also, aircraft and jet fighters with the training of Syrian military personnel.

## EVIDENCE OF MORAL CORRUPTION

In a cause and effect world, the sequence of events that started with the conspiracy to wage war against the Baltic States and Nordic country Finland in 1939-40 is still an active, serious war crime. The Soviet Union part in murdering 22,000 Polish nationals, prisoners of war, politicians, government officials, civil servants, and nationals is nothing less than genocide. A grave war crime. According to the Nuremberg Principles and International Law. That is still waiting to be acknowledged and reconciled by the Russian Government.

Molotov & Ribbentrop Pact, Between Nazi Germany foreign minister Ribbentrop, and the Soviet Union foreign minister Molotov, was a conspiracy and agreement to do the crime and wage war against peace in the Baltics and Nordic countries. They divided the regions into two separate spheres of influence to be regarded as their war spoil. From the Categorical Imperative Moral Philosophy perspective, that reveals the real intent, whether an action is moral or immoral. The measurable goal of the M&R Pact was a deliberately planned severe war crime, which led to a series of violent war crimes. It was a blatant willfully disconnect from the Spirit of the Natural Law. Both sides of the pact had rejected the Spirit of the Natural Law and the principles. Therefore the Soviets are guilty of their deeds in serious war crime and genocide. 1939-1945. Equally, as the Nazi German officers were hung for their convicted guilt in war crimes.

The Nazi German officers were arrested, taken to the Nuremberg court, trialed, and sentenced. The Soviet Union leaders have denied any wrongdoing. They are under the obligation to follow law principles as any other citizen in the international community. Unless they want to run away and hide away from the International community? E.g., behind the iron curtain? Or the Bamboo curtain? They hide because they don't want to admit Soviet Union-Russian war crimes and genocide guilt. They did build a wall in the Soviet Union, which was named the Iron Curtain. They continued to repress the real facts of history until the death of Joseph Stalin in 1955 and the collapse of the Soviet Union in 1991. Mikhail Sergeyevich Gorbachev did acknowledge many facts in the 1980s that Stalin had repressed for more than 40 years, and blatantly denied the spirit of truth.

## THE SPIRIT OF THE INTERNATIONAL LAW

To deliberately break international laws, as an aggressor, and to wage war. For what reasons? Selfish unlawful reasons, to benefit self from the proceeds of crime and murder. It is impossible to justify honestly or to explain away the criminal nature of the Molotov & Ribbentrop Pact. It was a conspiracy against the rule of law. Profiteering motivated it from the aggressive warfare and invasion of independent countries. Nobody denies that the Nazi German officers at Nuremberg Trials 1945-1946 were guilty of war crimes and crimes against humanity. Why? Because their deeds were such. Why would parallel war crimes and the crimes against humanity be nullified for the Soviet Union officers? It is not logical, rational, or moral to exempt the Soviet leadership for war crimes. Therefore, they are as guilty as the Nazi German Officers were guilty of the parallel war crimes, in the light of the Spirit of the Natural Law.

UNRESOLVED CRIME

For the people of Germany, 1944-1954 was an earth-shattering and humbling experience to live through. Similarly, for the people of Japan, it was a humbling experience for their nation to walk through. Their error was a severe error of judgment in giving their support for a political leader, that was spiritually bitter, misguided, morally corrupted, and in his worldview deceived. The peoples of those nations were all led into the gloomy guilt-ridden darkness of depression that many never came out of. Over 50 million people lost their lives during the 1939-1945 period. The main players that caused the catastrophic disaster on humanity were the same partners in crime, in the Molotov & Ribbentrop Pact. The main engine that drove Europe into the colossal conflict in 1939-41 was the criminal intent and conspiracy between two superstates to break the Spirit of the Natural Law blatantly.

After World War 2, Germany, people as a nation did acknowledge. They confessed the sins of their leaders, and they became healthier people as a result. They have also recovered economically in the last 75 years. They learned valuable lessons from 1914-1917 and 1939-1945. One of them is to respect the spirit of Natural Law. Crime does not pay. Victor's justice won't suffice in a world that has a Creator watching time and space. The only exception from the World War 2 war crimes is the Soviet Union – Russian leaders. They have not openly acknowledged the Soviet Union's spiritual reality, committing severe war crimes, and profiteering from it until 2018. Instead, the Russian leaders glorify USSR Nationalism, and they glorify Joseph Stalin as a national hero.

The deceived minds of the USSR leaders have not generally been renounced by the people of Russia. There is support for national leaders who opportunistically use lawlessness to advance Russian nationalism and territorial conquest. There is also some opposition that renounces corruption and lawless deeds, e.g., the annexation of Crimea and East Ukraine. The annexation of Crimea was deeply insulting to the Government and the people of Ukraine. If the Russian leaders are willing to act that way to their close relative neighbor, what would their actions be for a less relative? Therefore, the Russian people are keeping the same spirit of Stalin in power.

The current Russian leaders are toying with the same evil spirit as Joseph Stalin State Atheism. It has the same power of temptation, promising unlimited material resources and power if only they would go the whole hog for the Satan influence. The Russian leadership philosophy, and the military view of the power of Satan's evil to have more power than the power of the Creator of life. Death and destruction in that life philosophy are ascribed more power than the power of life.

The Russian leadership is suppressing the spiritual reality. And avoiding a realistic spirit of truth restitution. Russian leadership thinks to themselves, according to the lawless principles of the Nemesis, that they can deny and bluff out of the Soviets World War II war crimes. The Soviet Russians have a heritage of bluffing themselves out of being caught; they deny the rule of law. That is a trademark of Satan. That is one of the fringe benefits to his servants. Play the game by his cheating rules and never get caught because there are no absolute rules in the sphere of the Nemesis. Everything is an open game. Will they succeed in their bluff? Not when the Truth speaks out. (Judgement-of-Satan, AD)

The Soviet attempt to set it out long enough for people to forget World War 2 atrocities. Not only delayed the truth of being told to the nations but also increased their judgment. By the profiteering from Joseph Stalin extortion of territory (Karelia Isthmus, Old Salla Municipality, Petsamo Municipality, North Karelia, and the Japanese Kuril Islands. The spirit of truth will rule the affairs of men one day. Straightening out their corruptive minds thinking in relation to the spirit of truth, law, and justice.

The spiritual nature of life and reality is not human-made; it has been put in place by the will of the Creator

God. We are all accountable for our actions on the planet earth, whether they are moral or immoral, violent, or peaceful. Only through the open spirit of confession to the Creator of life can the past violations be nullified and forgiven. It undoes the spiritual shackles of sin and evil. There are spiritual principles that make way for life. How could the Western Alliance? England, France, the United States, and Russian people repress the facts of the Molotov & Ribbentrop Pact? It was a conspiracy, intent to make war against peace, to commit war crimes, during a time of peace The Russian leaders have said that the Molotov Ribbentrop Pact of 1939 was only political with political implications.

The current (2018) Russian President has said it that way. The Russian leader has also shared USSR communist ideology and worldview by admitting the following.

*"First and foremost it is worth acknowledging that the demise of the Soviet Union (1922 -1991) was the greatest geopolitical catastrophe of the century"* (Vladimir-Putin, 2005)

That is a diabolical worldview to hold and to acknowledge it as a personal value. Considering the 20 the century was the bloodiest century in human history. And that we in the 21 century now and have access to the records of the past human sufferings caused by the two despotic dictators. How can anyone glorify despotic dictators like Joseph Stalin and condemn Adolf Hitler at the same time? Nobody can if they have an understanding and respect for the Spirit of the Natural Law. That reveals the Intrinsic value of human life., created by the Creator of Life Elohim. (Blessings-and-Curses, AD)

Many walls went up in 1945, and in time many crumbled and fell down in 1991. The East and West wall of Berlin crumpled. The Iron curtain came down. Also, the bamboo curtain was removed from what it was during the 1950s. Satan's deceiving hold on people's minds was loosened for a time in 1991. The Spirit of Elohim delivered many souls from the torture of the Soviet Union prison dungeons in 1991. The demonic spiritual stranglehold with the darkness of the USSR leadership by Satan was released for a while.

The Nemesis is working overtime on the minds of Russian leaders, to tempt them, to deceive their minds into thinking that the Soviet Union was a glorious thing to worship. And it is in their best interest to return to those glorious power days of the Joseph Stalin USSR. Then they would have unlimited political and military power to rule the world, and far surpassing the annoying number One United States of American military and political power. The power of Nemesis to work the imaginations of leaders to a greater egocentric megalomaniac satisfaction and glory has no end until people come to their senses, by the grace of God. (Encyclopedia, Persecution of Christians in the Soviet Union, 2018)

Can you imagine what it would be like if the Soviet Union had remained in control of the Russian people? There would be no International Internet in Russia. No western digital electronics or other innovations in their society. It would be a closed society, behind an Iron curtain. Thousands of Gulags across the Soviets and Siberia. And the tormented prisoners of the underground churches with hundreds of thousands of political prisoners. All the people that have read the testimonies of Christians who suffered imprisonment, from the 1930s to the 20th century, all because of the Joseph Stalin Soviet Union ideology, that was controlled by the dictator's totalitarian State Atheism.

For anyone to say, *"First and foremost it is worth acknowledging that the demise of the Soviet Union was the greatest geopolitical catastrophe of the century,"* is really telling of their personal worldview.

- Dialectic materialism values
- State Atheism glorified
- Deceived mind.
- Heart and mind in a state of unbelief
- No respect for the millions of innocent victims that were murdered by the diabolical personality cult of Stalin.

Pretending, repressing, deceiving one's mind, into fabricated lies, that is a dangerous deception. It was a conspiracy, it was criminal intent, and it was implemented by both Nazi Germany and the Soviet Union leaders. The proof is in the hard evidence that can be read in books and online encyclopedias. Over 60 languages, such as The Ribbentrop and Molotov Pact 1939 – Wikipedia.

It was a conspiracy against the spirit of the rule of law. Once they agreed to it and signed it, both Nazi Germany and the Soviet Russian leaders disconnected themselves from the Spirit of the Natural Law. The Nuremberg principles apply to the Nazi Germany war criminals as well as the Soviet Union war criminals. Why would it not? The rational mind with reason compels it. There are no truth-based excuses from the Allied forces to deny the facts. Nuremberg Principle VI says it all. Guilty are those that violate the spirit of the law. It is not whom they know (Allied forces) but instead what they have done indeed?

There are four categories that the Soviet Union leaders were guilty of in 1939-1945.

- Crimes against peace
- War crimes
- Crimes against humanity, and genocide in Poland 1940.

To understand the Soviet Union leader's mindset and standards that would agree to the pact with the Nazi Germany leadership in 1939. To go on a violent rampage of the East European countries, we need to go back to the time of the birth of the Soviet Union State. Moreover, to understand what values and principles the State were founded on in 1917- 1922? That is the period of time when the spiritual seed of the future Russian State was building upon. The spiritual fruit would come 17 years later (1922-1939).

In the material world of plants and trees, the fruit of a tree is always consistent with the planted seed, likewise, in the spiritual realm. The spiritual seed will produce in kind the fruit of the spirit which was planted. Sow lawlessness and immorality, reap crime, and corruption. Cause and effect are consistent with the meta-knowledge and the spiritual laws of humanity. Their minds were seriously deceived into believing in the lies of their personal temptations. The temptations of Satan promised wealth, glory, and power. They both (Hitler and Stalin) fell for it, hook, line, and sinker. They went out on a limb, believing their own illusions of their own imagination. Also seeing and feeling the glory and praise that they did receive from the masses of their peoples. They did believe that the winner would take it all. They were lied to, and they lost everything. The reward for their effort was to be cursed by the millions of people for a hundred years. And to be rejected by the Creator of Life for eternity. The Nuremberg Trials convicted the Nazi German Officers for war crimes, according to the Nuremberg trials. but FAILED to apply the same principles of law to the Soviet Stalin totalitarian regime.

[16]

# NUREMBERG PRINCIPLES

NUREMBERG PRINCIPLES

**Principle I**
"Any person who commits an act which constitutes a crime under international law is responsible therefore and liable to punishment."

**Principle II**
"The fact that internal law does not impose a penalty for an act which constitutes a crime under international law does not relieve the person who committed the act from responsibility under international law."

**Principle III**
"The fact that a person who committed an act which constitutes a crime under international law acted as Head of State or responsible government official does not relieve him from responsibility under international law."

**Principle IV**
Main article: Superior orders
"The fact that a person acted under the order of his Government or of a superior does not relieve him from responsibility under international law provided a moral choice be in fact possible to him."
This principle could be paraphrased as follows: "It is not an acceptable excuse to say 'I was just following my superior's orders.'"
Previous to the time of the Nuremberg Trials, this excuse was known in common parlance as "Superior Orders." After the prominent, high-profile event of the Nuremberg Trials, that excuse is now referred to by many as the "Nuremberg Defense." In recent times, a third term, "lawful orders," has become common parlance for some people. All three terms are in use today, and they all have slightly different nuances of meaning, depending on the context in which they are used.
Nuremberg Principle IV is legally supported by the jurisprudence found in individual articles in the Universal Declaration of Human Rights, which deal indirectly with conscientious objection. It is also supported by the principles found in paragraph 171 of the Handbook on Procedures and Criteria for Determining Refugee Status, which was issued by the Office of the United Nations High Commissioner for Refugees (UNHCR). Those principles deal with the conditions under which conscientious objectors can apply for refugee status in another country if they face persecution in their own country for refusing to participate in an illegal war.

**Principle V**
"Any person charged with a crime under international law has the right to a fair trial on the facts and law."

**Principle VI**
The crimes from now on set out are punishable as crimes under international law:
Crimes against peace:

Planning, preparation, initiation, or waging of a war of aggression or a war in violation of international treaties, agreements, or assurances; participation in a common plan or conspiracy for the accomplishment of any of the acts mentioned under (i).

**War crimes:**
Violations of the laws or customs of war which include, but are not limited to, murder, ill-treatment or deportation to slave labor or for any other purpose of the civilian population of or in occupied territory; murder or ill-treatment of prisoners of war or persons on the Seas, killing of hostages, the plunder of public or private property, wanton destruction of cities, towns, or villages, or devastation not justified by military necessity.

**Crimes against humanity:**
Murder, extermination, enslavement, deportation, and other inhumane acts done against any civilian population, or persecutions on political, racial, or religious grounds, when such acts are done, or such persecutions are carried on in the execution of or in connection with any crime against peace or any war crime."

**Principle VII**
*"Complicity in the commission of a crime against peace, a war crime, or a crime against humanity as outlined in Principle VI is a crime under international law."* (Nuremberg_principles, 1945)

The above Nuremberg Trials were the bases for convinced the Nazi Germany Officers for their part in the conspiracy to commit war crimes. Likewise, the Soviet Union -Russian leaders need to judge according to the same standards of the International law and the moral code. According to the Spirit of the Natural Law. Nothing more, nothing less, that is the Spirit of true justice.

## FINLAND UNDER PERSECUTION

There is much evidence to prove that the Allied forces cowered before the Soviet Union leaders. Moreover, given his powers to do as he and the Nemesis wished on the Baltic States and The war-responsibility trials in Finland 1945,1946. (Encyclopedia, War-responsibility trials in Finland, 1945) The most obvious follow up the question in regard to the War-responsibility trials in Finland are these:

- Where were the War-responsibility trials of Soviet Union Russian 1939-1940 held?
- Where were the War-responsibility trials of Poland's Katyn Forest massacre held?
- Where and when were they held?
- When will the United States and England 1941-1945 war-responsibility trials be held?

The Western Alliance has often said they were the principled people? And that they are strutting on the moral high ground. That is the essence that they are referring to in the International War Crime Court of Nuremberg. They continue to arrest the Nazi Germany war criminals from 1939 – 1945. They arrest the Nazi German officers and take them out of the aged people's homes at the old age over 80 to 90's. On what basis are the old and frail being arrested? However, their judgment is one-sided and biased as the drunken despots were biased in Berlin 1945, 1946. Russian soldiers are raping the citizen women of Berlin, approved by their officers. (Rape, 1945). In the following chapter is the Axis personnel indicted for war crimes. The following is a list of War Crime Trials and the people suspected of committing war crimes on behalf of Nazi Germany or any of the Axis.

[17]

# INTERNATIONAL LAW TRIALS

The Nuremberg trials
The Doctors' Trial
The Milch Trial
The Judges' Trial
The Pohl Trial
The Flick Trial
The IG Farben Trial
The Hostages Trial
The RuSHA trial
The Einsatzgruppen Trial
The Krupp Trial
The Ministries Trial
The High Command Trial
The Auschwitz Trial
The Frankfurt Auschwitz Trials
The Dachau Trial
Buchenwald
Mauthausen
Flossenbürg
Mühldorf
Dora-Nordhaussen
The Belsen Trial
The Neuengamme Trials
Bucharest People's Tribunal
International Military Tribunal for the Far East
Khabarovsk War Crime Trials
Austrian
Croatian
Danish
Dutch
Finnish
German
Hungarian
Italian
Japanese
Latvian
Lithuanian
   World War II portal (Axis-War-Crimes, 1945)

## STALIN TRIALS IN FINLAND 1945-1946

The war-responsibility trials in Finland were trials of the Finnish wartime leaders held responsible by the allied forces view point and opinion, for "definitely influencing Finland in getting into a war with the Soviet Union and the United Kingdom in 1941 or preventing peace." From 1941 to 1945 England, France, and the USA were complicit in the conspiracy, war crimes and genocide that the Soviet Russian leaders committed during the Molotov & Ribbentrop pact 1939-40. Instead of taking Soviet Stalin to an International court of law, for the crimes against humanity (Genocide against Polish Nationals 1940) The Allied forces invited Stalin into their "club" and called Stalin "Good Old Joe."

The Brits should have stayed at home eating their own home made fish and chips on their own home island, away from their usual ambitious, provocative invasions, colony expansions and warmongering the local peoples, as in the Nordic region 1918 and 1941-45. The government leaders of Finland were responsible in defending Finland from the Bolshevik dictator Stalin, and his State Atheism totalitarian military leaders, who conspired during 1939 to 1941 with Adolf Hitler Nazi regime to exploit the Baltic States and Finland. There was nothing irresponsible about the leaders of Finland from 1917 to 1945 when they were fighting on the right side of the Spirit of the Natural Law. It was Adolf Hitler and Joseph Stalin that were doing violence to the Spirit of the Natural Law, from 1939 to 1945.

The allied leaders were weak and immoral for perverting the cause of justice; they skewed reality, tried to re define truth, justice, and world history, while justifying their own political imperialism, and nationalistic ambitions. They used Adolf Hitler and the Nazi war crimes to leverage themselves upwards into self-righteousness. And celebrated with one of the worst war criminals of World War 2, Joseph Stalin, their imperial victor's justice. Protecting and defending the war criminal Joseph Stalin from 1941 to 1953. During that time Stalin and the Soviet Union was committing war crimes against innocent peoples. The Allied forces victor's justice made them further proud, proud of self, their ears were not open to truth, nor their eyes could see the truth and reality from the East European perspective.

It was not the government leaders of Finland that were irresponsible between 1917 to 1945. How ignorant and stupid can they get? Claiming to be on the right side of the spirit of the law, while they are full of imperial bigotry. The Soviet Union leader Joseph Stalin was protected and given favoritism regardless of all the war crimes that he was guilty of. Why the obvious hypocrisy? Were the British and Americans so gutless with the court of the law that they had their tail between their legs when Stalin was around? What happened to the principles of the Rule of Law based on the Spirit of the Natural Law? Representing the Spirit of True Justice?

In the minds of the Allies victors, it was no longer valid, they had achieved their objectives, and they were then playing the role of gods according to their own nationalistic interests. Their worldview was black and white, the devil of their mind was slain with Hitler and the Nazi war criminals. They did not see their own corruption, being used by the same force that had worked Stalin since early 1900 to 1939. In the same spirit with the Hitler that destroyed millions of innocent lives in East Europe. The Allied forces did not see their own wrongs; they did not listen, or see the obvious truth, they patronized the Soviets leaders regardless of the crimes that they had committed between 1939 to 1945.

The Allied victors were also corrupted, they blended their own nationalistic politics with moral laws. In their own mind they thought they were morally upright, but, they were just playing their own political game for their own nationalistic advantage. But they only saw the world through their own short-sighted political colored lenses. And others did not have the same rights because of their own biases, they saw themselves as being morally on high ground, beyond the "evil doers." Therefore, they skewed the truth in history; they misrepresented the Spirit of the Natural Law. They did not defend or speak up for the Spirit of The Natural Law with those that were fighting against the spirit of Satan in Joseph Stalin and the Soviet Union state atheism totalitarian regime. They failed to represent True Justice. They cowered and did not want to offend the will and the territorial ambitions of Stalin, by questioning the Russian role in the Nazi German-Soviet Pact of Aggression.

The Soviet leadership committed severe war crimes, including genocide of Polish nationals, at the Katyn Forest Massacre, murdering 22,000 POW and civilians in 1940. Also exploited the people of several Baltic States in East Europe. There was real evidence presented of the Katyn forest massacre of the Allied forces, Roosevelt repressed it on the bases of Utilitarianism. Others did not want to think about it. The Soviet prosecutor at the Nuremberg Trials tried to offload the 1940 Katyn forest massacre as war crimes onto the Nazi officers, but the German military forces had provided sufficient evidence by then of the truth to the Red Cross, and the Allies members (except Russia) rejected the false claims. Therefore, the False Soviet documents were rejected. But nothing is done to defend the Spirit of the Natural law. Nothing said to defend the cause of the innocent that died due to the Soviet role in the Nazi German-Soviet Pact of Aggression 1939 – 1941.

"The chief Soviet prosecutor submitted false documentation in an attempt to indict defendants for the murder of thousands of Polish officers in the Katyn forest near Smolensk. However, the other Allied prosecutors refused to support the indictment, and German lawyers promised to mount an embarrassing defense. No one was charged or found guilty at Nuremberg for the Katyn Forest massacre. In 1990, the Soviet government acknowledged that the Katyn massacre was carried out, not by the Germans, but by the Soviet secret police." (Nuremberg-1945, Nuremberg trials, 1945)

FALSE ACCUSATIONS
Double standards, with false accusations made against the government leaders of Finland. Even the name used in the proposition, in the context of the 1939-1945 has fabricated a lie. A sure sign of the Nemesis, using the political influence and the military power of the Allied forces, to push false accusations onto innocent victims.

A FALSE BALANCE IS AN ABOMINATION

> "A false balance is an abomination to the LORD, But a just weight is His delight." Proverb 11:1 .

Satan's tactics have common characteristics as a deceiver of truth. The Holy Bible says this.

> "Woe unto them that call evil good, and good evil; that put darkness for light, and light for darkness; that put bitter for sweet, and sweet for bitter!" Isaiah 5:20. ( 500 BC)

THE WAR RESPONSIBILITY TRIALS & STATE ATHEISM

- There is no God in State atheism. (Anti-Christ-Campaign., 1928-1941).
- Moscow Trials 1936-38.There is no genuine justice in show trials. (Stalin-Show-Trials, 1936-1938)
- Conspiracy to Make War against Peace 1939-1941
- Nazi German-Soviet Pact of Aggression against peace. (Molotov- Ribbentrop-Pact, 1939)
- Aggression. War against peace. War crime.
- The Katyn Forest Genocide in 1940.
- 40,000 Polish nationals, civilian held as a POW and 22,000 executed. (Katyn- forest-Massacre, 1940)

THE ALLIED FORCES SHOW TRIALS 1945

The war-irresponsibility trials in Finland 1945, implied that the Finland government leaders were not responsible during the series of conflicts, initiated mostly by the Joseph Stalin Soviet Union aggression, during 1939 – 1941, and 1944. There were two totalitarian military dictators in 1939 that made a Pact together. How much did Uncle Sam and Uncle Joe get rewarded for the heist, the war crime and the genocide between 1939 to 1941? Allied forces Kangaroo court is a more appropriate name for the false accusations of the war-irresponsibility trials in Finland. Completely responsible leaders, and innocent of wrong doing between 1939 to 1945, in comparison to the Soviet Union leaders, politicians were sent to jail, according to the desire of the Soviet leadership. The many Baltic States folded at the same time under Stalin, and their nations were occupied for 50 years, until 1991. Allied leaders were self-serving and rotten to the core, patronizing Joseph Stalin, while millions of innocent people lost their lives.

How can anybody accuse the independent nation leaders of Finland of irresponsibility? When they only took back the territory that was legally theirs from 1941 to 1945. It was the Soviet Stalin who had immorally, ruthlessly stolen the land from Finland only 15 months earlier in March 1940. Extreme extortion demands by Stalin to claim 10% of the Finland territory, using the threat of the continuation of the war, if Finland representatives did not accept the terms and conditions of the peace agreement. Russian Bolshevik style extreme extortion were used in 1940. Who will show them a mirror of their actions? How can those Western hypocrites accuse the independent nation leaders being irresponsible? After the accusers, themselves had committed aggression (1939 to 1940), genocide (Katyn forest massacre 1940) the war against peace, and other war crimes against civilians during 1941 to 1945?

It was a severe error of judgment. A violation of reason in finding true justice. It was an Allied forces deviation from truth, a deviation from the categorical imperative in moral reasoning. Their failure to understand the spirit of the law, order, and true justice. Their failure to exercise responsible moral reasoning, lead to further errors of judgment by the allied forces. They compromised truth and justice. It does reveal the nature and the character of the Soviet Union leadership. They were immoral and severely corrupted as organized criminals since early 1900. They redefined moral laws, to suit their individual lawless goals and their godless state atheism materialistic worldview. They had no interest in moral reasoning or understanding of moral duty. The Soviet Union history from 1922 – 1940. The voice of reason and justice was not heard at the time that the USSR initiated the aggressive war in 1939-1940? There was also a very aggressive war against Poland in 1939.

The unprovoked aggressive war by the Soviet Union leader Stalin and his general was a severe war crime. As the result of the aggressive warfare attack on November 1939 – 1940 thousands of innocent people died in Finland alone.

- 25,904 dead or missing
- 43,557 wounded
- 800–1,100 captured
- 20–30 tanks destroyed
- 62 aircraft destroyed
  70,000 total human casualties. (Winter-War, 1939)

The war-responsibility trials in Finland in November 1945, did not raise the Soviet Union aggressive war against peace in 1939-40? It is disgraceful and morally disgusting. Shameful Western biases, appeasing a significant war criminal like Joseph Stalin.

### SOVIET UNION AGENDA

There is a consistent pattern that appeared for 39 years until it finally development and manifested much worse inside the Soviet Union and their neighbors. It started in early 1900, 1905, 1914, 1917 to 1922. If those immoral events were not a sign for morally responsible nation leaders to wake up, that things were going to get much worse, manifesting in lawlessness, disrespect to the rule of law, disrespect for religious practices and utter disregard to human rights in Russia. If that development for 22 years was not noticed as going from bad to worse, then the nation leaders are complete morons, with their heads inside their pet dog kennel. The Bolshevik violent behavior became a new norm inside the USSR, and routine for the political prisoners in Siberia, and the occupied territories. It was criminal intent, a war against peace. The Bolshevik criminal madmen had inverted the Russian government leadership, civil society structures and were expanding the same corrupted madness in East Europe with the help of Hitler's Nazi regime in 1939.

There are two sides to a coin, as a metaphor of the methods, the existence, and the influence of the Nemesis. People's minds and the soul that is being tempted and deceived into lawlessness behavior. The power of temptation works on the nation leaders living souls, the intellect, consciousness, imagination, will, ego and emotions. Also, on the natural human physical desires, that are potential areas of temptation, to make conscious compromises, towards carnal lawlessness. Moral compromises may come through, success, influence, wealth, a false worldview, heresies, superstitions, myths or bizarre life philosophies. Whatever it is, a temptation usually is like a doorway that person commits to and reaps the consequences of that moral compromise. The willing servants that do compromise spiritual reality morally, they become manipulated subjects by that spiritual power of temptation, even more of the same power of compromise.

The consistent pattern can be studied and learned from the experiences of the Russian monarchy, the Soviet Union leaders, the Baltic States experience and Finland history. There are many parallels in the Bolshevik strategic plan to invert the Russian government, that the Soviets implemented in East Europe and tried to do in the Nordic countries. The Bolsheviks succeeded in the inversion of the Russian government with the Russian revolution and the inversion of the Russian society with the 5-year civil war. Most hard-line criminals were released from prisons in Russia during the Russian revolution. Similarly, the Soviets released criminals from prisons when they occupied the Baltic States. It was in the same spirit of the Bolsheviks society inversion. Once the pattern is recognized, there are no other words to describe the Soviet Union than an empire influenced by evil. Where would such an idea come from? To invert the responsible structures of a government? And the responsible structure of a moral, law-abiding society? If not from the mind of Satan.

Also, why would anybody in their right mind aggressively expand the largest land area of any country in the world? Using methods that are so brutal, aggressive, inhuman and diabolical. The idea is irrational, a sinister force behind it, pushing the leaders towards destruction. Totalitarian dictators are not going to win over any moral law respecting human friends to their national cause. So why would their leaders use such crude methods and barbaric tactics? To capsize, to flip over the structures of society? That is characteristic and the intent of the spirit of the Nemesis. To cause destruction. And he can only work through willing subjects, given to his influence.

THE TRAIL OF THE NEMESIS DESTRUCTION
Early in the morning of August 24, 1939, the Soviet Union and Germany signed a ten-year non-aggression pact, called the Molotov–Ribbentrop Pact. The pact contained a secret protocol by which the states of Northern and Eastern Europe divided into German and Soviet "spheres of influence." (Molotov-Ribbentrop-Pact, 1939)

Nazi German-Soviet Pact of Aggression 1939 – 1941.

PARTNERS IN CRIME
*"In the north, Finland, Estonia, and Latvia assigned to the Soviet sphere. Poland partitioned in the event of its "political rearrangement"—the areas east of the Narev, Vistula and San Rivers going to the Soviet Union while Germany would occupy the west. Lithuania, adjacent to East Prussia, would be in the German sphere of influence, although a second secret protocol agreed in September 1939 assigned the majority of Lithuanian territory to the Soviet Union. According to this secret protocol, Lithuania would regain its historical capital Vilnius, previously subjugated during the inter-war period by Poland."* (Molotov-Ribbentrop-Pact, 1939)

Following the end of the Soviet invasion of Poland on 6 October, the Soviets pressured Finland and the Baltic states to conclude mutual assistance treaties. The Soviets were on a roll Westward, they were looking for any excuse, any cracks in the Baltic states defense to get a foot hold in, and for any excuse to doubt the neutrality of

Estonia; they found one in the escape of an interned Polish submarine on 18 September 1939. It is a most obvious thing, if anyone signs up for the Nazi German-Soviet Pact of Aggression, that the neighbors will run and scream wolf! So, therefore Soviets did not need to wait long after 23 August 1939 before they were spotted. They were in knee-deep under the will of the Nemesis from 1939 – 1991.

*"A week later on 24 September, the Estonian foreign minister was given an ultimatum in Moscow. The Soviets demanded the conclusion of a treaty of mutual assistance to establish military bases in Estonia. The Estonians had no choice but to accept naval, air and army bases on two Estonian islands and at the port of Paldiski. The corresponding agreement signed on 28 September 1939."* (Invasion, Occupation of the Baltic states, 1940)

LATVIA.

*"Latvia followed on 5 October 1939 and Lithuania shortly after that, on 10 October 1939. The agreements permitted the Soviet Union to establish military bases on the Baltic states' territory for the duration of the European war and to station 25,000 Soviet soldiers in Estonia, 30,000 in Latvia and 20,000 in Lithuania from October 1939."*...

Case #1.

*"In September and October 1939, the Soviet government compelled the Baltic states to conclude mutual assistance pacts which gave it the right to establish Soviet military bases. In May 1940, the Soviets turned to the idea of direct military intervention but still intended to rule through puppet regimes. Their model was the "Finnish Democratic Republic,"* (Invasion, Occupation of the Baltic states, 1940)

*The pseudo" Finnish Democratic Republic" was a Soviet puppet government farce, planned and set up by the Soviets for the first day of the 1939 aggressive war (Winter War) plan for the entire country take over to the global Communism doctrine."*......

The USSR-Russia was on the same Lenin & Stalin global communist takeover doctrine for 70 years. It is a crazy state atheism idea from the mind of Marx, Lenin, and Stalin.

Case #2.
LITHUANIAN

*"On 15 June 1940, the Lithuanian government had no choice but to agree to the Soviet ultimatum and permit the entry of an unspecified number of Soviet troops. President Antanas Smetona proposed armed resistance to the Soviets, but the government refused, proposing their candidate to lead the regime. However, the Soviets refused this offer and sent Vladimir Dekanozov to take charge of affairs while the Red Army occupied the state".* (Invasion, Occupation of the Baltic states, 1940)

Case #3.

*"On 16 June 1940, Latvia and Estonia also received an ultimatum. The Red Army occupied the two remaining Baltic states shortly after that. The Soviets dispatched Andrey Vyshinsky to oversee the takeover of Latvia and Andrei Zhdanov to oversee the takeover of Estonia. On 18 and 21 June 1940, new "popular front" governments were formed in each Baltic country, made up of Communists and fellow travelers. Under Soviet surveillance, the new governments arranged rigged elections for new "people's assemblies." Voters presented with a single list, and no opposition movements were allowed to file and to get the required turnout to 99.6% votes were forged."* It was a similar tactic used as in the pseudo-Finnish Democratic Republic takeover attempt. (Invasion, Occupation of the Baltic states, 1940)

POLAND

Their nation most gifted leaders in various organizations relocated, murdered and buried. Of the 22,000-total killed, about 8,000 were officers imprisoned during the Soviet invasion of Poland, their share of the Nazi German-Soviet Pact of Aggression 1939. Another 6,000 Polish nationals were police officers, and the rest were Polish intelligentsia that the Soviets deemed to be "intelligence agents, gendarmes, landowners, saboteurs, factory owners, lawyers, officials, and priests." The Soviets "deemed them to have been." Similarly as the Stalin purge and the Moscow Trials of 1936 to 1938.

- Estonia.
- Latvia.
- Lithuania.
- Romania.

Between 1922 to 1945, Joseph Stalin list of war crimes, atrocities, murder, and genocide are massive. The Americans and the British and the French were complicit in the Soviet war crimes and genocide, they were in alliance with Stalin, shaking hands with one of the worst war criminals of the World War 2. The Americans were over self-confident and arrogant when they were told by the people of the countries that have shared the Imperial Russian and Soviet Union border for many hundreds of years. The repetition of aggression and conflict, over 500 years, the nature of the violence, and intuitively the violent antagonism against the Spirit of the Natural Law. The conflict is spiritual in nature.

The American leadership did not believe it to be true. They were overconfident of the worldview and their mind perceptions of foreign cultures, politically and militarily ambitious Russian leaders. Roosevelt did not even believe the report about the Katyn Forest massacre; he was short-sighted and naive in his belief, his ability to judge character from formal meetings. Similarly, George Bush looked the Russian President in the eyes, and said, "he is a good man." Good men do not steal other people property, especially when the people are so close to the Russian story history, as Ukraine is. Good men do not go to the aid of dictators; especially they hang onto political power even after 400,000 casualties of the Syrian civil war, and many millions of refugees.

> "For God will bring every deed into judgment, with every secret thing, whether good or evil." Ecclesiastes 12:14.

The Western leaders said the same thing about Joseph Stalin, "a good man." They called him by a nickname, "Good Old Joe." How ignorant of the Western politicians, what foolish clowns the western leaders were. They were riding along with the deceptive spirit of Satan.

TIME MAGAZINE PERSON OF THE YEAR FOR 1939

The Time Magazine man of the year generally does speak for some sort of value? If nothing else, then thanks for the Nemesis working at New York, printing and selling the Time Magazine globally. They are everywhere. What's new? The American media serving the public was naive without knowing morally true facts of Joseph Stalin, from 1900 to 1939. It is shocking to consider the available facts that we have today. Thanks for the honest people, that have respect for truth at critical moments in history, such as Mikhail Gorbachev.

Stalin was devious and cunning, he was a hardened criminal, who concealed and denied his horrible leadership trail of violence, political repression, show trials, war crimes and genocide. The politically correct, people pleaser's in American leadership, called him the "Good Old Joe," at the time of the Nuremberg trials 1945. Stalin is named 'Time' magazine's person of the year for 1939, for switching the balance of power in Europe by signing the Nazi German-Soviet Pact of Aggression.

At New York, they had no idea when it was all going down. They knew at Berlin, and Moscow that there was a secret protocol signed, that said it all. It was a conspiracy to do crime against the Baltic States and Finland 1939 to 1941. They did not make the pact for the sake of peace, they signed the pact for the sake of the Nemesis, for exploitation of the innocent. The American's at New York saw it as Good Old Joe hooking up with Adolf. They saw it as appeasement, a nonaggression pact with Hitler, a decision that was later described as being "world- shattering." (Time-Magazine, 1939)

"Without the Russian pact," the magazine says, "German generals would certainly have been loath to go into military action. With it, the World War II began."

Conclusion, Stalin enabled Hitler to continue the destruction emboldened with a new partner in crime, USSR. A new paradigm and a new balance of power in East Europe 1939-1941.

[18]

# THE JUST WAR THEORY

The just war theory is central to this example. When is justified for a State government to employ military force against another State? Is there any difference in the Spirit of the Natural Law principles between a small nation of 3 million and the national population of 150 million? In Natural Law theory, the principles are constant, regardless of the population size. The law of the jungle logic may see that size difference as an opportunity for the bigger to exploit the smaller.

*"Just war theory today is a composite that has evolved from ideas developed by various religious figures. In the 5th century, St. Augustine discussed in the City of God, the circumstances under which killing could be justified, and empires legitimately expanded."* (Encyclopedia, Just War Theory, 426 AD)

In the 13th century, St. Thomas Aquinas laid out a more elaborate just war doctrine in his Summa Theologica. He wrote that three conditions were necessary to make a war just:

- a competent authority must order it;
- the cause must be just;
- moreover, the combatants must have "a right intention so that they intend the advancement of good or the avoidance of evil.

Modern just war guidance involves both the decision to go to war (jus ad bellum) and how to fight one (jus in bello). This latter set of criteria focuses on proportionality (how much force), targeting (avoiding non-combatants), and means (avoiding certain classes of weapons).

### WARS OF CHOICE
*"The question is whether wars of choice can also be justifiable. By definition, wars of choice tend to involve less than vital interests and the existence of alternative policies. Vietnam, Kosovo, and Bosnia were all wars of choice. So too was the second Iraq war, which began in 2003."*

*Are wars of choice ever justifiable? The answer is "yes," when using force is the best available policy option. The argument that the goal is worthy and that war is the best option for pursuing it should be strong enough to garner considerable domestic and international support. More importantly, the case should be persuasive that using military force will accomplish more good for more people at a lower cost than diplomacy, sanctions, or inaction.*

*However, what about the future? The concept of justifiable war is not merely one for history. Iran, North Korea, Pakistan, Afghanistan are all potential theaters for new or intensified U.S. military action. The question is not whether they would constitute just wars. That is too impractical a standard. The question in the real world is whether they would be justifiable to Congress, to the American people, to the world. It is a question the next President will have to answer."* (Richard.N.Hass, 2009)

## AMERICAN PRONOUNCE WAR ON JAPAN

Speech by the American President Roosevelt.

President Franklin Roosevelt called the unprovoked attack on Pearl Harbor a "date which will live in infamy," in a famous address to the nation delivered on December 8, 1941, after Japan's deadly surprise attack against U.S. naval and military forces in Hawaii. He also asked the Congress to declare war on Japan.

"The attack on Pearl Harbor was a surprise military strike by the Imperial Japanese Navy Air Service against the United States naval base at Pearl Harbor, Hawaii Territory, on the morning of December 7, 1941.

Japan intended the attack as a preventive action to keep the U.S. Pacific Fleet from interfering with military actions that were planned in Southeast Asia against overseas territories of the United Kingdom, the Netherlands, and the United States.

All eight U.S. Navy battleships were damaged, with four sunk. All but the USS Arizona were later raised, and six were returned to service and went on to fight in the war. The Japanese also sank or damaged three cruisers, three destroyers, an anti-aircraft training ship, and one minelayer. One hundred eighty-eight U.S. aircraft were destroyed; 2,403 Americans were killed, and 1,178 others were wounded.

The surprise attack came as a profound shock to the American people and led directly to the American entry into World War II in both the Pacific and European theaters. The following day, December 8, the United States declared war on Japan, "Yesterday, December 7, 1941—a date which will live in infamy—the United States of America was suddenly and deliberately attacked by naval and air forces of the Empire of Japan.

The United States was at peace with that nation and, at the solicitation of Japan, was still in conversation with its government and its emperor looking toward the maintenance of peace in the Pacific.

Indeed, one hour after Japanese air squadrons had commenced bombing in the American island of Oahu, the Japanese ambassador to the United States and his colleague delivered to our Secretary of State a formal reply to a recent American message. Moreover, while this reply stated that it seemed useless to continue the existing diplomatic negotiations, it contained no threat or hint of war or armed attack.

It will be recorded that the distance of Hawaii from Japan makes it evident that the attack was deliberately planned many days or even weeks ago.

During the intervening time, the Japanese government has deliberately sought to deceive the United States by false statements and expressions of hope for continued peace.

The attack yesterday on the Hawaiian islands has caused severe damage to American naval and military forces. I regret to tell you that very many American lives have been lost. Also, American ships have been reported torpedoed on the high seas between San Francisco and Honolulu.

Yesterday, the Japanese government also launched an attack against Malaya.

Last night, Japanese forces attacked Hong Kong. Last night, Japanese forces attacked Guam.

Last night, Japanese forces attacked the Philippine Islands. Last night, the Japanese attacked Wake Island.

Moreover, this morning, the Japanese attacked Midway Island.

Japan has, therefore, undertaken a surprise offensive extending throughout the Pacific area. The facts of yesterday and today speak for themselves. The people of the United States have already formed their opinions and thoroughly understand the implications to the very life and safety of our nation.

As Commander in Chief of the Army and Navy, I have directed that all measures be taken for our defense. However, always will our whole nation remember the character of the onslaught against us.

No matter how long it may take us to overcome this premeditated invasion, the American people, in their righteous might, will win through to absolute victory.

I believe that I interpret the will of the Congress and of the people when I assert that we will not only defend ourselves to the uttermost but will make it very sure that this form of treachery shall never again endanger us. Hostilities exist. There is no blinking at the fact that our people, our territory, and our interests are in grave danger.

With confidence in our armed forces, with the unbounded determination of our people, we will gain the inevitable triumph—so help us, God.

I ask that the Congress declare that since the unprovoked and dastardly attack by Japan on Sunday, December 7, 1941, a state of war has existed between the United States and the Japanese empire."

(President-Roosevelt, 1941)

SOME OF THE CRITICAL POINTS IN THE SPEECH ARE:

- Japan intended the attack as a preventive action to keep the U.S. Pacific Fleet from interfering

- All eight U.S. Navy battleships were damaged, with four sunk.
- All but the USS Arizona were raised, and six were returned to service and went on to fight in the war.
- The Japanese also sank or damaged three cruisers,
- three destroyers,
- an anti-aircraft training ship
- one minelayer.
- One hundred eighty-eight U.S. aircraft destroyed;
- 2,403 Americans killed
- One thousand one hundred seventy-eight others were wounded.
- 

PARALLEL COMPARISON OF THE UNPROVOKED AGGRESSION

The Soviet Union November 30, 1939-40, initiated the aggressive war against Finland.

Moreover, the 1941 Pearl Harbor surprise attack by Japan.

Which of the two events came first? Could it be that the U.S. Allies indifference and inaction to the Nazi Germany & USSR aggression in 1939-41 was viewed by Japan as justifiable? Free for all? Using the logic of, what is good for one, is suitable for all? Which of the two claimed more lives? Caused more damage?

The Imperial Super States, France, Britain, Russia, and the United States have highly polished porcelain over their national pride ego. Once that pride is cracked, the declaration of war follows. The smaller States are much humbler; they have human skin in the game. They are often bruised, lacerated, and scarred, but they must keep going regardless and suffer silently because the Imperials use the Victors justice to manipulate the ordinary people of the land and the smaller states.

How does the above destruction compare with the aggressive war against peace? That the Soviet Union committed to Poland in September 1939? Moreover, the aggressive war against peace in Finland in November 1939? Was not the Soviet Union aggression sufficiently extreme to reveal their intentions to exploit other's territory and property, to deny people their right to life, liberty, and property?

Here are the facts:

- Soviets cross over 1100 + km border,
- Used 21 divisions, totaling some 450,000 men in the invasion
- Air bombed the capital city Helsinki,
- Inflicting substantial damage and casualties to cities. 1000 civilians died.
- months war 25,904 dead or missing
- 43,557 wounded
- 800–1,100 captured
- 20–30 tanks destroyed
- 62 aircraft destroyed
- 70,000 total human casualties

President of Finland, Kyösti Kallio New Year speech 1940, four weeks after the Aggressive Soviet war against peace. The following page is a copy of a speech script, from the New Year 1940, given by the President of Finland, Kyösti Kallio. National burden of the aggressive war at the East front lines. The aggressive war that the Soviet Stalin had initiated on November 30. 1939.

[19]

# NEW YEARS DAY SPEECH 1940

The President of Finland Kyösti Kallio. (1937-1940). To Suomi people and friends! (Translated from Finnish to English by author).

*"As President of the Republic, it has been a tradition of mine that on the first day of the year to send out greetings message through our radio broadcasts, to create a brief overview of our societies and economic development. This time I have to give up on the practice because now there is only one thing that is on our mind, to rescue our fatherland from the attacker's reach that has struck its claws on our governing body. Our bodies. The old imperialist Russia, throughout history, has been a threat to the Finnish people, once again manifested its old instincts and without the slightest legitimate reason to attack our country.*

*Russian Tsar Imperialism has collapsed, but the imperialist practices have been inherited to its current rulers, even though their teacher guru Lenin declared when he came into power to be respectful of the sovereignty and self-determination of the peoples on the fringes of the old Tsar territory.*

*In practice, it has turned out to be words only. Initially, the sovereignty of the peoples who had the national strength to rise and watch over their independence, and they did gain independence, but now the Soviet Union leaders appear to be strong enough to demand influence over those countries as well. (growing military strength emboldens Soviet union leaders to demand control of the neighbors).*

*Such a request even though initially was cautious, was also made to Finland. From the experience of centuries, Finland was aware of what it was all about. Peace-loving-People like Finland, it tried to get the requests presented to us through negotiation, however, the apparent requests of the Soviet Union turned out to be demands on Finland's own security and interest were to be relocated and diminished.*

*The Soviet Union, as usual, made its claim under the guise of security of Leningrad, but in reality, it was the transport connections between the Gulf of Finland and Petsamo fjord control and disposal, weakening of Finland's defense capabilities in the Gulf of Finland, Karelian Isthmus and the Port of Petsamo.*

*None of the Leningrad's insecurity could have been the truth of the matter because already in Tartu's peace agreement it was agreed that Finland could not fortify Leningrad region, or the islands along the waterway and the shoreline area near Leningrad, nor the Finnish fishermen's island area at the Port of Petsamo.*

*In the negotiations, the Soviet representatives acknowledged these guarantees as sufficient about Finland but required additional guarantees that no superpower could take advantage of Finland's territory in a potential war against Russia. That was also an excuse because Finland is always there openly said that it wanted to stay away from the conflicts between the great powers and laments himself against every foreign power that seeks to offend his sovereignty.*

*Russia's invasion of Finland when the negotiations were still unfinished. Moreover, they delivered a demand for the appointment of the Communist government to our unconquerable country, shows that it had been presumptuously decided to occupy Finland and at the same time to engulf the country with the spirit of the Bolsheviks politics when the initial requests as they were, was not granted.*

*Our country was in a state of readiness that Russia did not get us by surprise, even though there is a non-fortified border over 1,000 kilometers. They attacked the border right away in some points, not caring less, and completely ignoring the agreements that we had with them, e.g., the resolution of mutual disputes by peaceful means.*

*Ruthlessly attacking using airplanes on the capital and other settlements by killing children, women and other civilians. Through these acts, the Soviet Union revealed at the beginning of its agenda. This raw assault brought together the front the whole of the Finnish people, whose national self-esteem and the blood felt love for the liberty of our independence, which every year we are increasingly strengthened.*

*Our defense is intact and indivisible. Our Parliament has unanimously drawn up laws that show its long-awaited consideration today. Defense work does not only involve men but also women who are sacrificing themselves; the versatile operation is of great value. The proportion of women today more noticeable when they are receiving, and part of the refugees and relocating process with incredible pride and with serenity adapted to both sides of the new conditions.*

*During this great trial of our nation, we have the consolation among us, cooperation and unity. It seems as if the people of Finland in the great distress found themselves. Moreover, that is why we need to rejoice. The sacrifice we now need everywhere is of high divine origin.*

*Sacrifice His work and resources for the neighbor is significant, but to sacrifice himself, the life of his country, and For his people is still much higher. In front of its vulnerability, we are silent, and we humble to thank God for great suffering and sorrows to awaken new life values.*

*We sincerely regret that we have been subjected to warfare that requires victims. But we have no other way to protect our independence than a sacrificial battle for our existence sake.*

*A couple of weeks ago, I had the opportunity to greet our superiors 'officers and crews and express our gratitude to our peoples for the different positions that stand for the protection of our home and the whole motherland.*

*These two fateful weeks that we have since lived have given us their own for our people and the whole world, new testimonies of the battle readiness of our defense Forces, perseverance and above all the unity and cooperation they have shown on land, at sea, and in the air. On behalf of our people, without mentioning anyone individually, or forgetting anyone, for everyone to our country defenders are heroic and deserves deep praise.*

*This equally grateful greeting is also presented to those wounded at the front lines, laying in the hospitals from their acts of courage. Which I have pointed out they are carrying the hard fate continually remembering their comrades who are on the front lines.*

*However, above all, we take a moment of silence to give respect to the many who have sacrificed their lives for our common homeland. Moreover, you, mothers, fathers, spouses, children, brothers and sisters, who are doing heavy work at home you will know this during this fateful Season, with greetings with the consent of knowing that every hand you know, that this is now about the existence of our nation and the future of which we all are Responsible for. Let us continue to carry our burdens each in place with the same unity and bravery. Every work for the motherland is now essential and necessary."*

(President Kallio, 1940)

[20]

# CONSTITUTIONAL LAW

"Constitutional law is a body of law which defines the role, powers, and structure of different entities within a state. Namely, the executive, the parliament or legislature, and the judiciary; as well as the fundamental rights of citizens and, in federal countries such as the United States and Canada, the relationship between the central government and state, provincial, or territorial governments." (Constitutional-Law, 2018)

### COMPARATIVE LAW
"Comparative law is the study of differences and similarities between the law of different countries. More specifically, it involves the study of the different legal "systems" (or "families") in existence in the world, including the common law, the civil law, socialist law, Canon law, Jewish Law, Islamic law, Hindu law, and Chinese law. It includes the description and analysis of foreign legal systems, even where no explicit comparison is undertaken. The importance of comparative law has increased enormously in the present age of internationalism, economic globalization, and democratization." (Comparative-Law, 2018)

### NATURAL LAW
"Natural law is a philosophy asserting that individual rights are inherent by human nature, endowed by nature—traditionally by God or a transcendent source and that these can be understood universally through human reason. As determined by nature, the law of nature is implied to be universal, existing independently of the positive law of a given state, political order, legislature or society at large. Historically, natural law refers to the use of reason to analyze human nature to deduce binding rules of moral behavior from nature's or God's creation of reality and mankind. The concept of natural law was first documented in ancient Greek philosophy, including Aristotle, and was referred to in Roman philosophy by Cicero."

### NATURAL LAW THEORY CAN BE DISCOVERED THROUGH DEDUCTIVE REASONING
Deductive reasoning, also deductive logic, logical deduction is the process of reasoning from one or more statements (premises) to reach a logically certain conclusion. The deductive reasoning goes in the same direction as that of the conditionals and links premises with conclusions. If all premises are correct, the terms are clear, and the rules of deductive logic are followed, then the conclusion reached is necessarily true. If we have no confidence in deductive logical reasoning, then we have no confidence in the ability to think about knowledge. If we have no confidence in thinking knowledge, then we are in the state of ignorance. People do have confidence in mathematics; it is a reliable design of the creation. The world that surrounds us is digital in the design, versus analog. It can be discovered mathematically, logically and with the ability to reason. (Natural-Law, 2018)

### THE LETTER OF THE LAW VERSUS THE SPIRIT OF THE LAW
The letter of the law versus the spirit of the law is an idiomatic antithesis. When one obeys the letter of the law but not the spirit, one is obeying the literal interpretation of the words (the "letter") of the law, but not necessarily the intent of those who wrote the law. Conversely, when one obeys the spirit of the law but not the letter, one is doing what the authors of the law intended, though not necessarily adhering to the literal wording. "Law" originally referred to legislative statute, but in the idiom may refer to any rule. Intentionally following the letter of the law but not the spirit may be accomplished through exploiting technicalities, loopholes, and ambiguous language." (Law, 2018)

### AN ORAL LAW

*An oral law is a code of conduct in use in a given culture, religion or community application, by which a body of rules of human behavior is transmitted by oral tradition and effectively respected, or the single rule that is orally transmitted.* (Law, 2018)

### CUSTOM LAW

Custom in law is the established pattern of behavior that can be objectively verified within a particular social setting. A claim can be carried out in defense of "what has always been done and accepted by law." Related is the idea of prescription; a right enjoyed through long custom rather than positive law. Customary law (also, consuetudinary or unofficial law) exists where:

- specific legal practice is observed and the relevant actors consider it to be law (opinion juris).

Most customary laws deal with standards of the community that have been long-established in a given locale. However, the term can also apply to areas of international law where specific standards have been nearly universal in their acceptance as correct bases of action – in the example, laws against piracy or slavery (see hostis humani generis). (Custom-Law, 2018)

### DICTATORS NARRATIVE INTERNATIONAL LAW

Citation: *"The Geneva Conventions of 1864, 1906, and 1929 had established international standards that were understood to encompass the humanitarian treatment of prisoners and of citizens in occupied territories during the war. Mitoma says, however, that at the time of the trials, criticism centered on the charges brought against the defendants for crimes against peace and crimes against humanity because such charges had not previously been established as part of the international law."*

*"The kind of guiding ideology of the Nuremberg Trials was laying down principles that there is a baseline of the natural law of universal human rights that are there at all times,"* he says. *"That guiding theory informs the emergence of human rights; the idea [is] that we have to advocate for human rights on a global level, and there are dimensions to our basic humanity that give us moral rights that form the fundamental basis of our morality and our humanity."* (Nuremberg-Legacy, 2018)

[21]

# LAMENTATIONS

The effects in the material world are often observable. The cause is, at the time is also observable and most undoubtedly knowable. The effect of soil erosion can be observed during and after rainstorms and floods. Flowing water carries away soil with its momentum. The morning sun heat melts away frost that can be observed. The head of a swinging golf club connects with the golf ball with a ping sound and is accelerated high up in the air for 300 yards. A pine tree during the winter snowfall has fallen over due to the weight of the snow on the branches. These signs can be described as cause and effect in a material world. But there is more than the material world. The spiritual dimension brings balance to the material world. Humans need a balance in their mind, body, and spirit. Humans are made in the image of their Creator; therefore, by design, there is a need for balance.

> "Woe to those who call evil good, and good evil; Who substitute darkness for light and light for darkness; Who substitute bitter for sweet and sweet for bitter!". Isaiah 5:20.

> "When the righteous increase, the people rejoice, But when a wicked man rules, people groan." Proverbs 29:2.

> "The LORD has made everything for its own purpose, even the wicked for the day of evil." Proverbs 15:4.

LAMENTATION
The date is July 5, 1941.
Nazi Germany military crossed the border on June 22, 1941. 2 weeks later, Joseph Stalin is being recovered from the shock and spoke to the Russian people through a radio broadcast in Moscow.
*"Comrades, citizens, brothers, and sisters, fighters of the army and Navy, my friends, I appeal to you.*
*The heinous attack by Hitler Germany continues; what has fascist Germany achieved by breaking the pact and attacking the USSR?*
*Its troops have achieved an advantageous situation, but politically they have lost because they have revealed themselves to the world to be bloodthirsty aggressors."*
– Joseph Stalin. (July 5, 1941).

Joseph Stalin's disgusting, immoral double standards. "have revealed themselves to the world to be bloodthirsty aggressors." How is the 22,000 Polish nationals genocide described? Genocide that Joseph Stalin and Rusian foreign minister Vyacheslav Molotov undersigned, and approved by Lenin, Trotsky, Zinoviev, Kamenev, Sokolnikov, and Bubnov, as members of the Soviet Politburo.

Only 20 months earlier, on August 23, 1939, Stalin with the Russian foreign minister Molotov, and the Nazi Germany foreign minister Ribbentrop signed the Nazi German-Soviet Pact of Aggression. What was Stalin thinking? Where was the Spirit of the Natural Law then? It was present, it was everywhere, but nobody had the interest to respect it. Only in deep desperation, the idea enters Stalin's mind to appeal for justice. He had no credit or standing for justice; he never offered it to others between 1917 to 1941. He denied life and justice for millions of innocent victims. Nazi Germany and Soviet leadership had agreed to a conspiracy to exploit the Baltic States, and with a secret protocol with divided spheres of influence regions between the two sides. The pact was illegal and immoral.

The first phase of the plan started from the German side; Poland's invasion began on September 1, 1939, one week after the signing of the Molotov–Ribbentrop Pact, followed by the Soviet part in the invasion of Poland on September 17, 1939. The Soviet capture 30,000 polish prisoners. On March 5, 1940, the Soviet Union secret police (NKVD) chief Lavrentiy Beria's sent a letter of proposal to execute all captive members of the Polish officer corps; it was approved by the Politburo of the Communist Party of the Soviet Union, including its leader, Joseph Stalin.

The 22,000 Polish prisoners requested to be executed, including landowners, saboteurs, factory owners, lawyers, officials, and priests". As the Polish Army officer class was representative of the multi-ethnic Polish state, the killed included Ukrainians, Belarusians, and Jews, including the Chief Rabbi of the Polish Army, Baruch Steinberg. The execution request was approved by Joseph Stalin, and the Soviet foreign minister Vyacheslav Molotov, and 3 Stalin's inner leadership circle.

APPEALING TO THE SPIRIT OF THE NATURAL LAW
**Scenario #1.** Germany -> USSR
Concerning the Spirit of the Natural Law, 1939, the leaders and the people of West Poland could have voiced the same words made by Stalin.

**Scenario #2.** USSR -> Poland
Two weeks later, the East Poland leaders and people could have echoed these words.
*"Comrades, citizens, brothers, and sisters, fighters of the army and Navy, my friends, I appeal to you. "The heinous attack by the Bolshevik criminals continues; what have the fascist Bolsheviks achieved by breaking the Spirit of the Natural Law and attacking the people of Poland? Its troops have achieved an advantageous situation, but politically they have lost because they have revealed themselves to the world to be bloodthirsty aggressors."*

**Scenario #3.** USSR -> Finland
Similarly, the leaders and the people of Finland could have voiced in November 1939.
*"Comrades, citizens, brothers, and sisters, fighters of the army and Navy, my friends, I appeal to you. The heinous attack by the Bolsheviks continues; what has the lawless Bolsheviks achieved by breaking the Spirit of the Natural Law and attacking Finland? Its troops have achieved an advantageous situation, but politically they have lost because they have revealed themselves to the world to be bloodthirsty aggressors."*

**Scenario #4.** USSR -> Estonia, Latvia, Lithuania
Similarly. Estonia. Latvia. Lithuania leaders and people could have voiced these words.
*"Comrades, citizens, brothers, and sisters, fighters of the army and Navy, my friends, I appeal to you. The heinous attack by Soviet Russia continues; what have the Russian Bolsheviks achieved by breaking the Spirit of the Natural Law and attacking the Baltic States? Its troops have achieved an advantageous situation, but politically they have lost because they have revealed themselves t the world to be bloodthirsty aggressors."*

## THE APPEAL FOR MORAL JUSTICE, AGAINST RANDOM EVIL

The point here is that Joseph Stalin appealed to the spirit of moral integrity and human value. Also, at the same time, he was appealing to a "legitimacy of an immoral pact" (Molotov & Ribbentrop Pact) that he had subjectively fantasized about being a self-serving crime against peace, And agreed to and signed it with his own hand, in the company of the Nazi Germany foreign leader Ribbentrop in October 1939.

The R&M Pact was immoral and illegal; it was immoral and subjectively delusional for Joseph Stalin. His appeal to a moral standard with immoral content is not valid. It was a contradiction of rational logic. Therefore, you cannot steal the property of another and appeal to a legitimate rule of law, to claim it as your own. The appeal made by Stalin reveals that his mind and heart were seriously deluded and morally irresponsible. The only organized criminal madman would deliberately commit serious crimes against humanity, and after committing crimes, would appeal to the law to defend his human rights. He expected justice from humanity, yet he was a brutal criminal towards humanity, by his actions destroying millions of human lives.

What was the Stalin appeal based on? His personality cult? Egotism? Or what? Certainly not based on the Spirit of the Natural Law. Stalin had none of it in him. If the law defends the illegitimate appeal and corruption of the lawbreaker, then the law becomes corrupted. Because a property generally does have a legitimate owner, therefore, when Stalin appeals to the people of Russia, with corrupted authority and a backlog of war crimes 1939-1941. The people who believe in the appeal have become partners in corruption and lies. The Soviet leader's intent had agreed to be a partner in crime, to violate the spirit of the moral law, and inflict pain and suffering onto millions of people in the Baltic States and Nordic countries. Stalin was a hardened criminal.

**Scenario #5.**

To go back in time to 1918. There is a legitimate appeal for justice heard, but the sounds are not allowed to be heard. Russian Tsar Nicholas II with his wife Alexandra and their five children, Anastasia, Tatiana, Olga, Maria, and Alexie, with their doctor. And three of their servants, that voluntarily chosen to remain with the family, also the Tsar's personal physician Eugene Botkin, his wife's maid Anna Demidova, and the family's chef, Ivan Kharitonov, and footman, Alexei Trupp, were eventually murdered by their Bolshevik guards on the night of 16/17 July 1918.

Nicholas II and his family could appeal to the Spirit of the Natural Law and deserve to be heard as a legitimate appeal for justice.

*"Comrades, citizens, brothers, and sisters, fighters of the army and Navy, my friends, I appeal to you. The heinous attack by the Bolsheviks continues; what has the lawless Bolsheviks achieved by breaking the Spirit of the Natural Law and attacking Russian Tsar Nicholas II and his innocent family? Its troops have achieved an advantageous situation, but politically they have lost because they have revealed themselves to the world to be bloodthirsty aggressors."*

The evidence is direct and unambiguous to understand. Words are empty without truth, integrity, and moral legitimacy. To make an appeal to the Spirit of the Natural Law for justice, the content of the appeal needs to have legitimacy and integrity. Joseph Stalin, in 1941, had zero legitimacy for a moral appeal to God; he had sold his soul to Satan many times over, from 1900 -1941.

## GOD'S RIGHTEOUS JUDGMENT

> "But because of your stubbornness and your unrepentant heart, you are storing up wrath against yourself for the day of God's wrath, when his righteous judgment will be revealed." "God "will repay each person according to what they have done." [a] To those who by persistence in doing good seek glory, honor, and immortality, he will give eternal life." "But for those who are self-seeking and who reject the truth and follow evil, there will be wrath and anger. There will be trouble and distress for every human being who does evil: first for the Jew, then for the Gentile;" "but glory, honor, and peace for everyone who does good: first for the Jew, then for the Gentile. For God does not show favoritism. "Romans-2:6-11.

Stalin violated and denied the fundamental human rights to millions of innocent civilians, right to life, right to liberty, and right to property. He took away the human rights of millions of innocent people for selfish, megalomaniac egocentric reasons that culminated in the Stalin personality cult. The Soviet Propaganda press continually praised Joseph Stalin, praising him as "Great," "Beloved," "Bold," "Wise," "Inspirer," and "Genius." Whom are they kidding? Nikita Khrushchev's speech to the 20th Congress of the Communist Party of the Soviet Union on February 25, 1956. Khrushchev's speech was sharply critical of the reign of deceased General Secretary and Premier Joseph Stalin, "Secret Speech" to the Twentieth Party Congress famously denounced Stalin's cult of personality.

*"One of those who heard the speech was the young Alexander Yakovlev, later a leading architect of perestroika, who recalled that it shook him to his roots. He sensed Khrushchev was telling the truth, but it was a truth that frightened him. Generations in the Soviet Union had revered Stalin and linked their lives and hopes with him. Now the past was being shattered and what they had all lived by was being destroyed. 'Everything crumbled, never to be made whole again.'"* (Khrushchev, 1953)

The Soviet Communism Worldview illusion was collapsing like a giant hollow clay statute. It failed and collapsed because it was built upon a false premise. The Soviet leaders violated the Spirit of the Natural Law, and offended the Creator of Life and His Written Word.

[22]

# SOVIET CONSPIRACY: WAR AGAINST PEACE

The conspiracy and the aggression of the Soviet Union in 1939 was the implementation of the Soviet Union share in the Nazi German-Soviet Pact of Aggression. Even before the two parties met to discuss the Pact, it was apparently a Crime against Peace conspiracy, intention to rob the innocent with military aggression, and forceful violence. Joseph Stalin was a willing partner in the plan to invade and take the Baltic States and Finland by force and to subjugate them under the totalitarian Soviet domination, just like they did with Poland 1939, Estonia, Latvia, Czechoslovakia from 1940 – 1991.

The Soviets military occupied the Baltic States for 50 years. The intent in the crime against peace and aggression was evident in the Molotov & Ribbentrop Pact. Both parties of the Pact agreed to benefit themselves from the aggression of warfare against the Baltic States and Finland. Many hundreds of thousands of innocent peoples died from the cause of the Nazi German-Soviet Pact of Aggression 1939-41. Why has such blatant crime against peace by the Soviet Union being treated with such indifference and nationalistic pride by the Russian leaders? Also, it was treated with indifference by the Allied forces during 1941-1991? To answer to that question is self-evident. First, there needs to be an established definition of truth and integrity. The absolute definition of what is a natural state, law of nature, and what are natural rights?

THE LAW OF NATURE
The only constraint given by the law of nature is that the rights that we have, the natural rights that we have, we can't give them up to another. It is a human moral responsibility under the Spirit of Natural Law. Nor can we take rights away from others. Under the state of nature, people are not free to take other's life, or their liberty, or their property. Those are the fundamental rights and the responsible, intelligent human character traits that humans are obliged to uphold spiritually. The human response is to be faithful to human qualities, more than animal reactions or responses.

Human beings do not even have the freedom to take their own life or liberty away. That would be morally irresponsible. The nature of the intelligent human mind is to have a free will with liberty, the ability to choose right. They do not have the liberty to violate the spiritual law of nature. They do not have the freedom to take their own life or to sell themselves to slavery. Or to give someone arbitrary power over them. Why is that? Where does such a human spiritual law of nature come from? There are absolute minimal constraints? It comes from the Creator of life. People are the creatures created by God. He has the last property rights to human beings and animals. They are living beings, created with a living soul. Intellect will, imaginations, consciousness, memory, and emotions.

The human mind with intellect and consciousness, created in the image of God. Enables the mind to understand with self-awareness what is right behavior and what is wrong behavior. The exercise of the will, with intelligent consciousness, makes a choice; it chooses to do that which is right. The obstacle to making the right choice can be self-will. Desire wants or coveting someone else's person or property. The mechanism of the self-will can submit the self to a higher cause. Truth, integrity, respect for other people's rights. Therefore, the intelligent, conscious person can quit the self-will, humble themselves, and maintain a respectable human character above the carnal flesh's selfish desires.

### THE STATE OF NATURE HAS A LAW OF NATURE TO GOVERN IT
*"That obliges every one: and reason, which is that law that teaches all mankind, who will but consult it, that being all equal and independent, no one ought to harm another in his life, health, liberty or possessions."* Jock Locke.

Natural rights are inalienable rights. Every human has a property in his own person. Therefore, nobody has any right to but to him/herself. The labor of his body and the work of his hands are also the property of his and her. Ultimately made only possible by the Creator of life.

That is the Spirit of the Natural law. Human Natural rights to live in harmony with the will of the Creator of life. Therefore, totalitarian dictators that are driven by selfish ambitions, populism, and nationalistic forces need to be condemned without any reservations because they are violating the Spirit of the Natural Law, Natural Rights, and the dignity of human life.

Most obviously, human rebellion and lawlessness against the Spirit of the Natural Law sow the seeds of anarchy, which works to do the Nemesis's will on earth. There is an ongoing violent conflict happening in human lives recruitment of people's souls to two opposing forces. Good and evil.

### LYING IS A DAMNING, DESTROYING SIN

"Men run into troubles by their own folly and then fret at the appointments of God." Proverbs 19:3-5.

"Delight is not seemly for a fool — To live in affluence, pleasure, and outward glory, doth not become him, nor suit with him; because prosperity corrupts even wise men and makes fools mad; and because it gives him more opportunity to discover his folly, and to make mischief both to himself and others." Proverbs 19:10.

"The integrity of the upright guides them, but the unfaithful are destroyed by their duplicity." Proverbs 11:3. (NIV)

"Better the poor whose walk is blameless than the rich whose ways are perverse." Proverbs 28:6. (NIV)

"The Lord detests lying lips, but he delights in people who are trustworthy." Proverbs 12:22. (NIV)

"To do what is right and just is more acceptable to the Lord than sacrifice." Proverbs 21:3. (NIV)

## STEALING AND LYING

"If a thief is found breaking in and is struck so that he dies, there shall be no bloodguilt for him, but if the sun has risen on him, there shall be bloodguilt for him. He shall surely pay. If he has nothing, then he shall be sold for his theft." Exodus 22:2-3. (ESV)

"The Lord saw that the wickedness of man was great in the earth and that every intention of the thoughts of his heart was only evil continually." Genesis 6:5. (ESV)
"Whoever walks with the wise becomes wise, but the companion of fools will suffer harm." Proverbs 13:20. (ESV)

"There is swearing, lying, murder, stealing, and committing adultery; they break all bounds, and bloodshed follows bloodshed." Hosea 4:2. (ESV)

"There are six things that the Lord hates, seven that are an abomination to him: haughty eyes, a lying tongue, and hands that shed innocent blood, a heart that devises wicked plans, feet that make haste to run to evil, a false witness who breathes out lies, and one who sows discord among brothers." Proverbs 6:16-19. (ESV)

"The Lord tests the righteous, but his soul hates the wicked and the one who loves violence." Psalm 11:5. (ESV)

## THE CORRUPTION OF THE ALLIED FORCES

A comparison of war crime/genocide committed by the Soviet Union against the Polish nationals in 1940.

Here is a comparison between the Soviet Union 1940 war crimes/ genocide against the Polish Nationals. And the Imperial Japanese Navy and Air Forces surprise attack against the United States naval base at Pearl Harbor. The point is the scale of the atrocity and damage, the severity of the attack by the aggressor.

When does it cross the war crimes red line? When is the declaration of war justified? Where is the red line boundary of lawlessness? The Spirit of the Natural Law is real. Natural rights come from human life intrinsic value. Why is it important for people everywhere to have a responsible moral duty for humanity?

The nationalism that is corrupted by the Soviet Union – Russia was, is not worthy of people's respect. It becomes a corrupted totalitarian lawless Pariah State. It has no authority to be in the government of millions of law respecting people. Truth respecting people deserve honest leaders, not corrupted criminals. Nationalism then becomes a dirty, corrupted word.

> "Righteousness exalts a nation, But sin is a disgrace to any people." Proverbs 14:34.

Where does the justified war action begin? Is it determined by political will? Do aggression and violence have any connection to justified war?

During World War 2, and after it, the Allied forces did not look or understand the European side Worldview, or did they seek true justice with the Spirit of the Natural Law. They presumed their own opportunistic imperialistic worldview as being a God-given privilege. Whereby their own self-interest and righteousness with their affectionate emotions justified the turning of the blind eye to the Soviet Union war crimes 1939-45. The Allied forces were not open or interested in real justice according to the Spirit of the Natural Law, but slightly more driven by their subjective victor's justice.

There are many examples in this book that points out the failures with evidence that the Imperials were playing the end game toward their own interest goals. They used law and justice to condemn the weaker and the lesser in the political power game. Moreover, turned a blind eye when the Imperial Super States commit genocide and war crimes. That is a grave crime of corruption globally, which means that corruption will continue to corrode the metal of the bridges in the International law, and no one is making an effort to renew and rebuild stronger bridges that can take and carry a load of the Spirit of the Natural Law true justice.

The Soviet Red Army's invasion of Eastern Poland on September 17, 1939, by a secret protocol of the Nazi German-Soviet Pact of Aggression, rendered the Polish plan of defense obsolete. The German-Soviet Frontier Treaty was a second supplementary protocol of the 1939 Hitler-Stalin Pact (known as the German-Soviet Treaty of Nonaggression. It was a secret clause as amended on September 28, 1939, by Nazi Germany and the Soviet Union after their joint invasion and occupation of sovereign Poland. It was signed by Joachim von Ribbentrop and Vyacheslav Molotov, the foreign ministers of Germany and the Soviet Union, in the presence of Joseph Stalin. The treaty was a follow-up to the first secret protocol of the Molotov– Ribbentrop Pact signed on August 23, 1939, between the two countries before their invasion of Poland and the start of World War II in Europe.

By September 17, the Polish defense was already broken, and the only hope was to retreat and reorganize along the Romanian Bridgehead. However, these plans were rendered obsolete nearly overnight, when the over 800,000-strong Soviet Red Army entered and created the Belarusian and Ukrainian fronts after invading the eastern regions of Poland in violation of the Riga Peace Treaty, the Soviet-Polish Non-Aggression Pact, and other international treaties, both bilateral and multilateral. (Invasion, Invasion of Poland, 1939)

[23]

# WAR CRIMES AND GENOCIDE

According to the Polish Institute of National Remembrance, Soviet occupation between 1939 and 1941 resulted in the death of 150,000 and deportation of 320,000 of Polish citizens, when all who were deemed dangerous to the Soviet regime were subject to Sovietization, forced resettlement, imprisonment in labor camps (the Gulags) or murdered, like the Polish nationals in the Katyn massacre. The Katyn massacre was prompted by NKVD chief Lavrentiy Beria's proposal to execute all captive members of the Polish officer corps, dated March 5, 1940, approved by the Politburo of the Communist Party of the Soviet Union, including its leader, Joseph Stalin and the Soviet Union foreign minister Vyacheslav Molotov.

- The number of victims is estimated at 22,000.
- The victims were executed in the Katyn Forest in Soviet Russia, the Kalinin and Kharkiv prisons, and elsewhere.
- Of the total killed: about 8,000 were officers imprisoned during the 1939 Soviet invasion of Poland,
- 6,000 were police officers,
- Polish intelligentsia that the Soviets deemed to be *"intelligence agents, gendarmes, landowners, saboteurs, factory owners, lawyers, officials, and priests."*

Would the Katyn massacre genocide, and war crimes be sufficient reason to declare war on those that perpetrated the crimes against humanity? If the crime were done against Britain, United States, France or the Soviet Union, it is reasonable to think that such unprovoked attack would be viewed as an insult to their nation. The human and material loss would be sufficient reason to declare war on the perpetrators. After the loss of the Pearl Harbor battleships, Navy vessels, the human loss of 2,403 Americans lives, and 1,178 wounded was a sufficient reason for American leaders to declare war on Japan. Is the American and British Western logic and reasoning at fault to declare war on those that attack them? It is a matter of Imperialist National pride; they would defend themselves if anyone dares to attack them. The above conclusion is right, that which is valid and justified war for the Imperialists, why then would it not be valid and justified for the smaller nations to do likewise? If they have the opportunity to do so.

DIFFERENT LOGIC APPLIED TO THE SMALLER POWERS

- Finland defended itself by a preemptive strike, hitting back at the war criminals, the perpetrators of the war against peace in 1939 to 1940.
- Finland military took back the territory that rightfully belonged to the 400,000 civilians inhabiting the Finnish Karelian municipality. The Karelian civilians were forced to evacuate in 1939. On the other hand, Joseph Stalin and the USSR military Generals committed war crimes during 1939-1940, they initiated the aggressive war against peace, in Poland and Finland.
- The USSR was operating under the Nazi German-Soviet Pact of Aggression (1939-1941). They were committing a conspiracy to do crime against innocent civilians, to the Baltic States and Finland.
- Where is the whistle? And who will blow it? War against peace is a war crime.
- Thousands of people perished due to the Nazi German-Soviet Pact of Aggression. The Soviets committed genocide in 1940, 22,000 Polish National prisoners were executed within two months.

It was a deliberate movement of anarchy from the 1917 to 1939 Bolsheviks lawlessness worldview and Joseph Stalin track record of crime and extreme violence. At the same time, France, England, United States were indifferent, and some 14 months later they became allies with those war criminals and providing the USSR with enormous amounts of military support. The Allied forces leaders were blind or repressing the true spiritual reality of the USSR leadership. What were the Allied forces thinking? Of the Russian events in 1917, 1922, 1936-38, 1939

-1941? There is an enormous river of blood flowing from Russia, during that time period. Did anyone in France, England, and the United States consider the Spirit of the Natural Law? Why would they become allies with such record of lawlessness? (1917 -1941). Where was the Creator of Life (Elohim) during those years? The Spirit of the Natural Law was active on the planet earth. And people in the western world went to church to worship God on their Shabbat. The moral error comes through humanism and subjective relativism. They trust their own mind understanding more than the principles taught in the Jewish Holy Scriptures, The Torah.

> "So be careful to do as the LORD your God has commanded you; you are not to turn aside to the right or to the left. You must walk in all the ways that the LORD your God has commanded you, so that you may live and prosper and prolong your days in the land you will possess." Deuteronomy 5:33 -32.

Stalin used criminal style extortion, he threatened to continue the 1940 aggressive war and made extreme territory demands. 1940 Moscow treaty was illegal; it used the threat of war as a lever for extortion of Finland territory. The Karelian Isthmus territory that had been inhabited for centuries by Finnish Karelian civilians. Why did the Allied forces punish the preemptive self-defense action of Finland in 1941, by taking the Finland government representatives to courts of law in 1945 and 1946? And jailing them with long sentences? Why?

Because the Soviet Union Joseph Stalin wanted it that way, in the same spirit as the 1939 Nazi German-Soviet Pact of Aggression. It was the Allied forces hypocrisy, corruption and double standards of Victors justice. But it is not good enough, it stinks to high heaven like an imperial dead carcass.

1. We could call it the Molotov and Stettinius Pact for the United States in 1945.
2. Or the Molotov and Mabane Pact for England 1945.
3. Or the Molotov and Pineau Pact for France 1945.

After their respective foreign ministers, uniting a pact with the Soviet Union foreign minister Molotov, for their united leisure of enjoying some cocktails. Whichever the case, the Allied forces had their tail between their legs when dealing with Joseph Stalin. And it was much easier to punish the small, the weak, and the innocent, that bring a severe war criminal to justice. They were inconsistent with the Spirit of the Natural Law. They apply one opportunistic rule law for themselves and impose another letter of the law for other peoples. To suit their own situation and circumstance. The truth is the Imperial pride, moral corruption, and self-righteous hypocrisy. Western Allied forces did not allow others to have the same privilege as they exercise themselves, for a preemptive strike for self- defense purpose. Here is one instance example of how the Allied forces hypocritically punished the small nation of Finland (population 3.1 Million)for taking a stand against the Soviet Union tyranny during 1939-1945. The responsible, consistent pattern of Finland government between 1917 to 1941 can be seen on the timeline. Considering Finland was invaded by Russia in 1707, and it became a subject of the Russian Monarchy rule for 100 years.

Finland declared to independent and free Grand Duchy of Finland Russian in 1917.
Tartu Peace agreement 1920. The treaty confirmed that the Finnish-Soviet border would follow the old border between the autonomous Grand Duchy of Finland and Imperial Russia.
1939 Nazi German-Soviet Pact of Aggression against the Baltic States, Finland, and the East Europe States. Was immoral, and organized a criminal conspiracy.
The aggressive war against Finland November 1939-40. Extortion with threats of continued war to surrender Karelian Isthmus territory to Soviet union including the city of Vyborg.
March 1940. Finland reluctantly, under further threat of war, agreed to the Soviet extortion and ceded 10% of Finland total territory to the Soviets.
June 1941 Finland takes back that which the Despotic Soviet leader Stalin extorted from them. by the threats of

continuation war. The 1920 borders of the legal Tartu Peace agreement was reached by Finland military within two weeks.

The above history timeline between 1917 – 1940 of Finland government is law respecting and legitimate. Finland was not an aggressor. Unlike the history of Imperial England, France, Russia, Sweden, or the United States in principle. They were the aggressors and making alliances with other aggressors. The history of Soviet Union between 1917 – 1940 is a murderous, bloody mess. Total lawlessness and anarchy. And the Allied forces went to bed with the bloodthirsty Bolsheviks. They called Stalin the "Good Old Joe." The Americans were naive, ignorant of the Bolsheviks 1917 to 1941 history.

The primary focal point regarding the violation of the rule of law and justice should have been the Immoral, criminal conspiracy made between Joseph Stalin and Adolf Hitler. That was a criminal conspiracy, a serious crime against the peace of the Baltic States and East Europe. The division of Poland between Germany and the Soviet Union was a severe crime against peace. It should have been stopped as a war crime there and then in 1939. Without waiting for the Western Utilitarian philosophy opportunities to advance themselves. If the 1939 Nazi German-Soviet Pact of Aggression had been stopped and condemned, with the support of the wider world, then the outcome would have been different. There would not have been the aggressive war by the Soviet Union against Finland in 1939.

Furthermore, there would not have been the slaughter of the 22,000 Polish nationals by the Soviets in April -May 1940. And the World War 2 would not have erupted and evolved the way it did. The Soviets would not have a partner in crime. Why was nothing said about the Soviet Union role in the Nazi German-Soviet Pact of Aggression conspiracy? The American did not believe it. Even after, they were told the truth by those that knew the nature and the traits of the real enemy, the Nemesis.

Roosevelt was told about the 1940 Katyn Forest massacre, but he refused to believe it. He trusted his own understanding more than those that had witnessed it. Similarly, President Bush looked into the eyes of the ex-Soviet KGB agent and said that there was a good man in there. "The Slovenian Summit was the first meeting between the U.S. President George W. Bush and the Russian President Vladimir Putin. It took place on June 16, 2001. At the closing press conference, in response to a question about whether he could trust Putin, Bush said,

"I looked the man in the eye. I found him very straightforward and trustworthy – I was able to get a sense of his soul." Bush's top security aide Condoleezza Rice later wrote that Bush's phrasing had been a serious mistake. "We were never able to escape the perception that the president had naïvely trusted Putin and then been betrayed." (Encyclopedia, Slovenia Summit 2001)

Next page map modified. Copyright © KARTTAKESKUS.fi

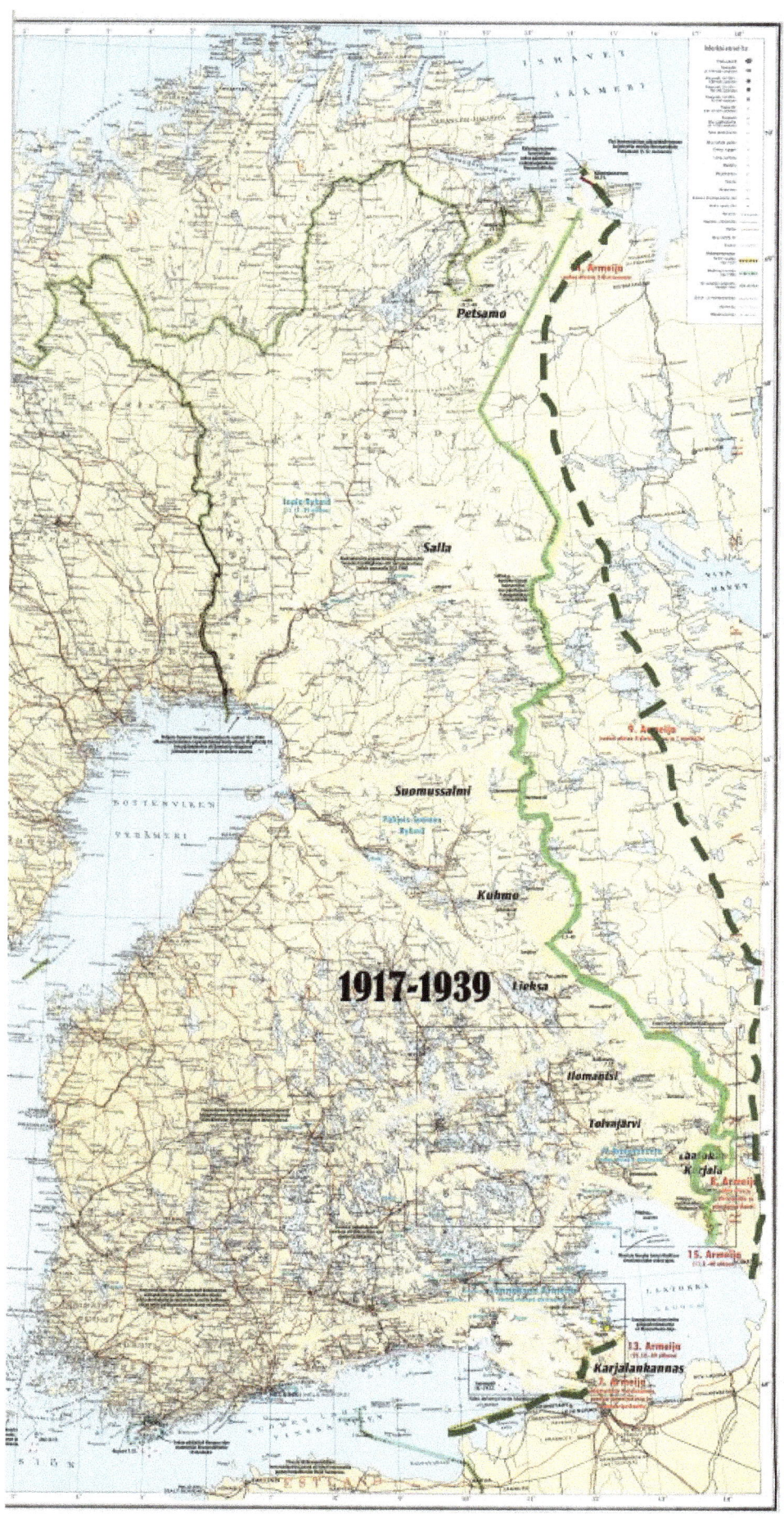

## WESTERN UTILITARIAN HYPOCRISY

However, the injustice gets much worse. Finland exercises her right to take preventative action against totalitarian despotic Soviet leaders in 1941. Finland drives the Soviet troops back to the legitimate borders of 1920, with the necessary military hardware supplies from Germany. For almost three years the borders remain stationary in the 1920 border trench positions. Finland attempts no significant new territory in the Karelian Isthmus. The 10% of the total area which was extorted from Finland in 1940 is claimed back. During the years 1941-45, England and the United States supply the Soviet Union with vast amounts of military equipment, planes, trucks, jeeps, clothing, boots, and food. They were directly assisting the totalitarian despotic war criminal. Why did they assist the severe war criminal? Because the Alliance forces naïve subjective self-interest. Without respecting the guidance of the Spirit of the Natural Law.

By 1945 Germany is defeated by the United Allied forces led by the United States, the British, France and pushed back from Russia by the Soviet Union forces to Berlin. The Soviet Union fury and revenge burned for a time and refocused up north to punish Finland for taking back what was legal, morally and rightfully belonged to the people of Finland. But the porcelain pride on Joseph Stalin head and shoulders had cracked and chipped, so he felt that he had to regain his former status as the father of the shining sun over the Soviet Union.

## SOVIET STALIN EXTORTION 1939-1940

With fire and fury, the Katyusha multiple rocket launchers, and long-range artillery, and the air bombers line up at the front line, to soften up the defenses and make a run for it with the Soviet T34 tanks, to break through the Finnish defenses across the Karelian Isthmus, from Lake Ladoga to the Gulf of Finland. Borders After Stalin Extortion 1940.

Next Page map modified. Copyright © KARTTAKESKUS.fi

## SOVIET ARTILLERY AT THE MAIN DEFENSE LINE 1944

"On 9 June 1944, the Soviet Leningrad Front launched a strategic offensive against Finnish positions on the Karelian Isthmus and the Lake Ladoga shores.

On the 21.7 km (13.5 mi)-wide breakthrough focus segment, the Red Army concentrated 3,000 guns and mortars. In some places, the concentration of artillery pieces exceeded 200 guns for every kilometer of the front or one for every 5 m (5.5 yds). Soviet artillery fired over 80,000 rounds along the front at the Karelian Isthmus. On the second day of the offensive, the artillery barrages and a superior number of Soviet forces crushed the main Finnish defense line."

"On 25 June, the Red Army reached the third line of defense, the Viipuri–Kuparsaari–Taipale line (VKT line), and the decisive Battle of Tali-Ihantala began, described as the most significant battle in Nordic military history.

At the end of 1944, the Finnish Army had retreated back to the city of Vyborg to approximately the same line of defense they had held at the end of the Winter War". ... (Encyclopedia, Continuation War 1941, 1941)

## CASUALTIES FROM THE SECOND PHASE OF THE 1939 SOVIET CONSPIRACY

A sizeable number of civilians who had been displaced after the Winter War had moved back into Karelia during the 1941 Continuation War. They had to be evacuated again;

of the 260,000 civilians who had moved back East with the continuation of war into the Karelia, only 19 chose to remain and become Soviet citizens.

Most of the Ingrian Finns together with Votes and Izhorians living in German-occupied Ingria had been evacuated to Finland in 1943–1944.

After the armistice, Finland was forced to return the evacuees.

Soviet authorities did not allow the 55,733 Karelia returnees to settle back in Ingria and instead deported them to central regions of the USSR.

According to Finnish historians, the casualties of the Finnish Defense Forces from 1941 to 1944 amounted to:

- 63,204 dead or missing
- 158,000 wounded.

A detailed list of Finnish dead is as follows:

- Dead and buried 33,565;
- Wounded, died of wounds 12,820;
- Dead, not buried, declared as dead 4,251;
- Missing, declared as dead 3,552;
- Died as prisoners of war 473;
- Other reasons (diseases, accidents, suicides) 7,932;
- Unknown 611.

## THE SOVIETS TIGHTENED THE SCREWS OF EXTORTION

The absurdity of the victor's justice to further punish those that dared to stand up against the Soviet dictator Stalin, along with the Allied forces they took the Axis powers to the courtrooms and judged them according to the victor's justice. Moreover, threw their imperialistic Super State self-righteousness evidence at them. It was their own nationalistic short-sighted pride and arrogance, without respect for the Spirit of the Natural Law.

The Soviet Union was the other half in the Nazi German-Soviet Pact of Aggression conspiracy, that caused loss of human life, and damage on a massive scale, in the Baltic States, East Europe, and Finland. Then only five short years later they, the USSR had morphed out of the Nazi German-Soviet Pact of Aggression, as if they were never part of it. That is corruption in England, France, the United States and the Russian leadership.

## DIALECTIC METAMORPHOSIS

*"Metamorphosis is a biological process by which an animal physically develops after birth or hatching, involving a*

*conspicuous and relatively abrupt change in the animal's body structure through cell growth and differentiation. Metamorphosis is iodothyronine-induced and an ancestral feature of all chordates".*

- 1905. Russians go through a metamorphosis and become Bolsheviks. Russians conspicuous and relatively abrupt change in their worldview and life philosophy structure, the transformation happens through Bolsheviks propaganda.
- For a time, 1905 -1922 they are the Bolshevik creatures.
- Further transformation, the metamorphosis continues, and they are turned into the Soviets by Joseph Stalin. They are marching to conquer the world for the sake of communism.
- The metamorphosis process has not stopped, (1939 – 1941) the Soviet leadership have committed themselves to march together and live in the same hive with the Nazi German-Soviet Pact of Aggression. The Soviets together with Nazi Germany are going to pillage East Europe and Finland.
- They march, pillage and destroy life together in the Nazi German-Soviet Pact of Aggression. Hundreds of thousands of lives are destroyed in Poland 1939, Finland from 1939 to 1940, and the Baltic States from 1940 to 1941.
- The Russian metamorphosis does not stop there. The Russian bear of 1900 – 1941, deeds of lawlessness, anarchy, genocide, war crimes, goes through a metamorphosis in the eyes of the Allied forces (England, France, United States) and now flies like a butterfly.
- The red-winged butterfly with a sickle and a hammer on its wings, lands on Franklin Roosevelt's shoulder, and Winston Churchill call out., don't move Frank! that's a keeper. We can sure use that on the home front.
- The red-winged butterfly is so adorable in the eyes of Franklin Roosevelt and Winston Churchill. They can't believe the historical facts that the East European people are telling them about the Russian metamorphosis during the years of 1900 to 1922. 1922 to 1939. So, they refuse to believe anything that is outside of their immediate interest.
- The Nuremberg International court is a convenient environment for the red-winged butterfly to flutter out of the window. Out of sight, out of mind.
- The partners in crime, Nazi German-Soviet Pact of Aggression. Their legal representatives are in the same space again; the only difference is that Joseph Stalin is in the will of Nemesis. And, Satan has pulled off the metamorphosis trick on the minds of the Allied forces. The Russian leaders are viewed as a red-winged butterfly, that has changed form, during the metamorphosis.
- The Russian metamorphosis continues with the theme of global Communism. They use their socialist philosophical influence over the other communist countries.
- The Berlin Blockade (24 June 1948–12 May 1949).
- Followed by the Korean War. 25 June 1950 – 27 July 1953).
- Vietnam War. 1 November 1955 to the fall of Saigon on 30 April 1975.
- Afghanistan War. December 1979 to February 1989.
- Russian Crimea annexation 2014.
- Russian engages in the Syria Civil War 2015.

At Nuremberg International court 1945 to 46, the Russian prosecutors accuse the guilty Nazi officers of their part in the 1939 Molotov & Ribbentrop Pact conspiracy. Their role in the aggressive war against peace in Poland from 1939 to 1941. Moreover, they also falsely blame others for the damage that they themselves had inflicted on the innocent civilians. 1940 Moscow peace agreement with Finland was criminal extortion, with threats for the war to continue if the Stalin terms of the peace agreement were not accepted and territory surrendered to the Soviets. 10% of the total Finland land area had to surrender to the Soviets. The 1939 Soviet aggression was the conspired criminal intent. The Imperial Western forces, England, France, United States, and generally Europe said nothing. Lawlessness could dictate the course of history for millions of innocent civilians in Europe.

## WAR REPARATION PAYMENTS

There were war reparations demanded by Soviet Stalin after both wars. After 1939 to 1940 war. At the Moscow terms of peace discussions, Stalin used extortion by the threat of continuation of war as leverage, to get large areas of land including 3 cities. Entire Islands, 38 municipalities. Enso wood pulp factory. Machinery from the Karelian Isthmus, 75 locomotives, and 2000 train cars was demanded by the Soviets as conditions for peace. It was appeasement for the Soviet-organized criminals.

The second lot of appeasements came in 1945. They wanted more of Finland territory, machinery, ships, trains, and much more. And the Allied forces were complicit to the Soviet Stalin extortion both occasion. 1940 and 1945. The Soviet demand for $600 million in reparations made in the spring of 1945 was reduced to $300 million. After the ceasefire, the USSR, however, insisted that the payments should be based on 1938 prices, which doubled the amount. Stalin was a shrewd, hard-hearted, ruthless demon for the cause of the Nemesis.

## NAZI GERMAN-SOVIET PACT OF AGGRESSION

The first conspiracy in 1939 between the Joseph Stalin and Adolf Hitler causes large-scale catastrophic damage to people and States that did not want anything to do with the Imperial politics of the Super States. The Soviet culprits that caused half of the damage in Europe walked away without even admitting their part in the conspiracy, the genocide, and war crimes, Stalin simply denied everything. Moreover, the Allied forces protected Joseph Stalin from admitting his role in the conspiracy, almost as if given amnesty.

The disrespect to the Spirit of the Natural Law did boomerang back to the Western Alliance, especially the Americans. They did pay with time and money after the Soviets Joseph Stalin withdrew back into the shell behind the iron curtain, and the Nemesis was back on the throne. It was beginning of the cold war of denial, the Soviets repressed the Spirit of the Natural Law, and suppressed people's voices from speaking out in the name of God for the truth. The new phase began with the suffering of hundreds of thousands of political prisoners denied their freedom to believe as the Creator of life intended for them to believe.

## THE WESTERN COLD WAR BACK-FLIP

What happened to their spirit of triumphalism that they gloated over the Axis Powers? They were quick to condemn the Nazi war criminals at Nuremberg because it was their direct enemy and turned a blind eye to the other war criminal guilty of the same war crimes and genocide during 1939-1941. They drank from the same cup as the victors with the despotic Soviet Joseph Stalin, that denied millions of people their right to life, and others liberty and denied almost everybody property. Self-interest ruled the actions of England, France, and the United States during 1941-1944. The bilateral damage were civilians on the fringes.

## CIVILIAN TARGETS. THE BATTLE OF HAMBURG

*"The Battle of Hamburg, codenamed Operation Gomorrah, was a campaign of air raids beginning 24 July 1943 and lasting for 8 days and 7 nights." "Operation Gomorrah killed 42,600 people, left 37,000 wounded and caused approx. One million German civilians to flee the city. The city's labor force was reduced by ten percent. Approximately 3,000 aircraft were deployed, 9,000 tons of bombs were dropped, and over 250,000 homes and houses were destroyed."*

*"Dwellings destroyed amounted to 214,350 out of 414,500. Hamburg was hit by air raids another 69 times before the end of World War II. In total, the RAF dropped 22,580 long tons of bombs on Hamburg."* (Wikipedia, The Battle of Hamburg, 1945)

## THE BATTLE OF DRESDEN

*"The bombing of Dresden was a British/American aerial bombing attack on the city of Dresden, in four raids between 13 and 15 February 1945, 722 heavy bombers of the British Royal Air Force (RAF) and 527 of the United States Army Air Forces (USAAF) dropped more than 3,900 tons of high-explosive bombs and incendiary devices on the city.*

*The bombing and the resulting firestorm destroyed over 1,600 acres (6.5 km2) of the city center. An estimated 22,700 to 25,000 people were killed, although larger casualty figures have been claimed."* (Encyclopedia, The battle of Dresden, 1945)

### SPIRIT OF THE NATURAL LAW JUSTICE

The keyword here is justice. What is justice? Justice is a rational human mind application of decisions, based on moral virtue. A decision that is not based on self-interest, but rather on real justice.

*"The idea of justice occupies center stage both in ethics and in legal and political philosophy. We apply it to individual actions, to laws, and to public policies, and we think in each case that if they are unjust, this is a strong, maybe even conclusive reason to reject them."* (Stanford-Edu, 2018) Justice and fairness should govern all human actions; human actions should be contained within the moral frame of justice.

### WHAT IS A PERPETRATOR?

*"A person who perpetrates, or commits an illegal, criminal, or evil act: The perpetrators of this heinous crime must be found and punished to the fullest extent of the law."*

*Millions voiced the above lamentation during 1939-1945. We can still read and hear the logic of lament, "The perpetrators of this heinous crime must be found and punished to the fullest extent of the law." But it was only voiced by those people that were inflicted. Nobody listened to the lament of the Baltic States people during 1939-1941. "The perpetrators of this heinous crime must be found and punished to the fullest extent of the law."*

There were no Super Powers built or motivated by the principles of Justice. They were all guilty of self-interest and selfish gain. The Imperial States grow stronger and more prominent, they use their arrogance and muscle to push others out of their smug way. They are utterly blind to the reality of their arrogance and pride that is the cause of World Wars. Their politically correct foreign ministers always holler,

*"The perpetrators of this heinous crime must be found and punished to the fullest extent of the law."*

In their board meetings, they discuss how to maximize the circumstances of the occasion. From 1939 to 1940 it was to do nothing to the victims of war crimes. Allow the Soviet dictator to run his course, has his way. In 1941-1944 they concentrated their resources to assist the War criminal Joseph Stalin, because of the convenience of the circumstances. They did not consider the principles of the rule of law and the Spirit of the Natural Law justice. How should the people of the world consider the Imperial powers such as England, France, United States? These superpowers indeed presume their self-righteousness. They have claimed for 75 years to have a high moral ground. Is there any spirit of truth in their presumptions claims?

They have brainwashed the Western World with the Western Hollywood style propaganda. The cliché about the German evil, and the opposed Imperial goodness. They have whitewashed themselves and their deeds like the Imperial whitewashed tombs. They found a convenient scapegoat during the World War 1 and World War 2. Oversimplified and polarized the reality of the spiritual battle in the heart and mind of humanity. When the Nemesis could no longer rage with the destructive muscle of the Nazi Germany military, it merely stepped out of the boots and into the boots of the Soviets war machine. The only prerequisite for the nemesis to enter was lawlessness. The Nemesis seeks out human hearts and minds are given to lawlessness, immorality, sin, wickedness, corruption, depravity, deceit, lies, and evil. Willing servants to do wholeheartedly deceitful deeds to the life on the planet earth, whether living plants, living animals, or human beings. It is a process of corruption that the Nemesis gains access to the human living soul.

### THE IMPERIAL SUPERPOWERS EXERCISE LAWLESSNESS

The Imperial Powers form alliances and fabricate their own rules and regulations that advance their interests. They use military power as a license to commit immoral deeds against innocent people on the fringes. The Soviets were guilty of genocide and war crimes; the Western Alliance protected the war criminal Joseph Stalin. The Soviets falsely accused the not guilty in the Nuremberg trials, regarding the Katyn Forest massacre, while in fact, they themselves had committed the genocide and the war crimes against the 22,000 Polish nationals in 1940.

[24]

# WAR RESPONSIBILITY TRIALS IN FINLAND

Finland War Responsibility Trials

The War Responsibility trials were conducted from November 1945 through February 1946 by a special court consisting of the presidents of the Supreme Court of Finland, the Supreme Administrative Court of Finland, a professor from the University of Helsinki, and twelve M.P.s appointed by the Parliament of Finland. It all sounds very proper, so did the open to media courts in Moscow 1936-1938, part of the Stalin purges, where people were forced to admit crimes that they had never committed.

Accused Status Punishment

- Risto Ryti Jukka Rangell 25th prime minister of Finland 6 years in prison 5th President of Finland 10 years in prison
- Edwin Linkomies 28th prime minister of Finland 5 years and six months in prison
- Väinö Tanner cabinet minister
- Toivo Kivimäki Finland's ambassador to Germany 5 years in prison
- Henrik Ramsay cabinet minister two years and six months in prison
- Antti Kukkonen cabinet minister two years in prison
- Tyko Reinikka cabinet minister two years in prison

## CRIMINALIZATION

Criminalization in criminology is the process by which behaviors and individuals are transformed into crime and criminals.

The Western Powers discriminated and demonized against anyone that was on the same side as the Germans. The West mindset was an overly simplified and self-centered worldview. They could not relate to the Baltics or the Nordic countries that have a long 700 years history regarding the Russians that attempt to invade any space that is left unchecked for a moment. The West selfishly protected a war criminal Joseph Stalin because it was advantageous to their Western interests. Moreover, as soon as the opportunity came for the blame game, they were there blaming anyone that had long-standing relations with German as a nation. They condemn the innocent in the name of the British Imperialism. They also had a discriminating worldview, as Imperialists naturally do.

Germany, from 1917 – 1918, played a decisive role in supporting Finland against the Bolshevik's absolute anarchy that flared during the Russian revolution and spread into East Europe and to Finland. Germany also was instrumental in supplying military equipment against the overwhelming totalitarian military State of the Soviet Union. The British could not relate laterally to anyone else except their Imperial interests and self-righteousness.

## CRIME

What is a crime? Just because the Western Imperialists call something a crime, or someone a criminal, and indict them for crimes, that is not necessarily so. Therefore, an exact definition is needed to stay on track with reasoning and logic. In ordinary language, a crime is an unlawful act punishable by a state or other authority. The term "crime" does not, in modern criminal law, have any simple and universally accepted definition, though statutory definitions have been provided for specific purposes. The common view is that crime is a category created by law; in other words, something is a crime if declared as such by the relevant and applicable law. The law of the land can be abused by dictators. One proposed definition is that a crime or offense (or criminal offense) is an act harmful not only to some individual but also to a community, society or the state ("a public wrong"). Such acts are forbidden and punishable by law.

## THE ALLIED CONTROL COMMISSION

The Allied Control Commission and the Communist Party of Finland raised the issue of the trials repeatedly during the spring and summer of 1945. They had their own skin in the game.

When the Treaty of London (London Charter) on August 8, 1945, defined three types of crimes:

1. war crimes
2. crimes against peace
3. crimes against humanity

On September 11, the parliament passed a law enabling the prosecution of those responsible for the 1941-1944 war. The Supreme Court of Finland and leading judicial experts protested the law as conflicting with the constitution of Finland and contrary to Western judicial principles (it was designed to apply retroactively), but they did not comment on the political necessity of it.

The Finnish public regarded it as a mockery of the rule of law. Juho Kusti Paasikivi, who was the prime minister of Finland at the time, known to have stated that the conditions of the armistice concerning this matter disregarded all laws. (Encyclopedia, Allied Commission, 1944)

## PARALLELS: SOVIET UNION 1939-40

- war crimes
- crimes against peace
- crimes against humanity

## MOLOTOV RIBBENTROP PACT 1939

Also known as the Nazi German-Soviet Pact of Aggression.

*"The pact delineated the spheres of interest between the two powers, confirmed by the additional protocol of the German-Soviet Frontier Treaty amended after the joint invasion of Poland."*

*"In addition to stipulations of non-aggression, the treaty included a secret protocol that divided territories of Poland, Lithuania, Latvia, Estonia, Finland, and Romania into German and Soviet "spheres of influence," anticipating "territorial and political rearrangements" of these countries."*

*"The Soviet Union sought to obtain parts of Finnish territory, demanding—among other concessions—that Finland cedes substantial border territories in exchange for land elsewhere, claiming security reasons, primarily the protection of Leningrad, 32 km (20 mi) from the Finnish border. Finland refused, and the USSR invaded the country."*

*"The League of Nations deemed the attack illegal and expelled the Soviet Union from the League."* (Molotov-Ribbentrop-Pact, 1939)

## EX POST FACTO LAWS

*"[Latin, "After-the-fact" laws.] Laws that provide for the infliction of punishment upon a person for some prior act that, at the time it was committed, was not illegal."*

"*Ex post facto laws retroactively change the rules of evidence in a criminal case, retroactively alter the definition of a crime, retroactively increase the punishment for a criminal act, or punish conduct that was legal when committed.*"

"*They are prohibited by the Article I, Section 10, Clause 1, of the U.S. Constitution. An ex-post-facto law is considered a hallmark of tyranny because it deprives people of a sense of what behavior will or will not be punished and allows for random punishment at the whim of those in power.*" (Legal-Dictionary, 2018)

"*The prohibition of ex-post-facto laws was imperative in colonial America. The Framers of the Constitution understood the importance of such a prohibition, considering the historical tendency of government leaders to abuse power. As Alexander Hamilton observed, "It is easy for men … to be zealous advocates for the rights of the citizens when others invade them, and as soon as they have it in their power to become the invaders themselves."*

"*The desire to thwart abuses of power also inspired the Framers of the Constitution to prohibit bills of attainder, which are laws that inflict punishment on named individuals or easily ascertainable members of a group without the benefit of a trial. Both ex-post facto laws and bills of attainder deprive those subject to them of due process of law—that is, of notice and an opportunity to be heard before being deprived of life, liberty, or property.*" (Legal-Dictionary, 2018)

"The Ex post facto laws, after the fact laws, is one more evidence of the Soviet Union corruption despotism. How they manipulated the circumstances to attain their selfish goals without any respect for the Spirit of the Natural Law. They started with an erroneous life philosophy and a false worldview in 1917-1922. From 1922- 1939, they had matured into an organized criminal movement, with no moral conscience left in them.

"*On March 5 1940, pursuant to a note to Joseph Stalin from Beria, six members of the Soviet Politburo. Stalin, Vyacheslav Molotov, Lazar Kaganovich, Kliment Voroshilov, Anastas Mikoyan, and Mikhail Kalinin signed an order to execute 25,700 Polish "nationalists and counterrevolutionaries" kept at camps and prisons in occupied western Ukraine and Belarus.*" (Katyn-forest-Massacre, 1940)

"*An investigation conducted by the office of the Prosecutors General of the Soviet Union (1990–1991) and the Russian Federation (1991–2004) confirmed Soviet responsibility for the massacres but refused to classify this action as a war crime or an act of genocide. The investigation was closed on the grounds the perpetrators were dead, and since the Russian government would not classify the dead as victims of the Great Purge, formal posthumous rehabilitation was deemed inapplicable.*" (Katyn-forest-Massacre, 1940)

"*Office of the Prosecutors General of the Soviet Union….and the Russian Federation ………..confirmed Soviet responsibility for the massacres but refused to classify this action as a war crime or an act of genocide.*"

In November 2010, the Russian State Duma approved a declaration blaming Stalin and other Soviet officials for ordering the massacre. Here we see a direct double standard, "*confirmed Soviet responsibility for the massacres but refused to classify this action as a war crime or an act of genocide.*"

Yet, in 1945 – 1946, at the Nuremberg trials, 9 of the Nazi Germany war criminals were sentenced to death. On what basis? On the basis of committing grievous war crimes. How come the law was applied to one group of war criminals, and the same law was not applied to another group of war criminals? That is favoritism, partiality, injustice, and cover-up. Inconsistent logic.

REACTION TO 1941 WAR RESPONSIBILITY TRIALS
Most Finns view the War Responsibility Trials as a kangaroo court set up by the Soviet Union to discredit the Finnish wartime leaders since the ex-post-facto law was against the Finnish Constitution. Even worse in the public opinion was the fact that the Soviet leadership, which had conducted a war of aggression, the Winter War, just 19 months before Finland started the Continuation War by attacking the Soviet Union, was not indicted at all, making the whole process hypocritical victor's justice in their view.

"*The conviction of Väinö Tanner did not shatter the Social Democrats as Zhdanov had predicted; on the contrary, it made him a martyr and hardened the anti-communist stance in the party. Communist sympathizers were ousted from the Social Democrats, and control of the labor unions was bitterly contested."*

*"Even President Paasikivi complained to his aide that the convictions handed down in the Trials were one of the biggest stumbling blocks to improving relations between Finland and the Soviet Union."* (Encyclopedia, War-responsibility trials in Finland, 1945)

### THE ALLIED CONTROL COMMISSION

*The Allied Control Commission (ACC) arrived in Finland on September 22, 1944, to observe Finnish compliance with the Moscow Armistice. It consisted of 200 Soviet and 15 British members and was led by Col. Gen. Andrei Zhdanov. Immediately after its inception, the commission required Finland to take more vigorous action to intern the German forces in Northern Finland. Finland's compliance with the commission resulted in a campaign to force out the remaining German troops in the area. Simultaneously, Finland was required to demobilize, which was also required by the commission.* (Encyclopedia, Allied Commission, 1944)

### THE MOSCOW ARMISTICE

The Moscow Armistice was signed between Finland on one side and the Soviet Union and the United Kingdom on the other side on September 19, 1944, ending the Continuation War.

Conditions for peace

The conditions for peace were like the extortion threats that had been reluctantly agreed in the Moscow Peace Treaty of 1940: Finland was obliged to cede all parts of the Karelian Isthmus and the Old Salla Municipality in Lapland, as well as individual islands in the Gulf of Finland. The new armistice also handed all Petsamo Municipality to the Soviet Stalin, and Finland was further compelled to lease the Gulf of Finland port Porkkala to the Soviet Union for fifty years (the area was returned to Finnish control in 1956).

Other conditions included Finnish payment of $300,000,000 ($4.2 billion in today's U.S. dollars) in the form of various commodities over six years to the Soviet Union as war reparations. Finland also agreed to legalize the Communist Party of Finland (after it had made some changes to the party rules) and ban the ones that the Soviet Union considered fascist. Further, the individuals that the Soviets considered responsible for the war had to be arrested and put on trial; the best-known case is that of the Finland President Risto Ryti.

The armistice compelled Finland to drive German troops from the Lapland territory, pressure from the Soviets led to the point of the Lapland War 1944–45. Finland military in armed conflict with the continuation war "brothers in arms," fighting the Soviets in the Lapland region from 1941 to 1944, against the Soviet forces led by the dictator Joseph Stalin. It was a shocking end for Finland, in a right defensive war that was fought on moral grounds, against a lawless despot, who initiated World War 2 with Nazi Germany, exploiting the weak and the innocent for the sake of lawless gain. The guilt of the Second World War rests equally on Stalin as it does on Nazi Germany. The same spirit of the Nemesis was the driving force behind the lawlessness and anarchy.

The Nemesis is deceitful, deceiving the mind of people to believe a lie. How is it possible that two equal partners in crime, in the conspiracy of the Nazi German-Soviet Pact of Aggression 1939 to 1941, are not punished for the war against peace and the genocide in 1940? It was possible because of the sinful rotten core nature of the Imperial power politics of the Western Alliance between 1941 to 1945. Not only was Stalin given protection, but none of the Soviet Union leaders were held accountable for their part in war crimes and genocide. At the same time, from the same time period, the Nazi German officers are taken to courts of law even after they are over 80 or 90 years ago.

Why the discrepancy? Why the silence on the Soviet-Russian crimes? It can't be because of the lack of evidence. The same spirit is active and working in the Crimea, East Ukraine, and Syria. The demonic spirits are always seeking volunteers, people that are given to lawlessness, rebellion, and anarchy. As soon as there are volunteers, then the demons manifest in lawlessness deeds and crime.

### THE PARIS PEACE TREATIES

The Paris Peace Treaties (French: Traité de Paris) was signed on February 10, 1947, as the outcome of the Paris

Peace Conference, held from July 29 to October 15, 1946. The victorious wartime Allied powers (principally the United Kingdom, Soviet Union, United States, and France) negotiated the details of peace treaties with Italy, the minor Axis powers (Romania, Hungary, Bulgaria), and Finland, following the end of World War II in 1945. The treaties allowed Italy, Romania, Hungary, Bulgaria, and Finland to resume their responsibilities as sovereign states in international affairs and to qualify for membership in the United Nations. The settlement elaborated in the peace treaties included payment of war reparations. Commitment to minority rights and territorial adjustments including the end of the Italian Colonial Empire in Africa, Greece, and Albania, as well as changes to the Italian–Yugoslav, Hungarian– Czechoslovak, Soviet–Romanian, Bulgarian–Romanian, Hungarian– Romanian, French–Italian and Soviet–Finnish borders.

During the Paris Peace Treaties, the allied members use clean white paper to dictate their desires, projecting their mind that is looking through their own nationalistic interests and politically colored lenses. They were reinventing basic principles of what is truth and what is true justice. They had to reinvent it because they did not have the moral courage to deal with the war criminals that acted aggressively from 1939 to 1940. They invented lies to justify themselves and to cover up corruption. The Allied forces covered up war crimes and genocide. They defended one of the two primary war criminals of world war 2 (Joseph Stalin) and punished the innocent. They did it because they were primarily inspired and guided by their own nationalistic false spirits. They did not consult the Spirit of the Natural Law, the Creator of Life (YHWH).

## A BLOODY MESS CAUSED BY THE SOVIET UNION AND NAZI GERMANY 1939-1941

It affected millions of people that never wanted anything to do with the Imperial Super Powers Politics. They are a curse on the ordinary people of the land that would never do such immoral acts to take part in political games at the expense of innocent people's lives. Not to mention executing hundreds, thousands, tens of thousands, hundreds of thousands, and even millions of innocent lives. Politicians are too often morally half-baked mindless people, disconnected from the world where people of the land live. Politicians too often are driven by selfish ambitions, greedy; they are often brutish, egotistic, narcissistic, and ruthless gluttons for power politics.

Millions of lives were affected, many millions of people dead, parents lost children, children lost parents, people wounded and crippled for life, and others imprisoned. The culprits are the politicians that play foolish political games. The Western propaganda is oversimplified in using Hollywood style scripts to demonize the Germans for all the Nazi evil that occurred during the World War. That is only one side of the coin. The other side of the coin looks almost as filthy greed and disgusting self-righteousness. Both sides are guilty of failing to respect the Spirit of the Natural Law.

It is the Spirit of the Natural Law and the Creator of Life that should be respected. Dictators are power-hungry and self-seeking; they will manipulate their human-made laws for their selfish goals and objectives; they do not respect the primary source of the Spirit of the Natural Law. The smallest of States are the most vulnerable; big Imperialists will manipulate the smaller for their own ends. Primitive brutes that go around like gorillas thumping others out of their drunken way. Rewriting laws to suit their own agenda. Judging the guilty innocent and the innocent guilty. They are lying to themselves, thinking that they have found success, and got away with murder.

[25]

# NATO ASSURANCE FOR THE RULE OF LAW

The NATO assurance for upholding the rule of law in East Europe is as complex as the elements of a living soul in humans. The will, imagination, consciousness, memory, emotions will not automatically tune itself to measurable goals in life without the power of the intellect. The will is blind and cannot choose the next objective without the intellect engaging the consciousness, imagination, and memory; information is vital for intelligent decision making. Once information is engaged, then the will can move into meaningful action. There are much self-interest and blindness in the International world of politics. The international world of sports is far more superior in their worldview, ethics, and equal opportunity for all competitors.

How many despotic dictators have there been in the individual sports of the last 100 years? Meaning, that they wrote the rules of the game for their advantage? The international sports world would not tolerate it? Because cheating in a fair rule game is not rational. Sport is all about fair competition with equal opportunity for all participants according to the written rules of the game. There is overall justice to the game. What about team sports? How many teams has there been with a dictator changing the rules for their own team advantage? The world of team sports would not tolerate it. They would not accept such a despotic team into their world of sports. It would be an irrational deviation from the Spirit of fair games. There have been many individuals cheating individuals; once caught, they are penalized according to the law.

## THE INTERNATIONAL WORLD POLITICS
Nationalism is often rooted in the Stone Ages, human carnal nature. The Bolsheviks communist ideology that commenced in 1917 – 1922 was a primitive and backward model for a government. It had a seriously erroneous worldview. Moreover, the life philosophy was flawed through the darkened minds of the atheistic dictators that selfishly placed themselves in the role that belongs only to the Creator of life. Humans cannot presume the role of a Creator of the universe, the first cause of life. An intelligent Creator of life does exist; in the beginning, the Creator, the first cause created, whether humans have the faith to believe the facts that are recorded in the Holy Scriptures or not.

Here is a scripture that describes what happens to the mind that does not respect the Creator of Life. When individual people do not appreciate the value of human life and disrespect the works of the Creator as found in the natural fauna and flora, then the mind is darkened to severe subjective errors in their worldview.

> "For although they knew God, they neither glorified him as God nor gave thanks to him, but their thinking became futile, and their foolish hearts were darkened. Although they claimed to be wise, they became fools and exchanged the glory of the immortal God for images made to look like a mortal human being and birds and animals and reptiles." Romans 1:21-25. (NIV)

## ROOT PROBLEM WITH POLITICS 1917 – 2017

The root problem with International Politics is the national biased self-interest, the use of the military force as a legitimate lever for imposing Nationalistic interests on other nations and cultures.

- 1939 Nazi Germany- Nazi German-Soviet Pact of Aggression
- Czechoslovakia
- Austria
- Poland
- Denmark
- Norway
- Belgium
- The Netherlands
- France
- Britain – the Channel Islands
- Italy
- 1939 Joseph Stalin USSR – Nazi German-Soviet Pact of Aggression
- 1939 USSR – Poland invasion.
- 1939 USSR — Finland invasion
- 1940 USSR – Estonia, Latvia, Lithuania, Romania invasion

The conflict between the Nordic region and Russia can be traced back to early 1400 when Russian started increasing their expansionist policies far and wide left right and center. The Russian expansionism led from Moscow clashed with the general Christian Worldview and values which were upheld by Sweden as early as the 12 century and has continued for 700 years. The Russia leader's and peoples have believed at times in the principles of the rule of law. The Soviet Union leaders did not believe in the principles of the rule of law that was derived from the Spirit of the Natural Law. The difference between the biased letter of the law and the Spirit of the Natural Law is essential to understanding true justice. The subjective biases in lawmaking. Making a written law for the sake of self-interest. The Spirit of the Natural law is unchangeable, always consistent, and impartial Universally.

## GEOPOLITICAL UNCERTAINTY

There is a persistent geopolitical expansionist jittering between the West and East. Internal Perpetuating movement, ever since early 1900. I has been ongoing in Russia to conquer the Baltic States and European territory. Even after Russian expanded from Moscow to be the largest land area of any other State which alone has not satisfied the nation's leaders insatiable lust for more territory. It is simplistic primitive preoccupation to value nothing else other than conquering other peoples territory. Who is perpetuating the unrest for more territory? It is the Nemesis behind the provocations, perpetuating the conflict with demonic influence. There is no rest for the wicked. They give in to temptations and go to corruption and crime and pervert the course of justice. Nation leaders appeal to the human ego, at times to satisfy their own nationalistic lust and pride in conquering territory. It appeals to the willful human carnal nature.

## THE UNMISTAKABLE INFLUENCE OF THE NEMESIS

The communist expansionism worldview is a false life philosophy, to gamble every other human moral value on the very narrow and primitive concept of success by eliminating others to grow self-interest nationalism. On these false principles, the Soviet Union fell into despotism and failed to function as a normal state with a democratic community. It had a pretense of "socialism," Biblically speaking, it was pseudo-socialism. It failed the spiritual content test.

## NEUTRAL STATE IS A MYTH

The study of History reveals the true nature of dictators that are allowed to operate with lawlessness. Humanism is often blind to the nature of spiritual rebellion and lawlessness. Humanism does not acknowledge the true nature of the human conflict between good and evil. They do not acknowledge their allegiance to the will of the Nemesis by denying God of the Universe. Humanism does foster respect for people but does not acknowledge the deeper realities of the spiritual life on the planet earth, and how the physical seeds are sown in the physical world. Parallel in the spiritual world. The seeds sown may take root and manifest and grow for a time in the physical world.

The metaphysical world contains a much larger proportion of reality than most people realize or want to admit. Human behavior also at the subconscious level plays a large role in the overall personality. What is in the subconsciousness comes out eventually in the manifestation of the personality. Therefore, the current events, e.g., 2014 Crimea, East Ukraine, and 2011 -1018 Syria, they have a connection to the seeds sown in the past spiritual reality. Connected to the USSR Joseph Stalin's lawlessness and corruption, that comes to the surface and manifests in the Russian politics.

In the spiritual sense, if the seedbed of the Soviet Union was not what it was in the spiritual reality, then the Russian leadership attitude towards the International law could not possibly be what it is today. Therefore, in one sense, the projector is in the past, on the lap of Stalin, and the policy is being played and projected to the viewing screen of today Both the Russian President Vladimir Putin and the Russian Prime Minister Dmitry Medvedev has studied law. How could they possibly appeal to being ignorant of the purpose of the law? Law is not a license to advance self. The purpose of civil law is to remind people of the Spirit of Natural Law. They do what they do because they love to break God-given laws more than they respect God. There is a spiritual link there to the Nemesis, through the power of temptation.

> "For those who are led by the Spirit of God are the children of God." Romans 8:14.

### VLADIMIR PUTIN
*"Putin studied Law at the Leningrad State University (now Saint Petersburg State University) in 1970 and graduated in 1975."* (Encyclopedia, Vladimir Vladimirovich Putin, 2018)

### DMITRY MEDVEDEV
*"In the autumn of 1982, 17-year-old Medvedev enrolled at Leningrad State University to study law. Although he also considered studying linguistics, Medvedev later said he never regretted his choice, finding his chosen subject increasingly fascinating: lucky "to have chosen a field that genuinely interested him and that it was really 'his thing."* (Wikipedia, Dmitry Anatolyevich Medvedev, 2018)

Nationalistic ruling spirits in the outer atmosphere. There is a link connection between the past Soviet Union leadership influence and the current Russian leadership worldview. From 1900 -1991 and from 1991 to today in 2018. What is the link connection? Stalin was influenced and gave himself to the influence and the powers of Satan. Similarly, in proportion to their disrespect of the Spirit of the Natural Law, the current Russian leadership will be violating the God-given Spirit of the Natural Law. The Russian leader's minds historically have been deceived by the influencing dark forces of the Nemesis.

Similarly, the people of the Russian nation have been influenced, but most often in a different area than their leaders. That is no excuse to be disrespectful of the Spirit of the Natural Law or to be deliberately breaking laws. Likewise, the servants of Satan today are influenced by the same characteristics of the Nemesis. Satan does not grow old and die, as Stalin did in 1953. Therefore, the Nemesis spirit that influenced the leaders of the USSR 1922-1953 to have the same power and methods of temptation to influence the Russian leaders from 2000 to 2020.

That is the link between people and the dark forces of the spirit world that serve the purposes of Satan. Russian leader's narrative often does not come from the rule of law-governed reality; they have and come from their own worldview propaganda reality, alibies that blame the another. They operate as organized criminals do, turning the truth into lies, and turning the lies into truth in the minds of those that listen to their propaganda. It is a seriously sinister game of perverting the course of justice.

THE VICTIMS

The victims during those periods were millions of innocent people. Specific events, Stalin great purge, 1936 – 1938 – Estimated 600,000 casualties. Soviet Pact with Nazi Germany 1939. Lawless pillage of East Europe – Victims: Poland, Finland, Estonia, Latvia, and Lithuania. War crimes: Winter War 1939, Katyn Massacre 1940 just to name two. Sweden was able to have a neutral status during the World War 2 because they didn't share a border with Russia. Finland took the brunt of the Soviet Union aggression 1939-1945.

Through the innovative technology the world has been changed, many other security threats are becoming apparent as the world becomes more reliant on digital technologies. The meta-physical world in the spiritual realm can activate people to lawless deeds, without being seen by anybody. Humanist philosophy believes that all people will start blogging about their local flower gardens and hobbies, and there won't be any lawless hackers violating people's rights. The life philosophy and the worldview of hardcore atheistic humanism do not acknowledge the rebellion will and anarchy that lurks in the deep depths of the underworld. Therefore, humanity needs to acknowledge the Creator of life and to give allegiance to the Creator, in so doing they eject the nemesis of humanity out of their personal space.

PEOPLE'S OPINION DEPEND ON RIGHT INFORMATION AND TRUE KNOWLEDGE

How can people vote on NATO, if in principle they are on the wrong side of the law? It is impossible. Therefore, half the battle is to inform people what the premise is for the rule of law? What are the foundations for State authority? What are the principles of the natural law? Implications

How does this help organizations like NATO and the European Union in the quest of drawing up an information policy on enlargement?

Firstly, the results allow for a new dimension of policy prioritization of countries according to their relative levels of public support and opposition to membership. As the issue of inviting new members to join both the European Union and NATO takes on increasing urgency, public attitudes in some of the prospective candidate countries are noteworthy. The following public opinion results from Central Europe and the Baltic states are drawn from the most recent Central and Eastern Eurobarometer, published by the European Commission in March 1997.

PROSPERITY AND SECURITY

Opinion polls are very popular ways of capturing the public mood of a country. The issue of the moment in the countries of Central Europe and the Baltic states is inevitably their overwhelming twin desires for prosperity and security, which translates into the political impulse by their governments to join the two principal organizations which they consider may help them in this regard – respectively the European Union and NATO.

What makes public opinion surveys on this matter even more important are that some governments are likely to put one or both enlargements if and when negotiations have been successfully concluded – to the test of a referendum. Slovakia is ahead of the game by planning to hold a referendum in May on NATO membership, even before NATO's Madrid Summit in July. Thus finding out how and why the public would vote at a given moment in time becomes essential in understanding and trying to cope with the debate that is increasingly taking place in candidate countries. To achieve that understanding, only two questions need to be asked in a typical public opinion survey. First, a simple "Would you vote for or against membership?" which we can then take much further with the obvious follow-up: "What are the main reasons why you would vote for or against?

[26]

# FINLAND ROAD TO EUROPEAN UNION MEMBERSHIP

Finland had been involved in European integration since 1961 when Finland joined the European Free Trade Association (EFTA) as an associate member of the FINEFTA agreement. In 1973, Finland entered into a free trade agreement with the European Economic Community (EEC) and became an EFTA full member in 1986. Finland began membership negotiations with the European Communities in February 1993 simultaneously with Sweden and Austria, negotiating with the Union on agriculture and regional policy in particular, as much else was already negotiated under the EEA Agreement. The hardship in the negotiations was the coordination of the agricultural sector with the Union's agricultural policy. Finland participated in the European Economic Area (EEA) from the beginning of 1994 to the end.

FINNS VOTED FOR MEMBERSHIP
In October 1994, an advisory referendum was held in Finland, where those in support of the Union membership won in votes. Reasons for accession were: security features and economic benefits: membership would allow Finnish companies to access the Union's internal market while at the same time providing overall stable economic development.

Furthermore, membership would guarantee Finland the opportunity to influence decisions that would, in any case, shape the content of our national policy. Arguments against accession included: membership would substantially curtail Finland's right to impose its affairs. Membership was also feared to deteriorate the pursuit of necessary labor, mainly agriculture. Also, fears about the consequences of opening borders and the weakening of social security were the reasons for resistance. On November 18, 1994, Parliament made the final decision. Since January 1, 1995, Finland, Sweden, and Austria became members of the Community, which became the European Union after entering into force of the Maastricht Treaty.

FINLAND A MEMBER OF ECONOMIC AND MONETARY UNION
When joining the EU in 1995, Finland joined the second phase of the European Economic and Monetary Union (EMU). In 1999, the EU approximated the economies of different countries so that the transition to the single currency would go as smoothly as possible. Since 2002, the Euro has been in circulation as a cash grant, replacing old national currencies.

FINLAND BELONGS TO THE SCHENGEN AREA
Finland signed an accession agreement with Schengen in December 1996, together with Sweden and Denmark. The Schengen acquis was applied in Finland and the other Nordic countries on March 25, 2001. In practice, the Schengen Agreement means that people can cross borders between the countries that are members of the Schengen Agreement without any checks at land borders, airports, and ports. The Schengen countries have agreed on the harmonization of their visa policy to facilitate the control of the external borders. Finland's accession to the European Union information package.

On November 18, 1994, the Parliament approved the accession of Finland with the vote result Share 152, No 45,

Empty 1, Off 1. The accession process to the European Union took several years. It was preceded by, and in part, at the same time the EEA process between the Member States of the European Community and the EFTA countries, which negotiated an agreement on the European Economic Area.

## ICELAND AND NATO

Iceland has been a member of the North Atlantic Treaty Organisation (NATO) since its foundation in 1949. Membership of the Alliance and the Defence Agreement with the United States of America has been the two main pillars of Iceland's security policy. With the changing security environment and the transformation of NATO, the contribution of Iceland to the Alliance has undergone a major change. While having no is standing army, Iceland contributes to NATO operations with both financial contributions and civil personnel.

## POLAND AND NATO

On 12 March 1999, Poland, the Czech Republic, and Hungary became full members of the North Atlantic Treaty Organisation. Diplomatic efforts and negotiations concerning Poland's accession to NATO were possible thanks to the historical events in Central and Eastern Europe in 1989. Before the fall of the Berlin Wall, which divided Europe into East and West, the first partly free elections to the Sejm and free elections to the Senate were held in Poland on 4 June 1989. The participants were the outcome of Round Table talks between representatives of communist authorities and the opposition which began in February and ended in April of the same year. These negotiations triggered the process of a peaceful transition of power in Poland.

As a result, the first non-Communist government in this part of Europe was formed, headed by Prime Minister Tadeusz Mazowiecki. Since its first days, the new government began to demonstrate its pro-Western orientation and started the long process of integrating Poland with Western organizations.

On 30 October 1989, the day of the meeting of the Foreign Ministers Committee of Warsaw Pact that had been planned long before the elections. The new chief of Poland's diplomacy Krzysztof Skubiszewski sent an encrypted cable to all Polish ambassadors, instructing them to call on the highest ranking officials in their host countries to inform them that Poland was in favor of "engaging in an all-European process of bridging divisions in Europe." The dissolution of the Warsaw Pact in 1991 and a positive response from NATO member states made Poland's accession to the North Atlantic Treaty Organization become a reality.

## THE IMPACT OF NATO MEMBERSHIP IN THE CZECH REPUBLIC

The Czech Republic, Poland, and Hungary joined the North Atlantic Treaty Organization (NATO) in 1999, in the alliance's first round of post-Cold War enlargement. Their accession represents a milestone in their integration into the trans-Atlantic community and recognition by long-standing NATO members that they had made a successful transition in establishing democratic political systems and market economies. Nevertheless, the Czech Republic's first two years of membership in NATO have had more than their share of problems.

Just like Poland and Hungary, the Czech Republic has had trouble fulfilling its obligations towards the alliance and has faced daunting problems in restructuring its Cold War legacy military into an organization compatible with the alliance framework. However, differentiating the Czechs from Hungarians and Poles, some foreign and security policies of the Czech Republic have seemed at times to dissent from NATO and have introduced doubts within NATO about the country's reliability as an alliance member.

To probe the deeper causes of the seeming Czech ambivalence about NATO and to assess the impact of NATO membership on Czech perceptions of security, a survey-based study was conducted to examine the extent to which the Czech public identifies with its responsibilities as a an alliance member. As NATO considers expanding membership to other post-Communist countries, this study provides some lessons regarding the impending next round of enlargement.

The study found that the main source of Czech hesitation towards NATO is a perception of a low level of influence that the public has on decision-making in security issues. This lack of of transparency and public debate in the Czech decision to join NATO, exemplified by the lack of a referendum on the issue, is the main source of the problem.

When taxpayers are neither consulted about their views on accession nor informed correctly about the costs of accession, as happened in the Czech Republic, both the quality of the new member's membership is damaged, and NATO has to deal with embarrassments that are potentially damaging to its operations. In other words, shortcomings in the democratic process in the Czech Republic continue to affect Czech attitudes and behavior toward NATO. This is the most pertinent lesson regarding the anticipated next round of enlargement and one that the alliance should not re-learn.

### SECURING THE NORDIC-BALTIC REGION

Russia's illegal annexation of Crimea in March 2014 and its military actions in Ukraine have led transatlantic policy-makers to reassess collective defense arrangements across what is frequently referred to as NATO's "eastern flank." Extending north partially beyond the "eastern Flank" is a region that comprises of eight Nordic and Baltic states, which have become increasingly interdependent in security terms. The region is of rising importance in the context of of Europe's changing security order.

NATO has a strong role in coordinating closer security ties between the region's states. Finland and Sweden are not members of the Alliance and are therefore not covered by NATO's collective defense clause. However, the Allies are working closely with both countries – two of NATO's most active partners – to assess security in the Baltic Sea region, to expand exchanges of information, including on hybrid warfare, coordinating training and exercises, and to develop better joint situational awareness.

The prospects are positive for improved NATO-Nordic-Baltic defense cooperation, yet some important challenges need to be overcome. The region will test NATO's flexibility in strengthening defense ties among its members and crucial partner states.

### CLOSER LINKS BETWEEN NATO AND NORDEFCO

Increasing links with NATO in a wider sense stands to widen the pool of expertise available for NORDEFCO's development. Finland and Sweden are already benefitting from enhanced opportunities for cooperation and dialogue with NATO since 2014. Moreover, Denmark and Sweden agreed to expand defense cooperation in January 2016, demonstrating the higher emphasis on defense policy within the mainstream Nordic political agenda.

As all militaries in the Nordic-Baltic region require similar specifications in procuring equipment, the NORDEFCO environment provides opportunities to reduce financial burdens by bringing greater economies of scale to bear for joint procurements.

With a strong argument present to advocate cold weather operations as a core focus, the NORDEFCO framework facilitates opportunities for a more significant number of joint military exercises that promise to hone better military interoperability in the Nordic-Baltic region.

The underlying compatibility between the Nordic and Baltic defence systems is strong. As is the case with Estonia and Lithuania, territorial defence planning in most Nordic states includes strong conscript elements.

Finally, from a wider NATO perspective, more NORDEFCO exercises should also be open to Allies from outside the region, such as Germany, France, Poland, the United Kingdom and the United States, which stand to be vital contributors under the RAP framework to defense in the Baltic Sea region. This type of broader security cooperation centered on Nordic leadership has previously been conducted to prepare for peace- support operations, for example, the Swedish-led "Viking" exercises. Given the Nordic-Baltic security situation, there should also be scope to widen this cooperation into the area of territorial defence.

### WHY IS FINLAND NOT IN NATO?

One reason is the political pressure from Russian officials, they have deemed Finnish NATO membership to be a red line and have threatened "necessary measures" using "military" means. There are many practical down to earth reasons why Finland has not joined the North Atlantic Treaty Organization.

There are six main reasons listed here:

1. The corruption of the Allied forces in World War 2. The allied forces patronized the Bolsheviks despotic dictator, the murderer of civilians, a war criminal guilty of genocide, with little respect for the Spirit of the Natural Law.
2. The Americans, British, and the French political leaders, revealed their sinful short-sighted souls.
3. The Atlantic Treaty is an American mold. Filled with their own interest.
4. The people and the government leaders of Finland suffered enormously from the Nazi German-Soviet Pact of Aggression. 430,000 war evacuees were caused by the 1939 to 1944 Soviet aggression.
5. The Americans, British, and the French were indifferent to the injustice of the war crimes and genocide, at the Soviet despot's spheres of interest, in the Baltic States and Finland.
6. The American, French, and England political leaders were corrupted to the core; nothing has changed in that regard. Their own societies have become more corrupted, sinful, and atheistic than they were 75 years ago. Where is their God? It is secular humanism. Self-righteous humanistic spirit of the world. That is not a reliable partner in the next global conflict

Also, a contributing factor is that Finland society has a similar mix of Russian Bolshevik lawlessness sympathizers as they did in 1918. Nothing has changed in that regard in the last 100 years. The Soviet Union leaders pressured Finland politically; the same Spirit has been activated by the current Russian leaders. It is a spiritual conflict in nature. Deep taproots are going down to the early 1900. Children of parents too often inherit the same Spirit and the mindset of their parents whether a child is enlightened spiritually in heart and mind or brainwashed with pseudo-socialism.

The Finnish civil society structure is often naively polite; or extremely rude; they pamper all babies, whether the orientation is the Bolsheviks red and left, or a Christian worldview, with a strong sense of God-given justice. The current Russian leaders are dictating No! To the question, should Finland join NATO? The legitimate question for everyone is, what has Finland's independence, and self-determination has anything to do with the lawless and immoral Russian nationalistic leaders? The Soviet Russian leaders are manipulative, lawless, and immoral. The facts prove it.

The Russian leaders have no respect for the small East European Baltics States or the Nordic countries. They don't even respect the International standards of the International law that the bigger Western States observe. The Russian leader's deeds and actions from the last 100 years prove them to be misguided, anti-God, anti-Christian values and immoral, without any respect for the Spirit of the Creator God, or the Spirit of the Natural Law.

Finland leaders have no obligations to be a slave to the untamed Spirit of the Nemesis, which is actively influencing and manipulating the Russian leaders to further corruption and deceit. Such as their military activities in Syria, Ukraine Crimea Peninsula, and East Ukraine. That is according to the Spirit of the Natural Law. Satan and his demons host are always desiring to deceive people, to cause destruction on earth. That is only possible through willing human agents like the lawless Soviet Russian leaders that have hearts and minds that are given to deceitful corruption, to steal, kill, and destroy the innocent peoples of the land.

It is the same core spirit problem that the Swedes confronted the Russians when they built the Nyenschantz fortress in 1611, in the Gulf of Finland, at the mouth of the Neva River. Nothing has changed in the psyche of the Russian leaders over 300 years. The European region is like a magnet that they are drawn to, and the desire to conquer it. There were the original pioneers, people living in the Gulf of Finland region, including the Karelian Isthmus. But the Russian, not so great Peter, lusted for it. He coveted and lusted the region that already belonged to the people of the land. He never took the message from God, given to Moses 3400 years ago, as in the Torah. The instructions from God.

Instead, people have lived according to their own will, as they saw fit without giving any credit to the Creator of

Life, no respect to the Spirit of the Natural Law. They became deceived by Satan and his demon host. Why does the 400-year spiritual conflict between military superpowers and the people of the land in history keep looping over and over, in East Europe and in Finland? When will the Russian leaders get off it? It keeps looping over and over because they keep reading their own leader's history, their Imperial Russian storybooks. Their pride and ego are rooted in their nationalistic idolatry, in their leader's unbelief, godlessness, and state atheism.

The Russian leaders are not 100 years behind times; they are almost 2000 years behind the real-time. That is the square one, where the rules are written and readout; it sets the rules for the Creator of Life board game on the planet earth. Dictators bluff is all it takes to change people's minds. After all, it has only been 79 years, when there was a conspiracy, war crimes, genocide, and extortion of the homes and property of 430,000 people of Karelia and Lapland. It was a total war at the borders of Finland, only two short generations ago. The Spirit of fear entered millions of people during World War two years, and many will keep it in their soul for the rest of their life.

The Continuation War began 15 months after the end of the USSR aggression against Finland in 1939 Winter War. It was fought for the sole reason of taking back the territory that USSR had lawlessly stolen from Finland, with extreme demands of the Moscow peace agreement in 1940. Stalin demanded to hand over the Karelian Isthmus, including the entire historical Finnish/Swedish city of Viipuri (Vyborg).

Easier ways could be a crippling random cyber attack, or at the bare minimum a repositioning of Russian forces on the Finnish border, or a trade blockade. These kinds of threats appear in the minds of people. They are risks most people in Finland do not want to take. The nature of the beast is predatorial. It does not need to plan much; it just waits for the prey to come. An aggressive military response on Finnish territory cannot be ruled out. It is the nature of the beast. The general attitude in the society of Finland toward Foreign Policies can be viewed in four categories:

1. Pro-Western.
2. Pro-Soviet Union – Russia.
3. Purely opportunist business.
4. Indifferent/not interested.

The 200-year historical record has left an imprint on the psyche of the Finnish people's consciousness. They know that the imperial powers politics are infamously arbitrary and capricious. In 1939 the population of Finland was 3.5 million; the Soviet Union population at the time was 184 million. The dictator's mind felt threatened by Finland. Almost as if Finland was a floating iceberg and was threatening to sink the Soviet ship. The Soviet leadership was hallucinating; Finland was perfectly still, without moving. It was the Bolsheviks that sank the Russian Monarchy ship in 1917. A guilty conscience can project one's misdeeds to others.

The Imperial superpowers leaders preach the need for education and the need for sophisticated politics to the people of the land peasants, and they talk about the virtues of rules, law, and policy. However, they have no spiritual sense of the sense of justice according to the Spirit of the Natural Law.

Ambitious Politicians have been a significant curse to the planet earth like no other people. The worst 25 dictators of history have all been ambitious politicians. They were a mass curse to the people's lives and the land because they had a false self-centered worldview and erroneous life philosophy. They gained popularity and power through the people; they coveted political and military power; they built up the forces and used it capriciously to steal, kill, and destroy. They also jailed the opposition that voiced the truth about lawless politicians being undesirables, uncivilized and unregenerate.

### MAP OF THE SUOMI PEOPLE

The correct worldview that respects the Spirit of the Natural Law is in the Holy Scriptures. Primarily the Spirit of the Natural Law has existed since the beginning, but the human living soul, with a will, imagination, consciousness, emotions, memory, and intellect, rarely seeks the truth and justice in the Spirit of the Natural Law. Enlightened people have understood the Spirit of the Natural Law, and they respected it and did no harm to other people.

They did to others as they wished others do to them, the golden rule. There was capacity in their living soul for lateral thinking. They built relationships, families, villages, and at times a beginning of a nation. The Spirit of the Natural Law is unchangeable. Therefore it is reliable and impartial regardless of the time, circumstances, or status. It cannot be bribed, influenced, or bought-out for selfish gain.

## FINLAND RELUCTANCE TO JOIN NATO?

There are unresolved issues with double standards and Western leader's hypocrisy that need to be straightened out. The West has lost credibility and Truth and Justice during the 1900 -1950 World Wars. They have an inclination for utilitarianism as a life philosophy. They are prone to be opportunists and revel in the Victors Justice.

- Unresolved Soviet Union war crimes against Finland between 1939 -1945.
- Unresolved Soviet Union war crimes against the Baltic States between 1939 – 1945.
- The Western Alliance was complicit in protecting a severe war criminal Joseph Stalin.
- The Western Alliance was complicit in the war crimes committed by the Soviet Union.
- The Western Alliance exercised biased victor's justice in the War Responsibility Trials in Helsinki. They sentenced the Finnish government Politicians to jail. The trials were conducted from November 1945 through February 1946.
- Risto Ryti, 5th President of Finland, ten years in prison.
- Jukka Rangell 25th prime minister of Finland 6 years in prison
- Edwin Linkomies 28th prime minister of Finland for five years and six months in prison
- Väinö Tanner cabinet minister five years and six months in prison
- Toivo Kivimäki, Finland's ambassador to Germany, five years in prison
- Henrik Ramsay cabinet minister two years and six months in prison
- Antti Kukkonen cabinet minister two years in prison
- Tyko Reinikka cabinet minister two years in prison

The War Responsibility Trials in Helsinki was like the show trials of Joseph Stalin, with no grains of truth to it. The Soviets were organized criminals with fabricated show trials and false accusations. Orchestrated to suit their ends. The Soviet leadership repeated the same flimflams over and over in the Baltic States, rubber stamping Stalin authority to judge and replace the legitimate representative government of an independent State. Whatever the Baltic State the Soviets system had access to, it dug its claws and ripped up the legitimate government structure and replaced it with communist representatives.

The Soviets did not make it to the Finland Capital 1939-40. Therefore they were not able to disable the legitimate government of Finland. So the Soviet propaganda machine created a puppet representative for the people of Finland. Absurd as it appears, but they were serious in their efforts to demolish legitimate governments and replace them with Communist governments to start a global revolution for communism. This was intended for Finland by the Soviets during November 1939.

## THE SOVIETS PSEUDO FINNISH DEMOCRATIC REPUBLIC

The "Finnish Democratic Republic" was a pseudo-government regime located near Stalingrad, created and recognized only by the Soviet Union leaders. The appointed leader was the Finnish-born politician Otto Ville Kuusinen (a leftist communist); the Finnish Democratic Republic was Joseph Stalin's planned means to conquer the strings to Finland and to use it for his ends. The Soviet Union argued that it was the only legitimate government for all of Finland that was capable of ending the Winter War and restoring peace, which was the Soviet Foreign Policy at the time, to manipulate Independent East European Baltic States, under the control of the Rogue Soviet state.

There was no let-up in Joseph Stalin Soviet efforts to expand and unroll the red carpet of communism into

Europe and further afield. The tenacious and diabolical effort which was inward, materialistic that eventually curled up inside the Iron and Bamboo Curtains. Thank God it was constrained to those geographical areas. Their life philosophy was atheism with a purely materialistic worldview. No Creator of life or the Spirit of the Natural Law gave license to the arbitrary and capricious use of violence against human rights, right to life, right to liberty, and right to property.

## THE SOVIET UNION STRATEGY

The Great Purge or the Great Terror was a campaign of political repression in the Soviet Union that occurred from 1936 to 1938. For the ambitious Bolsheviks politicians "Communism," it required a large-scale purge of the Communist Party and government officials, repression of peasants and the Red Army leadership, widespread police surveillance, suspicion of "saboteurs," "counter-revolutionaries," imprisonment, and arbitrary executions.

"Mobile gas vans were used to execute people without trial. It has been estimated at 600,000 people died at the hands of the Stalin led the Soviet government during the Purge." (Encyclopedia, Great Terror, 1936)

The internal purge of the Joseph Stalin political environment in the Soviet Union was a strategic plan that would be repeated in everywhere that the Soviet Union expanded to. There was no shortage of people that had a different worldview from those of the Bolshevik Communists. The State leaders would be removed from office, killed, relocated, or executed. The purging would continue with grooming for a Soviet puppet state. It was a diabolical plan to milk a nation of their resources to a foreign ruler.

## A PUPPET STATE

"A puppet state is a state that is supposedly independent but is, in fact, dependent upon an outside power. It is nominally sovereign but effectively controlled by a foreign or otherwise alien power, for reasons such as financial interests."

"A puppet state preserves the external paraphernalia of independence like a name, flag, anthem, constitution, law codes, and motto but in reality is an organ of another state which created or sponsored the government. Puppet states are not recognized as legitimate under international law." (Wikipedia, Puppet State, 2018)

The puppet state plan was put into effect in the early days of the Winter War against Finland. The Soviets set up the pseudo-Finnish Democratic Republic, a puppet regime set up by the Soviets on the first day of the Winter War.

## THE WESTERN ALLIANCE AND THE SOVIET UNION

WWII experience (no outside help in Winter War '39-'40) in particular taught Finns not to trust the Imperial States during the extreme crisis, no matter what formal treaties say. In other words, they do not fundamentally believe NATO would help them when World Wars break out. It is the Western Utilitarian life philosophy, the more significant cause to win favor. Principles and treaties are not respected. Such national self-sufficiency has also turned so that Finns are suspicious of joining any organization that might force them to send soldiers abroad for unclear or Imperial ambitious causes. This is a further impediment to joining NATO.

## THE BALTIC STATES AND NATO?

First off, all of the Baltic States joined NATO. Moreover, most of it boils down to protection. Former Communist Eastern Europe and the Baltics, in particular, wanted to get as far away from Russia as possible because of the lawlessness. Keep in mind that for the Baltics, the USSR not only invaded these countries but integrated the countries into the Union and tried to destroy their culture and replace it with Russian/ Communist culture (Russification). Moreover, the average citizens of Estonia, Latvia, or Lithuania are still very wary, if not fearful, of Russia. The Ukraine conflict only heightened these fears; among all of the members of NATO, the Baltics and Eastern European countries reacted with the most hostility. So with NATO, the Baltic States get Western protection from Russia, so Russia could not annex a part of Estonia with a large Russian population without retaliation, perse.

Many, many countries simply don't trust Russia and their supposed expansionist goals hence the "need" to join NATO. NATO membership essentially guarantees an few options:

- Security from the wealthiest, most powerful country on the globe. E.g., the US is spending about $3 billion on reinforcing Europe, or more specifically the Baltic states, for additional equipment, brigades, etc.
- Being allowed to "slack off" on their defense budget. If I am not mistaken, NATO nations are «suggested» to pay 2% of their GDP on defense. If they weren't NATO members, I suspect they would be paying more than 2%, but that is for a different day.
- Upgrading and training of their forces and being allowed to be sold certain weapons otherwise restricted to those nations.

THE DEBATE FOR AND AGAINST NATO MEMBERSHIP

The dominating argument among interviewees for joining NATO is its image as a guarantor of security and stability in the region. The desire for security guarantees is most widely held in Poland and Lithuania. In Poland and Estonia, many people also refer to security and protection from Russia as a reason for entering NATO. However, a considerable number of interviewees also link NATO membership with hope for more general progress and cooperation, this non-military interpretation being most prevalent in Romania.

Another set of of interviewees expect that NATO will help to control and reform the army and the military industry as well as the same percentage stating simply that their country needs NATO support. The most frequent reason given for a vote against NATO membership is people's preference for their country having a neutral status. The view is shared in particular by about one-fifth of Latvians, Hungarians, Slovaks, and Bulgarians.

On the other hand, Poles and Romanians do not show much sympathy towards neutrality. A general antipathy against the military and war is invoked as an argument against joining NATO more frequently than average in Estonia, the Czech Republic, Hungary, and Slovakia. This kind of reasoning is by contrast practically absent in Poland and Romania. The perceived expense of NATO membership is a deterrent factor particularly in the Czech Republic, Estonia, Slovakia, and Hungary.

FOR THE RULE OF LAW:

- NATO respects the principles of the rule of law.
- They support the principles of the Natural law.
- NATO respects the right to life, liberty, and property.
- NATO defend the small states that are being manipulated by the larger military states.
- The defender of the defenseless.
- NATO seeks solutions to conflicts with true justice.
- NATO supports the International Law.
- Train military for self-defense against terrorism

AGAINST THE RULE OF LAW:

- Oppose NATO
- Oppose the rule of law
- Bolsheviks. Soviet Union lawlessness 1900-1991.
- The USSR opposes the rule of law. 1939-1941.
- Deny the principles of the Natural Law.
- Exploited, manipulated and invaded small States.

- Committed War crimes but did not acknowledge them as such.
- Profiteering from Stalin War crimes. Annexed lands. 1939-45.
- Support dictators that murder civilians. E.g., Syria, East Ukraine.
- Disregard for the International law.
- Disregard for the International Bill of Rights.

ETERNAL SPIRIT OF THE LAW

The world has become more complex, but the rule of law and the principles of the natural law have not changed and will not change as long as there is the rule of law. The evidence of law and lawlessness in many specific countries is real. In international affairs, there is blatant disrespect for the sanctity of human life. The principles of the International Bill of Rights are not respected.

The Bill of Rights is based on the Spirit of Natural Law. No matter which way one looks at it, there is no excuse for denial or escape from the obvious conclusion that many state leaders are perpetuating blatant lawlessness. The same pattern is visible from the last 100-year history. The problem is not where people generally think; the historical narrative, like Hollywood propaganda, fiction books, and comics, have often oversimplified the reality and hide the agents of the Nemesis in the process.

What is the answer to the misleading information? True justice, according to the Spirit of the Natural law, is the answer. To be impartial in the judgment of the WW2 war crimes. Those countries that we're guilty of severe WW 2 war crimes and were let off by the Allied forces without any accountability for their leaders disrespect for the Spirit of the Natural Law are the same countries that are perpetuating lawlessness again since the early year 2000.

It was the Bolshevik leaders that manifested lawlessness; then, it evolved into the USSR from 1922 – 1991. The same pride for lawlessness and the arrogance of criminality is manifesting in Russia, Syria, Iran, and North Korea. There is an underground connection that has a spiritual association, namely the Nemesis. The nemesis of humanity does use people to do his will, in an attempt to make the world under his dominion – e.g., a rogue State under control of the Nemesis dark underground spirit forces.

There is a Creator of life, in the beginning, Life was created, humanity was created. Therefore the way up is to acknowledge the Creator of Life and learn how to respect the laws of life and the Natural Law. Metaphysical world is significant to the logic and rationale of life philosophy and a correct worldview. Human in self-will and subjective experience is a sure cul-de-sac. Dictators have closed circuit minds that do not foster the respect fo the International law, or give the rule of law opportunities for others. Dictators throughout history have come to steal rob and destroy life on earth.

IS NATO READY TO DEFEND THE BALTIC STATES?

In any case of war against Russia, the Baltic States are expected to be overrun by Russia fairly quickly, only due to the sheer numerical superiority of men and equipment that Russia has in the region and because the supply lines of their forces was across the border.

*"Sir Richard Shirreff argued that his plot is plausible, noting that "we have seen recently, regularly, Russian so-called snap exercises of 30-40,000 troops in which the exercise scenario is the occupation of the Baltic states."*

*"Indeed, NATO and other organizations have been war-gaming such scenarios for years; after a series of war games in 2014 and 2015, for instance, the Rand Corporation concluded that NATO currently had not mobilized enough resources to defend the Baltic states from a Russian invasion. It's an assessment that Shirreff agrees with, despite NATO's plans to rotate four battalions (around 4,000 troops) through Poland and the Baltic states."* (Atlantic-Council, 2018)

Moreover, look at the geographical location of the Baltics; they are directly next to the Russian border. A Russian blitzkrieg style attack would quickly overwhelm the NATO token forces in the three countries. So unless NATO builds up a serious force in the 3 Baltic countries with bases and an increase on the number of troops deployed there (which will increase tensions with Russia immensely), NATO is not ready to defend the Baltics.

# [27]
# WORLDVIEW CONFLICTS IN 2020

Worldview Conflicts in 2020

Conflicting Worldviews are the primary reason for unrest, rebellion, and wars in the world. Worldview preference, presumptions, illusions, and choice are always present in human psychology and demonstrated in society with life values, relationships, education, beliefs, ethics, religion, endeavors, and Nationalism. Most often individual people may not be conscious of their own Worldview in detail or how different it may be from other people in their own society or other people's and Nation society. There are International events that do draw people together from all over the world, whether it is around government, religion, sports, natural disasters, Media event, or some kind of cultural festival event.

Worldview is often absorbed through national identity and hidden behind decades of family values, from parents, relationships in society. People are generally ushered in, conformed, and molded into a society with a national identity and a culturally learned Worldview. The spirit of Nationalism often overrides the details of specific ethics and moral values. Nationalism can override ethics and moral values if the spirit of Nationalism is lifted up blindly with zeal as a higher value. Historical National narrative is often the motivator to compel people into a nationalistic Worldview. Suppose a Worldview has a moral and ethical framework that Nationalism must abide inside. In that case, it can be a good and positive power that keeps the people united with a common purpose.

Historical interpretation of World War One and World War Two. National biases and government leader's corruption has manipulated the actual facts of history away from Truth. Victor's justice is a mechanism that government leaders have used to manipulate history's facts to suit their own interests, political, and economic agenda. From Moses's times on mount Sinai 3460 years ago, the Holy Scriptures are explicit and clearly present and define what is acceptable and what is prohibited by the Creator of Life on Earth. Holy God does not tolerate hardcore atheism in government leaders that are the false prophets of people society. Isaiah, the prophet, saw and felt the same confusion at the time in his society. He explicitly spoke out what the mind and the Word of the Lord were regarding what is morally right and what is Morally Wrong.

> Isaiah 5:18-24. "Woe to those who begin by pulling at transgression with a thread, but end by dragging sin along as if with a cart rope.
>
> They say, "We want God to speed up his work, to hurry it along, so we can see it! We want the Holy One of Isra'el's plan to come true right now, so we can be sure of it!"
>
> Woe to those who call evil good and good evil, who change darkness into light and light into darkness, who change bitter into sweet and sweet into bitter!
>
> Woe to those seeing themselves as wise, esteeming themselves as clever. Woe to those who are heroes at drinking wine, men whose power goes to mixing strong drinks,

> who acquit the guilty for bribes but deny justice to the righteous! Therefore, as fire licks up the stubble, and the chaff is consumed in the flame; so their root will rot, and their flowers scatter like dust; because they have rejected the Torah of Adonai-Tzva'ot, they have despised the word of the Holy One of Isra'el."

That is precisely what Isaiah warned the people of Israel against. And it is exactly what the Bolshevik leaders committed in Russia 1900-1922. Creating the Soviet Union State Atheism. They violated every God-given principle in the most potent blatant ways, torturing, imprisoning, and murdering millions of God's people. It did not stop with the collapse of the Soviet Union in 1991. Russian leaders have the same spirit of the Soviet Union State Atheism, with Joseph Stalin Communism Worldview's principles, as the driving force of Russian Nationalism. They do not recognize the Spirit of the Holy God or the instructions and commands given with the Oracles of God in the Torah. In fact, the Soviet Union leaders were the enemies of God in every way imaginable.

Expansion of False Worldview Information

Whether a cause is good and has merit, people get together and share their circumstances, life experiences, hopes, and ideas. Leaders also share publicly, market, and promote their ideas, products, and services or a particular Worldview. Usually either a liberal or a conservative Worldview. A Liberal Worldview usually without an ideology and also fewer rules and constraints for moral behavior. Conservative Worldview most often has a Worldview, with rules and constraints for morally right behavior.

Populist movements are quickly whipped up by leaders by promising people more money, freedom, rights, or civil action in society. Politicians in history have been the most destructive and have done the most damage to Humanity, causing millions of deaths. Why are the politicians? Because they can get a grip on an Entire nation and use the financial and military resources of a Nation to do war. Political leaders can manipulate the spirit of Nationalism in a way to convince the people that a False Worldview is a True Worldview, according to the manipulated spirit of Nationalism. That is precisely what Joseph Stalin managed to do in Russia. Karl Marx, Vladimir Lenin Joseph Stalin, and the Bolsheviks duped the Russian people into believing in erroneous ideology and a false Worldview.

The only preventative blockage between the Bolsheviks State Atheism and Russia's people was the Jewish Holy Scriptures Bible. Therefore, the Bolsheviks had to do violence to the established religious structures, Churches, religious leaders, and believers. Soviet Union State atheism led by Joseph Stalin wiped out religious services and congregations in Russia. Why did they wipe out religion? Because the God-given Jewish Holy Scripture True Worldview stood in the way of the Bolsheviks rebellion and Anarchy. Can you now begin to understand how a False Worldview is in conflict with a True Worldview? A True Worldview is in line with the revealed Truth of the Holy scriptures.

What if someone refuses to believe in the revealed God-given True Worldview? Then the person is refusing to believe God at His word. There may be several reasons why someone refuses to believe in Truth. The possibility that the person has been brainwashed into believing a lie cannot recognize Truth over error. This is another reason why the Soviet Union blew up and demolished church building, burnt bibles, and forbid the distribution and publication of bibles in the Soviet Union. The Soviet leaders wanted the minds and the spirits of people in the Satanic darkness.

God of Abraham, Isaac, and Jacob has used the written word to bring people out of darkness into light for the last 4000 years. It is God's written word that gives light to the path and enlightens understanding and the knowledge of God so that we may know God personally. Established relationship by the lamb of God.

> Jeremiah 9:23. "Here is what Adonai says: 'The wise man should not boast of his wisdom, the powerful should not boast of his power, the wealthy should not boast of his wealth; instead, let the boaster boast about this: that he understands and knows me — that I am Adonai, practicing grace, justice and righteousness in the land; for in these things I take pleasure,'" says Adonai."

> Jeremiah 23:29 (CJB). "Isn't my word like fire," asks Adonai, "like a hammer shattering rocks?"

> Isaiah 40:8 (CJB). "The grass dries up, the flower fades; but the word of our God will stand forever."

> Isaiah 55:10-11 (CJB). "For just as rain and snow fall from the sky and do not return there, but water the earth, causing it to bud and produce, giving seed to the sower and bread to the eater; so is my word that goes out from my mouth —it will not return to me unfulfilled; but it will accomplish what I intend, and cause to succeed what I sent it to do."

Defenders of the False Worldview Blame God's Way Being the Wrong Way.

From early 1900 the Bolsheviks rebellion in Russia blamed the legitimate Russian Government and the Monarchy for the injustice in the Russian society. The Bolsheviks rebellion wanted Karl Marx, Vladimir Lenin, and Joseph Stalin Worldview. Also, for Russian people to conform to the Bolsheviks Communist Worldview.

What travels first, the horse, or the cart? Typical for rebellious people they posses a spirit of rebellion, and are looking for some excuse to manifest Anarchy. According to the Holy Jewish Scriptures, human rebellion is as the sin of witchcraft, and incorrigible obstinate stubbornness is a sin of idolatry (1 Samuel 15:23).

> 1 Samuel 15:23 (KJV). "For rebellion is as the sin of witchcraft, and stubbornness is as iniquity and idolatry. Because thou hast rejected the word of the Lord, he hath also rejected thee from being king."

Karl Marx and Lenin were of Jewish descent. They obviously had no interest in reading the five Books of Moses. Or believing in the existence of YHWH. Many of the Bolsheviks were Jews. Is it any wonder that in Germany the lawless rebellion and anarchy of the Bolsheviks galvanized the German leaders attitude and resistance to the Bolsheviks Worldview. The German people knew by heart that the Bolsheviks Worldview was seriously erroneous and despicable. It was only 400 years after Martin Luther reformation in Europe. There were many spiritual revivals in Germany during those 400 years leading up to the First World War.

Russian Civil War followed the Bolsheviks uprising and overthrow of the Russian Tsar. First World War, which claimed the lives of about 3 million Russians, among some 15 million across the world as a whole. Compare that to the Bolsheviks orchestrated Russian Civil War casualties. The conflict raged across Eurasia for four years; the human cost was astronomical. It claimed approximately 15 million lives and reconfigured the whole of 20th-century history. That was before Joseph Stalin established the Soviet Union State Atheism.

"In his new book, historian Norman Naimark argues that the definition of genocide should include nations killing social classes and political groups. Naimark, the author of the controversial new book Stalin's Genocides, argues that we need a much broader definition of genocide, one that includes nations killing social classes and political groups. His case in point: Stalin. The book's title is plural for a reason: He argues that the Soviet elimination of a social class, the kulaks (who were higher-income farmers), and the subsequent killer famine among all Ukrainian peasants – as well as the notorious 1937 order No. 00447 that called for the mass execution and exile of "socially harmful elements" as "enemies of the people" – were, in fact, genocide.

I make the argument that these matters shouldn't be seen as discrete episodes, but seen together," said Naimark, the Robert and Florence McDonnell Professor of Eastern European Studies and a respected authority on the Soviet regime. "It's a horrific case of genocide – the purposeful elimination of all or part of a social group, a political group" Stalin had nearly a million of his own citizens executed, beginning in the 1930s. Millions more fell victim to forced labor, deportation, famine, massacres, and detention and interrogation by Stalin's henchmen."

**Deceived Human beings deceiving the unaware.**

> Deuteronomy 11:16 (ASV). "Take heed to yourselves, lest your heart be deceived, and ye turn aside, and serve other gods, and worship them; "

> Obadiah 3 (CJB). "Your proud heart has deceived you, you whose homes are caves in the cliffs, who live on the heights and say to yourselves, 'Who can bring me down to the ground?'"

> 1 Timothy 2:14 (CJB). "Also it was not Adam who was deceived, but the woman who, on being deceived, became involved in the transgression."

> Galatians 6:7-8 (CJB). "Don't delude yourselves: no one makes a fool of God! A person reaps what he sows. Those who keep sowing in the field of their old nature, in order to meet its demands, will eventually reap ruin; but those who keep sowing in the field of the Spirit will reap from the Spirit everlasting life."

> 1 John 1:8 (CJB). "If we claim not to have sin, we are deceiving ourselves, and the truth is not in us."

Russian leaders maintain the same attitude and the spirit of hostility against the will of God on Earth. Because they continually violate the Spirit of the Natural Law and repress the Written Commandments of God. The evidence from the year 2000 to 2020 proves that Russia, as a Nation, has not changed from the Soviet Union State Atheism principles and the Joseph Stalin Worldview. The annexation of Crimea proves it, east Ukraine proves it, and the deaths of five hundred thousand people in Syria proves it. Russian leaders continue to take the opportunity where the spirit of Soviet Union State Atheism Worldview leads them. Russian leaders will even challenge the Western Worldview, saying that the Soviet Union Communism Worldview is a Moral Worldview. And the Western World Worldview is Immoral Worldview. Russian leaders accuse the Western nations of Western biases and racism against Russian.

The one thing that the Russian leaders and the Russian people that vote their leaders in do not accept or understand. Soviet Union State Atheism was an insult for the Creator of Life. The God of Abraham, Isaac, and Jacob. How could anyone blow up and demolish hundreds of churches, burn millions of bibles, and imprison, torture, and murder hundreds of thousands of priests and Christians? And still, think that the Soviet Union Way is Morally superior, and the Western way with Religious freedom is the wrong way. People can only think that way if their mind has been duped and blinded by Satan's diabolical schemes. And that is precisely what has occurred in Russia since the early 1900. Even today, Russian leaders are spiritually blind, and their hearts are hardened and calloused. They cannot perceive Spiritual Truth in the light of the Torah or Yeshua Hamashiach.

Russian Leaders Bluff.
What should the people of the Western Nations do? When Russian leaders bluff the people of the world with the Soviet Union Worldview. They need to pushback when Russian leaders present Soviet Union-style lies as the Truth. To expose the darkness of the Soviet Union evil empire. By confronting the lies, speaking out the Holy Jewish Scriptures to those that repress and suppress the Truth of God's word in any given situation. Whether it is Crimea, East Ukraine, Syria, Germany, Japan, the United States, Canada, Australia, New Zealand, Korea, Poland, Denmark, Sweden, Estonia, Finland, or Norway.

Suppose Nationalism abandons ethics and moral values as they did in Russia from 1914 to the formation of the Soviet Union State Atheism in 1922. In that case, it is immoral and violating the Spirit of the Natural Law, given by the Creator of Life on the planet Earth. The Holy Jewish Scriptures reveal God's mind and the expectations that a Holy God has put on Humanity. As a spirit of force motivator, Nationalism often claims to be on a high moral ground when the people respect their father and mother, grandparents, and elders and obey the civil land laws.

These are the three pillars that provide the people of a nation with the illusion that their Nation is moral, without repentance and rejection of the Soviet Union State Atheism, war crimes, and genocide. Russian is guilty of the Soviet Union State Atheism and making a safe haven for Satan on Earth. Of course, the minimum of human society's core values is essential. They must be respected for the people of a society to have moral values in their lives. People to abandon these ethics would be immoral. It is also possible for organized criminals to commit a crime, steal, and murder, continue to love their father and mother and respect the elders. Truth requires an authentic spirit to be valid. God is not a physical being, judging people by outward appearance. God is a Spirit, a transparent Spirit that no human can conceal or hide their deeds or attitudes.

The three core moral values are taught, trained, and disciplined to the children of families early in life when the human mind and heart is tender and malleable. The family environment with children is emotionally empathetic to each family member. They maintain a spirit of unity with care and love.

After the toddler stage to the late teenage years, human beings become influenced by the world's people's standards and norms. Suppose they are no input into their lives outside, emphasizing the importance of ethics and moral values above personal favoritism, short-term financial or material gains. In that case, there will be a compromise to the point where law-breaking and immorality are rationalized and justified by personal wants, desires, and needs.

Moral corruption will inevitably occur when ethics and moral values are not respected and esteemed by people's families of a society. People do get corrupted by the influence of other corrupted people in the world. Then the disconnect from ethical and moral values, because of the lesser agenda and purpose in life, whether it is barely to make a living and survive, or to secure a better position by climbing up the rank and file, or for more personal power. Different sexes use different means to advance their self-interests and to secure better future prospects. Quality personal relationships are vital in keeping people alive ethically in tune with moral harmony, respecting God-given life on Earth.

What is the hidden secret that keeps strong bonds in people with ethics and morality in society?

The hidden secret for many people is the Creator of Life instructions, message. It promises to those that keep His covenant. Information from the Creator of Life to Humanity. Clearly spelled out how and where where the living soul functions of the mind need to be focused on in life.

- Intellect
- Conscience
- Imagination
- Will
- Memory
- Emotions.

The focus of human life should not be self-serving. Some of the world's most miserable people have trusted their feelings, the soul desires, wants, and physical lusts in life. Without guiding principles, they abuse alcohol, drugs and slide into deeper depravity. The human soul appetites can lead to pleasures that eventually corrupt and destroy their physical, spiritual, and soul lives. Millions of people with addictive lifestyles, as priorities in their Worldview that they serve. Pleasure seeking can become an addiction that no longer delivers the desired contentment, satisfaction, and highs.

> Ephesians 5:17-19 (ESV) "Therefore, do not be foolish, but understand what the will of the Lord is. And do not get drunk with wine, for that is debauchery, but be filled with the Spirit, addressing one another in psalms and hymns and spiritual songs, singing and making melody to the Lord with your heart,"

> Proverbs 20 New International Version. "Wine is a mocker and beer a brawler; whoever is led astray by them is not wise."

> Proverbs 23:29-35 (CJB) "Who has misery? Who has regret? Who fights and complains all the time? Who gets bruised for no

good reason? Who has bloodshot eyes? Those who spend their time over wine, those always trying out mixed drinks. Don't gaze at the red wine as it gives its color to the cup. It may glide down smoothly now; but in the end, it bites like a serpent —yes, it strikes like a poisonous snake. Your eyes will see peculiar things, your mind will utter nonsense."

Isaiah 5:11 (CJB). "Woe to those who get up early to pursue intoxicating liquor; who stay up late at night, until wine inflames them."

Isaiah 5:22 ESV. "Woe to those who are heroes at drinking wine, and valiant men in mixing strong drink,"

Hosea 4:11 (CJB). "Whoring and wine, both old and new, take away my people's wits."

1 Corinthians 6:10 (ESV). "Nor thieves, nor the greedy, nor drunkards, nor revilers, nor swindlers will inherit the kingdom of God."

1. Creator of Life does exist. He is an Eternal Spirit, not a physical being.
2. He knows as the Creator of Life what human beings are made of.
3. The Creator of Life requires that Humanity give respect to the Creator of Life.
4. By learning the names and the attributes of the Creator of Life, we express faith in God.
5. It is impossible to please God without any interest, acquired knowledge, or expressed faith in Him.
6. Creator of life instructs Humanity to go to God as the First source for life instructions.
7. By taking the time to learn from the Master instructions in the Torah, Humanity can make better life choices.
8. Making a life commitment to know the Truth that Yeshua Hamashiach presented, it is possible to have a new life. Holy Spirit breaking negative habits and addictions that self-serving life attaches to.

[28]

# UNITED STATES LIGHT UPON A HILL

Matthew 5:14-16. CJB

> Matthew 5:13. CJB. "You are salt for the Land. But if salt becomes tasteless, how can it be made salty again? It is no longer good for anything except being thrown out for people to trample on.

> Matthew 5:14-16. CJB "You are light for the world. A town built on a hill cannot be hidden. Likewise, when people light a lamp, they don't cover it with a bowl but put it on a lampstand, so that it shines for everyone in the house. In the same way, let your light shine before people, so that they may see the good things you do and praise your Father in heaven."

Worldview conflict can cause conflict on a large scale all the way down to individual relationships and everything else between the two far ends of the scale. There are people in the world that stand up for what is ethically and morally right, most often because they have faith in the God of Abraham, Isaac and Jacob. They accept and acknowledge that the Jewish Holy Scriptures are divinely inspired messages, contained in the books of the Bible. Therefore, they are a resource of information that instructs people how to live and behave ethically and morally, in the will of God. United States of America, historically are known as people who believe in the the God of the Bible. Unlike many other Nations, they openly acknowledge God on their dollar, "In God We Trust".

The United States 2020 Election once again has brought up the conflicting polarized Worldviews that even the United States people have in their nation value systems, such as a life philosophy, and a Worldview. The two main political parties divide the people in many ways into two opposing groups. Conservative (Republican) values on one side, and the liberal (Democrats) values on the other side. The Republican Worldview in many ways reflects the Judaeo-Christian Worldview.The Evangelical Christians support the Republican party policies. The life philosophy and worldview of the Republican Party can be read in the Republican 2016 Platform.

Republican Party Platform 2016

**Preamble**

*We believe in American exceptionalism.*
 *We believe the United States of America is unlike any other nation on earth.*

*We believe America is exceptional because of our historic role — first as refuge, then as defender, and now as exemplar of liberty for the world to see.*

*We affirm — as did the Declaration of Independence: that all are created equal, endowed by their Creator with inalienable rights of life, liberty, and the pursuit of happiness.*

*We believe in the Constitution as our founding document.*

*We believe the Constitution was written not as a flexible document, but as our enduring covenant.*

*We believe our constitutional system — limited government, separation of powers, federalism, and the rights of the people — must be preserved uncompromised for future generations.*

*We believe political freedom and economic freedom are indivisible.*

*When political freedom and economic freedom are separated — both are in peril; when united, they are invincible.*

*We believe that people are the ultimate resource — and that the people, not the government, are the best stewards of our country's God-given natural resources.*

*As Americans and as Republicans, we wish for peace — so we insist on strength. We will make America safe. We seek friendship with all peoples and all nations, but we recognize and are prepared to deal with evil in the world.*

*Based on these principles, this platform is an invitation and a roadmap. It invites every American to join us and shows the path to a stronger, safer, and more prosperous America.*

*This platform is optimistic because the American people are optimistic.*

*This platform lays out — in clear language — the path to making America great and united again.".................................*

Source: https://www.presidency.ucsb.edu/documents/2016-republican-party-platform

Why do the Republicans believe the following?

- We believe in American exceptionalism.
- We believe the United States of America is unlike any other nation on earth.

Primarily because they have adopted the Judaeo-Christian Worldview from the Jewish Holy Scriptures of the Bible.

Secondly, because of their chronological history, their founding fathers were sufficiently enlightened spiritually to understand that there is a Creator of Life that either allows nations to prosper or to experience setbacks.

Theologically that could be described as the Sovereignty of God. The principles of obedience lead to blessings, and disobedience leads to setbacks and frustrations.

The third scenario is the worst-case scenario. The incorrigible obstinate and willful to trust their own understanding of the visual material world to be all there is in life.

Nowhere in the Bible does it say that the Creator of Life is a material being. The Bible says that G-d is a Spirit being, not a physical being.

Therefore, if you look for evidence of God's existence, you won't find Him. He is nowhere to be seen.

However, there are the works of God that point to the intelligent design of life. The works of God are the evidence of Intelligent design that does point to the Creator of Life outside of time and space.

What is the US Democratic Party Worldview?

In many respects, they are asymmetrically opposite, especially regarding the Jewish Holy Scriptures. Whether we call it the Jewish Holy Scriptures, The Tanakh, or the Torah. These are the original terms to describe the books of the Bible distributed to the Western world. According to the will of the Creator of Life, many people in the Western world have accepted the Jewish Holy Scriptures as the information source with instructions to humanity on how to live morally on the planet earth. It takes faith to believe and to take on God at His Word. It is faith in God that leads people to learning the Instructions given in the Torah, and it is faith to place higher value on the Written Instructions from God, in order to live a life that is in line with the will of the Creator of Life. That what obedience to God looks and feels like. There needs to be traction, and not only wheel spin.

It was the Democratic Party leaders that wanted to remove Bibles from the US Schools. Also to stop prayer at schools. Most recently (December 2020) the Senate voted on Legalizing marijuana, The Democratic party was all in for legalizing marijuana. The Republican party was against.

House Passed Bill to Legalize Marijuana, but Senate Vote Unlikely.

Party:

| PARTY. | YEA. | NAY. |
|---|---|---|
| DEMOCRATS: | 222. | 6 |
| REPUBLICANS: | 5. | 158. |
| INDEPENDENT: | 1. | |
| TOTALS: | 228. | 164. |

The above Bill to Legalize Marijuana chart numbers and the Political Parties reveals many things about the Political Party policy, philosophy and their Worldview. On one side you have a Political Party that have shaped their party values according to the Judaeo-Christian Worldview that is described in the 66 books, written by some 40 authors of the Bible canon. Drugs use should not be indulged, because it corrupts human behavior. Reference is found in the Letter to the Ephesians. Chapter 5:

> "Therefore, pay careful attention to how you conduct your life — live wisely, not unwisely. Use your time well, for these are evil days. So don't be foolish, but try to understand what the will of the Lord is. Don't get drunk with wine, because it makes you lose control. Instead, keep on being filled with the Spirit — sing psalms, hymns and spiritual songs to each other; sing to the Lord and make music in your heart to him; always give thanks for everything to God the Father in the name of our Lord Yeshua the Messiah." Ephesians 5: 18-20.

People will always get defensive and object to everything that may limit their life pleasures, philosophy and Worldview. Therefore, some will say, the above bible verse does not say marijuana, it says "don't get drunk with wine". Wisdom always considers many variables, reading between the lines, does mention that being drunk makes you lose self control. In other words, drunken state, drugs alter the mind, and the altered mind state compromises moral values and ethics. Other Bible translations use the word debauchery.

> "And do not get drunk with wine, for that is debauchery; but ever be filled and stimulated with the [Holy] Spirit." Ephesians 5:18.

**Jewish Holy Scripture Bible Republican Worldview**

Some 60 million Evangelical Christian in United States are active members of a local or International Church, they have a Biblical Worldview. They know Bible verses from the New Testament, Philippians 3:17-21. They pay attention to the letters of the Apostles.

> "Brothers, join in imitating me, and pay attention to those who live according to the pattern we have set for you. For many — I have told you about them often before, and even now I say it with tears — live as enemies of the Messiah's execution-stake. They are headed for destruction! Their god is the belly; they are proud of what they ought to be ashamed of, since they are concerned about the things of the world. But we are citizens of heaven, and it is from there that we expect a Deliverer, the Lord

> Yeshua the Messiah. He will change the bodies we have in this humble state and make them like his glorious body, using the power which enables him to bring everything under his control."

### Counterfeit Worldviews

The protest pattern of populist movements always tries to throw the responsible Classic Worldview baby out with the dirty water. That is telling. It reveals how populist understanding of a responsible Worldview is shallow. And how little respect and empathy for reality-based Government leaders.

On the other hand, the blame of populist movements could be pointed at the rivaling political parties. They are often competing with other political parties trying to outdo each other, with promises that create false expectations and delusional realities for the voters. Politicians fail to deliver on their promises, which directly blows those who placed their hopes on the politicians' promises. Therefore, the game of politics is often a corrupting exercise.

What is the answer to the corrupting effects of cheap political rivalry?

The answer is found in a reality check of the intellectual power of the voter. The voter should have their head screwed on, with the ability to think straight in line with a responsible reality of reason and logic. Suppose they don't wake up to the emotional roller coaster ride of irresponsible politics. In that case, they will be put over the barrel repeatedly until they accept their own error of judgment.

### Failure to Accept the Realities of Life as it is.

To know which Information is correct from false, people need to rediscover logic and reasoning basics. They need to learn the basic principles of rational and logical thinking.

To know which is correct from false, people need to rediscover the basics of logic and reasoning. They need to learn the basic principles of rational and logical thinking. Even with the fundamental First Four Principles of Logic, it needs a truth-based frame in the reality of healthy living, in the will of the Creator of Life.

Here are the First Principles of Logic to fresh the memory, from Being Logical: A Guide to Good Thinking book. By McInerny, D.Q.

The First Principles of Logic:

1. Identity.
2. Excluded middle
3. Sufficient reason.
4. Contradiction.

THE PRINCIPLE OF IDENTITY
Stated: A thing is what it is.
Explanation: The whole of existing reality is not a homogenous mass. It is a composition of individuals, and the individuals are distinguishable from one another.

THE PRINCIPLE OF THE EXCLUDED MIDDLE
Stated: Between being and nonbeing there is no middle state.
Explanation: Something either exists or it does not exist; there is no halfway point between the two. The lamp sitting on my desk is either really there or it is not. There is no other possibility. We might ask: How about becoming? Isn't the state of becoming between those of being and nonbeing? The answer is no. There is no such

thing as just becoming; there are only things that become. The state of becoming is already within the realm of existence.

THE PRINCIPLE OF SUFFICIENT REASON
Stated: There is a sufficient reason for everything.
Explanation: The principle could also be called "the principle of causality." It states that everything that actually exists in the physical Universe has an explanation for its existence. What is implied in principle is that nothing in the physical Universe is self-explanatory or the cause of itself. (For a thing to be a cause of itself, it would somehow have to precede itself, which is absurd.)

THE PRINCIPLE OF CONTRADICTION
Stated: It is impossible for something both to be and not be at the same time and in the same respect.
Explanation: This principle could be regarded as a fuller expression of the principle of identity, for if X is X (principle of identity) it cannot at one and the same time be non-X (principle of contradiction).
Source: McInerny, D.Q. Being Logical: A Guide to Good Thinking.

In everyday modern life with machines, devices, gadgets, appliances, people have no issues to consult a competent service provider. When there is a need to get a device serviced, upgraded, or repaired. It is understood that a qualified technician has the necessary knowledge of the device, machine, or appliance operations to get the necessary task completed. The service person's qualifications are based on technical knowledge and skills. Processing of technical Information by a qualified technician. That is taken; it is a no-brainer. People understand the process of servicing machines and devices to be a logical, rational process.

The world of devices, gadgets, appliances, and machines is at a lower level than other life priorities. E.g., voting for a Political Party to manage National Security, Banking, Economics, Human and Religious Rights, and investments. Why then is it that people are not consulting a rational, logical process in their decision making? People often make a voting decision on emotional impulses. Feelings, the emotions of their soul, hardship, poverty, independent rights, and other social issues are why they vote for a particular political party candidate.

Again, it could be argued that it is the fault of the Political party candidates that hype up the people's emotions about voting. In their long one year, political campaigns, sale pitches, and false hope promises. The United States is renowned for the political hype over its presidential candidates. They are over the top in their campaign budgets.

"Campaigning to be elected president of the U.S. is an expensive undertaking. During the 2012 presidential race, Barack Obama and Mitt Romney spent a combined sum of nearly $1.12bn, according to the Centre for Responsive Politics. Although U.S. elections have almost always been a costly affair, the costs have only spiraled over time. Between Abraham Lincoln's 1860 campaign and Donald Trump's in 2016, the amount spent to be elected president increased more than 250-fold, even when the numbers are adjusted for inflation." (worldfinance.com).

Democratic presidential elects spent US$1.120,000,000 in 2012 presidential race. That is an outrageous amount of money. It shows how much they coveted to be in the office of a president. Therefore they hyped up the people with their high ticket campaigns to trawl people into their political camps.
What about 2020? How much did they spend?

"Total 2020 election spending to hit nearly $14 billion, more than double 2016's sum. According to the nonpartisan Center for Responsive Politics, the amount spent on both the presidential and congressional campaigns will hit nearly $14 billion." (CNN)

AMERICAN DOLLAR.

What did the presidential candidates talk about on their campaigns? Economics, national security, border security, people trafficking, American people Worldview, and national employment. The U.S. Republican Party candidate Donald Trump did most of the talking. The Democratic party candidate Joe Biden only had small crowds to share his vision with on his campaigns. Republican party Trump talked mostly about himself and far too little about the values, politics, and the Republican party's values. Why not? Maybe because he could not help it. Maybe because he was not a professional politician, he did not see the value of promoting the republican party. Trump would have won more people if he had talked more about the Republican party and less about himself. Anyone knows that a political party's real powerhouse is the party's people and not just one individual leader. That is a principle of good leadership.

2020 Conflicts Within a Nation

The anarchy protest pattern that emerged in early 1900 in Russia has spread worldwide, including the United States. People without faith are more likely to be given to anarchy. Because they have no external moral code to follow, they go by the seat of their pants emotions. Many influential people glorify people, demonstrations, and revolutions. Why? Because it is perceived to advance their cause and their Worldview.

The validity of populist movements, demonstrators' emotional reactions.

The populist movement may have a lot of passion for their cause, emotional thrust to drive their Worldview through to a future Government. A populist movement like Karl Marx Socialism is a seriously erroneous Worldview. Despite how passionately his followers may believe in his philosophy. It is a utopian pie in the sky. Disconnected Idealism from the real world created by Intelligent, conscious being. Creator of Life, the First cause of the Universe.

God does not apologize for His infinite existence outside of time and space. He has provided life on planet earth, allowed humanity to interact, see, and experience life. It is a free will choice of the mind and heart to believe and give respect and honor to the Creator of Life. The primary evidence of the Intelligent being is found in the natural world.

Obstinate Unbelievers

By repressing the primary external evidence of intelligent design in Creation, the unbelievers conclude that their desired Worldview lens's conflicting perception can only be cleared up by recreating a more liberal worldview according to their own desires and imaginations. So they attempt to recreate the external Universe and life on earth according to the aberration of their inner being. Contrary to accepting the moral value-based Worldview given by the Creator of Life over 3460 years ago at Mount Sinai.

By What Function is Repression of Information Performed?

It is found in the human living soul functions of the mind.

- Intellect
- Consciousness
- Imagination
- Will
- Memory
- Emotions

When analyzing the arguments and the debates, we find that the specific areas of repression and denial surface for all humanity to see. Shockingly it is the one and the same, as it was 100 years ago. And the one and the same as it was 1000, 2000, 3000, and 4000 years ago. Precisely the same repression and expressed denial by the human mind. It is evident in the predisposition. The objectors who have preloaded themselves with a mind-set. They are saying between the lines. The objectors do not accept or want to see the primary evidence. They already know that they would be forced to admit the Primary Evidence representative and the Creator of Life law Principles by accepting the evidence.

For the Russian Bolsheviks in early 1900, the evidence was in the Creation. The representative was the Russian Monarchy-Nicholas II. The problem was the Classic Worldview. According to integrity, honesty, represented by the classic rule of law principles. Meaning, objective Truth and honesty is a golden rule that should never be disconnected from personal responsibility. Because it is an integral part of the individual person's identity that gives purpose and meaning in life. The same rule applies to all levels of society, from the King down to whoever. It's the golden rule. It shows no partiality. Why not? Because all human beings are subject to the ultimate authority, the King of Righteousness.

> Romans 12: 19. "Never seek revenge, my friends; instead, leave that to God's anger; for in the Tanakh it is written, "Adonai says, 'Vengeance is my responsibility; I will repay.'"

Rejecting the Proposal

People evaluate all the time what is on offer. Regarding the U.S. 2020 elections, they have had over 4 years to evaluate the United States 2020 proposal. Before that, they have a long history of the Political Party proposals by the Republican and the Democratic Party. Populist proposals trawl populist people. All voting people's souls operate and react to reasonable proposals. What is a reasonable proposal by a Political party? There are many levels to a Political Party's values.

Many of the political party proposals are strategic moves with objective goals. Political party long term objective goals can be hidden, convoluted with other alibis that smokescreen the political objective. Two such hidden agendas of the U.S. Democratic party was the Mexico open borders strategy. Legalize marijuana is another one. Legalize marijuana is a populist move to reach a populist group of voters. The open Mexico borders policy has a hidden agenda that may work for the U.S. Democratic Party for harvesting more votes.

According to the Pew Research Center, they estimated the illegal immigrant population to be 11.1 million in 2014 or approximately 3 percent of the U.S. population. During the last 4 years of the Trump Presidency (2016-2020), the number of foreign-born people living in the U.S. rose by about 3% from 43.7 million the year before Mr. Trump's election to 45 million last year. The number of people living in the U.S. born in Mexico has fallen steadily since Mr. Trump's election. Comprehensive coverage of the U.S. Mexico border crisis. The data for 2019 suggests that would-be migrants continue to cross undeterred. The number of detentions at the border was more than double the number for the previous year, mainly driven by a considerable rise in the number of families attempting to make the crossing.

The US-Mexico border is an emotional issue for tens of millions of people. The question is this, is the emotional well-being of migrants the highest priority in securing United States borders? The right answer is? Of course not. The people crossing the Mexico border would be passionate about the US-Mexico border policy. Therefore it becomes a political hot button that the U.S. Democratic party cannot resist. They are all over it because they are in it for political reasons, driven by political gain, even to the extreme of undermining the Constitution of the United States in effect. They are in the role of an agitator ready and willing to put a spanner in the gears of a Super State.

U.S. 2020 Elections Corruption and Fraud

The same repression and expressed denial. It is evident in the predisposition. The objectors have preloaded themselves with a mind-set to do whatever it takes to win. They were sold the idea over the last 4 years that the Republican candidate was a lousy deal for America. It was heard worldwide, including Australia, Radio National programs ranted crack-pipe hate-Trump comments for years. Why would National Radio editors and program hosts in Australia go on with the hate-Republican Party narrative for years?

For a straight forward answer to that question, you would want to ask a psychiatrist or a psychologist. Based on the number of times they repeated the same line on Australia's National radio while they were on air. At least one program host is smug about being an atheist during that same period, with no qualms regarding his obstinate unbelief in the primary evidence of the creator of Life. Also boasting of him being a member of the communist party in the early '60s. Every U.S. Republican Party President since Ronald Regan is bagged as misfits.

Why? Because they do not believe or represent the Classic Worldview. A Worldview based on the moral values presented in the Jewish Holy Scriptures of the Bible. The Judeo-Christian Worldview is an adaptation of the same Biblical Worldview. They both have absolute moral values, with the responsibility to the Creator of Life that gave Torah's instruction to humanity in the first place, some 3460 years ago. That is a classic Worldview. Have faith in God, believe, and respect YHWH's word. Honor your parents. Do not steal. Do not covet. Do not commit adultery. As it is written in the book of Exodus, chapter 20.

[29]

# THE ILLEGITIMATE AUTHORITY

Soviet Union leaders acted outside of the Spirit of the Natural Law, or the legal rule of law; they were NOT responsible for civil authority during 1922-41. The Bolsheviks movement started as rebellious outlaws and ended up as an organized crime mob in the Russian leadership vacuum. A vacuum that the Bolsheviks engineered themselves. There is only one legitimate neutral authority regarding the spirit of the law, which is the Spirit of the Natural Law. The rule of law is regarded and respected by many nations. A legal rule of law is entirely dependent on the spirit of Natural Law. The spirit of the law does not conform to the personal agenda of dictators whims. The spirit of the natural law is constant and not a respecter of persons.

The lawlessness that the Soviet Union manifested in 1922-1945 renders its authority invalid. It was corrupted, immoral, and discriminated against the spirit of peace. The Soviet Union leader's worldview was misguided. Their life philosophy was false. Their methods and tactics to persuade people's minds to their philosophy were the schemes of organized criminals. Therefore the territorial claims and treaties that it forced upon neighbors with the use of threats. The threat to the continuation of the aggressive war that the Soviet Union had initiated in November 1939. It can be described as being extortion by the use of military aggression.

NATURAL LAW THEORY THROUGH DEDUCTIVE REASONING
Deductive reasoning, also deductive logic, logical deduction is the process of reasoning from one or more statements (premises) to reach a logically certain conclusion. The deductive reasoning goes in the same direction as that of the conditionals and links premises with conclusions. If all premises are correct, the terms are clear, and the rules of deductive logic are followed, then the conclusion reached is necessarily true. If we have no confidence in deductive logical reasoning, then we have no confidence in the ability to think about knowledge. If we have no confidence in thinking knowledge, then we are in a state of ignorance. People do have confidence in mathematics; it is a reliable design of the creation. The world that surrounds us is digital in the design versus analog. It can be discovered mathematically, logically, and with the ability to reason.

THE LETTER OF THE LAW VERSUS THE SPIRIT OF THE LAW
The letter of the law versus the spirit of the law is an idiomatic antithesis. When one obeys the letter of the law but not the spirit, one is obeying the literal interpretation of the words (the "letter") of the law, but not necessarily the intent of those who wrote the law. Conversely, when one obeys the spirit of the law but not the letter, one is doing what the authors of the law intended, though not necessarily adhering to the literal wording.

"Law" originally referred to legislative statute, but in the idiom may refer to any rule. Intentionally following the letter of the law but not the spirit may be accomplished through exploiting technicalities, loopholes, and ambiguous language.

INTERNATIONAL LAW
Quote: *"The Geneva Conventions of 1864, 1906, and 1929 had established international standards that were understood to encompass the humanitarian treatment of prisoners and citizens in occupied territories during the war."*

*"Mitoma says, however, that at the time of the trials, criticism centered on the charges brought against the defendants for crimes against peace and crimes against humanity because such charges had not previously been established as part of the international law."*

"The guiding ideology of the Nuremberg Trials was laying down principles that there is a baseline of the natural law of universal human rights that are there at all times," he says. "That guiding theory informs the emergence of human rights; the idea [is] that we have to advocate for human rights on a global level, and there are dimensions to our basic humanity that give us moral rights that form the fundamental basis of our morality and our humanity." (Wikipedia, International Law, 2018)

NUREMBERG TRIALS CRITICISED
These quotes from The Nuremberg Trials and the Holocaust.
DO THE 'WAR CRIMES' TRIALS PROVE EXTERMINATION?
By Mark Weber.
*"Robert Jackson, the chief US prosecutor and a former US Attorney General declared that the Nuremberg Tribunal "is a continuation of the war effort of the Allied nations" against Germany. He added that the Tribunal "is not bound by the procedural and substantive refinements of our respective judicial or constitutional system ..." /5*

*"Judge Iola T. Nikitchenko, who presided at the Tribunal's solemn opening session, was a vice-chairman of the supreme court of the USSR before and after his service at Nuremberg. In August 1936, he had been a judge at the infamous Moscow show trial of Zinoviev and Kamenev."/6. "At a joint planning conference shortly before the Nuremberg Tribunal convened, Nikitchenko bluntly explained the Soviet view of the enterprise: /7.*

*"We are dealing here with the chief war criminals who have already been convicted and whose conviction has been already announced by both the Moscow and Crimea [Yalta] declarations by the heads of the [Allied] governments... The whole idea is to secure quick and just punishment for the crime..." - "Judge Iola T. Nikitchenko (USSR).*

*"The fact that the Nazi leaders are criminals has already been established. The task of the Tribunal is only to determine the measure of the guilt of each particular person and mete out the necessary punishment — the sentences."*

*"In violation of the first Nuremberg count of "planning, preparation, initiating or waging a war of aggression," the Soviet Union attacked Finland in December 1939 (and was expelled from the League of Nations as a result). A few months later, the Red Army invaded Lithuania, Latvia, and Estonia and ruthlessly incorporated them into the Soviet Union. The postwar French government violated international law and the Nuremberg charge of "maltreatment of prisoners of war" by employing large numbers of German prisoners of war as forced laborers in France."*

*" In 1945 the United States, Britain, and the Soviet Union jointly agreed to the brutal deportation of more than ten million Germans from their ancient homes in eastern and central Europe, a violation of the Nuremberg count of "deportation, and other inhumane acts committed against any civilian population." /26.*

*Chief US prosecutor Robert Jackson privately acknowledged in a letter to President Truman that the Allies (/25). have done or are doing some of the very things we are prosecuting the Germans for. The French are so violating the Geneva Convention in the treatment of [German] prisoners of war that our command is taking back prisoners sent to them [for forced labor in France]. We are prosecuting plunder, and our Allies are practicing it. We say aggressive war is a crime and one of our allies asserts sovereignty over the Baltic States based on no title except conquest.*

*"Mikhail Vozlenski, a Soviet historian who served as a translator at the Nuremberg Tribunal in 1946, later recalled that he and the other Soviet personnel felt out of place there because of the alleged crimes of the German leaders were "the norm of our life" in the Soviet Union. /29 The Soviet role in the proceedings, which the United States fully supported, moved American diplomat and historian George F. Kennan to condemn the entire Nuremberg enterprise as a "horror" and a "mockery."/30.*

*"Nuremberg's double standard was condemned at the time by the British weekly The Economist. It pointed out that whereas both Britain and France had supported the expulsion of the Soviet Union from the League of Nations in 1939 for its unprovoked attack against Finland, just six years later, these same two governments were cooperating with the USSR as a respected equal*

at Nuremberg. "Nor should the Western world console itself that the Russians alone stand condemned at the bar of the Allies' justice," the Economist editorial went on. It continued:"/31.

..."Among crimes against humanity stands the offense of the indiscriminate bombing of civilian populations. Can the Americans who dropped the atom bomb and the British who destroyed the cities of western Germany plead "not guilty" on this count? Crimes against humanity also include the mass expulsion of populations. Can the Anglo-Saxon leaders who at Potsdam condoned the expulsion of millions of Germans from their homes hold themselves completely innocent?. The nations sitting in judgment [at Nuremberg] have so clearly proclaimed themselves exempt from the law which they have administered".

"German guilt for the killing of thousands of Polish officers in the Katyn forest near Smolensk was similarly confirmed by Nuremberg document USSR-54." This detailed report by yet another Soviet "investigative" commission was submitted as proof for the charge made in the joint indictment of the four Allied governments. As a Soviet prosecutor explained:

"We find, in the Indictment, one of the most important criminal acts for which the major war criminals are responsible was the mass execution of Polish prisoners of war shot in the Katyn forest near Smolensk by the German fascist invaders." /44

(Interestingly, two of the eight members of the Soviet Katyn Commission were also members of the Soviet Auschwitz commission: Academician N. Burdenko and Metropolitan Nikolai.) It was not until 1990 that the Soviet government finally acknowledged that the Katyn massacre was carried out, not by a German unit, as "proven" at Nuremberg, but by the Soviet secret police. "/45

The same sentence could be proclaimed to the Soviet Union Leaders from the mouth of Judge Iola T. Nikitchenko. On the basis, he was prepared to proclaim the innocent of Katyn forest massacre guilty and the guilty innocent at Nuremberg 1945 innocent. The Spirit of the Natural Law was seriously violated by the Bolshevik spirit Soviet Union leaders from 1917 -1940. The Russian Judge Iola T. Nikitchenko also committed Perjury. (Nuremberg-1945, Nuremberg trials, 1945)

WHAT IS PERJURY?

Perjury is a crime that occurs when an individual willfully makes a false statement during a judicial proceeding after he or she has taken an oath to speak the truth. The Nuremberg Trials of 1945, 1946 was the most significant International court trials in history. The Russian Judge Iola T. Nikitchenko showed his true colors, no respect for the Spirit of the Natural Law.

We are dealing here with the chief war criminals who have already been convicted and whose conviction has been already announced by both the Spirit of the Natural Law and the authority of the Holy Scriptures in principles... The whole idea is to secure quick and just punishment for their war crimes...The fact that the Soviet Union leaders are criminals has already been established. The task of the Tribunal is only to determine the measure of the guilt of each particular person and mete out the necessary punishment — the sentences.

[30]

# MOSES DEUTERONOMY CHAPTER 32 (CJB)

DEUTERONOMY CHAPTER 32 (CJB)
 "Parashah 53: Ha'azinu (Hear) 32:1–52
 "Hear, oh heavens, as I speak! Listen, earth, to the words from my mouth!
 May my teaching fall like rain. May my speech condense like dew, like light rain on blades of grass, or showers on growing plants.
 "For I will proclaim the name of Adonai. Come, declare the greatness of our God!
 The Rock! His work is perfect, for all his ways are just. A trustworthy God who does no wrong, he is righteous and straight.
 "He is not corrupt; the defect is in his children, a crooked and perverted generation.
 You foolish people, so lacking in wisdom, is this how you repay Adonai? He is your father, who made you his! It was he who formed and prepared you!
 (ii) "Remember how the old days were; think of the years through all the ages. Ask your father — he will tell you; your leaders too — they will inform you.
 "When 'Elyon gave each nation its heritage, when he divided the human race, he assigned the boundaries of peoples according to Isra'el's population;
 but Adonai's share was his own people, Ya'akov his allotted heritage.
 "He found his people in desert country, in a howling, wasted wilderness. He protected him and cared for him, guarded him like the pupil of his eye,
 like an eagle that stirs up her nest, hovers over her young, spreads out her wings, takes them and carries them as she flies.
 "Adonai alone led his people; no alien god was with him. (iii) He made them ride on the heights of the earth. They ate the produce of the fields.
 He had them suck honey from the rocks and olive oil from the crags, curds from the cows and milk from the sheep, with lamb fat, rams from Bashan and goats,
 with the finest wheat flour; and you drank sparkling wine from the blood of grapes.
 "But Yeshurun grew fat and kicked (you grew fat, thick, gross!). He abandoned God his Maker; he scorned the Rock, his salvation.
 They roused him to jealousy with alien gods, provoked him with abominations.
 They sacrificed to demons, non-gods, gods that they had never known, new gods that had come up lately, which your ancestors had not feared.
 You ignored the Rock who fathered you, you forgot God, who gave you birth. (iv) "Adonai saw and was filled with scorn at his sons' and daughters' provocation.
 He said, 'I will hide my face from them and see what will become of them; for they are a perverse generation, untrustworthy children.
 They aroused my jealousy with a non-god and provoked me with their vanities; I will arouse their jealousy with a non-people
and provoke them with a vile nation.

"'For my anger has been fired up. It burns to the depths of Sh'ol, devouring the earth and its crops, kindling the very roots of the hills.

I will heap disasters on them and use up all my arrows against them.

"'Fatigued by hunger, they will be consumed by fever and bitter defeat; I will send them the fangs of wild beasts, and the poison of reptiles crawling in the dust.

Outside, the sword makes parents childless; inside, there is panic, as young men and girls alike are slain, sucklings and graybeards together.

"'I considered putting an end to them, erasing their memory from the human race; but I feared the insolence of their enemy, feared that their foes would mistakenly think, "We ourselves accomplished this; Adonai had nothing to do with it."

"'They are a nation without common sense, utterly lacking in discernment. (v) If they were wise they could figure it out and understand their destiny.

After all, how can one chase a thousand and two put ten thousand to rout, unless their Rock sells them to their enemies, unless Adonai hands them over?

For our enemies have no rock like our Rock — even they can see that!

"'Rather, their vine is from the vine of S'dom, from the fields of 'Amora — their grapes are poisonous, their clusters are bitter; their wine is snake poison, the cruel venom of vipers.

"'Isn't this hidden with me, sealed in my storehouses?

Vengeance and payback are mine for the time when their foot slips; for the day of their calamity is coming soon, their doom is rushing upon them.'

"Yes, Adonai will judge his people, taking pity on his servants, when he sees that their strength is gone, that no one is left, slave or free.

Then he will ask, 'Where are their gods, the rock in whom they trusted? Who ate the fat of their sacrifices and drank the wine of their drink offering?

Let him get up and help you, let him protect you!

See now that I, yes, I, am he; and there is no god beside me. I put to death, and I make alive; I wound, and I heal; no one saves anyone from my hand!

(vi) "'For I lift up my hand to heaven and swear, "As surely as I am alive forever, if I sharpen my flashing sword and set my hand to judgment, I will render vengeance to my foes,

repay those who hate me.

I will make my arrows drunk with blood, my sword will devour flesh — the blood of the slain and the captives, flesh from the wild-haired heads of the enemy."'

"Sing out, you nations, about his people! For he will avenge the blood of his servants. He will render vengeance to his adversaries and make atonement for the land of his people."

(vii) 44 Moshe came and proclaimed all the words of this song in the hearing of the people and of Hoshea the son of Nun.

When he had finished speaking all these words to all Isra'el, he said to them, "Take to heart all the words of my testimony against you today, so that you can use them in charging your children to be careful to obey all the words of this Torah. For this is not a trivial matter for you; on the contrary, it is your life! Through it you will live long in the land you are crossing the Yarden to possess.""

(Moses, Deuteronomy 32: 1-47, 1446 AD)

## MORAL PHILOSOPHY CONSEQUENTIALIST MORAL REASONING

Consequentialism is the class of normative ethical theories holding that the consequences of one's conduct are the ultimate basis for any judgment about the rightness or wrongness of that conduct. Thus, from a consequentialist standpoint, a morally right act (or omission from acting) is one that will produce a good outcome or consequence. In an extreme form, the idea of consequentialism is commonly encapsulated in the saying, "the end justifies the means," meaning that if a goal is morally important, any method of achieving it is acceptable. (Wikipedia, Consequentialism, 2018)

## REASON OF RIGHT AND WRONG?

The consequential moral reasoning is used by politicians and dictators; they justify the means by the ends. Consequentialist Mora reasoning (Utilitarian doctrine)Locates morality in the consequences of an act.

Jeremy Bentham February 1747 – 6 June 1832) was an English philosopher, jurist, and social reformer regarded as the founder of modern utilitarianism. Bentham defined as the "fundamental axiom" of his philosophy the principle that "it is the greatest happiness of the highest number that is the measure of right and wrong." He became a leading theorist in Anglo-American philosophy of law, and a political radical whose ideas influenced the development of welfarism. (Encyclopedia, Jeremy Bentham, 1748)

[31]

# CATEGORICAL MORAL REASONING

*"Locates morality absolute moral requirements, in certain duties and rights, regardless of the consequences."* (Harward-Edu, 2018)

*The categorical imperative (German: kategorischer Imperative) is the central philosophical concept in the deontological moral philosophy of Immanuel Kant. Introduced in Kant's 1785 Groundwork of the Metaphysics of Morals, it may be defined as a way of evaluating motivations for action. According to Kant, human beings occupy a special place in creation, and morality can be summed up in an imperative, or ultimate commandment of reason, from which all duties and obligations derive. He defined an imperative as any proposition declaring a specific action (or inaction) to be necessary.* (Encyclopedia, Categorical Imperative, 2018)

### EVASIVE SKEPTICISM

*"And so maybe it is just a matter of, each person having his or her principles and there's nothing more to be said about it, no way of reasoning." That is the version of skepticism, to which I would offer the following reply. It is true, these questions have been debated for a very long time, but the very fact that they have recurred and persisted may suggest that, though they are impossible in one sense, they are unavoidable in another. Moreover, the reason they are unavoidable is that we live some answers to these questions every day. So skepticism, just giving up on moral reflection, is no solution. Immanuel Kant described the problem with skepticism when he wrote, "Scepticism is a resting place for human reason, where it can reflect upon its dogmatic wanderings, but it is no dwelling place for permanent settlement...Simply to acquiesce in skepticism can never suffice to overcome the restlessness of reason."* (Harward-Edu, 2018)

### LOGIC AND REASON EXPLAINED

LOGIC IS ABOUT clear and effective thinking. It is a science and an art.

*"The whole purpose of reasoning, of logic, is to arrive at the truth of things. This is often an arduous task, as truth can sometimes be painfully elusive. But not to pursue truth would be absurd since it is the only thing that gives meaning to all our endeavors. It would be equally absurd to suppose that truth is something forever to be pursued but never to be attained, for that renders our activity purposeless, which is to say, irrational, and turns truth into a chimera."*

*"Many mistakes in reasoning are explained by the fact that we are not paying sufficient attention to the situation in which we find ourselves. A fact is something made or done. It has a clear objective status."* (McInerny, 2004) (p. 4).

#### Objective facts

*"There are two basic types of objective facts, things, and events. A "thing" is an actually existing entity, animal, vegetable, or mineral.*

*A subjective fact, to the subject experiencing it, is self-evident under normal circumstances. However, through such mechanisms as self- delusion or rationalization, a person could fail to get straight a fact even about himself. We all tend to favor our own ideas, which is natural enough. They are, after all, in a sense our very own babies, the conceptions of our minds.*

*But conception is possible in the thinking subject only because of the subject's encounter with the world. Our ideas owe their existence, ultimately, to things outside and independent of the mind to which they refer: objective facts).*

*"Our ideas are clear, and our understanding of them is clear, only to the extent that we keep constant tabs on the things to which they refer. The focus must always be on the originating sources of our ideas in the objective world. We do not really*

*understand our own ideas if we suppose them to be self-generating, that is, not owing to their existence to extramental realities."* (McInerny, 2004)

### Subjective Ideas

*"The more we focus on our ideas in a way that systematically ignores their objective origins, the more unreliable those ideas become.*

*"The healthy bonds that bind together the subjective and objective orders are put under great strain, and if we push the process too far, the bonds may break. Then we have effectively divorced ourselves from the objective world.*

*Instead of seeing the world as it is, we see a projected world, one that is not presented to our minds but which is the product of our minds."*

### Establishing a fact

*"When we speak of "establishing a fact," we do not refer to establishing the existence of an idea in mind. The idea in mind, as we have seen, is a subjective fact, but the kind of fact we are concerned with establishing is an objective fact. To do so, we must look beyond our ideas to their sources in the objective world. I establish a fact if I successfully ascertain that there is, for a particular idea I have in mind, a corresponding reality external to my mind."*

### Match Ideas to Facts

*"Match Ideas to Facts: There are three basic components to human knowledge: first, an objective fact (e.g., a cat); second, the idea of a cat; third, the word we apply to the idea, allowing us to communicate it to others (e.g., in English, "cat"). It all starts with the cat. If there were no real cats, there would be no idea about them, and there would be no word for the idea."* (McInerny, 2004) (p. 9).

### The clear idea in reality

*"It is a clear or sound idea to the extent that we can relate it to the objective world. But many things in the objective world go together to compose the rich meaning of the idea of democracy: persons, events, constitutions, legislative acts, past institutions, present institutions."*

*"If my idea of democracy is going to be communicable to others, it must refer to what is common to me and others, those many things in the objective world that are its originating source."*

*"To prevent my idea from being a product of pure subjectivism, in which case it could not be communicated to others, I must continuously touch base with those many facts in the objective world from which the idea was born."* (McInerny, 2004) (p. 10).

### Bad ideas

*"Bad ideas can be informative, not about the objective world— for they have ceased faithfully to reflect that world— but about the subjective state of the persons who nourish those ideas.*

*Bad ideas do not just happen. We are responsible for them. They result from carelessness on our part, when we cease to pay sufficient attention to the relational quality of ideas, or, worse, are a product of the willful rejection of objective facts."* (McInerny, 2004) (pp. 10-11).

### Order of things

*"As we have seen, first comes the thing, then the idea, then the word. If our ideas are sound to the extent that they faithfully represent the thing, then they will be clearly communicable only if we clothe them in words that accurately signify them.*

*Ideas, as such, are not communicable from one mind to another. They have to be carefully fitted to words so that the words might communicate them faithfully.*

*Putting the right word to an idea is not an automatic process, and sometimes it can be quite challenging. We have all had the experience of knowing what we want to say but not being able to come up with the words for it."* (McInerny, 2004) (p. 11).

## SPIRIT OF THE LAW VERSUS THE MAN-MADE LAW

The Ten Instructions of Torah are all about self-control. To master self-control, to respect life, other people, and life-giver. Self-control and discipline should be a priority in life.

> "Whoever is slow to anger is better than the mighty, and he who rules his spirit than he who takes a city." Proverbs 16:32. (ESV)

## THE TEN INSTRUCTIONS

> "And God spoke all these words:
>
> "I am the Lord your God, who brought you out of Egypt, out of the land of slavery. "You shall have no other gods before [a] me."
>
> "You shall not make for yourself an image in the form of anything in heaven above or on the earth beneath or in the waters below. You shall not bow down to them or worship them; for I, the Lord your God, am a jealous God, punishing the children for the sin of the parents to the third and fourth generation of those who hate me, but showing love to a thousand generations of those who love me and keep my commandments."
>
> "You shall not misuse the name of the Lord your God, for the Lord will not hold anyone guiltless who misuses his name."
>
> "Remember the Sabbath day by keeping it holy. Six days you shall labor and do all your work, but the seventh day is a Sabbath to the Lord your God. On it, you shall not do any work, neither you, nor your son or daughter, nor your male or female servant, nor your animals, nor any foreigner residing in your towns. For in six days, the Lord made the heavens and the earth, the sea, and all that is in them, but he rested on the seventh day. Therefore the Lord blessed the Sabbath day and made it holy."
>
> "Honor your father and your mother so that you may live long in the land the Lord your God is giving you."
>
> "You shall not murder."
>
> "You shall not commit adultery."
>
> "You shall not steal."
>
> "You shall not give false testimony against your neighbor."
>
> "You shall not covet your neighbor's house. You shall not covet your neighbor's wife, or his male or female servant, his ox or donkey, or anything that belongs to your neighbor."
>
> Exodus 20: 1 -17.

## BACK TO THE BASICS

Why is Proverbs chapter 16, verses 32, right?

"Whoever is slow to anger is better than the mighty, and he who rules his spirit than he who takes a city."

It is true because it will save the person from causing a lot of grief to him/her self. It is a protection from self-inflicted harm.

### TO BELIEVE AND TO WORSHIP GOD A PREVENTATIVE ACTION

- Avoid getting into mind-numbing idolatry
- The Intellectual mind enlightened by a law
- Responsible in word, deed, and actions
- Organized to rest one full day of a 7-day week
- Respect for parents
- Avoid murdering a human being
- Avoid adultery
- Avoid stealing
- Avoid lying

- Avoid coveting and lusting for things.

## VLADIMIR LENIN AND JOSEPH STALIN DEEDS

They could have chosen to do the morally right thing. Instead of being driven by the self-carnal nature, that led to rebellion and anarchy. They should have listened to the spirit of wisdom and obeyed the voice of the Creator God in their heart of hearts. That is the morally responsible duty of all mankind. But they chose to side with the Nemesis and lost their souls in the process.

> "And he said to me: 'This is the word of the Lord to Zerubbabel, saying: Not by might nor by power, but by My Spirit, says the Lord of Hosts." Zechariah 4:6. (MEV)

> "But whoever looks intently into the perfect law that gives freedom and continues in it-not, forgetting what they have heard, but doing it— they will be blessed in what they do." James 1:25. NIV

> "When the righteous increase, the people rejoice, But when a wicked man rules, people groan." Proverbs 29:2.

> "God will repay each person according to what they have done. To those who by persistence in doing good seek glory, honor, and immortality, he will give eternal life.
> But for those who are self-seeking and who reject the truth and follow evil, there will be wrath and anger." Romans 2:6-8. (NIV)

## WHERE ARE THE RUSSIAN CHRISTIANS AT A TIME OF LAWLESSNESS?

> "Submit yourselves, then, to God. Resist the devil, and he will flee from you." James 4:7. (NIV)

> "Have nothing to do with the fruitless deeds of darkness, but rather expose them." Ephesians 5:11. (NIV)

> "To fear the Lord is to hate evil; I hate pride and arrogance, evil behavior, and perverse speech." Proverbs 8:13. (NIV)

The Christian worldview addresses all areas of life. There is a universal purpose for national leaders to do right.
Politics are unavoidable. Government restrains evil and promotes good. A genuine need to love our neighbor. Leaders need to build upon civilized principles or a society.

The Holy Bible instructs the mind on what is morally right. The Holy Spirit enables believers to do that which is right. Believers need to be healthy and courageous, not to believe in bluff.

Christians are in spiritual warfare against Satan representatives on earth. It has to be confronted with the Word, faith, and the Spirit.

## WHAT IS A CHRISTIAN ACCORDING TO YESHUA?

> "But when they arrest you, do not worry about what to say or how to say it. At that time, you will be given what to say, for it will not be you speaking, but the Spirit of your Father speaking through you." Matthew 10: 19,20.

> "So, do not be afraid of them, for there is nothing concealed that will not be disclosed or hidden that will not be made known. What I tell you in the dark, speak in the daylight; what is whispered in your ear, proclaim from the roofs. Do not be afraid of those who kill the body but cannot kill the soul. Rather, be afraid of the One who can destroy both soul and body in hell." Matthew 10: 26-28.

> "Whoever acknowledges me before others, I will also acknowledge before my Father in heaven. But whoever disowns me before others, I will disown before my Father in heaven." Matt 10: 32-33.

> "Whoever does not take up their cross and follow me is not worthy of me. Whoever finds their life will lose it, and whoever loses their life for my sake will find it." Matt 10:38.

Christians need to be wise, making the most of any opportunity to expose the spiritual darkness. The wicked unbelievers will use whatever means to manipulate the naïve and innocent. That is another reason why absolutes need to be established; otherwise, life becomes a merry go around the manipulation of the devil's will.

Vladimir Lenin and Joseph Stalin did not accept the instructive principles given in the Book of Romans, chapter 13. It applies to believers and non- believers alike. The chapter is about the purpose of the Rule of law. People in civil society need to respect the established Rule of law.

"Let everyone be subject to the governing authorities, (Including the Russian Tsar Nicholas II 1917) for there is no authority except that which God has established. The authorities that exist have been established by God. Consequently, whoever rebels against the authority is rebelling against what God has instituted, and those who do so will bring judgment on themselves, for rulers hold no terror for those who do right, but for those who do wrong. Do you want to be free from fear of the one in authority? Then do what is right, and you will be commended. For the one in authority is God's servant for your good. But if you do wrong, be afraid, for rulers do not bear the sword for no reason. They are God's servants, agents of wrath to bring punishment on the wrongdoer. Therefore, it is necessary to submit to the authorities, not only because of possible punishment but also as a matter of conscience." Romans 13:1-6.

[32]

# REBELLIOUS ANARCHY

Vladimir Lenin and Joseph Stalin were anarchists; they rebelled, that is why Stalin was often in prison, and Lenin had to flee from Russia. They were anti-Christ and anti-God. The Bolsheviks took the authority from the Monarchy by force. Some may think that was a good thing to do. However, was it moral? Was it legal? Was it ethical? Was it done in the Spirit of the Natural law? And did it give glory to the Creator of Life? If not, then it was a curse on their people and the nation. The casualties alone from the Russian Civil war were approx. 1.3 Million on the Red side, and 1.5 million on the White Russian side. Total approx. 2,800,000 casualties.

The Russian revolutions of 1905 and 1917 also cost many lives. All that happened even before the Soviet Union Stalin's meat grinder was established in 1922. Many more millions of lives lost due to the materialistic leadership of Vladimir Lenin and Joseph Stalin. Vladimir Lenin and Joseph Stalin did not submit to the legitimate governing authority of their nation. Once in power, they ruled with a totalitarian iron fist, demanding a total submission from everyone. Stalin caused over a tenfold amount of casualties to the Russian people that Nicholas II ever did. It goes to show how empty the human mind is if it does not submit to legitimate authority. Rebellions, anarchists, and dictators always cause much more damage by their willful self-appointments.

Leaders abuse power. The natural reaction from ordinary people is to remove the leaders that are abusing privilege and power. How the change takes place makes all the difference between right and wrong, which side of the natural law the people end up on. Outside of the law or inside the Spirit of the Natural law.

MAJOR POLITICAL MURDERS IN RUSSIAN HISTORY
How many? At least 22.

- Peter III, Emperor of Russia 1762
- Paul I Emperor of Russia, 1801.
- Mikhail Miloradovich, military Governor of Saint Petersburg. 1825.
- Nikolay Mezentsov, Executive Director of the Third Section, 1878.
- Nikolay Alekseyev, Mayor of Moscow. 1893.
- Alexander II of Russia, Tsar of All Russia. 1881.
- Nikolai Ivanovich Bobrikov, Governor-General of Finland 1904.
- Vyacheslav von Plehve, Russian Interior Minister. 1904.
- Grand Duke Sergei Alexandrovich Romanov, former Governor-General of Moscow. 1905.
- Pyotr Stolypin, Russian Prime Minister 1911.
- Tsar Nicholas II and his family, 1918.
- Elizabeth of Hesse, Grand Duchess of Russia, 1918.
- Grand Duke Sergei Mikhailovich, 1918.

- Princes John Constantinovich, Constantine Constantinovich, and Igor Constantinovich, poet and prince. 1918.
- Sergei Mironovich Kirov. 1934. A prominent early Bolshevik leader in the Soviet Union.
- Grigory Zinoviev. 1936. Most prominent former communist party leader.
- Lev Kamenev, 1936. Most prominent former communist party leader.
- Yuri Piatakov. Anti-Soviet Trotskyite-centre. 1937.
- Grigory Sokolnikov, anti-Soviet Trotskyite-centre. 1937.
- Nikolai Bukharin, Russian Bolshevik revolutionary. 1938.
- "The Great Purge or the Great Terror was a campaign of political repression in the Soviet Union, which occurred from 1936 to 1938. It involved a large-scale purge of the Communist Party and government officials, repression of peasants and the Red Army leadership, widespread police surveillance, suspicion of "saboteurs," "counter-revolutionaries," imprisonment, and arbitrary executions.
- Solomon Mikhoels, Chairman of the Jewish Anti-Fascist Committee. 1948.

The above list leads to a question about the connection between the Nemesis and the people's hearts and minds. What drives people to rebellion, lawlessness, and anarchy?

> "You have plowed wickedness, you have reaped injustice; you have eaten the fruit of lies. Because you have trusted in your way, in your numerous warriors." Hosea 10: 13.

[33]

# KARELIAN REFUGEES 1939-1944

The Soviet Stalin aggression on November 30, 1939, was pre-planned in advance, with the support of the Nazi German-Soviet Pact of Aggression. The invasion attempt of Finland by the Soviet forces during winter 1939. How much time would it require to mobilize 21 Soviet divisions? A total of 450,000 troops. With all the logistics needed to invade Finland across the 1100 km border, to occupy all the way to the capital Helsinki. There is a lot of logistics needed to supply 450,000 troops with munitions, fuel, field hospitals, and food. Therefore, the decision to invade across the border from the Gulf of Finland to the Arctic Sea was in the making for a considerable time. It was not what the Soviets claimed at the time, a reaction to Finland's aggression.

The highest populated region of Finland, in the path of the Soviet Union military invasion, was the Karelian Isthmus land bridge. The region was populated by 407,000 Karelians; they had to be evacuated at short notice and leave their family homes behind. Leaving behind their farms, stocks, and lifelong memories to escape from being annexed by the invading Soviet military forces crossing the Finland border from the Russian side.

The 407,000 War refugees from Karelia families were taken to safety away from the Soviet Russian invasion into the Finland interior. Early in December, many children were separated from their families and placed in foster care in the Scandinavian countries. During the 1939-40 Winter War and Continuation War in 1941-44, nearly 80,000 children transferred to Sweden, Denmark, and Norway. About 72,000 children were taken to or left in Sweden, 4 200 in Denmark, and about one hundred children and mothers in Norway. About 15,500 of them did not return to Finland; they were adopted by the families that had fostered them. The initial Winter War that started in November 1939 and ended in March 1940 only lasted three months (104 days). Many of the children returned home to Finland in 1940 once the threat of war was over.

## RESETTLEMENT FROM SOVIET EXTORTION

The Finland Karelia region, where the 407,000 Karelian Finns had evacuated from, had to be re-settled in Finland. It was a large-scale operation to organize and manage, primarily because of the winter season. November to March is mid-winter, the Nordic land is covered in snow and ice, and extremely cold.

War refugee families by the thousands had to be found accommodation hastily, in whatever building was available at the time, within a short notice. Temporary accommodation at schools and community halls, later to be moved to rural communities sharing housing. Many people lived in small quarters that had to be made available for sharing with many other peoples, and at times families, parents, or grandparents. During the winter of 1939 to 1940, re-accommodating hastily evacuated 407,000 war refugees was a tall challenge during the cold winter. It was a double inconvenience to the innocent peoples, extraordinarily shattering, depressing, and annoying as if life was not challenging enough without some megalomaniac despot dictator creating extra burdens on the honest, hard-working peoples and their families of the land. It started on November 30, with Christmas, and all the family time celebrations, gifts, and delicious homemade foods, only three weeks away. How could anybody be such a moron? He would have to be an unspiritual pagan, unbelieving atheist, that was totally uncivilized, and most likely illiterate, that had never read the Good News of the Gospel story.

Karelia War refugees. The National Archives of Sweden. Riksarkivet.

Imagine that, to plan and start a war across 1100 km border, with 450,000 troops, the war against peace, with only three weeks to Christmas? It was a well-planned, diabolically inspired strategic move to hit the people hardest, where it hurts the most, at home, and the families. Fathers of the families were not able to be at home, warm near the fireplaces, spending time with the families. Instead, the men had to be at the front lines, out in the dark, in the extreme cold, keeping watch to stay alive. Such is the evil desires and the unfolding manifestations of the diabolical mind of the Nemesis.

The devil's volunteers may have desired to grab the presents, and the food from the tables, from people that cared for the Christmas celebrations. Whichever way we look at it, it was a diabolical evil move to violate the peace of Christmas, which such a violent act of aggression. Tens of thousands of men and fathers never saw their families again, never felt the warmth of the spring season or the summer sun. It was the end of the line for their life. Caused by drunken Soviet Bolsheviks leaders and a despotic dictator. After the Winter War had started, not everyone escaped the Soviet invasion; the municipality was Suojärvi, where 1700 civilians were captured by the invading Soviet troops at Hyrsylä and other villages of the Lake Suojärvi. These villagers were taken to the Russian concentration camp in the village of Interposolka, south of Petrozavodsk, and to the Kaimaoja camp west of Kondopoga.

Soviet officers took the trapped Finn civilians as war prisoners and transported the prisoners to eastern Soviet Karelia in heavy trucks that were unprotected against the winter cold. Many children died in cold carts because there was no protection. The villagers were taken to prison camps where dozens of people died. Fortunately, those that were still alive, they returned to Finland after the peace agreement of 1940. At the remote East region corner (Suojärvi) of Finland, for many, the evacuation notice was short when people woke up to the explosion of bombs, and the escape from their homes was immediate. Then there was no time to think about what to do; the priority was only to keep alive. Many people only had time to put on clothes for themselves and their children. Talk about a rude awakening.

Everywhere, evacuations did not go without tragedy. In many villages, the enemy surprised the civilians, and people were shot in the front yard of their homes. People fled their homes on foot and some on horses. The goal was to get to the train stations where people filled both passenger and freight wagons. Fear and distress reflected on people's faces as they waited for transport at the train stations in the middle of the night in the snow and the sleeting rain. November 30, 1939. Even when they had escaped the enemy for a while, there was a growing fear of the aerial bombings on the railway, and the trains were in the people's minds. Most of the men at the frontlines, the fleeing refugees, were mostly women, children, and the elderly.

A total of 1,700 civilians were left behind at the border area of Suojärvi, of which less than half of the villages of the Hyrsylä bend. Following the repatriation of prisoners under the terms of the Moscow peace agreement, on May 25, 1940, a total of 102 civilians had died at the prison camps in five months. During early **December 1939**, the temperatures dropped down to minus 20C in Lapland and later also in South Finland.

**January 1940**, the first 1-9 days were clear skies and cold, followed by warmer change for five days. Then a long span with freezing temperatures dropping minus 30 Celsius to minus 40 Celsius through most areas. February 1940, the extreme cold continued with little cloud cover. In Lapland for the entire month, the temperatures stayed steady at minus 30 Celsius to minus 40 Celsius. In the south, extreme cold lasted until February 20.

**March 1940**, the extreme cold continued for 20 days, persisted from the cold jetstreams originating from Siberia. The extreme sub-zero temperatures around minus 15 Celsius to minus 40 Celsius makes it extremely difficult for the civilians to flee from the war zones during the transportation and the temporary shelters. People get frostbite and can die from exposure to the extreme cold, especially when there are over 407,000 of them. It was a human-made, dictators disaster inflicted on innocent peoples, families, and children.

Extreme cold affects people's health; they do not stay healthy for long unless the shelters and housing have sufficient heating to keep the people from freezing and catching cold-related influenza. The elderly suffered from hard physical labor related to aching joints and arthritis. The cold winter snow cover season in the Nordic countries south typically is from the beginning of December to the end of March. In the Northern Lapland region, the winters are more prolonged, from November to May. There is much variation in the 1000+ kilometer stretch (South to North). The snow and ice-covered grounds can last between 5 to 6 months of the year, some variations from year to year.

The hastily arranged temporary accommodation was not the best option for children, that is why many were housed in suitable shared housing with families. Also, 80,000 children were sent to other Nordic countries as foster children, to Denmark, Sweden, and Norway, as temporary foster children, and some were adopted permanently by the foster care families. It was an extremely testing time for the spirits of the families, for the people of Karelia. They had to leave almost everything that they and their parents and grandparents had worked for during their lifetime. Many families had inherited properties from their grandparents to their parents, and suddenly at the whim of a despotic dictator, the 407,000 refugees lost their inherited proper geographical location in the world.

In the 1940 Moscow peace agreement, Stalin extorted the territory with the threats of a continuation of the war. Demanding all the Finland Karelian territories to be handed over, the entire area where 407,000 Karelian war refugees had escaped the 1939-40 Winter War. Further, 23,000 evacuees came from North Finland Lapland, Municipality of Petsamo, Salla, and Kuusamo during 1939 and 1944 evacuations caused by the second Soviet invasion attempt and annexation of the Finland territory.

The Karelian Isthmus and the City of Vyborg cessation were core demands by Stalin in terms of the peace agreement. If the Stalin territory demands were not ceded, then Stalin threatened to continue the Soviet aggression of war and again attempt to invade and occupy the entire Finland territory. It was clearly extortion, demanding an independent country to hand over territory under military threat. At the same time, the British government was backing Joseph Stalin all the way. It was the British government representatives that were sitting at the table during the 1944 Moscow Armistice. The Brits were driving their own interests regardless of the seriousness of Soviet Stalin lawlessness, war crimes, and genocide.

Allied Control Commission

"The Allied Control Commission (ACC) arrived in Finland on September 22, 1944, to observe Finnish compliance with the Moscow Armistice. It consisted of 200 Soviet and 15 British members and was led by Col. Gen. Andrei Zhdanov." "Immediately after its inception, the commission required Finland to take more vigorous action to intern the German forces in Northern Finland. Finland's compliance with the commission resulted in a campaign to force out the remaining German troops in the area. Simultaneously, Finland was required to demobilize, which was also required by the commission".

"The ACC provided Finland with a list of "war criminals" against whom Finland had to start judicial proceedings. Although this required Finnish post-facto legislation,". But it was not according to the Spirit of the Natural Law. Soviet Stalin dictated the list of war criminals against whom Finland had to start judicial proceedings". (Commission, 1944)

Typical to the Soviet Spirit and diabolical propaganda, they showcase formality to the letter of the law, but there is no spirit of truth or justice to their proceedings. They did in the same Spirit as the Moscow trials and the Stalin purge 1936-38. They worked together with the communist sympathizers in Finland to jail the innocent.

The Allied Control Commission consisted of 200 Soviets and 15 British members. It was a false spirited fiasco, the communists barking at the wrong tree. At the root level, it was the same Spirit as the Bolshevik's progression to the Soviet Union military superpower. From 1917 to 1922, 1936 to 1938, 1939 to 1941. They had no respect for the Spirit of the Natural Law. The timeline is littered with lawlessness, rebellion and anarchy, war crimes, and genocide. The British went along with because it served their own interest. They saw themselves as the Imperialists, the Royal Monarchist, being permanently on the Queen's moral high ground, above the law, they were playing God. They were reinventing laws to serve their own and the Soviet's nationalistic interests. The Allied forces had a common enemy; the laws were rewritten to punish the rest in order to serve the Imperialist nationalistic interests and pride. In the process, they failed to recognize the Spirit of the Natural Law. Therefore the innocent were punished, and the war criminals were rewarded, and it continues up to the current 2018.

Soviet Russian leaders have not acknowledged their leader's past war crimes. Their mind does not perceive or recognize that which is immoral, that which is wrong because of their morality; their character is so corrupted that they deny everything. They are always on the defensive, repressing, suppressing, or blatantly rejecting truth as being a false spirit. Their government leaders have established themselves as representatives of corruption on earth. Because they do not acknowledge the apparent evil, instead, they hide it, nurse it, propagate it and export it. Selling it as a desirable virtue.

> "Woe to those who call evil good and good evil, who turn darkness to light and light to darkness, who replace bitter with sweet and sweet with bitter." Isaiah 5:20.

The British, the French, and the Americans are the guilty cause of that discrepancy; they gave the Soviet war criminal Stalin their blessing and amnesty from war crimes in 1940 and 1945. The Spirit of the Soviet's lawlessness during World War 2 returned like a boomerang to haunt the Allies during the cold war. Everything changed in 5 years. The massive American 17.4 Million Tons of supplies aid to the Soviets, and British military equipment, with 15 million pairs of boots and much other material support from 1941 to 1945 left no impression; there were no strings vibrating inside the stone heart of Stalin.

During 1940, threats of the continuation of the war were taken seriously by the Finnish government. The extortion demands reluctantly agreed to during March 1940 in Moscow. Some 12 months later, the pact between Nazi Germany and the Soviet Union was disintegrating, and the Nazi Germany leaders were planning to Invade Soviet Union Russia. Stalin was going to be on the receiving end in more ways than one, not a surprise Christmas party.

Finland's government leaders took the offer to join the eastward push against the Soviet's aggression and take back all the territory that Stalin had extorted from Finland with the threat of war in 1940. Finland's government representatives agreed to join Germany as a co-belligerent, meaning that Finland would take the front lines along with Finland and Russian border only and push the Soviet back all the way to the agreed and legally recognized 1920 Treaty of Tartu borders.

It also agreed on the access to some 100,000 German military troops into the Arctic region of Finland, and they would form the front line up the top end and push the Soviet back to the Port of Murmansk and over the Murmansk railway towards the shores of the White Sea. In the summer of 1941 (June), the German war plan Operation Barbarossa was sent off, heading into Russia's heart, which was Moscow. Once Germany attacked Russia, then Russia started an air bombing the major capital cities of Finland. Once the bombing of the cities of Finland started, then Finland declared war on Russia. The Finnish military went over the 1940 Russia border on June 25, 1941.

By September 1941, Finland's effort to push back Russia from the 1939 Finland territory in East Karelia was completed. The offensive had reversed the post-winter War concessions to the Soviet Union in the region of the Karelian Isthmus and the shores of Lake Ladoga Karelia. The war evacuees of Finland Karelian were forced to evacuate in November 1939. About 50 % returned to their homes in 1941-42. Moreover, three years later, again, they were forced to evacuate the same territory for the second time in four years, in 1944.

It was an emotionally extremely testing time for the Karelians to have such a roller coaster ride with mixed emotions, loss of everything, followed by restoration of future hope. They were forced to leave their family heritage behind with great disappointment and despair in 1939. Most of the buildings were burn and destroyed, not all but most. And to have their hopes restored in 1941 during the continuation war, they returned back to their family homes.

How does a rational moral human being justify such immoral action, as the war against peace, that Stalin initiated in 1939? It was an action plan from a diabolical mind, to be condemned by all the moral powers of human living soul capacity. The intellect, consciousness, imagination, will, memory, and emotions. Nothing in human moral virtue defends such irresponsible despotic action as the Soviet Stalin aggression against innocent peoples. Ignorant people were brainwashed in the Soviet Union into serving the Nemesis spirit personality cult, personified in Stalin. Many municipalities had work groups rebuilding destroyed houses and buildings during 1941-43. The course of war turned against the Finland defensive war as the German forces were driven out of Russia by the Allied forces and the Soviets.

Once the German forces were driven back to Berlin in 1944, the Soviets turned their available military forces to the front line of Finland. And the Stalin imperial nationalism came back with a demonic vengeance again to punish and claim back their 1939 war crimes and the extortion of much-coveted Finland Karelia territory. It was Stalin's egotism and self will thrust upon the Soviet neighbors. To steal, kill, and destroy innocent people. How does God see Joseph Stalin? According to God's Holy nature. He is the same today, yesterday, and tomorrow. His character does not change. Therefore there is no escape from judgment. Evil people are causing harm to innocent people of the land directly or indirectly will be punished with eternal judgment. Glory be to God that his character is consistent.

> "Behold, God will not reject a blameless man, nor take the hand of evildoers." Job 8:20. (ESV)

> "Sing to God! Sing praises to His name. Exalt the One who rides on the clouds—His name is the LORD—and rejoice before Him. A father of the fatherless and a defender of the widows is God in His holy habitation". Psalm 68: 5.

The arrogance and pride of Stalin, returning from the Nazi German-Soviet Pact of Aggression invasion of Finland 1939-40, also being supported by the Allied forces. Just like the Pharaoh of Egypt that would not let the people of Israel go. Stalin arrogantly, selfishly and egotistically, had committed war against peace and war crimes in 1939. Also, lawlessly extorted territory from Finland in 1940. The Soviet Union was condemned by the International League of Nations in 1939.

[34]

# LEAGUE OF NATIONS

League of Nations
December 14, 1939
"The Winter War began when the Soviet Union ruled by dictator Josef Stalin attacked Finland on November 30, 1939, three months after the invasion of Poland by Germany that started World War II. Because the attack was judged as illegal, the Soviet Union was expelled from the League of Nations on December 14." (Winter-War, 1939)

LEAGUE OF NATIONS EXPULSION OF THE USSR, DECEMBER 14, 1939
*The Council,*
*Having taken cognizance of the resolution adopted by the Assembly on December 14, 1939, regarding the appeal of the Finnish Government, Associates itself with the condemnation by the Assembly of the action of the Union of Soviet Socialist Republics against the Finnish State, and for the reasons set forth in the resolution of the Assembly, in virtue of Article 16, paragraph 4, of the Covenant, finds that, by its act, the Union of Soviet Socialist Republics has placed itself outside the League of Nations. It follows that the Union of Soviet Socialist Republics is no longer a Member of the League."* (Historical-Resource, 1939)

There were many war crimes committed by Stalin from 1939 to 1940. War against peace, and genocide against the Polish National in 1940. Yet, the Allied forces were supplying Stalin with military hardware, tens of thousands of planes, tens of thousands of trucks and jeeps, and hundreds of tons of food and clothing supplies. The allied forces did it all for an extreme war criminal; they supported a war criminal while the war criminal was once again waging aggressive war against Finland in 1944.

The Allied forces were self-serving in their short-sighted imperial bigotry. It took several years before the Allied forces woke up to the spiritual reality of the Bolsheviks USSR leadership corruption. They did not believe the facts that the Nordic and the Baltic States shared with the Americans about the reality of the Bolsheviks USSR spirit of anarchy, 1900 to 1941 history. In recent times the head of Stalinism lawlessness has raised its head. The Western Nation leaders have complained about the lack of moral integrity in the Russian leadership, and it was the Western support and aid that made it possible for Stalinism to grow and flourish from 1917 to 1945. The western leaders were short-sighted and naive; they did not understand the deceiving nature of the Nemesis. They trusted the Bolshevik representatives of the Nemesis as some kind of truth base worldview to build an empire upon. It was an anti-God atheism establishment from the deceiver of humanity. It rejected absolute moral values and downplayed the need for integrity.

The cold facts of rebellion, lawlessness, and disrespect of moral virtues lead to a downward spiral morally. Making violence in the process against the Spirit of the Natural Law. The aggression and the spirit of anarchy were written all over the wall of truth from 1900 to 1953. The Nemesis dragon, true to its evil nature, creating deceit, chaos, and destruction, soon started biting the western hand that had been feeding it, during the time leading up to the cold war.

First, it was the Russian Tsar and the Romanov family that became the victim of the Russian lawlessness and anarchy; it was a war against the Spirit behind the rule of law. The same spirit of the Nemesis, with the spirit of rebellion, lawlessness, and anarchy, was behind building the iron curtain and the Berlin wall at the beginning of the cold war. The methods do matter how a society develops a better spirit for all. It is not achieved by volunteering to do the work of the Nemesis, to steal, kill, and destroy. The Nemesis demon helpers do offer many lucrative temptations to win over many volunteers.

## BETWEEN A ROCK AND A HARD PLACE

The building up of the Soviet Union military from 1941 to the 1960s was made possible by the Allies' victory over Germany and Japan in 1945; the Soviet Union military bounced back with a vengeance. It became the sole superpower rival to the United States. Then came the Cold War between the Soviet Union and the United States; the posturing and saber-rattling between the two Super Powers led to further military buildups, the nuclear arms, and the Space Race. By the early 1980s, not surprisingly, the Soviet military had more troops, more tanks, and more artillery guns and nuclear weapons than any other nation on earth. And they still felt threatened by their small neighbors, like Finland, Estonia, Latvia, Poland, and Japan.

During the 1920 – 1939, the Treaty of Tartu between Finland and the Soviet Union was in effect; there was a mutual understanding that covered various aspects of concerns. The Treaty had clauses that constrained Finland from building up the military defense lines and forces or strengthening the defense lines on the Gulf of Finland Islands and other parts that were seen as sensitive and potentially threatening areas by the Soviet leadership. In many ways, it made Finland more vulnerable and created mistrusts in the minds of many people towards the Soviet Union leaders in general. At the time, Finland had a population of 3.4 million, and the Soviet Union population was 184 million.

It only goes to show that there is an invisible force behind the Soviet leader's minds agenda, that was pushing them to the unthinkable, the insane aspirations of world domination. They play a zero-sum game in their mind. As if the measurable goal of humanity is to win over others, to conquer the world from others. That is insanity, considering what the Creator of Life has said and made. It is not our world to decide; everything belongs to the Creator of Life; he has the last word.

## THE SALPA-DEFENSE- LINE

The construction of the Salpa Line began at the end of the Winter War in 1940. At first, volunteers worked there—then people ineligible for the war service were mobilized. The maximum number of workers on-site was near 35,000 in the spring of 1941. The Salpa-Line stretches northwards from the Gulf of Finland to the Barents Sea, 1200 kilometer distance. It was not secured evenly along with the entire distance, only on the map, it continued for 1200 km.

They built 728 various concrete installations along the defensive line, 315 km of wire obstacles, 225 km of anti-tank obstacles, 130 km of anti-tank ditches, more than 3000 entrenchments, 254 concrete infantry shelters, trenches, rifleman's cells, and dugouts composed the power and strength of this defensive line. Numerous lakes, marshes, and quarried rock pillars were also incorporated in the defensive line. For example, the Lake Saimaa area is a labyrinth of lakes of varying sizes, islands, straits, and rivers, making the area very easy to defend during the summer and other thawed out seasons. During the winter, lakes are frozen sufficiently solid for tanks to run over the top of the ice.

90% of all the concrete installations of the Salpa-Line were on the line between the Gulf of Finland and the Lake Saimaa waterway system. Grey Nordic granite quarried into 2 to 3-meter-long oblong shapes, which were stood upright, with 1-meter length buried underground. It was a practical tank stopping barrier during that time. (SALPA, 1940)

SA Picture (War Archives). War Museum of Finland. Granite boulder Enemy Tank obstacle.

FOUR MAIN DEFENSE LINES KARELIAN ISTHMUS 1944
The four lines of defense prepared to defend Finland in 1944 against the Soviet invasion.

1. The main front line, Finland – USSR border
2. V-T line
3. V-K-T LINE
4. SALPA-Line (1100 length)

During the 1939 Soviet War against Peace, there were two defensive lines to block the Soviets from invasion. Main Defense-Line

THE MANNERHEIM DEFENSE LINE
"The Mannerheim Line was a defensive fortification line on the Karelian Isthmus built by Finland against the Soviet Union. During the Winter War, it became known as the Mannerheim Line, after Field Marshal Baron Carl Gustaf Emil Mannerheim. The line was in two phases: 1920–1924 and 1932–1939. By November 1939, when the Winter War began, the line was by no means complete." (Defense, 1939)

1940 STRATEGIC DEFENSE
The Commander-in-chief of Finland 1940 Military Baron Carl Gustaf Mannerheim ordered Edvard F Hanell as the head of the new Eastern border fortification at the end of March 1940. He worked during the Winter War at the headquarters as a pioneer commander for the defense constructions. Hanell was Jager officer, pioneer, engineer, and concrete expert. He studied in France for his Education. The practical planners of the fortress would be armed defense groups of the military. The underlying idea was that the groups that designed and built the defensive obstacles would be fighting in their own group fortifications. Thus, motivating at all stages and the most efficient

way to get the job done. The central principle was to build a fortress backstop, sufficiently far away from the border out of reach of the enemy's guns. In most part, it was located out of reach of the Soviet high caliber guns, with the only exception of the southernmost part along the Gulf of Finland. The eastern Salpa-line fortress plan under Hanelli, approved on May 11, 1940.

### VKT DEFENSE LINE

The VKT-line or Viipuri–Kuparsaari–Taipale line was a Finnish defensive line on Karelian Isthmus during the Continuation War, spanning from Viipuri (Vyborg) through Tali and Kuparsaari along the northern shore of Vuoksi River, Suvanto and Taipaleenjoki to Taipale on the western shore of Lake Ladoga, using natural benefits of the eastern part of the destroyed Mannerheim Line. (Defense, VKT DEFENSE LINE, 1944)

### VT-DEFENSE LINE

"The VT-line or Vammelsuu–Taipale line was a Finnish defensive line on the Karelian Isthmus built-in 1942–1944 during the Continuation War and running from Vammelsuu on the northern shore of the Gulf of Finland through Kuuterselkä and Kivennapa and along Taipaleenjoki to Taipale on the western shore of Lake Ladoga." (Defense, V-T-DEFENSE-LINE, 1944)

### SALPA-LINE DEFENSE

"The construction of the Salpa Defense Line was an enormous effort for war-torn Finland in the 1940s, which Edvard Hanell, head of the fortification itself, described as a show of strength from the entire Finnish engineering team." In the fortification work, some different mining and concrete construction techniques developed, which have since become useful in peace-building work. In the construction of the Salpal-line, the latest technologies in the field combined with the experiences gained during the Winter War, creating a united effort for the defense of Finland by optimizing the natural terrain for defense against the Soviet aggression. The combined effort uniting the workforce for the fortification line over 1200 kilometers is impressive."

A total of 728 different types of reinforced concrete bunkers, gun bill boxes, and gun pits, and underground wood reinforced tunnels. Built-in Salpalinja; more than 3,000 underground accommodation facilities, about 315 kilometers of tank blocking obstacles cut out of grey granite, 315 kilometers of barbed wire obstacles, 130 kilometers of anti-tank trenches, and 350 kilometers of connecting trenches for fighting. In the battles of the summer of 1944, among Finnish soldiers, the Salpa-line was seen as a last resort against the worse scenario of the Soviets breaking through the other three defense lines across the Karelian Isthmus. Salpa's defense line was the Last defense line, which was said to have formed the military backbone of the Army in the fight against the summer of 1944. The soldiers knew that the Salpa line was far behind their backs there was the most strong ground defense line ever built in Finland by the defense engineers, which would allow the troops to delay fighting and drawback further while concentrating on the changing situations of the defensive, even when the front was broken.

During the Second World War, the Finnish Army proved highly capable of defending its country for a time, even with limited preparation for a major war that nobody believed would come against the none threatening Finland. Undoubtedly, the Salpa-line would also have been a tough obstacle for the Soviets to defeat, which would have created even a greater military concentration by the Soviets and increased their own casualties many times over. The practical obstacle of the Salpa-line was respected in the Soviet leadership. It was not possible to circumvent the Salpa-line, and after the massive battles of the 1944 early summer months, there was less willingness to try, in the high probability of significant casualties, to attempt to break the Salpalinja.

The Soviet leadership had noticed that the Finns' defense was not easily broken with even overwhelming numbers of foot soldiers and armory. The Soviet troops along the Finnish front were decided to conserve and send to more priority missions to strike Germany in Central Europe. That decision indeed saved a large number of lives on both sides. The significant Soviet offensive started to invade Finland on June 9, 1944.

"On June 9, 1944, the Soviet Leningrad Front launched an offensive against Finnish positions on the Karelian Isthmus and in the area of Lake Ladoga, timed to coincide with Operation Overlord in Normandy as agreed during the Tehran Conference."

"The Red Army penetrated the second line of defense, the Vammelsuu– Taipale line (VT line), by the sixth day and recaptured Vyborg almost without resistance on June 20." "On June 25, the Red Army reached the third line of defense, the Viipuri– Kuparsaari–Taipale line (VKT line), and the decisive Battle of Tali- Ihantala began, which was the largest battle in Nordic military history."

## TAIPALE BEACH

The VKT line, the Vyborg-Kuparsaaren-Taipalee line, was the third and last defensive position of Finns in the Karelian Isthmus during the Continuation War (June 25, 1941, to 1944). When the second Defensive line, Vammelsuun-Taipalee VT line, was broken by the Red Army on June 9, 1944.

A major offensive with the Red Army 450,000 men, 10,000 cannons and mortars, and 800 tanks and assault guns combined in the Karelian Isthmus offensive. To the defense came 75,000 Finnish troops ready to absorb the invasion by the Red Army, at the minimal fortified VKT line, which fortifications had started in early 1944.

- The VKT line broke in June-July 1944, at the besieged Vyborg, then moved to the Battle of Ihantala and Tienhaara in the Battle of Talin- Ihantala and in the Bay of Vyborg. Moreover, later at the beginning of July in Vuosalmi. However, the primary Soviet offensive was successfully absorbed and stopped on all fronts of VKT, except at the city of Vyborg.
- The VKT line did not break along the Lake Ladoga side, but the troops were forced to retreat as the terms of the cease-fire agreement dictated in September 1944.
- The Taipale corner of Lake Ladoga held firm during the 1939 -1940 war, and also during the 1944 Red Army Major Offensive to break through the Finland defenses across Karelian Isthmus.

Fortunately, the Soviet Red army never broke through the third defensive line. Therefore the SALPA- Defense- Line was not required to use. It was built to be the last line of defense in the face of the Soviet Red Army invaders. (Taipale, 1944)

## WHITE ISLAND ASSAULT

The Red Army attack on the 6.7 km long Valkea-Saari (white Island) block was prepared with a three sections Soviet guard, supported by three regiments of armored tanks and assault tank guns. In addition to the artillery divisions, there were six artillery regiments, as well as cannons and rocket launchers. The battlefield was prepared to support with 1,208 over 75mm caliber cannons or grenade launchers. The Soviet concentration of cannon positions per kilometer at the Valkea-Saari front line was over 200 cannons per kilometer section.

On June 9, 1944, the Red Army commenced the destruction of Finnish positions by the use of air force, which was a shock to the Finnish 10th Division, that was positioned in the area and immediately had to engage the reserves to the battle. At the Finnish headquarters, the leadership did not believe that a significant Red army invasion had begun. The next day, on June 10, at 5 o'clock in the morning, began the red Army cannon fire assault with the preparation that lasted 135 minutes, which involved 3,000 cannons and grenade launchers. The Suomi positions were pulverized almost wholly.

According to the Finnish War Archive database, Valkeasaari casualties from June 9 to June 14, there were 163 dead. The Red Army broke that line of defense, and the remaining Suomi soldiers had to withdraw back to a second defense line at the VT-line or Vammel-Suu– Taipale line.

The Taipale River meets the Lake Ladoga; it was a stronghold for the Suomi forces. It came under massive assault during the Winter war of 1939 to 1940 and the Continuation War of 1944. But the Red Army never broke the defensive line at Taipale. After both wars and the securing of the peace treaty, the Suomi troops at the Taipale positions had to walk back towards the interior of Finland, out of their positions some 100 + kilometers to the agreed new Finland and Russian border, according to the Stalin's extortion territory demands.

It is unusual after a peace treaty for the soldiers to withdraw from the positions that they held secure during the war. Stalin used military threats to extort territory from the Finland government representatives at the peace agreement negotiations in Moscow. Finland and German total casualties and losses for the three years continuation war on the border and Finland territory are the following.

WAR CASUALTIES
June 25, 1941, to December 30, 1941.

- 17,000 – fallen – (2833 per month)
- 63,000 – wounded – (10,500 per mth)
- 3000 – missing – (500 per mth)
- June 25, 1941, to September 19. 1944.
- 430,000 Karelian and Lapland Finn evacuees.

Finnish:

- 63,204 fallen or lost,
- 158,000 wounded
- 2,377- 3,500 imprisoned
- 1,129 dead civilians

German soldiers in Finland

- 14,000 fallen or lost, 37,000 wounded

SOVIET UNION STRATEGIC GOALS IN 1939-40.
Many naive people in the world always repress truth in the face of evildoers. Even in Finland, there are generations of Soviet Union Communism sympathizers that have always denied the reality about Joseph Stalin and the evil deeds of the Soviet Union Communism. Similarly, some people repress the truth; they escape from the truth into their own imaginary subjective rabbit hole imaginary world. Truth can be known; the Jewish Holy Scriptures testify to the truth. Jesus from Nazareth also said that he was obedient to the written Torah, and by following the instruction of the Torah and the instructions given by Yeshua Hamashiach. Those that are obedient will know the truth. The disobedient will never know the truth because they refuse the conditional terms of living with truthful actions and deeds. Disobedience effect the mind brain, continues compromises affect the heart and mind, so that the grip on rational logic and reasoning can slip away by immoral behavior. People can sin against other people, and they can also sin against their own living soul. Those that compromise truth will always lose out in the end.

The general objective goals for Finland were already determined for Stalin's with the Nazi Germany & Soviet Union Aggression pact in Moscow, August 23, 1939. The entire purpose of the pact for Adolf Hitler and Joseph Stalin was the invasions, occupation, and exploitation of small East European countries, e.g., Denmark, Norway, Poland, Latvia, Estonia, Lithuania, Karelia, Romania and Ukraine. The Soviet Union would sometimes ask for a permission of the East European/Nordic countries; if they obliged, then occupation was effortless. The occupation lasted over 50 years in Estonia by the Soviet Union military.

Military occupations by the Soviet Union
"During World War II, the Soviet Union occupied and annexed several countries effectively handed over by Nazi Germany in the secret Molotov–Ribbentrop Pact of 1939."
These included the eastern regions of Poland

- Poland incorporated into two different SSRs,
- as well as Latvia (became Latvian SSR,

- Estonia (became Estonian SSR,
- Lithuania (became Lithuanian SSR,
- part of eastern Finland (became Karelo-Finnish SSR,
- and eastern Romania (became the Moldavian SSR
- and part of Ukrainian SSR).
- 

Apart from the Molotov–Ribbentrop Pact and post-war division of Germany, the USSR also occupied and annexed Carpathian Ruthenia from Czechoslovakia in 1945 (became part of Ukrainian SSR).
  (Wikipedia) See web link. https://en.wikipedia.org/wiki/Military_occupations_by_the_Soviet_Union
  Objective Goals: Karelian Isthmus. OCCUPY AND TAKE CONTROL.
  Karelian Isthmus breakthrough to the Capital Helsinki.

- USSR 7th ARMY
- USSR 13th ARMY.
- USSR 15th ARMY
- USSR 8th ARMY

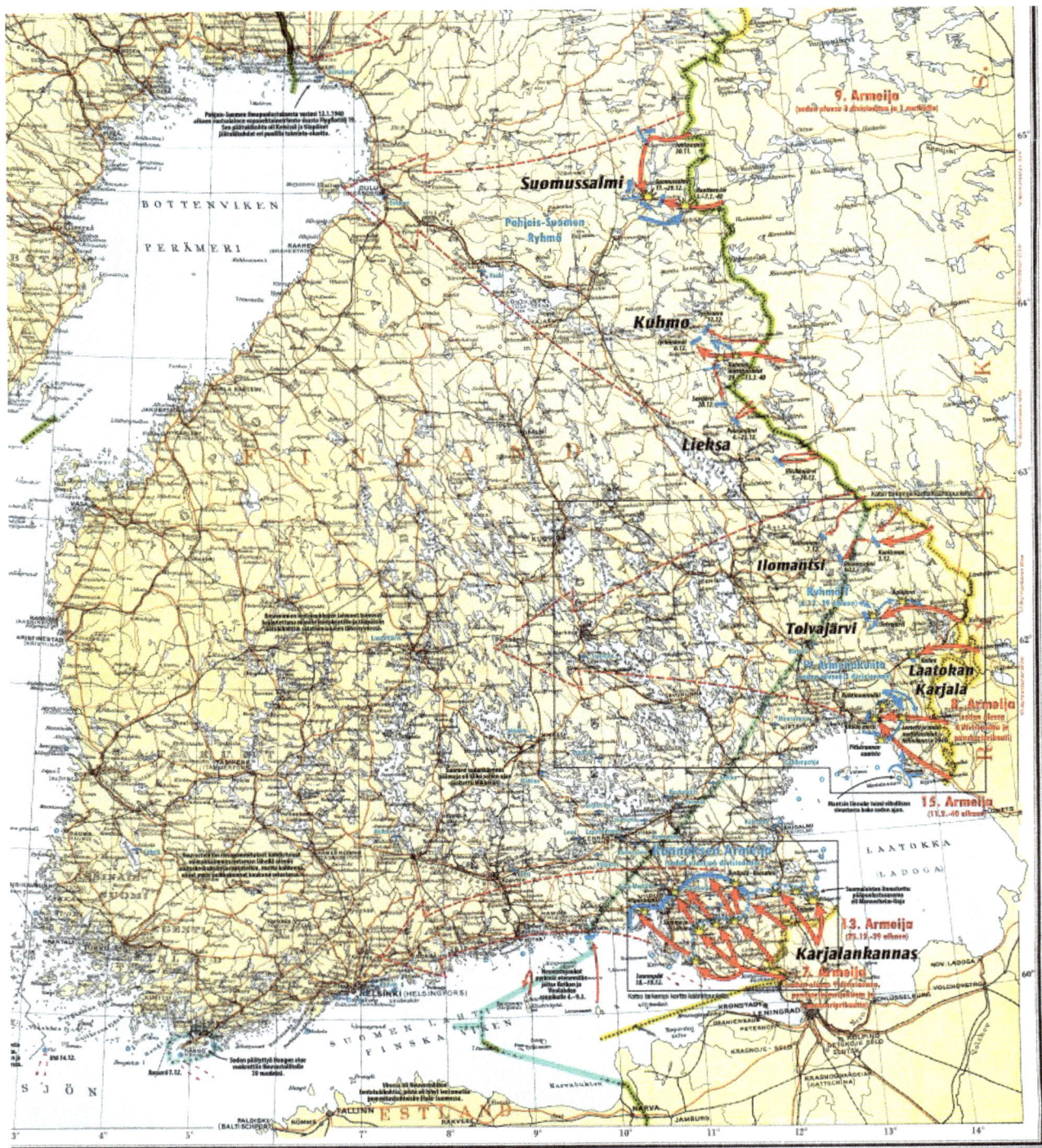

Objective Goals: OCCUPY AND TAKE CONTROL

Kuolajärvi, Savukoski, Pelkosenniemi, Jousijärvi, Kemijärvi, Rovaniemi breakthrough to the City of Kemi. Gulf of Bothnia Port.

Suomussalmi and Kuhmo regions breakthrough to City of Oulu and the Hailuoto Island.

- USSR 14TH ARMY
- USSR 9TH ARMY

Objective Goals: OCCUPY AND TAKE CONTROL
Ladoga Karelia, Tolvajärvi, Ilomantsi brekthrough to the heart of Finland at Pieksämä

- USSR 14TH ARMY

Copyright © KARTTAKESKUS.fi

Objective Goals: OCCUPY AND TAKE CONTROL
Breakthrough to the Barents Sea Port of Petsamo, and drive the Finnish forces down the Arctic Ice Road to level of the Arctic Circle at Rovaniemi.

WHAT CAN WE LEARN FROM HISTORY?
There is much to be learned from history about human behavior, corrupted leaders, dictators, and how the Nemesis uses them to cause destruction and influence the good, the bad, and the ugly. Meaningful and factual

events in human history have been recorded for us to read and study since 1500 BC. Over 3500 years of reliable, truth-based recorded human history, with profound insights into the failings, flaws, sins, the hubris, atrocities, hidden mysteries, victories, and human vulnerability to the diabolical deceitfulness of the human mind. Often entirely self-determined by the program of the master, that he or she chooses to covet, love, follow and commit to in life.

What does the Bible say about the corrupt nature of the human heart and mind? Especially when individual people have ascended into positions of political authority and military power over the ordinary people of the land. Ordinary people of the land generally cannot destroy on a massive scale; they do not have the interest, ambitions, or the time for it. They have their own life to live according to God's will, seeds to sow, plants to care for, and crops to harvest.

The destruction on a massive scale comes with political and military power, namely by lawless totalitarian dictators. History reveals it to be so. 'What comes first, is it the power or corruption? The potential for corruption is in human nature already present, unless the intellect, self-will, and consciousness have enlightened. The self-will may be dormant, like silently sleeping corruption, waiting for the opportunity to manifest. The Nemesis is drawn to the power players of global politics, preying on the potential opportunity for mass destruction. Destructive power can be used as a lever for negotiations. The Nemesis evil lust is after destructive power; it's a fantasy of destroying every living thing that God has created.

Why do nation leaders plan lawlessness and deliberate violence against the people of the global community? It is a mystery, without the temptations of the Nemesis. The destructive acts add no value to the individual person or contribute anything to the individual status as a leader, or as a human being, created in the image of God. Those that cause harm to the innocent. In essence, it is a battle in the human heart and mind, whom will it respect and serve? If there is a fear of God, then the person will respect the intrinsic human value. Alternatively, it is to be calloused and indifferent to human suffering, and that becomes a secondary concern after personal ambitions.

On the side of the Creator of life, that offers a new life, a spiritual new birth? Or the fatalistic human carnal nature, a slave to the law of entropy, a lost soul in immense size universe, without hope of eternity, without a savior. For the Creator of life? Or against the will of the Creator, Elohim. The other option is rebellion, self-will, living outside of the will of God.

Humans are self-determining free-willed agents. According to their intellect, consciousness, imagination, and will. They do have a free will, and at the same time, they are determined. It may sound like a contradiction, to have a free will, and at the same time to be determined. It is not a contradiction; it reveals the intricate architecture of the brain design hardware, with the human mind psychology software. It is not a direct system to the will or a human-made machine controlled by the pulling of levers. That would be too simple for it to be functional with human consciousness.

> "But Jesus did not entrust Himself to them, for He knew all men. He did not need any testimony about man, for He knew what was in a man". John 2: 24.

> "The Wickedness of Man," Then the LORD saw that the wickedness of man was great on the earth and that every intent of the thoughts of his heart was only evil continually. "The LORD was sorry that He had made the man on the earth, and He was grieved in His heart." Genesis 6:5,6.

> "Then he called the crowd to him along with his disciples and said: "Whoever wants to be my disciple must deny themselves and take up their cross and follow me." Mark 8:34 NIV.

### THERE IS HOPE IN THE FREE WILL

There is an encouraging promise of freedom, from the slavery of sin, in the human free will concept. That does not mean that man in the fallen state can save himself or to become righteous by his free will alone. No, that is not possible. Yet the human intellect, consciousness, imagination and the free will, in each individual person needs to work with moral responsibility. It is an act of the free will. Because all humans have a carnal nature, in large part, humans are carnally minded. They seek carnal pleasures without an equalizing balance with spirituality. Therefore, if the carnal nature is not kept in check, the law of entropy takes over, and moral corruption follows.

> "Now the works of the flesh are evident: sexual immorality, impurity, sensuality, idolatry, sorcery, enmity, strife, jealousy, fits of anger, rivalries, dissensions, divisions, envy, drunkenness, orgies, and things like these. I warn you, as I warned you before, that those who do such things will not inherit the kingdom of God." Galatians 5:19 ESV.

> "for all have sinned and fell short of the glory of God," Romans 3:23 NIV.

Salvation comes from the Lord. Lost humanity needs to be spiritually drawn and awakened to see the sinful condition of their living soul by the Spirit of the Creator of life, Elohim.

> "No one can come to Me unless the Father who sent Me draws him, and I will raise him up at the last day." John 6:44.

There needs to be a spark, a kindling by the Holy Spirit in the heart of man, woman, and child, to be inspired to seek the Lord for the redemption and Salvation of their living soul. There needs to be a spiritual desire, a hunger for truth, for love, and for sin-free life.

The most crucial data access into the human mind is the eyes, ears, and the mouth that speaks. The saying goes, when the mind input is garbage, then the mind will further create garbage out. From the thoughts, ideas, and speaking it out, perpetuating the carnal human mind cycle with sinful actions.

> "Yet they did not obey or incline their ear, but walked in their counsels and the stubbornness of their evil heart, and went backward and not forward." Jeremiah 7:24.

The fallen state of the human living soul is not as if it is a clean slate without any prior inclinations, prejudice, or disposition. Physical and spiritual human beings come to the world through a slow process of conception, birth, and experiment with learning, to develop consciousness, and to be physically autonomous to move about freely in a physical world. The first nine months, followed by 12 months, then three years, and five years, nine years, and 13 years.

During the first thirteen years of a healthy physical body, the underlying physiology is learned through the laws of the physical environment. Also, the opportunity for the healthy human mind to develop through the meaningful input, to learn what it means to be more human than an animal. The mind needs to be developed sufficiently strong with nurture, guidance, Education, information, and knowledge to know what it means to be a human being made in the image of the Creator God. For the self-determining healthy individual, the environment input does have the power to influence how the person becomes to be more like a morally responsible human being made in the image of the Creator God. Then a lessor wild animal. However, most animals do not behave so poorly, relatively as some humans do.

The disciples of Yeshua Hamashiach spent three years with the teaching of Torah, ethics, and love as a Jewish Rabbi, observing and learning a Torah -based worldview and the Elohim, Ruach Ha-Kodesh Spirit-filled new life. How much the 13 people group time they spent together was not exclusive all the time, e.g., Peter was a married man. The human free will and the freedom to choose is critical to the development of the individual's mind and personality. Because a human being is self-determining, therefore the correct worldview input needs to be factual and truth based.

The information and data input of the mind will reproduce, metaphorically speaking, its own species, type, and kind, whether carnal pleasures or spirituality orientated life values. An analogy, a meat grinder is a mechanical machine; if you feed it meat, then the meat will come out the other end. However, if you feed it dried bread crumbs, then breadcrumbs will come out the other end.

WHAT IS THE WRONG INPUT?

Wrong input for the mind is wrong information. At a young age, it is the parent's responsibility to make sure that children do not get the wrong input values established in their hearts and mind. Also, to train the mind of a child with the ability to know the real value of virtues. And to train the young minds with the ability to make the right moral decision with confidence every time. Where do the parents get the right information? So that they can teach it to their children? They must get it in order to be able to teach it to the minds and hearts of their children.

It is also a question of confidence with self-esteem, to know what is right. To know what is morally right is the right information for the human living soul; intelligence, consciousness, imagination, will, memory, and the emotions. The right information from the Bible to the human heart, soul, and mind. By now, we well know that dictators are full of false information. There is a difference between morally right and morally wrong.

The wrong information is to believe a subjective lie based on the human experience. A lie is to represent the right as being wrong and to represent the wrong as being right. It is morally irresponsible. In a protected spiritual family environment, teenager's minds are protected and remain with a clear mind and a good conscience. The challenge of the mind is to learn the difference between truth and falsehood. The challenge for the mind and will is to choose that which is right and true, regardless of the temptation to choose the false or the morally wrong choice at the time.

The power of temptation is in the indecision. If your mind is morally weak, and never received the right information, or never had to choose that which is morally right, then the temptation will try and persuade towards the wrong choice. That is why temptations lead to the broadways. The easy way. Without consciously thinking and knowing the value of moral virtue, the natural inclinations and disposition of the carnal human nature can quickly lead the individual astray to immoral behavior.

MORALLY RIGHT INPUT

The mind must take control of decision making; it is through the intellect, consciousness, and the will, that the mind is made secure with the willpower to choose that which is morally right, every time. It is a challenge for the central executive section of the frontal lobe, of the mind intellect, to pioneer and claim and master new territory in moral decision making. Through the exercise of it, it becomes a familiar skill, a strength of the mind. Then it can be used in faithful service according to the individual's call. For some, it may be cleanup or renovating, and for others, maybe a complete rebuilding of their ability to think straight. The neuron cells of the mind reinforce the right choice by establishing connections to new cell connections, associated with making the right moral decisions and choosing ethically and morally right values. It really is that straight forward.

If an individual has faith in the Creator of the Universe, Elohim, according to the Holy Scriptures, and has been delivered from their own unbelief, then they need to work at establishing the right decision connections, with the right input, the instructions of the Torah inside their thinking mind. Making moral decisions, based on information, and the information is found in the instructions of the written Torah. The written instructions of the Torah, are not a human opinions. It is morally pure information to humanity, from the Creator of Life (YHWH), at Mount Sinai.

> "Yeshua said to him, "If you can believe,[a] all things are possible to him who believes." Immediately the father of the child cried out and said with tears, "Lord, I believe; help my unbelief!" Mark 9:23-25.

> "What then shall we say in response to these things? If God is for us, who can be against us?" Romans 8:31.

**The Spirit of God is intimately involved with drawing people to Salvation.**
**THINK ON THESE THINGS**

> "And the peace of God, which surpasses all understanding, will guard your hearts and your minds in Christ Jesus. "Finally, brothers, whatever is true, whatever is honorable, whatever is right, whatever is pure, whatever is lovely, whatever is admirable — if anything is excellent or praiseworthy — think on these things." Philippians 4:7,8.

> "For if you live according to the flesh, you will die; but if by the Spirit you put to death the deeds of the body, you will live. For all who are led by the Spirit of God are sons of God." Romans 8: 13,14.

[35]

# WHAT DOES THE BIBLE SAY ABOUT THE SATAN?

What Jesus Said About Satan. Jesus said a good deal about Satan.

> He called him: the enemy, Matthew 13:39.

"The evil one," Matthew 13:38

> "The prince of this world," John 12:31; 14:30

"A liar," and "the father of lies," John 8:44.

> "A murderer," John 8:44.

He said that he "saw him fallen from heaven," Luke 10:18.

> That he has a "kingdom," Matthew 12:26.

That "evil men are his sons," Matthew 13:38.
  That he "sowed tares among the wheat," Matthew 13:38,39.
  He "snatches Word from hearers," Matthew 13:19; Mark 4:15;
  The "bound a woman for 18 years", Luke 13:16.
  That he "desired to have Peter," Luke 22:31.
  That has "angels," Matthew 25:41.
  That "eternal fire is prepared for him," Matthew 25:41
  THE BIBLE REPRESENTS SATAN AS:

"The Tempter," Matthew 4:3
"The prince of demons," Matthew 12:24; Mark 3:22; Luke 11:15.
"Source of demoniacal possession," Matthew 12:22-29; Luke 11:14-23
That he put the betrayal into the heart of Judas, Jn 13:2,27.
That he perverts the Scripture, Matthew 4:4; Luke 4: 10,11
That he is "the god of this world," 11 Cor. 4:4.
That he is "the prince of the power of the air," Ephesians 2:2
That he "fashions himself into an angel of light," 11 Cor. 11:14.
That he is our "adversary," 1 Peter 5:8.
He is "the deceiver of the whole world," Rev. 12:9; 20: 3,8,10.
Calls him "the great dragon," "the old serpent," Revelation 12:9; 20:2.
The "seducer of Adam and Eve," Genesis 3:1-20.
That he will "flee if resisted," James 4:7.
That he caused "Paul's thorn in the flesh," 11 Cor. 12:7.
Hindered Paul's missionary plans, 1 Thess. 2:18.
Caused Ananias to lie, Acts 5:3.
That Gentiles are under his power, Acts 26:18.
That he blinds the minds of unbelievers, 11 Cor. 4:4.
False teachers are "a synagog of Satan," Rev. 2:9; 3:9.
Can produce false miracles, 11 Thes. 2:9.
Is the moving spirit of the "Apostasy", 11 Thes. 2:9
As a roaring lion seeks to devour Christians, 1 Peter 5:8
Is overcome by faith, 1 Peter 5:9.
Is Wiley, Ephesians 6:11.
Is the spirit that works in the disobedient, Ephesians 2:2
Moved David to sin, I Chron. 21:1.
Caused Job's troubles, Job 1:7-2:10.
Was the Adversary of Joshua, Zech. 3:1-9.
Gets the advantage of Christians, 11 Cor. 2:11.
Evil men are his children, 1 John 3:8,10. (Baptist, 2020)

[36]

# HOW DOES THE NEMESIS GET ACCESS TO SOULS?

For most people, it is the choice of the will, by their choosing, even if they choose not to be conscious of the moment consequence, or if they repress truth from themselves. Human life and soul are most vulnerable at the beginning as a newborn and slowly develop and grows under the protective umbrella of parental love, nurture, and goodwill. The development of the newborn Spirit, heart, and soul ideally grows under the protective cover of the parents, family, friends, and community.

The living soul in this context is found in the core functions of the mind, intellect, consciousness, imagination, will, memory, and emotions. The intellect is vital for survival; the consciousness is everything on the earth experience. The will is blind, utterly dependent on the other functions of the mind, like consciousness, intellect, imagination, memory, and emotions. They commit to the intelligent process, communicating to the will, contributing to the decision-making process, to use the will. The consciousness and the intellect commit the will to action, interacting, and confabulating with the will to further decisions.

Similarly, to the human ten internal organ systems, they are vital for consciousness. Yet, the intellect and consciousness are at a higher level and supreme for survival. There are biological systems at lower levels that make life possible. Human consciousness, intellect, and will, need to be proactive, to search out and understand the ethical, moral environment that they live in. It is vital for spiritual survival. To know what the purpose of human life is on the planet earth. According to the Creator of life, Elohim will.

The influence of the Nemesis comes from outside with distractions to the healthy mind, intellect, and consciousness, Presenting distractions with temptations with opportunity for the human to sin. Both extreme ends of the subjective human behavior are prone to outside influence, such as loneliness, personal failure, depression, ill health, rejection, and bitterness of the soul. The other extreme is a personal success, naturally gifted or highly talented personality, popularity, friends and favoritism, egotism, and unconstrained without accountability to moral absolutes.

The third extreme is hubris, arrogance, hard-hearted, cynicism, unbelief, and self-centered narcissism. The human soul is vulnerable to the enemy of the soul at every extreme. Whether personal success, personal failure, or hardness of heart, these personality character traits and conditions of the human heart, are all vulnerable to the enemy of the soul deception, that can lead to further extremes. The personal talent success is most obviously seen on screen in cinemas, and on the stage of the pop culture, artists, musicians that are a talented or experienced personal success. In some individual cases, in order to maintain their performance, relieve stress, or to experiment with higher emotional states and feelings, they experiment with drugs, and before long become addicted to the substance abuse. Substance abuse is a sure sign of a past temptation and failure to resist. Then coming under the further influence and the power of the enemy of the soul, the Nemesis, the devil, and Satan.

How is it so? It is so because the individual person has lost some level of control, of the consciousness, imagination, intellect, and the self- controlled will. That can quickly happen through a disconnect between children and parents. Children during the teenage years may disconnect from parents, relative to the close bond that they had as young children. The enemy of the soul will take that disconnect as an opportunity to drive a wedge between the child and a parent. The human soul is vulnerable to being wounded by the negative impact on the emotions. And the reaction is by hiding personal experiences, concealing the truth with secrecy, and searching out a way for escapism.

Binge drinkers have a habit of drinking to the point where they lose consciousness. Whatever the circumstance, or pleasure-seeking, they push the limits to the extreme, where the mind is completely overwhelmed by the influence of the substance. They escape for a time outside of their ordinary consciousness, into an excited state for a time. Their experienced high may be drawn like a bell curve after the effects have worn off, and the normal state of mind and consciousness is returning back down to ordinary consciousness.

They may feel remorse after a day or two, the sick feeling that comes from alcohol poisoning. The temptation of pleasure was such a strong driving force that it pushed the buttons for other carnal pleasure to such extreme bordering on insanity. Losing control of the mind with drugs is crazy. Lack of control of the mind by natural means is a vulnerability. The human living soul is entirely dependent on the functions of a healthy mind, the intellect, imagination, consciousness, will, memory, and emotions. The most apparent substance temptations in modern western society are alcohol, illegal recreational drugs, and prescription drugs. The power of temptation can be augmented by the tempter's promise of immediate gratification of pleasures of the physical senses, as well as altering the state of an anxious mind.

HOW IS THE NEMESIS SO ELUSIVE?

- The Nemesis is elusive for many reasons:
- Satan is a deceiver by nature; it is what he does best
- The cultural glorification of sexual seduction, temptation, and Sin
- The commercial value of Sin as entertainment
- The separation between the visible and the invisible worlds
- Human beings have been given the authority to rule the physical world.

> "Then God said, "Let us make mankind in our image, in our likeness, so that they may rule over the fish in the sea and the birds in the sky, over the livestock and all the wild animals, [a] and over all the creatures that move along the ground." Genesis 1: 26.

The western hedonistic culture is self-determining, creative programs and entertainment pleasures, from the human carnal heart and mind, to satisfy the insatiable lust demands for pleasure. Most western societies entertain and flaunt blatant Sin. Sin is marketed openly and widely as a commercial commodity for entertainment purposes. Hollywood has marketed Sin with heroes and herons. In the entertainment world, people are portrayed as loving Sin is positive and enjoyable. Is it any wonder why the enemy of the soul is elusive? Because the devil is sleeping under the same bed-sheets.

The arrow of time flows in a forward direction. The flow of time can be backtracked with stored memory and documented timeline history. Cooking is a process, whether steaming, poaching, boiling, scrambling, baking, or frying eggs. It is impossible to undo the cooking process of material food items. Only the miracle substance of water can be changed from one form to another and reversed from liquid water to solid water and from solid water to liquid water. Also, from liquid to steam, and from steam to liquid, and liquid to solid, or steam to solid. The versatile and flexible, colorless, transparent, odorless, unique substance of water. The cooking method of food decisions needs to be made before the cooking starts, not after the event. That is the nature of the window and the reality of time. The window of real-time is essential for the right conscious decision making, most crucial for future outcomes. Likewise, greater temptations appear at specific locations at specific times. Depending on the window of opportunity presented.

The temptation is restricted and limited to the window of opportunity and the speed of time. It is limited to one window frame of time, in step with the real-time reality. If the individual's mind is distracted and opens his or her soul by entertaining the mind with Sin, then the power of temptation will be so much more overwhelming with the will cooperating. A conscious mind will need to decide whether to sin or not to sin. The Bible says that if we voluntarily sin, then Sin will find us out. We cannot deny it; therefore, it is best to make up the mind to believe what the Bible says about Sin. And to fear God and to shun evil. With the conscious decision of free will, we choose to believe the truth. The truth is written in the Holy Scriptures.

> "Do not be wise in your own eyes; fear the LORD and shun evil." Proverbs 3:7.

> "you will certainly sin against the LORD, and you may be assured that your sin will find you out." Number 32: 23.

Satan's influence will try to come in and exploit that window of time that may influence the individual person living soul, intellect, consciousness, imagination, will, memory and emotions, and start to cause moral decay. Therefore, the power of temptation works in partnership with distraction. The human mind functions, intellect, imagination, consciousness, will, memory, and emotions, are vulnerable functions of the mind for the devil to invade with immorality. Also, to take control of those functions of the mind and to use it for his purposes. And over time, destroy them in the process, debilitating the human living soul mind.

Alternatively, the living soul mind is powerful God-given tools to resist the temptations if those tools are sharp and focused on resisting the devil's deceitfulness. It is vital for the mind to be conscious and to know what temptation to Sin is? Before, a protective wall can be built in the heart and mind. The reason why the devil gets access to peoples living souls and their physical body is that people open the window and let the influence involuntarily as if they did not know better? That is how addictions get access to the human living soul.

People choose to sin. Generally, people love to sin in the mind, heart, soul, and body. That is the prime reason why the enemy of the soul is so elusive. Because people have invited the influence of Satan into their lives, they have blended the God-given moral absolutes into a puree of subjective relativism, with postmodernism and denial of the existence of the first cause. In the beginning, God, Elohim. Genesis 1:1.

It is impossible to unscramble cooked eggs and convert them into boiled eggs. Therefore, before the cooking stage, make up your mind, with understanding, what outcome do you desire? What is the result? Depends entirely on the cooking method you choose to use. It is true that people cook eggs for their nutritional needs, that comes from cooked food. They do not do the cooking process as a ritual for the cooking method's sake. Various cooking methods are not equal; some methods are quicker and possibly more convenient than other methods. How is that relevant to the temptation of the Nemesis? It is to do with the power of distraction of the consciousness. To make the mind dull without understanding what the Lord requires from the human heart, mind, and soul.

> "He has shown you, O mortal, what is good. And what does the Lord require of you? To act justly and to love mercy and to walk humbly with your God." Micah 6:8.

Satan will sell rotten eggs for the price of premium eggs. Satan comes to steal, kill, and destroy anything and everything. From chicken eggs to the chooks, and even the chook pen. None of that will satisfy the Nemesis for long, and it will be back with more temptations if Satan is invited to home with entertainment for Sin. Whenever those three deeds are being committed (steal, kill, destroy), you can be sure that Satan's influence is there at work.

YESHUA HAMASHIACH

> "The thief comes only to steal and kill and destroy. I came that they may have life and have it abundantly." "I am the good shepherd. The good shepherd lays down his life for the sheep." John 10:10-29. (ESV)

People do need a strong motivation to keep striving with work and to survive in life. Strong motivation can also clear the mind from distractions, at least when there is working to do. Meaningful work can be a strong motivator rewarding the efforts with positive experiences along the life journey.

TREASURES IN HEAVEN

> Yeshua said, "Do not store up for yourselves treasures on earth, where moths and vermin destroy, and where thieves break in and steal. But store up for yourselves treasures in heaven, where moths and vermin do not destroy, and where thieves do not break in and steal. For where your treasure is, there your heart will also be." Matthew 6:19- 21. (NIV)

A BIBLICAL WORLDVIEW

A Biblical worldview with a moral life philosophy can bring spiritual meaning, natural health, and physical longevity to life. Life is a balancing act, there is objective truth, and there is objective love. There is also the subjective carnal truth and subjective carnal love.

They are not equal in the realm of the human experience and being created in the image of the Creator God, with an intellect, consciousness, imagination, will, memory, and emotions. The Creator of the Universe God also has an intellect, consciousness, imagination, will, memory, and emotions. That is the primary reason why and how the conscious human mind has such a powerful capacity to think and understand many idea concepts outside the immediate human life four-wall box. The evidence of the works of God is found in the natural environment. Psalm 104

TRUTH TO LIVE ON

Truth can be discovered; it requires an effort and cooperation of the human will, intellect, consciousness, heart, mind, and soul. The importance of logic and reason is often underestimated; here, it is again confronting the mind.

"The whole purpose of reasoning, of logic, is to arrive at the truth of things. This is often an arduous task, as truth can sometimes be painfully elusive. But not to pursue truth would be absurd since it is the only thing that gives meaning to all our endeavors. It would be equally absurd to suppose that truth is something forever to be pursued but never to be attained, for that renders our activity purposeless, which is to say, irrational, and turns truth into a chimera".

McInerny, D.Q. Being Logical: A Guide to Good Thinking (McInerny, 2004)

I hope these grains of truth with logic and reasoning. The Spirit of the Natural Law, used in this book, and the many references are pointing to the Holy Scriptures as an authoritative guide to understanding so that the mind may be enlightened by the Spirit of grace and strengthened for the battle of the human souls.

## ALL SCRIPTURE IN THE BIBLE IS GOD-BREATHED

"All Scripture is God-breathed and is useful for instruction, for conviction, for correction, and for training in righteousness, so that the man of God may be complete, fully equipped for every good work." 2 Timothy 3:16,17.

"Seek the Lord while he may be found; call on him while he is near. Let the wicked forsake their ways and the unrighteous their thoughts. Let them turn to the Lord, and he will have mercy on them, and to our God, for he will freely pardon. "For my thoughts are not your thoughts, neither are your ways my ways," declares the Lord. "As the heavens are higher than the earth, so are my ways higher than your ways and my thoughts than your thoughts. As the rain and the snow come down from heaven and do not return to it without watering the earth and making it bud and flourish so that it yields seed for the sower and bread for the eater, so is my word that goes out from my mouth: It will not return to me empty, but will accomplish what I desire and achieve the purpose for which I sent it." Isaiah. 55: 6 -11.

**Seek Truth, and Truth Will Set the Human Soul Free.**

"So Jesus said to the Jews who had believed him, "If you abide in my word, you are truly my disciples, and you will know the truth, and the truth will set you free." John 8: 31,32.

[37]

# ABOUT THE AUTHOR

Victor John Leinonen is a Finnish born author with a diverse background. His family migrated from Finland when he was nine years old and moved to Australia, where he later became a citizen. Victor's parents were Christians and influenced family life by example, with Christian values. Victor experienced the migration from a Finnish speaking Nordic country to the English-speaking school in Australia as being eruptive to his education and learning. He left school at the age of 15 and started working on building sites as a labourer, one of the sites was the high court of Australia, Canberra, in 1977.

Victor's carnal nature got the better of him, and he went the broad way of the Spirit of the world from 1975 to early 1981. Utterly a lost soul without a spiritual anchor in life. Regular work during the week and the recreational weekends with playing music, coastal surf trips, and consuming alcohol and smoking drugs for recreation. After a few years, life became more chaotic; regular abuse of alcohol, driving a car under the influence, locked him up in a corrective prison camp for a few weeks.

The short lifestyle the correction did not bring about permanent change. Soon enough, another violation of the law from drinking and resisting police arrest. Took him to the same corrective prison camp for a month. The culture of drinking was losing the appeal fast; it made no sense to him long term. It was a harmful addiction without any lasting rewards. Furthermore, it brought no satisfaction to his living soul. And it did not give answers to the ultimate question about the meaning of life. Addiction to drugs makes no sense; it is just another type of escapism deceiving the mind. To make one believe that the temporary feelings produced by alcohol or illegal drugs could add any meaning or value to human life is a dangerous carnal error. That also has the power through addiction to permanently destroy people's lives. Too many lives have been destroyed by addiction to harmful drugs.

While working in forestry in a small New South Wales country town in 1981, one Saturday morning, Victor visited a news agency, and his eye caught an article in the Readers Digest. The Readers Digest article was about a political prisoner's life experience in the Soviet Union. Victor bought the Readers Digest magazine and read it. The author of the article was Richard Wurmbrand. A Romanian Christian minister of Jewish descent. He shared his life experiences in the book of being imprisoned by the Soviet Communists in Romania for being a Christian minister. He was severely tortured and coerced to give up his faith in Jesus and to stop talking about him to others. The persecution came by the Communist regime of Romania from 1948 to 1967.

Wurmbrand passed through the penal facilities of Craiova, Gherla, the Danube–Black Sea Canal, Văcărești prison, Malmaison, Cluj, and ultimately Jilava, spent three years in solitary confinement. The article communicated the unimaginable suffering of political prisoners and Christians everywhere in the Soviet Union. Richard Wurmbrand spent a total of fourteen years in Soviet prisons.

*"Wurmbrand was released from his first imprisonment in 1956, after eight and a half years. Although he was warned not to preach, he resumed his work in the underground church."*

*"He was arrested again in 1959 and sentenced to 25 years. During his imprisonment, he was beaten and tortured. Physical torture included mutilation, burning, and being locked in a largely frozen icebox. His body bore the scars of physical torture for the rest of his life. For example, he later recounted having the soles of his feet beaten until the flesh was torn off, then the next day beat again to the bone. This prolific writer said there were no words to describe that pain."*

(Richard Wurmbrand).

## THE TRAITS OF THE NEMESIS

*"Secret police visited Richards wife Sabina in 1959 and posed as released fellow prisoners. They claimed to have attended Richard's funeral in prison. During his second imprisonment, his wife Sabina was given official news of Richard's death, which she did not believe. Sabina herself had been arrested in 1950 and spent three years in penal labour on the canal. Sabina's autobiographical account of this time is titled The Pastor's Wife. Their only son, Mihai, by then a young adult, was expelled from college-level studies at three institutions because his father was a political prisoner, an attempt to obtain permission to emigrate to Norway to avoid compulsory service in the Communist army was unsuccessful."*

*"Eventually, Wurmbrand was a recipient of an amnesty in 1964. Concerned with the possibility that Wurmbrand would be forced to undergo further imprisonment, the Norwegian Mission to the Jews and the Hebrew Christian Alliance negotiated with Communist authorities for his release from Romania for ten thousand American dollars."*

(Richard-Wurmbrand, 1948)

*"Richard Wurmbrand wrote more than 18 books, the most widely known being Tortured for Christ. Variations of his works have been translated into more than 60 languages. He founded the international organization Voice of the Martyrs, which continues to aid Christians around the world who are persecuted for their faith."*

(Voice-Of-The-Martyrs, 2018)

Victor sent away for the free book titled Tortured For Christ-By Richard Wurmbrand in 1981. After receiving it and reading it, he ordered another book and some audiotapes. After reading a few books and listening to the tapes, the scriptures started to affect his life, heart, mind, and soul. He well knew in his inner being that he wanted a changed life. To find meaning and purpose and give up drinking alcohol because it was so detrimental to everything practical, like the need to have a regular work commitment. What comes first, the horse or the cart? Sometimes people have neither, and they fill the need with other substitutes. Drinking is often filling a vacuum of spiritual needs. Learning to give up self-will and old habits are not always natural. It is the self will that get people trapped into addictions in the first place. Going outside of God's will early in life is often caused by self-will. Learning what it means to believe can be found by following Yeshua Hamashiach for genuine spiritual needs. In hindsight, the Holy Spirit of God drew Victor to a God-centered Spiritual reality, with a New Holy Spirit influenced life.

The Bible-based teaching and the testimony of Richard Wurmbrand started to influence Victim thinking and decision-making and turn his life slowly back towards God's will. Eventually, to receive the grace of Ruach Ha-Kodesh. Enabling him to believe and to receive Yeshua Hamashiach as his personal savior for Salvation. In 1982 Victor moved back to Canberra to live. He was invited by a family friend to a youth meeting at the Canberra Missionary Church. After a few meetings, the Ruach Ha-Kodesh's conviction came, convicting Victor to surrender self-will at the foot of the cross and follow the teaching of Yeshua. The Spirit reached the core, heart, mind, and soul, a more profound surrender to the Holy Spirit of God.

Going to the Canberra Missionary Church became regular, eventually publicly accepting Jesus Christ as his personal savior and Lord. Victor was water baptized in 1983 as a sign of self-surrender to God's will and repentance. The following year Victor went on to study and work with Youth With A Mission in 1984 until 1990.

1993 Victor returned to studies as an adult, a student completing his HSC, and in 1995 trained at the School of Tourism and Hospitality in Canberra, where he completed his training to become a qualified chef. Victor has spent over 20 years working in many excellent 4 to 5-star hotel restaurants in Australia and Finland Lapland until New Year 2017. Since 2010, Victor has been working with the internet, social media, blogging, websites, advertising, and information marketing, using photography and video services for local business advertising.

Victor's passion for the peace-loving Nordic people's traditions led him to write his first book, The Inkeri Land (2012). His second book, The Nemesis (2018), and the third book title, Bloggers guide To Arctic Finland (2019). The Second Edition of the Nemesis is titled A Claim For A True Worldview (2020).

**A Claim For A True Worldview** book edition is for anyone who desires to know what a True Worldview is and how it can be discovered. It uses the history of the ancient people of Nordic Finland as a modern case study. To reveal how people have been duped into believing false Worldviews. This case study reveals how and where the battle rages over integrity and truth; the battle rages against the 4000-year-old narrative and the truth claims found in the Jewish Holy scriptures.

Humans beings are constantly bombarded with distractions and false information. Power-hungry dictators and tyrants desiring to exploit those weak or ignorant of the God-given truth for humanity. The Creator of Life does exist outside of time and space. He has high expectations for humanity to use their intellect, consciousness, imagination, will, memory, and emotions in a way that God intended it to be used. The primary evidence of the existence of God is found in the works of God. Living things, plants, insects, birds, fish, mammals, and humans. To reject the primary evidence is to repress the truth. And to put the human soul experience above the knowledge of God.

The people of Finland over 500 years have experienced unbelievable struggles and injustice by dark forces and conquering Imperials. Invasions and many hundred years of submission and subjugation. Battles with losses and victories over the dark, sinister forces of Bolsheviks State Atheism and Communism. The brazen hard-core atheism of the Soviet Union was inspired by insidious evil at all levels. The philosophy, the spirit, and the Worldview of Communism were Anti-Christ spirited, violating the Spirit of the Natural Law.

It was the most diabolical anti-God government on earth that has gotten off the ground in the last 400 years. Every word from the Creator of Life in the Jewish Holy Scriptures was blasphemed, rejected, and explained away as unreliable nonsense. Karl Marx's brainchild utopian communism was an ego-centric fantasy that came to deceive, steal, kill, destroy the land's people, and the peace on earth. Karl Marx, Vladimir Lenin, and Joseph Stalin were deceived by Satanic temptations. They were used by Satan to establish an evil empire on earth and to make war on the Kingdom of God.

The Imperialist powers are also driven by human carnal nature, political power, military conquest, avaricious greed for riches, natural resources, and territorial takeover. They are often empowered by the deceiving spirits, and the deceiver of humanity called Satan, directly or indirectly. People need to be sober and learn to think logically and rationally. Consider what Yeshua said about his mission on earth.

> 1 John 3: 8. ESV. "Whoever makes a practice of sinning is of the devil, for the devil has been sinning from the beginning. The reason the Son of God appeared was to destroy the works of the devil."

**Authors books online.** https://www.amazon.com/AUTHOR-VICTOR-LEINONEN/
Family background.

Victor Leinonen is the son of a mechanic, and his Father was a lumberjack. Victor's pride for the Spirit of the Natural Law, Biblical Christian values, and real justice is evident in his writing and the pursuit to learn and share the mysteries of a Biblical worldview and Biblical life philosophy. With the Good News of the Yeshua Hamashiach Gospel. New spiritual life is to be found for those that seek it. The mind, heart, and soul that seeks the truth and lines up with the teaching of Yeshua Hamashiach. Jesus said to the Jews, if they follow his teaching, then they will know the truth, and the truth will set them free.

The God of Abraham, Isaac, and Jacob is the same YHWH that Yeshua was walking with and teaching on 2000 years later. The First Cause of the material Universe, YHWH.

Victor's mother and three sisters were forced to evacuate Finland, Karelia, in 1939. They became war refugees during the Soviet invasion in November 1939. They were fortunate, for far too many were unable to escape. One thousand seven hundred civilian people were trapped inside the same Suojärvi municipality by the undeclared war against peace, an invasion attempt by the Soviet Union in November 1939.

THANK YOU FOR TAKING THE TIME TO READ A CLAIM FOR A TRUE WORLDVIEW BOOK 2020

I hope that the grains of truth, with the logic and reasoning, found in this book, with the Scripture quotations as a guide, to lead, instruct and inform the mind. So that the mind and heart may be enlightened by the Spirit of truth and grace, and enable Christians to speak up with their beliefs, stand up for A True Worldview, and defend true justice and the Christian faith with understanding. And to know how to be on the right side of the Spirit of the Natural Law.

> Yeshua said to his disciples. "Look, I am sending you out as sheep among wolves. So be as shrewd as snakes and harmless as doves." Matthew 10:16.

Victor John Leinonen. December 12. 2020.

[38]

# GOSPEL ACCORDING TO MATTHEW

"Blessed are they which are persecuted for righteousness' sake: for theirs is the kingdom of heaven. Blessed are ye, when men shall revile you, and persecute you, and shall say all manner of evil against you falsely, for my sake. Rejoice, and be exceeding glad: for great is your reward in heaven: for so persecuted they the prophets which were before you.Ye are the salt of the earth: but if the salt has lost his savor, wherewith shall it be salted? it is thenceforth good for nothing, but to be cast out, and to be trodden under foot of men. Ye are the light of the world. A city that is set on a hill cannot be hidden.Neither do men light a candle, and put it under a bushel, but on a candlestick; and it giveth light unto all that are in the house.Let your light so shine before men, that they may see your good works, and glorify your Father which is in heaven." Matthew: Chapter 5:11-16. (Yeshua Hamashiach)

[39]

# THE ARMOR OF GOD

"Finally, be strong in the Lord and in his mighty power. Put on the full armor of God, so that you can take your stand against the devil's schemes. For our struggle is not against flesh and blood, but against the rulers, against the authorities, against the powers of this dark world and against the spiritual forces of evil in the heavenly realms. Therefore put on the full armor of God, so that when the day of evil comes, you may be able to stand your ground, and after you have done everything, to stand. Stand firm then, with the belt of truth buckled around your waist, with the breastplate of righteousness in place, and with your feet fitted with the readiness that comes from the gospel of peace. In addition to all this, take up the shield of faith, with which you can extinguish all the flaming arrows of the evil one. Take the helmet of salvation and the sword of the Spirit, which is the word of God. And pray in the Spirit on all occasions with all kinds of prayers and requests. With this in mind, be alert and always keep on praying for all the Lord's people." Ephesians 6: 10-18. (Apostle-Paul )

# [40]

# TERMINOLOGY

**Adonai**: A Divine name, translated "Lord," and signifying, from its derivation, "sovereignty."

**Elohim**: Elohim is a Hebrew word that denotes "God" or "God. Genesis 1:1. "In the beginning, "Elohim."

**YHVH** (Yehovah: Yud-he-vah-he). Mentioned 6807 times in the Jewish Holy Scriptures. Significant name of Elohim to consider.

**Yeshua**: Yeshua means salvation. It was suggested that the name Yeshua could be found hidden within the Tetragrammaton YHVH, as "Yeshua HaNazarei Vemelekh HaYehudim" which in Hebrew translates as, "Jesus of Nazareth, King of the Jews," which is the same as the familiar Latin inscription INRI seen written on the notice that was nailed to the cross above Jesus per Pontius Pilate's instruction, "Iesus Nazarenus Rex Iudaeorum." "The name 'Jesus' did not yet exist when Jesus Christ was on Earth, approximately 4 BC to 29 or 34 AD. It did not come into existence until configured by the Council of Nicea of the Roman Catholic Church in the 4th century." " (Yeshua.org).

**Jesus**: "Yeshua is the Hebrew name, and its English spelling is "Joshua. Iesous is the Greek transliteration of the Hebrew name, and its English spelling is "Jesus." Thus, the names "Joshua" and "Jesus" are essentially the same; both are English pronunciations of the Hebrew and Greek names for the Lord." (Gotquestions.org)

**Nemesis**: arch-enemy, arch-rival, enemy, rival, foe, adversary, opponent, antagonist, combatant.

**Spirit of the Natural Law**: It is the Spirit of the Transcendent Eternal Creator of Life order, presented to humanity as an organized structure of the Law, according to the nature of God.

It is also experiential knowledge for understanding God's ways.

> "So He said to the Jews who had believed Him, "If you continue in My word, you are truly My disciples. Then you will know the truth, and the truth will set you free." John 8: 31, 32.

To know the truth, and to be free, is a spiritual journey and discovery. Yeshua walked in the Spirit of obedience to the Torah (instructions of God). And he overcame the devil by speaking out the Torah with faith.

**Torah**: Instructions from the Spirit of the Elohim.

*"Torah, in Judaism, in the broadest sense the substance of divine revelation to Israel, the Jewish people: God's revelation teaching or guidance for humankind. The meaning of "Torah" is often restricted to signify the first five books of the Old Testament, also called the Law (or the Pentateuch, in Christianity). These are the books traditionally ascribed to Moses, the recipient of the original revelation from God on Mount Sinai. Jew-ish, Roman Catholic, Eastern Orthodox, and Protestant canons all agree on their order: Genesis, Exodus, Leviticus, Numbers, and Deuteronomy. "* (www.britannica.com)

To understand and benefit of the wisdom and the guidance from the instructions of the Torah, essentially, it requires the Spirit of the Elohim for spiritual interaction with the human living soul: Intellect, imagination, will, memory and emotions. To think like God thinks, to imagine as God imagines, and to feel like God feels. It can be summed up by the phrase, inspired by the Spirit of Elohim. To understand the five books of the Bible requires the same Spirit that was active when the books of the Bible were played out in real life, and the events later recorded and written for future generations. To unlock the mystery of Elohim, it requires revelation, natural and supernatural revelation, by the Spirit of the Elohim that has inspired, interacted, and created it through His influence.

**Natural Law:** In the end, where does Law come from? *"The Theory of Natural Law maintains that certain moral laws transcend time, culture, and government. There are universal standards that apply to all mankind throughout all time. These universal moral standards are inherent in and discoverable by all of us and form the basis of a just society."* Wikipedia.

**Satan:** The description of Satan is used in the same context as what is used and written in the Holy Bible scriptures, and also in the same context as Yeshua used it on Earth, nothing more, nothing less. Satan is the adversary of God's message and messengers on Earth. The Good News message needs to be known and done on Earth. When it all has been accomplished, then the devil's time on Earth will be over. And human minds and hearts will no longer be deceived into unbelief, ignorance, rebellion, and lawlessness. People will know in the end that there is a Creator of Life, as it is written, in the beginning, Elohim.

**True Worldview.**

A reality-based worldview that is according to the Image and the mind of God. He has shared information with humanity, that is logical and rational:

- Reality. Truth based, factual knowledge about human nature and life on earth.
- Beliefs. That which is True?
- Values. That which is Right?
- Behavior and habits. That which is according to right behavior?

Foundational instructions given over 3460 years ago at mount Sinai. The Jewish Holy scripture Worldview, according to the Creator of Life Creative order. Human beings are made in the image of God. Made to be morally responsible for their deeds and actions. The human living soul functions of the mind; intellect, conscience, imagination, will, memory, and emotions. Mammals also have the same functions of the human living soul mind, but play a different role in life according to the Creator of Life will.

[41]

# IMAGE INDEX

Book cover.   All Rights Reserved ©Vesa Leinonen 2020.
1. Page 48.    Spirit of the Natural Law to the Rule of Law in Society Graphic. Rights Reserved. Design by Vesa Leinonen.
2. Page 69.    Finland Delegation at Tartu 1920.
3. Page 70.    Soviet Union Delegation Tartu 1920.
4. Page 88.    Nazi Germany & Soviet union Aggression Pact. Graphic by Victor Leinonen.
5. Page.89.    Map of Arctic Finland 1939. Karttakeskus.fi Map, used with permission.
6. Page 90.    Map of South Finland 1939. Karttakeskus.fi Map, used with permission.
7. Page.100.   Kemijärvi to Salla railway. SA Picture (War Archives). War Museum of Finland. Used with permission.
8. Page 102.   Karelia Isthmus, and Ladoga Isthmus map. Karttakeskus.fi Map, used with permission.
9. Page 146.   Blood stained hand graphic. Stock photo.
10. Page 149.  Ladoga Karelia map. Karttakeskus.fi Map, used with permission.
10. Page 151.  Finland border map 1917-1922. ©Karttakeskus.fi Map, used with permission.
11. Page 152.  USSR Invasion Attempt 1939. ©Karttakeskus.fi Map, used with permission.
12. Page 153.  Finland Push back USSR annexation. ©Karttakeskus.fi Map, used with permission.
13. Page 154.  Rebound borders 1944. ©Karttakeskus.fi Map, used with permission.
14. Page 208.  War refugee children from Karelia. The National Archives of Sweden. Used with permission. Riksarkivet.
16. Page 215.  Granite boulder enemy tank obstacle. SA Picture (War Archives). War Museum of Finland.
17. Page 226.  Gulf of Bothnia Sea Invasion Objective. ©Karttakeskus.fi Map.
19. Page 220.  Ladoga Karelia Invasion Objective. ©Karttakeskus.fi Map.
20. Page 221.  White Sea to Gulf of Bothnia Invasion Objective. ©Karttakeskus.fi Map.
21. Page 222.  Port of Petsamo Invasion Objective. ©Karttakeskus.fi Map.
21. Page 234.  Author. Victor Leinonen

# BIBLIOGRAPHY

Treaty of Rapallo(1922)Retrieved from https://en.wikipedia.org/wiki/ Treaty_of_Rapallo_ (1922)

Anti-Christ-Campaign. (1928-1941). USSR anti-religious campaign (1928– 1941). Retrieved from www.en.wikipedia.org:/wiki/USSR_anti- religious_campaign

Apollos. (2018, May 20). Hebrew. Retrieved from Bible Gate: www. biblegateway.com/Hebrews

Apostle. (2018, May 21). Philippians 4. Retrieved from www.biblegateway. com/Philippians

Apostle-Paul. (AD, May 22). Romans 8:14. Retrieved from www.biblegateway.com:https://www.biblegateway.com/Romans

Atlantic-Council. (2018, May 22). Atlantic Council. Retrieved from www. atlanticcouncil.org/nato

Aunala, A. (2018, May 21). The University of Jyväskylä Finland. Retrieved from www.://jyx.jyu.fi:

Axis-War-Crimes. (1945). List of Axis war crime trials. Retrieved from www.en.wikipedia.org/wiki/List_of_Axis_war_crime_trials

Baptist, R. (2018, May 22). What Jesus Said About Satan. Retrieved from www.richmondhillbaptist.org:

Blessings-and-Curses. (AD). Deuteronomy 27:25. Retrieved from www. biblegateway.com:Deuteronomy

Comparative-Law. (2018, May 21). Comparative Law. Retrieved from www. en.wikipedia.org: Comparative law

Constitutional-Law. (2018, May 21). Constitutional Law. Retrieved from www.en.wikipedia.org: Constitutional law

Custom-Law. (2018, may 21). Custom Law. Retrieved from www. en.wikipedia.org: Custom (law)

Dynasty, L. o. (2018, May 21). Who Shall Be The Emperor of Russia? Retrieved from www. russianlegitimist.org/who-shall-be-the-emperor-of- Russia/

Elohim. (1000-BC). Psalm 24:1. Retrieved from www.biblehub.com/ psalms/24-1.htm

Encyclopedia. (2018, May 21). Immanuel Kant. Retrieved from www. en.wikipedia.org/wiki/Immanuel_Kant

Encyclopedia. (1748). Jeremy Bentham. Retrieved from www.en.wikipedia. org/wiki/Jeremy_Bentham

Encyclopedia. (1918, March 3). Treaty of Brest-Litovsk. Retrieved from www.en.wikipedia.org/wiki/Treaty_of_Brest-Litovsk

Encyclopedia. (1926, May 21). Treaty of Berlin. Retrieved from www. en.wikipedia.org/wiki/Treaty_of_Berlin_(1926)

Encyclopedia. (1932, January 21). Soviet–Finnish Non-Aggression Pact. Retrieved from www.en.wikipedia.org: https://en.wikipedia.org/ wiki/ Soviet_Non-Aggression_Pact

Encyclopedia. (1936). Great Terror. Retrieved from www.en.wikipedia. org/wiki/Great_Purge

Encyclopedia. (1939, August 23). German-Soviet Frontier Treaty. Retrieved from www.en.wikipedia.org/ wiki/German_Soviet_Frontier_ Treaty

Encyclopedia. (1939, November 26). Shelling of Mainila. Retrieved from www.en.wikipedia.org/wiki/Shelling_of_Mainila

Encyclopedia. (1941, June 25). Continuation War 1941. Retrieved from www.en.wikipedia.org/wiki/Continuation_War

Encyclopedia. (1944, September 22). Allied Commission. Retrieved from www.en.wikipedia.org/wiki/Allied_Commission#Finland

Encyclopedia. (1945, February 13). The battle of Dresden. Retrieved from www.en.wikipedia.org/wiki/Battle_of_Dresden

Encyclopedia. (1945, November 15). War responsibility trials in Finland. Retrieved from www.en.wikipedia.org/wiki/War-responsibility_trials_in_Finland

Encyclopedia. (2001, June 16). Slovenia Summit 2001. Retrieved from www.en.wikipedia.org/wiki/Slovenia_Summit_2001

Encyclopedia. (2018, May 21). Abolition of Monarchy. Retrieved from www.en.wikipedia.org:/wiki/Abolition_of_monarchy

Encyclopedia. (2018, May 20). Baltic Fleet. Retrieved from www.en.wikipedia.org/wiki/Baltic_Fleet_During_the_October_Revolution_and_Russian_Civil_War

Encyclopedia. (2018, May 21). Bar Mitzvah. Retrieved from www.en.wikipedia.org/wiki/Bar_and_Bat_Mitzvah

Encyclopedia. (2018, May 22). Categorical Imperative. Retrieved from www.en.wikipedia.org/wiki/Categorical_imperative

Encyclopedia. (2018, May 21). Deception. Retrieved from www.en.wikipedia.org/wiki/Deception

Encyclopedia. (2018, May 20). Huittisten meijerikahakka. Retrieved from www./fi.wikipedia.org/wiki/Huittisten_meijerikahakka

Encyclopedia. (2018, May 21). Joseph Stalin. Retrieved from www.en.wikipedia.org/wiki/Joseph_Stalin

Encyclopedia. (2018, May 21). Karl Marx. Retrieved from www.en.wikipedia.org/wiki/Karl_Marx

Encyclopedia. (2018, May 21). Natural Law. Retrieved from www.en.wikipedia.org/wiki/Natural_law

Encyclopedia. (2018, May 21). Nikolay Bobrikov. Retrieved from www.en.wikipedia.org/wiki/Nikolay_Bobrikov

Encyclopedia. (2018, May 21). Persecution of Christians in the Soviet Union. Retrieved from www..en.wikipedia.org/wiki/Persecution_of_Christians_in_the_Soviet_Union

Encyclopedia. (2018, May 20). Red Guards. Retrieved from www.en.wikipedia.org/wiki/Red_Guards_(Finland)

Encyclopedia. (2018, May 21). Social Democratic Party. Retrieved from www.en.wikipedia.org/wiki/Social_Democratic_Party_of_Finland

Encyclopedia. (2018, May 21). Socialism. Retrieved from www.en.wikipedia.org/wiki/Socialism

Encyclopedia. (2018, May 21). Territorial Dispute. Retrieved from www.en.wikipedia.org/wiki/Territorial_dispute

Encyclopedia. (2018, May 21). Viena Expedition 1918. Retrieved from www.en.wikipedia.org/wiki/Viena_expedition

Encyclopedia. (2018, May 22). Vladimir Vladimirovich Putin. Retrieved from www.en.wikipedia.org/wiki/Vladimir_Putin

Encyclopedia. (426 AD). Just War Theory. Retrieved from www.en.wikipedia.org/wiki/Just_war_theory

Encyclopedia, W. (2018, May 20). Pietism. Retrieved from www.en.wikipedia.org/wiki/Pietism

Good-News. (AD). John 3:16. Retrieved from www.biblehub.com/john/3-16.htm

Harris, B. (2018, May 21). Joseph Stalin. Retrieved from www.moreorless.net.au/killers/stalin.html

Harward-Edu. (2018, May 22). Michael J. Sandel. Retrieved from www.hls.harvard.edu/faculty/directory/10761/Sandel/

Historical-Resource. (1939, December 14). Historical Resources About The Second World War. Retrieved from www.historicalresources.wordpress.com/2008/12/01/league-of-nations-expulsion-of-the-ussr-december-14-1939/

History. (2018, May 20). World War I. Retrieved from www.en.wikipedia.org/wiki/World_War_I

History, H. (2016). Russian Revolution: A Concise History From Beginning to End. In H. History, Russian Revolution: A Concise History From Beginning to End (p. (p. 7).). Amazon Kindle Edition.

Invasion. (1939, September 1). Invasion of Poland. Retrieved from www.en.wikipedia.org/wiki/Invasion_of_Poland

Invasion. (1940, June). Occupation of the Baltic states. Retrieved from www.en.wikipedia.org/wiki/Occupation_of_the_Baltic_states

Invasions. (2018, May 21). Invasion list. Retrieved from www.en.wikipedia.org/wiki/List_of_invasions

Isaiah. (700 BC). Bible Hub. Retrieved from www.biblehub.com/kjv/isaiah/5.htm

Isaiah-truth. (700 BC). Isaiah 5. Retrieved from www.biblehub.com/kjv/isaiah/5.htm

Jean_Sibelius. (2018). Retrieved from www.en.wikipedia.org/wiki/Jean_Sibelius

Jehoshaphat. (1450 BC). 2 Chronicles 20: 5,6. Retrieved from www.biblegateway.com/Chronicles

John. (2018, May 21). Revelation 18:12. Retrieved from www./biblehub. com/revelation/18-12.htm

John-3:20. (AD). John 3:20. Retrieved from www.biblehub.com/john/3- 20.htm

Joseph-Stalin. (1894, November). Joseph Stalin. Retrieved from www. en.wikipedia.org/wiki/Joseph_Stalin

Judgement-of-Satan. (AD). Judgement of Satan. Retrieved from www. biblegateway.com/Revelation

Katyn-forest-Massacre. (1940, April). Katyn Forest Massacre. Retrieved from www.en.wikipedia.org/wiki/Katyn_massacre

Khrushchev. (1953, May 21). Khrushchev. Retrieved from www. historytoday.com/Khrushchev

Kreeft, P. (2018, May 21). Peter Kreeft.com. Retrieved from www. peterkreeft.com: http://www.peterkreeft.com/featured-writing. htm

Kuril. (1945, August 18). Invasion of the Kuril Islands. Retrieved from www.en.wikipedia.org/wiki/Invasion_of_the_Kuril_Islands

Kuusinen. (1939). Otto Wille Kuusinen. Retrieved from www.en.wikipedia. org/wiki/Otto_Wille_Kuusinen

Kuusinen. (1939, November 30). Terijoki Hallitus. Retrieved from www. en.wikipedia.org/wiki/Terijoen_hallitus

Law. (2018, May 21). Law. Retrieved from www.en.wikipedia.org/wiki/ Law

Legal-Dictionary. (2018, May 22). Ex Post Facto Laws. Retrieved from www.legal-Dictionary.thefreedictionary.com/Ex+Post+Facto+Laws

Leino, E. (2018, May 20). Lapin kesä. Retrieved from Kainuun Eino Leino -seura ry. www.kainuuneinoleinoseura.fi/Eino- leinon- runoja/lapin-kesa/

Locke, J. (2009, September 5). THIS LAND IS MY LAND. Retrieved from Harvard University: https://www.youtube.com/watch?v=MGyygiXMzRk

Locke, J. (2018, May 20). John Locke. Retrieved from www.en.wikipedia. org/wiki/John_Locke

Luther, M. (2018, May 20). Martin Luther. Retrieved from www. en.wikipedia.org/wiki/Martin_Luther

McInerny, D. (2004). Kindle Edition. In D. McInerny, Being Logical: A Guide to Good Thinking (p. (p. 19).). New York: Random House Publishing Group.

Mill, J. S. (1863). Utilitarianism. Retrieved from www.utilitarianism.com/ socrates.html

Molotov-Ribbentrop-Pact. (1939, August 23). Nazi German-Soviet Pact of Aggression. Retrieved from www.en.wikipedia.org/wiki/ Molotov%E2%80%93Ribbentrop_Pact

Moscow. (1940, March 12). Moscow Peace Treaty. Retrieved from www. en.wikipedia.org/wiki/Moscow_Peace_Treaty

Moses. (1446 AD). Deuteronomy 32: 1-47. Retrieved from www.biblegateway.com/Deuteronomy

Moses. (1446 BC, May 21). Deuteronomy. Retrieved from www. biblegateway.com/Deuteronomy

Natural-Law. (2018, May 21). Natural Law. Retrieved from www. en.wikipedia.org/wiki/Natural_law

Nemesis, T. (1945, November 15). War-responsibility trials in Finland. Retrieved from www.en.wikipedia.org: https://en.wikipedia.org/ wiki/ War-responsibility_trials_in_Finland

NKVD. (1940). The People's Commissariat for Internal Affairs. Retrieved from www.en.wikipedia.org/wiki/NKVD

Noebel, D. (n.d.). Understanding the Times. In D. Noebel, The Collision of Today's Competing Worldviews (Kindle Location 2). Kindle Books.

Nuremberg-1945. (1945, November 1). Nuremberg trials. Retrieved from www.en.wikipedia.org/wiki/Nuremberg_trials

Nuremberg-1945. (1945, November 20). Nuremberg_principles. Retrieved from www.en.wikipedia.org /wiki/Nuremberg_principles

Nuremberg-Legacy. (2018, May 21). The Legacy of Nuremberg, 70 Years On. Retrieved from www./today.uconn.edu/2015/11/the-legacy-of- Nuremberg-70-years-on/

Operation-World. (2018, May 22). Finland. Retrieved from www.operationworld.org/country/finland/text.html

Paul, A. (2013, May 21). Ephesians. Retrieved from www. biblegateway.com: https://www.biblegateway.com/passage/?search=Ephesians+6%3A12&version=NIV

President-Roosevelt. (1941, December 8). President Roosevelt's Infamy Speech. Retrieved from www.time.com/pearl-harbor-franklin- roosevelt-infamy-speech-attack/

Presidentti-kallio. (1940, March 14). Tasavallan presidentti Kyösti Kallion puhe 14.3.1940. Retrieved from www.histdoc.net/historia/ kallio1940-03-14.html

Berlin Rape, W. (1945, October 21). Rape during the occupation of Germany.

Retrieved from Encyclopedia: www.en.wikipedia.org/wiki/ Rape_ during_the_occupation_of_Germany

RC-Sproul. (2018, May 22). What is Free Will. Retrieved from https:// www.youtube.com/watch?v=bcyttnC6cjg

Richard.N.Hass. (2009, May 5). When is War Justifiable? Retrieved from www.onfaith.cow/onfaith/2009/05/05/when-is-war- justifiable/6626

Richard-Wurmbrand. (1948, February 29). Richard Wurmbrand. Retrieved from www.en.wikipedia.org/wiki/Richard_Wurmbrand

Romans-2:6. (2018, May 21). God's Righteous Judgment. Retrieved from www.biblegateway.com/Romans

Russia. (2018, May 20). Alexander II of Russia. Retrieved from www. en.wikipedia.org/wiki/Alexander_II_of_Russia

Sakhalin. (1945, August 9). Sakhalin. Retrieved from www.en.wikipedia.Org/wiki/Invasion_of_South_Sakhalin

Sandel, D. (2009, Sep 8). Harward Video. Retrieved from YouTube: ttps://www.youtube.com/watch?v=MGyygiXMzRk

Saressalo, L. (2000, May 20). Antikvaari. Retrieved from www.antikvaari.fi/naytatuote.asp?id=1191273

Stalin-Show-Trials. (1936-1938). Moscow Trials. Retrieved from www. en.wikipedia.org/wiki/Moscow_Trials

Stanford. (2018, May 21). Kant's Moral Philosophy. Retrieved from www. plato.stanford.edu/entries/kant-moral/

Stanford-Edu. (2018, May 22). Justice. Retrieved from www.plato. stanford. edu./entries/justice/

Sweden. (2018, May 20). Grand Duchy of Finland. Retrieved from www. en.wikipedia.org/wiki/Grand_Duchy_of_Finland

Sweden. (2018, May 20). Finnish War. Retrieved from www..en.wikipedia. org/wiki/Finnish_War

Sweden. (2018, May 20). Henry (Bishop of Finland). Retrieved from www..en.wikipedia.org/wiki/Henry_(bishop_ of_Finland)

Their-Fruit-Yeshua. (AD). You Will Know Them by Their Fruits. Retrieved from www.biblegateway.com_Matthew

Time-Magazine. (1939). Time Person of the Year. Retrieved from www. en.wikipedia.org/wiki/Time_Person_of_the_Year

Treaties, S. (2018, May 20). Treaty of Nöteborg. Retrieved from w w w. en.wikipedia.org/wiki/Treaty_of_N%C3%B6teborg

UN. (2018, May 21). Universal Declaration of Human Rights. Retrieved from http://www.un.org/en/universal-declaration-human-rights/

Vladimir-Lenin. (1918, May 22). Socialism in One Country. Retrieved from www.en.wikipedia.org/wiki/Socialism_in_One_Country

Vladimir-Putin. (2005, April 26). Putin calls collapse of Soviet Union 'catastrophe'. Retrieved from www.washingtontimes.com/ news/2005/apr/26/20050426-120658-5687r/

Voice-Of-The-Martyrs. (2018, May 22). Voice of the Martyrs. Retrieved from www.VOM.com: https://vom.com.au/

Wikipedia. (1918-25). Allied intervention in the Russian Civil War. Retrieved from www.en.wikipedia.org/wiki/Allied_intervention_in_the_ Russian_Civil_War

Wikipedia. (1920, October 14). Treaty of Tartu (Russian–Finnish). Retrieved from Treaty of Tartu: www.en.wikipedia.org/wiki/ Treaty_of_ Tartu_Russian_Finnish

Wikipedia. (1922, May 21). Treaty of Rapallo. Retrieved from www. en.wikipedia.org/wiki/Treaty_of_Rapallo_(1922)

Wikipedia. (1939, August 23). Nazi German–Soviet Pact of Aggression. Retrieved from www.en.wikipedia.org / wiki/ Molotov%E2%80%93Ribbentrop_Pact

Wikipedia. (1945, April 18). The Battle of Hamburg. Retrieved from www. en.wikipedia.org/wiki/Battle_of_Hamburg_(1945)

Wikipedia. (2018, May 21). Alfred Kordelin. Retrieved from www. en.wikipedia.org/wiki/Alfred_Kordelin

Wikipedia. (2018, May 21). Casus belli. Retrieved from www. en.wikipedia. org/wiki/Casus_belli

Wikipedia. (2018, May 22). Consequentialism. Retrieved from www. en.wikipedia.org/wiki/Consequentialism

Wikipedia. (2018, May 22). Dmitry Anatolyevich Medvedev . Retrieved from www.en.wikipedia.org/wiki/Dmitry_ Medvedev

Wikipedia. (2018, May 22). International Law. Retrieved from www. en.wikipedia.org/wiki/International_law

Wikipedia. (2018, May 21). Natural Rights. Retrieved from www. en.wikipedia.org/wiki/Natural_and_legal_rights

Wikipedia. (2018, May 22). Puppet State. Retrieved from w w w. en.wikipedia.org/wiki/Puppet_state

Wikipedia. (2018, May 21). Russification. Retrieved from www.en.wikipedia.org/wiki/Russification

Wikipedia. (2018, May 21). State of Nature. Retrieved from www. en.wikipedia.org/wiki/State_of_nature

Wikipedia. (2018, May 21). The early life of Joseph Stalin. Retrieved from www.en.wikipedia.org/wiki/Early_life_of_Joseph_Stalin

Wikipedia. (2018, May 21). Utilitarianism. Retrieved from www.en.wikipedia.org/wiki/Utilitarianism

Wikipedia. (2018, May 21). Vladimir Lenin. Retrieved from www. en.wikipedia.org/wiki/Vladimir_Lenin

Wikipedia, E. (2018, May 20). Chernobyl disaster. Retrieved from www. en.wikipedia.org/wiki/Chernobyl_disaster

Wikipedia, E. (2018, May 21). Franz Albert Seyn. Retrieved from www. en.wikipedia.org/wiki/Franz_Albert_Seyn

Winter-War. (1939, November 30). Winter War 1939. Retrieved from www.en.wikipedia.org/wiki/Winter_War

Wisdom, S.-o. (1945). Proverbs 11:11. Retrieved from www.biblehub. com: http://biblehub.com/proverbs/11-

Wisse, R. (2018, May 21). Was Lenin Jewish? Retrieved from www. myjewishlearning.com/article/was-lenin-jewish/

Word, G. I. (2018, May 21). www.biblegateway.com. Retrieved from Bible Gate .com: https://www.biblegate_Exodus

World, O. (2018, May 22). Operation World. Retrieved from www. operationworld.org: http://www.operationworld.org/country/ russ/owtext.html

Yeshua. (2018, May 21). Bible Gateway.com. Retrieved from www..biblegateway.com: https://www.biblegateway.com/John

Yeshua. (30 AD). Matthew 11:29. Retrieved from www. biblegateway.com/ Matthew Yeshua. (AD). Recorded by Matthew Chapter 5:. Retrieved from www. biblegateway.com/Matthew

**Soviet Russian Leadership Worldview Question**

The people of Finland, Sweden, and Norway unequivocally know the truth about Soviet Russia. The accumulated knowledge over many generations of cultural experience that the Soviet Russian leadership has been leading their people with an erroneous State Atheism Worldview. Why does it matter, and why should outsiders' care? It matters because of the false premise of the Soviet Russian leader's lack of respect for the intrinsic value of human life.

Historically, Soviet Russian is known for its character. That they are not content as a nation to be preoccupied with looking after their own people's national affairs and improving their own lot. Soviet Russia's leadership historically has coveted other people's wellbeing and then transgressed moral laws to exploit and steals others' territory, property, and people. Soviet Russian leadership does not have the mind, heart, or spiritual harmony to respect life and submit to God's national leadership laws. So they are tempted with covetousness of territory and material wealth, and they have to adhere to no moral code or internal Spirit that respects the principles of God-given law. So they side with the transgressors and the violaters against the Spirit of the Natural Law.

Because they are outside the Spirit of the Natural Law. They object to the people adhering to and respecting the Spirit of the Natural law. Because they have no invested interest in God-given laws regarding transparent integrity, they have no internal integrity. Their natural human heart and mind oppose the Spirit of the Natural Law, which is spiritual in essence. The love for life and love for truth be known among people. Meaning, no more grey areas between true and false. No more lying, cheating, and stealing. Why not?

Because the moral code, from the Creator of Life, commands people to respect the One true living God of the Universe. Information regarding God's instruction to humanity can be found in the Jewish Holy Scriptures. The Torah, Tanach, and the Spirit of truth as revealed by Yeshua from Nazareth.

---

Exodus 20 CJB. "Then Elohim said all these words, "I am YHWH your Elohim, who brought you out of the Land of Egypt, out of the abode of slavery. "You are to have no other Elohim before me.
You are not to make for yourselves a carved image or any kind of representation of anything in heaven above, on the earth beneath, or in the water below the shoreline.
You are not to bow down to them or serve them; for I, YHWH your Elohim, am a jealous Elohim, punishing the children for the sins of the parents to the third and fourth generation of those who hate me, but displaying grace to the thousandth generation of those who love me and obey my mitzvot."

---

"How blessed are the meek! For they will inherit the Land! Matthew 5:5 (CJB).

## How can the leaders of Nordic countries know what is right? And what is false?

How can they know what is brilliantly right, and what is erroneous?

The leaders of Finland, Sweden, and Norway have been aware of the truth for over 500 years. How did they know?

The truth was spelled out over 3460 years ago by Moses.

Exodus 20

Complete Jewish Bible

---

Exodus 20:1-16.

"Then YHWH said all these words:

2 א "I am YHWH your God, who brought you out of the land of Egypt, out of the abode of slavery.

3 ב "You are to have no other gods before me. You are not to make for yourselves a carved image or any kind of representation of anything in heaven above, on the earth beneath or in the water below the shoreline. 5 You are not to bow down to them or serve them; for I, YHWH your God, am a jealous God, punishing the children for the sins of the parents to the third and fourth generation of those who hate me, 6 but displaying grace to the thousandth generation of those who love me and obey my mitzvot.

7 ג "You are not to use lightly the name of YHWH your God, because YHWH will not leave unpunished someone who uses his name lightly.

8 ד "Remember the day, Shabbat, to set it apart for God. You have six days to labor and do all your work, but the seventh day is a Shabbat for YHWH your God. On it, you are not to do any kind of work — not you, your son or your daughter, not your male or female slave, not your livestock, and not the foreigner staying with you inside the gates to your property. 11 For in six days, YHWH made heaven and earth, the sea and everything in them; but on the seventh day he rested. This is why YHWH blessed the day, Shabbat, and separated it for himself.

12 ה "Honor your father and mother, so that you may live long in the land which YHWH your God is giving you.

13 ו "Do not murder.

14) ז "Do not commit adultery.

15) ח "Do not steal.

16) ט "Do not give false evidence against your neighbor.

"Do not covet your neighbor's house; do not covet your neighbor's wife, his male or female slave, his ox, his donkey or anything that belongs to your neighbor."

(A: vii) All the people experienced the thunder, the lightning, the sound of the shofar, and the mountain smoking. When the people saw it, they trembled. Standing at a distance, they said to Moshe, "You, speak with us; and we will listen. But don't let God speak with us, or we will die." Moshe answered the people, "Don't be afraid, because God has come only to test you and make you fear him, so that you won't commit sins."

---

## Soviet Russian Leaders Always Blames the West

They often use the blame game as an alibi to commit more violations to small independent countries. The Soviet Russian monologue is one way that they can justify to their people and to themselves more bad deeds. The same manner of blaming others over 100 years. The Russian Monarchy and the Tsar was the cause of the Russian Civil war. Then they blamed the small Independent European and Nordic countries for not cooperating with the Bolsheviks to establish and spread Communism across National borders.

Stalin blamed the people of Russia and everybody else that disagreed with him regarding the Soviet Union Superpower. Stalin and the USSR blamed the Polish Nationals in 1940 for not cooperating with Soviet Worldview.

He blamed the Finns, the Estonians, the Germans, the British, and the Americans for being biased and unfair. The truth of life is more direct to cause and effect. Joseph Stalin was in denial, repressing the Spirit of truth. He was a misguided individual who was sold out to the devil, working to establish Satan's kingdom on earth. He was seriously deceived and believed in the power of evil and darkness.

In a similar tone, modern Soviet Russian leaders very often blame the Western World for being anti-Russia. What is the point of such false accusations? They say it to justify themselves. The real reason for the anti-Russian sentiment globally has a historical track record. Soviet Russia has not come clean from their Leaders World War Two war crimes. They have not even come close spiritually to what Germany, Japan, and many other Nation leaders have done. If you inspect the integrity of Nations after the Second World War, the only country that has benefited from their War crimes over 75 years is Russia. How can we know that? How do we know that to be the case? And is it true?

For starters, the truth can be known. Jesus said to the Jews almost 2000 years ago.

> "John 8:31-40 NAS
> "So, Jesus was saying to those Jews who had believed Him, "If you continue in My word, then you are truly My disciples; and you will know the truth, and the truth will set you free."

There it is. Torah. Disciples. Truth. Freedom.
Jeremiah also declared the Truth of YHWH 2600 years ago.

> Jeremiah 9:24 ESV "but let him who boasts boast in this, that he understands and knows me, that I am the Lord who practices steadfast love, justice, and righteousness in the earth. For in these things I delight, declares the Lord."

There it is again, to know YHWH. And to know His character traits. Yeshua spelled it out again and again with explicit words.

> 1 John 3:8 ESV "Whoever makes a practice of sinning is of the devil, for the devil has been sinning from the beginning. The reason the Son of God appeared was to destroy the works of the devil."

Soviet Russian Leadership Have Suppressed, Repressed and Denied Truth for over 100 years

So much that they have become trapped in the cocoon of their own unbelief and spiritual darkness. Their faculties of reason have become darkened. They no longer can discern what is morally right and what is immoral. So, they blame everybody that disagrees with their ways. They experience it as discrimination and racism. Who is to Blame?

The Soviet Russian leadership is to be blamed. They are the ones that dug a deep hole for the people of Russia to fall into and become spiritually trapped. The declaration of the Soviet State Atheism in 1922 was a pivotal moment for the Bolshevik's cause in Russia. Joseph Stalin became their proud, hardened criminal leader.

Reality Check

People in the Nordic countries, Europe, and elsewhere, as of 2015, Christianity had approximately 2.4 billion church-going believers out of a worldwide population of about 7.5 billion people.

Russian leaders have a population of 144.5 million people. Maybe 122 million are honest Bible believers.

Soviet Union leaders had a population of some 287 million people. Maybe 144 million were NOT honest Bible believers.

That is such an insignificant percentage (16%) of the current 2.4 billion church-going believers.

Here is the kicker. The Soviet Russian leaders were such a minority. Incorrigibly obstinate with their obsession. They tried to obliterate the Jewish Holy Scriptures from Russia and the Communist political power country arena. They went about as a deviant representation of anarchy, and a minority, forcing people to adopt their life philosophy and the Stae Atheism worldview. That was an evident demonstration of the diabolical influence on their minds and hearts.

The Soviet Russian leaders did unimaginable evil; they did the unthinkable and violated the people that belonged to the Creator of Life, YHWH. The Ancient Holy One, the God of Abraham, Isaac, and Jacob. The Bolsheviks, Soviet State atheists, with the leadership of Joseph Stalin, did violence to the Spirit of the Natural Law on earth. They were the enemies of God, doing the dirty deeds for the kingdom of Satan on earth.

**Russian leadership from 2000 to 2020?**

What is the Russian leadership Worldview? They continue to gravitate towards the Worldview of the Soviet Union. Why? Because of the Russian Nationalism spirit, they are trapped in the spiritual hole that the Bolsheviks and Joseph Stalin State atheism dug for them about 100 years ago. Does that mean that the Russian have the same worldview? Of course not. There are genuine, honest peace-loving Russian people, that believe in the Creator of Life. And they believe in the Jewish Holy Scriptures that contain the instructions and the Oracles of YHWH. Those genuine believers that have been enlightened. They also know what is morally right and what is immoral. They do not suppress, repress, or deny the Spirit of the Natural law.

YHWH of the Holy Scriptures Also Hates Workers of Iniquity.

The Jewish Holy Scriptures in the Bible teach to hate evil.

> Proverbs 8:13 ESV "The fear of the Lord is hatred of evil. Pride and arrogance and the way of evil and perverted speech I hate.".

Next time you hear Russian leaders blaming the Western world for being biased, or racist, think again. Remember that for over 4000 years, the God of Abraham, Isaac, and Jacob has been speaking and leading people towards His ways and away from evildoers. In effect, what the Russian leaders have been saying for 100 years, is this, the God of the Bible (YHWH) and his Son (Yeshua from Nazareth) is biased, ostracizing, and racist towards Russian leadership. What the Russian leadership perceives and experience as ostracizing, sanctions, is in fact, God of the Bible making His will known on earth by His Spirit.

**God of the Bible is the same yesterday, today, and forever.**

> Jeremiah 5: 18-23.
>
> "Woe to those who begin by pulling at transgression with a thread, but end by dragging sin along as if with a cart rope. They say, "We want God to speed up his work, to hurry it along, so we can see it! We want the Holy One of Isra'el's plan to come true right now, so we can be sure of it!"
>
> Woe to those who call evil good and good evil, who change darkness into light and light into darkness, who change bitter into sweet and sweet into bitter!
>
> Woe to those seeing themselves as wise, esteeming themselves as clever.
>
> Woe to those who are heroes at drinking wine, men whose power goes to mixing strong drinks, who acquit the guilty for bribes but deny justice to the righteous!
> Therefore, as fire licks up the stubble, and the chaff is consumed in the flame; so their root will rot, and their flowers scatter like dust; because they have rejected the Torah
> of Adonai-Tzva'ot, they have despised the word of the Holy One of Isra'el."

**For God So Loved the World**

John 3: 16-21. ESV

> John 3: 16-21. ESV "For God so loved the world, that he gave his only Son, that whoever believes in him should not perish but have eternal life. For God did not send his Son into the world to condemn the world, but in order that the world might be saved through him. Whoever believes in him is not condemned, but whoever does not believe is condemned already, because he has not believed in the name of the only Son of God. And this is the judgment: the light has come into the world, and people loved the darkness rather than the light because their works were evil. For everyone who does wicked things hates the light and does not come to the light, lest his works should be exposed. But whoever does what is true comes to the light, so that it may be clearly seen that his works have been carried out in God."

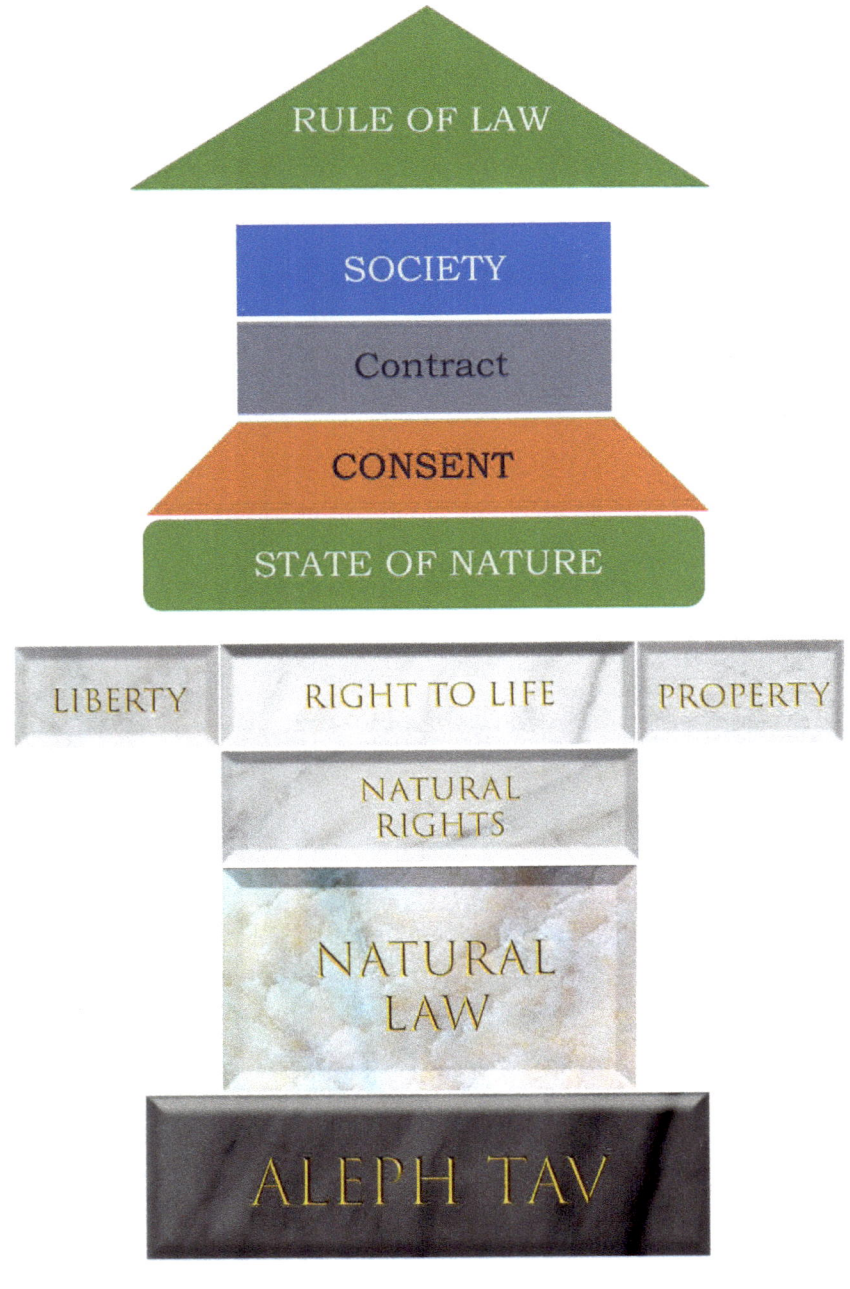

Graphic. All Rights Reserved. Victor Leinonen. 2020.

www.ingramcontent.com/pod-product-compliance
Lightning Source LLC
Chambersburg PA
CBHW061747290426
44108CB00028B/2917